business accounting

Jill Collis and Roger Hussey

business accounting

an introduction to financial and management accounting

First published 2007 by
PALGRAVE MACMILLAN
Houndmills, Basingstoke, Hampshire RG21 6XS and
175 Fifth Avenue, New York, N.Y. 10010
Companies and representatives throughout the world

PALGRAVE MACMILLAN is the global academic imprint of the Palgrave
Macmillan division of St. Martin's Press, LLC and of Palgrave Macmillan Ltd.
Macmillan® is a registered trademark in the United States, United Kingdom
and other countries. Palgrave is a registered trademark in the European
Union and other countries.

ISBN-13: 978–1–4039–4886–1
ISBN-10: 1–4039–4886–0

This book is printed on paper suitable for recycling and made from fully
managed and sustained forest sources. Logging, pulping and manufacturing
processes are expected to conform to the environmental regulations of the
country of origin.

A catalogue record for this book is available from the British Library.

12 11 10 9 8 7 6 5 4 3
16 15 14 13 12 11 10 09 08 07

Printed in Great Britain by
The Cromwell Press, Trowbridge, Wiltshire

contents

list of figures

list of tables

preface

Accounting information lies at the heart of business, regardless of whether the user of the information is the owner, the manager or an external party, and irrespective of the size of the business. Therefore, it is not surprising that accounting is a core module on programmes that include the study of business. *Business Accounting* provides an introduction to financial and management accounting in an accessible, non-technical style that is suitable for non-specialist undergraduate and postgraduate students. The active-learning approach seeks to convey an understanding of the subjectivity inherent in accounting and the ability to evaluate financial information for a range of business purposes.

The chapters are presented in a logical teaching sequence and each chapter has a clear structure with learning objectives, key definitions and activities within the text. The latter are used to illustrate the principles, encourage reflection and introduce the next learning point. At the end of each chapter there are exam-style practice questions to test the learning outcomes. Answers to these questions, together with additional materials, PowerPoint slides and interactive progress tests for use in a virtual learning environment are available on the lecturers' website.

Part I of the book sets the scene with three chapters that introduce the student to the world of accounting and finance in a business context, whilst Parts II and III cover the key aspects of financial and management accounting respectively. The wide range of topics offered allows the lecturer to select those that are relevant to the syllabus and the level of study. On some programmes, the two main branches of accounting are studied at different stages (for example introduction to financial accounting in semester 1 or year 1 and introduction to management accounting in semester 2 or year 2); on other programmes, the topics are drawn from both branches (for example introduction to accounting), with a follow-up module as a core or elective at the next stage. The use of the book on successive modules offers the advantage of continuity as well as cost savings for students. The following examples illustrate some of the ways in which the book can be used.

EXAMPLE 1 **Choice of topics where the two branches of accounting are taught separately**

Module 1	Module 2
Introduction to financial accounting	*Introduction to management accounting*

Part I The world of accounting and finance
  1 Nature and purpose of accounting
  2 Accounting principles and rules
  3 Importance of cash
	Part III Management accounting
	 12 Importance of cost information
	 13 Costing for product direct costs
	 14 Costing for indirect costs
	 15 Costing for specific orders and
	     continuous operations

Part II Financial accounting
  4 The accounting system*
  5 The trial balance*
  6 Measuring financial performance
  7 Measuring financial position
  8 Financial statements of a sole trader
  9 Financial statements of a partnership
 10 Financial statements of a limited
     company
 11 Analysing financial statements
	16 Activity-based costing
	 17 Marginal costing
	 18 Budgetary control
	 19 Standard costing
	 20 Capital investment appraisal
	 21 Discounted cash flow

* Optional if bookkeeping is not required

EXAMPLE 2 **Choice of topics where both branches of accounting are taught together**

Module 1	Module 2
Introduction to accounting	*Advanced accounting*

Part I The world of accounting and finance
  1 Nature and purpose of accounting
  2 Accounting principles and rules
  3 Importance of cash
	Part I The world of accounting and finance
	  2 Accounting principles and rules
	     (revisited)

Part II Financial accounting
  4 The accounting system*
  5 The trial balance*
  6 Measuring financial performance
  7 Measuring financial position
  8 Financial statements of a sole trader
	Part II Financial accounting
	  9 Financial statements of a partnership
	 10 Financial statements of a limited
	     company
	 11 Analysing financial statements

Part III Management accounting 12 Importance of cost information 13 Costing for product direct costs 14 Costing for indirect costs 17 Marginal costing 20 Capital investment appraisal	*Part III Management accounting* 14 Costing for indirect costs (revisited) 15 Costing for specific orders and continuous operations 16 Activity-based costing 18 Budgetary control 19 Standard costing 21 Discounted cash flow

* Optional if bookkeeping is not required

Acknowledgements

We would like to acknowledge the invaluable help given to us by our students, who have given us their opinions on this book and its associated learning resources. We are also grateful to the anonymous reviewers for their thoughtful feedback on the draft text.

We are indebted to a number of friends and colleagues, who have given us the benefit of their experience; in particular Rachel Jones for her insightful comments and careful checking of the first draft and Laura Davies and Bian Tan for their support and encouragement. Finally, we are grateful to Martin Drewe, our editor, for his enthusiasm in ensuring that this transatlantic writing duo achieved their aims.

Every effort has been made to trace all the copyright holders but if any have been inadvertently overlooked the publishers will be pleased to make the necessary arrangements at the first opportunity.

Acronyms

ABC	activity-based costing
ACCA	Association of Chartered Certified Accountants
AIM	Alternative Investment Market
ARR	accounting rate of return
ASB	Accounting Standards Board
ASC	Accounting Standards Committee
BEP	breakeven point
b/f	brought forward
c/f	carried forward
CA85	Companies Act 1985
CA89	Companies Act 1989
CIMA	Chartered Institute of Management Accountants
CIPFA	Chartered Institute of Public Finance and Accountancy
CWA	continuous weighted average
DCF	discounted cash flow
DTI	Department of Trade and Industry
EPS	earnings per share
FIFO	first in, first out
FRC	Financial Reporting Council
FRS	Financial Reporting Standard
FRSSE	Financial Reporting Standard for Smaller Entities
GAAP	generally accepted accounting principles
HP	hire purchase
IAS	international accounting standard
IASB	International Accounting Standards Board
IASC	International Accounting Standards Committee
ICAEW	Institute of Chartered Accountants in England and Wales
ICAI	Institute of Chartered Accountants in Ireland
ICAS	Institute of Chartered Accountants in Scotland
IFRIC	International Financial Reporting Interpretations Committee
IFRS	International Financial Reporting Standard
IOSCO	International Organization for Securities Commissions
IRR	internal rate of return
JIT	just-in-time
LLP	limited liability partnership
LSE	London Stock Exchange
Ltd	limited
NBV	net book value
NPV	net present value
NRV	net realizable value
P/E	price/earnings
PAT	profit after tax
PBIT	profit before interest and tax
Plc	public limited company
PV	present value
ROCE	return on capital employed
ROE	return on equity
SAC	Standards Advisory Committee
SBS	Small Business Service
SME	small and medium-sized enterprises
SoP	Statement of Principles for Financial Reporting
SSAP	Statement of Standard Accounting Practice
STRGL	Statement of Total Recognized Gains and Losses
WIP	work in progress

the world of accounting and finance

nature and purpose of accounting

When you have studied this chapter, you should be able to:

- Explain the purpose of accounting in a business context
- Distinguish between financial accounting and management accounting
- Compare different types of business entity
- Explain the importance of financial information to management
- Identify the main users of published financial statements.

1.1 introduction

This book focuses on accounting in a business context and everyone knows that business is about trying to make money. An accounting system can be used to record what has happened to the money in the business over time and provide financial information on the performance and position of a business. Financial information is needed by the owners and managers of the business, as well as others outside. Precisely who the users are depends to a large extent on the type and size of the business. For example, financial information relating to a small convenience store is likely to be used only by the owner and the tax authorities. However, financial information relating to a large, global company will have a much wider range of users. A user's level of interest depends on the purpose for which the financial information is needed. For example, a manager working in a division of a large company is likely to require detailed information in order to run the department; a bank lending officer contemplating lending £1m to a business is likely to need information for assessing the risk that the business will not be able to repay the loan with interest when it falls due.

Whether you decide to start your own business when you complete your studies, or become an employee, you will need a basic understanding of accounting so that you can make the best use of the financial information that the accountants provide. In this chapter we introduce you to the purpose of accounting. We provide an overview of the work involved in the two main branches of accounting and the accountancy profession. We also describe the different types of business organization and the principal sources of financial information about a business, before going on to consider the potential users of the information.

1.2 purpose of accounting

Even if you have not studied business or management before, you are likely to be familiar with some of the terminology associated with this subject. The phrase *accounting and finance* is often used to describe the subject you are studying. In general terms, finance refers to sources and management of money and we shall look this more closely in Chapter 3. In this chapter we will focus on what we mean by the term *accounting*. In everyday language, accounting for something means giving an explanation or report on something, and this lies at the heart of the subject, as the following brief history shows.

history of accounting

'The earliest records of financial information, in Mesopotamia and later in Egypt, date from the fourth millennium BC. Records are more abundant from Greek and Roman times. They are often merely lists of expenditure on major projects or lists of income from taxation. However, even before sophisticated accounting had been invented, some of the functions of accountants had become well established. "Keeping account" has always been part of ordered society. "Giving account" has always been the duty of chancellors and stewards to whom responsibility has been delegated. From time to time, the kings or lords would *audit*, or hear the accounts. Sometimes the lord was illiterate and innumerate and relied considerably on the skills of his steward, or accountant.

The essential purpose of accounting is still to communicate relevant financial information to interested persons. Today, the owners of companies (the shareholders) expect to see an account from their stewards (the directors) which has already been audited by independent accountants (the auditors). The original purpose of accounting was to explain what had been going on – how the stewards had collected and used their lord's money. This accountability or stewardship role still applies, though there are now additional roles for accounting information.'
Source: Nobes and Kellas, 1990, p. 10.

In its broadest form, we might say that accounting is a service that is provided for those who need financial information about the business. However, we need a more authoritative explanation. The following definition is taken from the *Oxford Dictionary of Accounting* (Hussey, 1999):

KEY DEFINITION   Accounting is the process of identifying, measuring, recording and communicating economic transactions.

In a business context, the term *economic transactions* refers to the commercial dealings of the organization that are concerned with creating wealth for the owner(s); in other words, money-making activities. We shall now consider each of the activities in the accounting process separately:

- *Identifying* economic transactions in most cases is fairly straightforward. Examples include selling goods or services to customers, paying wages, purchasing stock and buying machinery or equipment. It is also important to distinguish between the personal economic transactions of the owner(s) and/or managers and the economic transactions of the business, and focus solely on the latter.
- *Measuring* economic transactions is done in monetary terms. This convention began when more people learned to read and write and society moved from a bartering system where goods and services were exchanged without using money. For example, a farmer might exchange 10 pigs for 1 cow and measure the transaction in those very simple quantitative terms. Using money, the transaction might be 10 pigs sold at £10 each, and the sale recorded as £100; 1 cow purchased at £100 and the purchase recorded as £100. Measuring transactions in monetary terms makes it easier to aggregate, summarize and compare similar types of transaction.

- *Recording* economic transactions is essential. Traditionally they were recorded in hand-written books of accounts known as ledgers, but today most businesses keep computerized records.
- *Communicating* economic transactions is done by producing a variety of different financial statements. These are drawn from the records and set out in a particular format that summarizes a particular financial aspect of the business. The three main forms of financial statement are the cash flow statement, profit and loss account and balance sheet. We shall be looking at each of these financial statements in more detail in Part II.

The following activity allows you to carry out the basic accounting procedures of identifying, measuring and recording the economic transactions involved in building some office shelves:

activity

A business buys 5 litres of paint, 20 metres of timber and employs a carpenter for two days to build shelves in an office. Paint costs £4 per litre, timber costs £2.50 per metre and the carpenter charges £50 per day. What is the total cost of the shelves?

The cost can be calculated in a number of stages. You need to multiply the cost of paint per litre by the amount used. You also need to multiply the cost of timber per metre by the amount used. Finally, you need to calculate the cost of employing the carpenter by multiplying his daily rate by the number of days. The order in which you work out the figures does not matter, as long as you arrive at three figures which, when added together, make up the total cost of the job:

	£
Cost of paint (£4 × 5 litres)	20
Cost of timber (£2.50 × 20 metres)	50
Cost of labour (£50 × 2 days)	100
Total cost of the shelves	170

In more complex examples it is not so easy to identify and measure the economic events in monetary terms. We shall be looking at some of these problems in subsequent chapters.

1.3   main branches of accounting

The 18th century saw the start of an industrialization process in Europe that began to change many countries from rural to urban economies. During the 19th century new technologies were developed for commercial and industrial purposes, such as engineering and applied science, and industrialization spread to other continents through the colonialist policies pursued by the more powerful European countries as they competed for raw materials, new markets and diplomatic advantage (*Oxford Paperback Encyclopedia*, 1998). Another dramatic change took place during the 1970s and 80s, when the reduced cost of electronic hardware helped bring about a revolution in the commercial and personal use of information technology that has transformed the storage and processing of data and electronic communication systems. By the mid-1990s many commercial and public organizations had their own websites on the internet for publicity, sales and publishing. Thus, the internet has created a global market place for many businesses.

The formation of the European Union (EU), which has its roots in the Treaties of Rome (1957), has been another significant influence on the internationalization of business, together with the development of international markets for raising finance. Such changes have meant that instead of operating in local or national markets, businesses in many countries around the world operate in a global economy. Indeed, some businesses have become huge conglomerates with complex activities and international operations that were unimaginable in the days when transactions were based on simple bartering.

Not surprisingly, accounting has had to develop in response to these changes in the business environment and the subject can now be divided into many specialist areas. However, there are two main branches: *financial accounting* and *management accounting*, as shown in Figure 1.1.

FIGURE 1.1 **Main branches of accounting**

We are going to start by looking at a definition of financial accounting.

KEY DEFINITION	Financial accounting is the branch of accounting concerned with classifying, measuring and recording the economic transactions of an entity in accordance with established principles, legal requirements and accounting standards. It is primarily concerned with communicating a true and fair view of the financial performance and financial position of an entity to external parties.

From this definition you can see that the purpose of financial accounting is to provide financial information to meet the needs of *external users*. The term 'true and fair view' implies that the financial statements produced at the end of a financial period (usually a year, but sometimes less) are a faithful representation of the economic activities of the organization. The financial statements are drawn up within a regulatory framework, which is very important for businesses that have been formed as limited liability entities. Therefore, the organization must prepare the financial statements according to legislation and other regulations. In addition, the financial statements are prepared using a number of accounting assumptions which have been established as general principles. We shall be looking at these assumptions in the next chapter. Generally, an organization's financial statements are considered to give a true and fair view if they comply with the regulatory framework and normal accounting principles. However, in a very small number of cases, the organization may have to ignore specific rules to ensure that the financial statements give a true and fair view so that the users of the financial statements are not misled.

Financial accounting can be divided into a number of specific activities, such as the following:

- bookkeeping, which focuses on the recording of business transactions
- auditing, which is the thorough examination of the financial systems and records to confirm that the financial statements give a true and fair view (an audit is a legal requirement for all large companies and for some small and medium-sized companies that are not eligible for exemption)
- corporate recovery, which is concerned with the provision of insolvency services and advice to businesses in financial difficulties
- taxation advice, which is governed by legislation.

activity

A financial accountant can give advice on the following matters (tick the appropriate box):

	True	False
(a) How to arrange financial affairs so that the least amount of tax is incurred	☐	☐
(b) The best way to borrow money for a specific project	☐	☐
(c) The likely profit to be made on a music festival	☐	☐
(d) Carrying out financial transactions in foreign currencies	☐	☐
(e) Deciding on the best way to provide for a pension	☐	☐
(f) Calculating VAT payments	☐	☐
(g) Trading in stocks and shares	☐	☐

You may have been puzzled by some of these statements, but you would be right if you said that they are all the concern of the financial accountant. However, as in other professions, there are specialists who may concentrate on specific areas within financial accounting.

We will now look at a definition of management accounting.

KEY DEFINITION

Management accounting is a branch of accounting concerned with collecting, analysing and interpreting quantitative and financial information. It is primarily concerned with communicating information to management for planning, controlling and decision making.

Whereas financial accounting is concerned with providing financial information to external users, the above definition indicates that management accounting focuses on providing financial information to *internal users*: those responsible for managing the business. We shall be looking at management accounting in some detail in Part III of this book. A management accountant is concerned with identifying why the information is required so that the most appropriate technique can be used to supply information to managers. The managers of the business need this information to enable them to plan the progress of the business, control the activities and understand the financial implications of any decisions they may take. Unlike financial accounting, management accounting is not governed by legislation or regulations and the emphasis is on providing information for decisions that will help the business achieve its financial targets.

Cost accounting is an important part of management accounting and incorporates techniques for planning, control and decision making. Large organizations may employ a specialist cost accountant whose job it is to ascertain the cost of operating the various cost centres in a business and the cost of products, services and other cost units. This allows management to make important decisions, such as setting selling prices, production and/or sales targets, and deciding which products or services are the most profitable to produce or supply. Another important aspect of cost accounting is establishing budgets and standard costs, and comparing them with the actual costs incurred.

To illustrate the difference between financial accounting and management accounting we can look at the example of the office shelves again:

- A financial accountant would be interested in the total cost of £170 so that it can be recorded as the economic transaction.
- A management accountant would be more concerned with informing managers how much the individual elements cost, such as the paint, the timber and the labour. A management accountant would also want to calculate how much the shelves actually cost and compare it with the planned or budgeted figure (what it was estimated they would cost).

---

activity

Classify the following activities (tick the appropriate box):

	Financial accounting	Management accounting
(a) Auditing the books of an organization	☐	☐
(b) Managing the tax affairs of a business	☐	☐
(c) Analysing the financial implications of management decisions	☐	☐
(d) Preparing financial statements at the end of the year	☐	☐
(e) Ensuring compliance with legal and other regulations	☐	☐
(f) Providing financial information for managers	☐	☐
(g) Keeping the financial records of the organization	☐	☐

By now you are probably more confident about deciding which activities involve financial accounting and which can be classified as management accounting. With the exception of (c) and (f), all the above activities are concerned with financial accounting.

The purpose of management accounting is to provide managers with financial and other quantitative information to help them carry out their responsibilities. The responsibilities of managers in any organization can be classified as planning, controlling and decision making. Therefore the financial information they require should help them to control the resources for which they are responsible, plan how those resources can be most effectively used and decide what course of action they should take when a number of options are open.

activity

Imagine you are a manager and decide whether you would require the following information for planning, controlling or decision making:

(a) The amount claimed for taxi fares by staff last month

(b) The prices charged by a new supplier for services or materials

(c) The cost of running the office photocopier

(d) The cost of employing subcontracted staff, compared with your own employees

(e) The cost of making a component, compared with buying it from a supplier

Items (d) and (e) should be easy to define because in both circumstances you are choosing between alternatives and therefore you are making decisions. With items (a) and (c) you are mainly concerned with controlling costs, although you might want the information to make plans for future expenditure. Item (b) could be concerned with planning future costs or you may be about to decide whether to change to another supplier. This decision may have arisen because you are trying to control costs. Although the boundaries between planning, controlling and decision making are blurred, financial and statistical information has a very important role to play and it is the management accountant who provides this information.

As management accounting is concerned with providing information that is useful to managers, it offers a number of general advantages, such as helping a business become more profitable (or ensuring that a not-for-profit organization provides value for money).

activity

What other advantages do you consider management accounting information offers to managers? Draw up a list of the ways in which management accounting information can be used by managers under the headings of planning, controlling and decision making.

Your list may include some of the following advantages:

Planning
- the price of products or services
- the number of employees and what they should be paid

- the quantity of each product or service that must be sold to achieve a desired level of profit.

Controlling
- unnecessary expense and waste
- the amount of investment in machinery or equipment
- the cost of running different departments.

Decision making
- whether to make or buy a particular component
- whether it is worth investing in new technology
- which products or services to offer if there is a shortage of skilled labour.

1.4 accountancy and the profession

Although accounting can be divided into financial and management accounting, you should not be misled into thinking that there is no relationship between these two activities, since they both draw on the same data sources and both generate financial information. However, there are some important differences, which relate to the accuracy, level of detail and timing of the information produced. Financial accounting operates on the basis of an annual reporting cycle. As you will see in the next section, for some businesses (limited liability entities) it is strictly regulated because the information must be as accurate as possible. For most businesses, it is often some months after the end of the financial year before the financial statements are issued. The financial statements are drawn up for the entire business and contain aggregated information that is presented in the way required by legislation. By contrast, management accounting is not regulated and the aim is to present the information to managers when they want it and in the form they want it. In most management accounting systems, reports for each activity in each part of the organization are produced on a monthly or more frequent basis. Consequently they are very detailed. Because the reports are produced frequently, some figures may be based on estimates.

In a large business where the accounting systems are well designed and operate efficiently, if the periodic management accounts for the different parts of the business were aggregated, the resulting totals would be very similar to the figures in the financial accounts. However, there would be some differences. For example, the financial accounts would contain details of interest payments, dividends paid to shareholders and tax payments. There may also be minor differences due to some figures in the management accounts being estimated. If there were any significant differences, they would be investigated by the firm's accountant.

Another difference is that a large business is likely to employ specialists to deal with different aspects of accounting and finance, whereas a medium-sized business may have one qualified accountant who carries out both financial and management accounting functions, perhaps with the help of other staff, such as a credit controller and bookkeeper. In a small business, it may be more cost effective for all the accountancy work, except some simple record keeping, to be carried by an external accountant. However, this does not mean that smaller businesses do not make use of management accounting information. Although the most widely used sources of financial information in smaller businesses relate to cash (bank statements and cash flow information), the large majority use monthly or quarterly management accounts and budgets (Collis and Jarvis, 2002).

In the UK, a qualified accountant must have passed a number of rigorous examinations set by one of the recognized accountancy bodies. He or she then pays an annual subscription to become a member of that particular institution, and thus joins the accountancy profession. Table 1.1 shows the qualified membership of the six British chartered accountancy bodies in 2002:

TABLE 1.1 **Qualified membership of the British accountancy bodies 2002**

	No. of members	%
Institute of Chartered Accountants in England and Wales (ICAEW)	123,719	38
Association of Chartered Certified Accountants (ACCA)	95,416	30
Chartered Institute of Management Accountants (CIMA)	59,896	19
Institute of Chartered Accountants in Scotland (ICAS)	15,166	5
Chartered Institute of Public Finance and Accountancy (CIPFA)	13,471	4
Institute of Chartered Accountants in Ireland (ICAI)	12,932	4
	320,600	100

Source: Adapted from Edwards, 2003, p. 59.

Membership of the ICAEW rose by about 10% between 1998 and 2002, but the ACCA grew by almost 40% in the same five-year period (Fisher, 2003). The ACCA is unusual because approximately half its members are based outside Britain. It also has the highest proportion of female members (36%). Although all the accountancy bodies have shown steady increases in the number of qualified female members, women are outnumbered by men in the accountancy profession.

Accountants can work in professional practice (for a firm of accountants or in their own practice), in commerce and industry or in the public sector. A qualified accountant is not necessarily restricted to one area of work. However, an accountant in a professional practice is likely to be a member of ICAEW, ACCA, ICAS or ICAI. Membership of CIMA would be most appropriate for a management accountant in industry. Membership of ACCA or CIPFA would be appropriate for a treasurer in a local authority, or an accountant in the National Health Service or other public sector organization with funding from national or local government.

1.5 classifying businesses

Accounting provides important information that is used in all kinds of organizations, regardless of the nature of their activities, their financial objectives or their size. This is because accounting information helps organizations to achieve their economic objectives. All entities strive to ensure that the revenue generated and the costs incurred are at acceptable levels, but what is an acceptable level varies. In the profit-making sector the economic objective of some business owners is to maximize wealth and they pursue what we call *profit maximization* strategies. Others place limitations on the amount of wealth they want to create and follow strategies they hope will give them sufficient profit to maintain a certain lifestyle and no more. Recent research shows that 53% of small and medium-sized entities (SMEs) (defined as those with up to 250 employees) do not intend to grow (SBS (Small Business Service), 2004). This type of economic rationality can be called *satisficing* (Simon, 1960). Although we are looking at accounting in a business context, you should be aware that in the not-for-profit sector the economic objective is to break even. This means that managers working in organizations in the public sector and in social organizations, such as clubs, will be concerned with generating enough revenue to cover costs rather than making a profit.

The size of business entities ranges from very small, such as a florist's shop with one owner and no employees, to a large multinational company with thousands of owners (the shareholders) and thousands of employees. Government statistics show that of the estimated 4.3 million business enterprises in the UK in 2004, 99% were small (a small enterprise is defined as having 0–49 employees) (SBS, 2005). However, Britain is not the only country where small firms dominate to such a large extent. In continental Europe, 99% of the 19.3 million enterprises in the European Economic Area and Switzerland are small (European Communities, 2004).

As well as providing a living for their owners, small firms make a significant contribution to the economy. In the UK they provide 47% of employment, despite the fact that 73% consist solely of the self-employed owner-manager(s) (SBS, 2005). Comparing these to the European statistics, we find that the small firms account for 56% of employment (European Communities, 2004). With an average size of 5 employees, European enterprises are smaller than in the USA, for example, where the average number is 20. This is because in Europe approximately 50% of firms with fewer than 10 employees are sole proprietorships, compared to 80% in the USA. Regardless of their global position, most countries recognize the significant contribution to economic growth made by smaller entities.

The majority of smaller entities are owner-managed and family-owned (Collis, 2003; SBS, 2004). In larger businesses, ownership and control tends to be separated, as the owners appoint managers to run the business on their behalf. Businesses also differ in terms of their legal status and in the groups of people who are likely to be interested in financial information about them. Before we look at the users and uses of financial information, we need to consider the three main types of enterprise in the UK:

- sole proprietorships
- partnerships
- companies and corporations.

Figure 1.2 shows how the four million UK enterprises are dispersed among these categories.

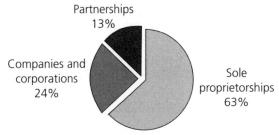

FIGURE 1.2 **UK enterprises by legal status**
Source: Adapted from SBS, 2005, Table 2.

As you can see, the majority of enterprises are *sole proprietorships*. A sole proprietorship is an unincorporated entity because it has not gone through a process of incorporation by which it is registered as a limited liability entity. It is owned by one person, who is in business with a view to making a profit. A sole proprietor may be providing a service (for example a window cleaner, hairdresser or business consultant), trading goods (for example a newsagent, florist or grocer) or making goods (for example a cabinet maker, potter or dress designer). Alternatively, the business may have activities in the primary sector (agriculture, forestry or fishing). A sole proprietor may run the business alone or employ full-time or part-time staff. The owner of this type of business may experience difficulty in obtaining the finance to start the enterprise, as the capital is restricted to what he or she has available to invest plus any loans. However, there are no legal formalities to set up this type of business and no obligation to disclose financial information to the public. One key characteristic is that a sole proprietor has *unlimited liability*, which means that the owner is personally liable for any debts the business may incur. This liability extends beyond any original investment and could mean the loss of personal assets.

A *partnership* is an entity in which two or more people join together in business with a view to making a profit. Examples range as widely as those cited for sole traders but partnerships are a popular form of business for professional firms such as accountants, doctors, dentists and solicitors. The maximum number of partners in a firm used to be restricted to 20, but this limit was removed in 2002. In a general partnership the partners have 'joint and several' liability. This means that the partners have *unlimited liability* for each other's acts in terms of any debts the business may incur. The capital invested in the business is restricted to what the partners have to invest, supplemented by what they can borrow. The partners may run the business alone or employ full-time or part-time staff. The Business Names Act 1985 requires the names of the partners to be shown on business stationery, but they need not be used in the business name. The partners must keep accounting records and in the absence of a written or verbal *partnership agreement*, the Partnership Act 1890 applies. A written partnership agreement is a deed of contract that relates to the agreement to form a partnership.

activity

What sort of financial matters do you think partners ought to agree on before starting the business?

The most obvious matters to agree are as follows:

- How to divide the profit
- How much money (capital) each partner will invest in the business
- Whether any of the partners will be entitled to a salary
- Whether any interest will be payable on the capital invested by the partners
- Whether any interest will be payable on any loan made to the partnership by any of the partners.

If the partners are in dispute and there is no partnership agreement, the Partnership Act 1890 provides rules on the relationship between the partners. We will be looking at partnership law in more detail in Chapter 2.

activity

To help you identify the similarities and differences between the two types of business organization, decide whether the following characteristics apply to a sole proprietor, a simple partnership, or both:

	Sole proprietorship	Partnership
(a) The entity is an unincorporated business	☐	☐
(b) There is only one owner	☐	☐
(c) There is no maximum number of owners	☐	☐
(d) There are no formalities involved when starting the business	☐	☐
(e) There should be a contract of agreement	☐	☐

What they have in common is that they are both unincorporated businesses. The first important difference to note is that a sole proprietor is the sole owner of the business, whereas a partnership has at least two owners with no maximum. Another important difference is that there are no formalities involved in setting up a business as a sole proprietor, whereas the relationship between partners in a partnership must be formalized in a contract of agreement. You might argue that partners do not need a contract of agreement, because in the absence of such a deed the Partnership Act 1890 sets out the relationship. This means that a standard agreement is applied, although this may not be appropriate in all circumstances. You may have thought of some other differences such as:

- A partnership can raise more capital than a sole proprietorship to start the business because there is more than one owner.
- For the same reason, a greater range of skills is likely to be available in a partnership.
- The pressures of managing the business are shared in a partnership, whereas a sole trader must bear them alone.
- Any loss made by a partnership is shared among the partners, whereas a sole trader suffers the whole of any loss the business incurs.
- In a partnership, responsibility for debts incurred by individual partners, or the business as a whole, is shared; a sole trader must carry responsibility for debts incurred by the business alone.
- The individual partners are responsible for the actions of the others in a partnership, whereas a sole trader has none of these worries.

Perhaps the most important characteristic these two types of business have in common is that the owners have unlimited liability, which is the case for all unincorporated businesses.

We will now move on to look at two types of business that have *limited liability*: a *limited liability partnership (LLP)* and a *limited company*. A limited liability entity is a business that, through the process of legal incorporation, is considered to have a legal identity that is separate from its owners, who are known as members. The capital invested in the business is raised by selling shares to members (hence the term *shareholder*) and can be supplemented by loans and other forms of debt finance. Members have limited liability, which means that even if the business fails owing significant amounts, the owners' liability for those debts is limited to the capital they have invested.

the concept of limited liability

'The Limited Liability Act 1855 was the first to establish the principle of limited liability subject to certain safeguards, but it was only in force a few months before the Joint Stock Companies Act 1856 superseded it and became the first in the line of statutes which culminated in the concept of limited liability as we know it today.

The concept of limited liability relates to the members of a company being liable to contribute towards payment of its debts only to a limited extent. The amount of members' liability is determined by the liability clause contained in a company's memorandum of association, and differs in its nature according to whether the company is one which is limited by shares, limited by guarantee, or unlimited.

The vast majority of companies registered under the Companies Act are companies "limited by shares". This means that the shareholders or members have a limited liability to pay the debts of the company. When new shares are issued by a company, the person who takes the shares must agree to pay for them. Usually payment will be made immediately but sometimes shares will be issued "unpaid" or "partly paid", in which case payment must be made later. If the company goes into liquidation and is insolvent, the members are liable to pay for their shares in full if they have not already done so ...

Complementary to the concept of limitation of the members' liability is the notion that the company is a separate "legal person" distinct from the members and the directors. It is the company that buys and sells, owns land, employs workers, makes profits or losses, and not the individuals who make up the company. The company itself is owned by the members, and its directors act on its behalf, but the debts are the debts of the company and the only assets which can be used to satisfy those debts are the assets owned by the company ... These complementary rules of limited liability and legal personality, therefore, combine to confer enormous advantages on the sole proprietor who turns his [or her] business into a company.'

Source: Mallett and Brumwell, 1994, pp. 6–7.

LLPs were introduced by the Limited Liability Partnership Act 2000 and the Limited Liability Partnership Regulations 2001 (after the above article was written). In the first two years 4,442 of this new type of partnership were registered, many of which are professional firms offering services, such as accountants, doctors and solicitors. LLPs are allowed to organize themselves internally in the same way as a general partnership. However, in their external relations, most of the requirements that apply to limited companies (modified as appropriate) apply.

Limited companies and LLPs are more closely regulated than sole proprietors and general partnerships. On formation they must file two documents with the Registrar of Companies at Companies House, which is part of the Department of Trade and Industry (DTI):

- *Memorandum of association*, which gives details about the constitution of the business and its objects.
- *Articles of association*, which gives details about its internal regulation, including the voting rights of shareholders, how shareholders' and directors' meetings will be conducted and the powers of management.

Under the Companies Act 1985 all limited liability entities are required to make public disclosure of financial information. They are obliged to keep accounting records and prepare an *annual report and accounts* which must be filed with the Registrar of Companies and distributed to every shareholder. The annual report and accounts is a comprehensive source of financial information on a limited liability entity and includes the annual financial statements (with some simplifications and disclosure concessions for qualifying smaller entities). We will be looking at the annual report and accounts in more detail in Chapter 2.

Companies can be divided into *private companies* and *public companies*. Most public companies are converted from private companies under the re-registration procedure in the Companies Act 1985. Of the 1.6 million companies on the register in 2003, only 0.7% were public limited companies, 99% were private limited companies and 0.3% were unlimited private companies (DTI, 2003). The main differences between a private company and a public company are:

- A public company must state in its memorandum of association that it is a public company.
- A public limited company's name must end with the words 'public limited company' or the abbreviation 'Plc' or 'Ccc' the Welsh equivalent; a private limited company's name must end with the word 'limited' or the abbreviation 'Ltd'.
- A public limited company can advertise its shares and invite the public to buy them, and its shares can then be freely bought and sold; a private limited company's shares are only available privately.

The shares of a UK public limited company are listed on the London Stock Exchange (LSE) and may also be listed on any of the international stock exchanges. Investors can buy and sell shares in person through a broker, a bank, a share shop or on the internet. Most financial institutions try to keep the process as informal and fast as possible. When shares are issued, an advertisement is placed in the newspapers in the form of a prospectus and application coupon. It is best to obtain professional advice before buying shares, since every investment carries some risk as well as the chance of making a gain. Because limited companies are so important to the economy, information about them, particularly public limited companies, is readily available. We will look at this in more detail in Chapter 2.

Figure 1.3 summarizes the different types of business entity we have described.

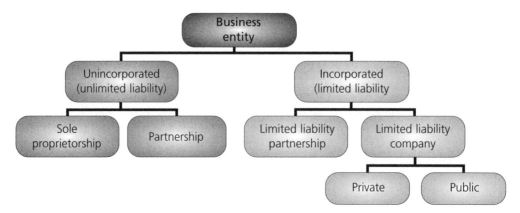

FIGURE 1.3 **Types of business entity**

What do you think are the main advantages of an LLP or limited
company over a general partnership?

One of the main advantages is that the members of an LLP or limited company have their
liability limited to the amount they have agreed to invest, even if the company goes into
liquidation. With a general partnership, the partners are liable for the debts of the business,
even if they were not personally responsible for incurring them. There are two main exceptions to this restriction on liability that apply to LLPs:

● If the member of an LLP was personally at fault, he or she may have unlimited liability
  if he or she accepted a personal duty of care or a personal contractual obligation.
● If an LLP becomes insolvent, the members can be required to repay any property withdrawn from the LLP, including profits and interest, in the two years prior to insolvency.
  This is only applicable where it is reasonable that the member could not have
  concluded that insolvency was likely.

A limited liability entity usually finds it easier to raise finance than a general partnership. Public limited companies raise finance by issuing shares on a stock exchange. Private
limited companies cannot do this and can only raise capital from selling shares privately.
Once they are established, limited liability entities find it relatively easy to raise loans
because the financial regulations imposed on them give lenders some confidence in the
financial information they provide, which they use to assess and monitor the lending risk.
Limited liability entities have an unlimited life, whereas a general partnership has a finite
life. When a member of a limited liability entity dies, his or her shares can be transferred to
someone else and the company or LLP continues; when a partner in a general partnership
dies, the old partnership ceases. Of course, the remaining partners are free to reform the
business as a new partnership, with or without additional partners.

1.6   importance of financial information to management

Before looking at the potential uses of financial information, we need to establish what we mean by *financial information*. For our purposes, financial information can be considered to be information about something expressed in terms of money. We are confronted with financial information at home and at work. We may be so used to reading and hearing it that we do not think about what messages we are being given and why. For example, if you have gone shopping today, you may have compared prices and been given receipts which itemize and total your purchases. At home you may have received your bank statement or a telephone bill and decided that you must cut back on your spending. At work you may have received a quotation that you intend to use to help you decide which supplier to order from. These are examples of financial information that have a direct impact on your activities. Other items may have less direct impact. For example, if you have read the newspaper or looked at news programmes on television or the internet, you will probably have heard about how much a particular celebrity earns, the state of the economy, changes in interest rates or record profits made by a particular company. If you have no association with that company, you may simply conclude that it indicates the state of a prosperous economy which may bring you some indirect benefits. If you are a shareholder or an employee of the company concerned, you will probably have a much greater interest.

To understand how financial information can be helpful, we need to identify the uses to which it can be put. One way of doing this is to define the responsibilities involved in any job or activity.

---

activity

Sally Lunn is the manager of a small coffee shop. Here is a list of her responsibilities:

- ordering and controlling stock
- supervising two full-time and two part-time staff
- ensuring the security of the premises
- keeping cash records and daily banking
- general display and maintenance of the shop
- serving customers
- resolving customers' complaints.

Think of a job you have held in the past or present and jot down a list of your responsibilities. If you have not had any work experience, think about any voluntary job you may have done, such as helping in a charity or organizing a student event.

No matter what work you are describing, it is likely that your responsibilities can be classified under one of the following major activities:

- *Planning* – Without plans and policies a business has no sense of direction or purpose. Financial information allows plans and policies to be formulated and helps people in the organization understand the targets and standards it intends to achieve. For example, a manager needs to know what profit it is hoped the business will make; on a personal level you need information in order to plan holidays, whether you need to take a weekend job, and so on.

●   *Controlling* – A large number of responsibilities at work are concerned with ensuring that the organization makes progress towards its set objectives. For control to be effectively maintained, financial information is required on such matters as the various costs of products and processes, monitoring labour efficiency and identifying the sources and purpose of all expenditure. Similarly for social activities, such as organizing a student ball, information is needed to ensure that a loss is not made.

●   *Decision making* – In establishing plans, it is necessary to decide which of the various courses of action should be taken. We need to know the financial implications of our actions in order to select the most appropriate plan. In business, a manager may need to make a decision between using machinery and labour on an activity; on a personal level we may need to make a decision between buying a car and using public transport.

activity

Consider any financial information you currently receive and classify it according to whether it helps you in controlling, planning or decision making. The information can be financial information you receive at work or at home, such as your bank statement or household bills. You may find that some types of information help with more than one activity.

Once you have completed your list, compare it with the one you drew up for the previous activity. The information should match. For example, if you decided that most of your responsibilities are concerned with controlling, then most of the information you receive will be ticked under that heading in your list. On the other hand, you may have identified financial information that you require but do not currently receive, or financial information you receive but cannot use because you do not understand it. In later chapters we shall be looking at different types of financial information and identifying those that are most relevant to your responsibilities.

1.7   users of financial statements

We are now ready to consider the main users of financial information produced by different types of business entity.

activity

List the various groups of people who might find financial information about a business useful and give some examples of how they might use it.

The contents of your list will depend to a large extent on the type of organization you had in mind. It is easy to appreciate that management will have an interest in financial information about the business, as we have already discussed that they need it in order to run the business and carry out their responsibilities of planning, controlling and decision making. In general, financial information about a business is important to its owners, lenders, suppliers, employees and customers to assess the financial strength of the business. It is also important to the government to evaluate its economic and fiscal policies and to government agencies, such as those responsible for collecting taxes, regulation or keeping statistical records. Financial information about the business may also be used by competitors, potential purchasers, pressure groups and members of the public who are interested in its activities.

Whether financial information is readily available depends upon on the type of business and, to some extent, its size. Since sole proprietorships and general partnerships are not required to make public disclosure of financial information, the main user of their financial statements is management. In other words, their financial statements are prepared for those responsible for running the business.

On the other hand, limited liability entities have a statutory obligation to publish annual financial statements by sending a copy to shareholders and filing them at Companies House. The communication of the financial statements to external parties in this way is known as *financial reporting*. The following list summarizes the main users of the financial statements published by limited liability entities (ASB, 1999):

- Present and potential investors for assessing investment risk and return
- Employees for assessing job security, job opportunities and for pay bargaining
- Lenders for assessing and monitoring lending risk
- Suppliers and other trade creditors for assessing and monitoring credit risk
- Customers for evaluating continuity of supply, after sales service/warranties
- Governments and their agencies for allocating resources, taxation, regulation, national statistics and so on
- The public for evaluating such things as the impact of the entity's activities on the local economy, the community and the environment.

Because of the importance of financial reporting, we shall be examining the needs of the users of the financial statements in more detail in the next chapters.

1.8 conclusions

In this first chapter of the book we have described the two main branches of accounting and looked at the roles of financial and management accountants. We have examined and contrasted the main characteristics of two types of unincorporated business (sole proprietorships and general partnerships) and two types of incorporated business (limited liability partnerships and limited liability companies). We have also compared a private limited company with a public limited company. This has allowed us to draw out the financial implications resulting from the choice of business type, with a particular focus on raising capital and disclosure of financial information.

Our discussion of the importance of accounting in providing financial information to internal users allowed us to draw the general conclusion that it is useful because it aids management in their responsibilities for planning, controlling and decision making. Finally, we have examined the users of the financial statements of limited liability entities.

practice questions

1. Explain why students studying business or management subjects should learn about accounting.
2. Define accounting and explain the difference between the two main branches of accounting.
3. Compare the advantages and disadvantages of sole proprietorships, general partnerships and limited liability entities.
4. Explain the concept of limited liability.
5. Identify the seven main users of the financial statements of limited liability entities and briefly describe their information needs.

references

ASB (1999) *Statement of Principles for Financial Reporting*, December, London: Accounting Standards Board.

Collis, J. (2003) *Directors' Views on Exemption from Statutory Audit*, URN 03/1342, October, London: DTI, www.dti.gov.uk/cld.

Collis, J. and Jarvis, R. (2002) 'Financial information and the management of small private companies', *Journal of Small Business and Enterprise Development*, 9(2): 100–10.

DTI (2003) *Companies in 2002–2003*, July, London: The Stationery Office.

Edwards, J. R. (2003) 'The accountancy profession: Where they came from', *Accountancy*, June, pp. 58–60.

European Communities (2004) *Highlights from the 2003 Observatory, 2003/8*, Luxembourg: Office for Official Publications of the European Communities, http://europa.eu.int/comm/enterprise/enterprise_policy/analysis/observatory_en.htm.

Fisher, L. (2003) 'Institutes vie for slice of growing profession', *Accountancy*, June, p. 62.

Hussey, R. (ed.) (1999) *Oxford Dictionary of Accounting*, Oxford: Oxford University Press.

Mallet, N. and Brumwell, J. (1994) 'The concept of limited liability', *Credit Control*, 15(10): 6–9.

Nobes, C. and Kellas, J. (1990) *Accountancy Explained*, London: Penguin Books.

Oxford Paperback Encyclopedia (1998) Oxford: Oxford University Press.

SBS (2004) *Annual Small Business Survey 2003*, URN 04/390, www.sbs.gov.uk/analytical.

SBS (2005) *Small and Medium Enterprises (SME) Statistics for the UK 2004*, URN 05/92, www.sbs.gov.uk/content/statistics.

Simon, H. (1960) *Administrative Behaviour*, 2nd edn, London: Macmillan – now Palgrave Macmillan.

accounting principles and rules

Learning objectives

When you have studied this chapter, you should be able to:

- Explain the need for regulation

- Describe the main accounting principles for financial accounting

- Identify the key regulations for partnerships and limited liability entities in the UK

- Explain the importance of international accounting standards and the associated conceptual framework to users.

2.1 introduction

In Chapter 1 we explained that accounting is a process that involves identifying, measuring, recording and communicating the economic transactions of an organization and identified the main users to whom the information is communicated. All users, but external parties in particular, need to know that the accounting information they receive is of high quality and reliable. They also need to be able to understand how the figures have been calculated and be able to compare financial statements in the knowledge that they have been prepared on the same basis.

In this chapter we introduce the main accounting principles and rules that provide the regulatory framework for financial accounting in the UK. This framework is rooted in common practices that have evolved over many years and today some elements are codified in law, whilst others are either non-mandatory regulations or regarded as good practice. We start by looking at the importance of financial reporting and the need for regulation. This is followed by an explanation of some of the fundamental principles that apply to the financial statements of all business entities. We then go on to examine the rules and regulations that apply to partnerships and limited liability entities. The next section discusses the role of accounting standards, which have a major influence on financial reporting, since they specify how particular financial transactions and events should be reflected in the financial statements. We also discuss the move towards international convergence of financial reporting through the use of international accounting standards. The final section explains how the development of accounting standards is underpinned by a conceptual framework, which assists in improving the quality of financial reporting.

2.2 need for regulation

All businesses produce financial statements to report on their business, although the content and format differs according to whether they are a sole proprietorship, partnership or limited liability entity. We shall be looking at these differences in subsequent chapters. The financial statements set out the financial progress (or lack of it) and give an indication of the financial health of the business at a specific date. For sole traders and partnerships the distribution of annual financial statements is often restricted to the owners of the business and those with a direct interest, such as the bank and the tax authorities. You will remember from Chapter 1 that we used the term *financial reporting* to refer to the communication of the financial statements of an organization to external parties and this is a key part of financial accounting. Users of the financial statements rely on the integrity and judgement of management to provide high quality and reliable information.

Over the years it has been found that a *regulatory framework* is needed to ensure that all members of the accountancy profession prepare financial statements in a standard way and produce high quality, reliable information. The regulatory framework is known as *Generally Accepted Accounting Principles (GAAP)*. GAAP provides guidance to accountants on the work they do in preparing and presenting the financial statements. Over the years, individual countries have developed their own regulatory frameworks, which can be described as UK GAAP, US GAAP and so on. Some countries in the developing world have minimal legislation, whilst other countries, such as the USA, have a highly developed and prescriptive system. This state of affairs is not satisfactory in today's increasingly global marketplace and has led to the development of International GAAP, which has been adopted as the basis for financial reporting by listed group companies in all 25 members of the EU. In total nearly 100 countries are committed to adopting International GAAP, including Australia, China and Hong Kong, Norway, South Africa and Switzerland.

The focus of GAAP in most countries is on financial reporting by large companies (Big GAAP). In UK GAAP there are concessions and exemptions for smaller companies (Little GAAP) and there is work in progress on developing something similar at the international level. UK GAAP is based partly on principles and partly on rules. This means there are both mandatory and non-mandatory elements. The main elements are:

- Accounting standards
- Company legislation
- Stock exchange rules.

KEY DEFINITION	Generally Accepted Accounting Principles (GAAP) in the UK are the accounting standards, the requirements of company legislation and stock exchange rules.

Before we start looking at the role of the different elements of UK GAAP, we will examine the end product of financial reporting. The financial statements of limited liability entities are included in a document called the *annual report and accounts* because it contains narrative reports (such as a report from the directors that explains its activities and operations throughout the year and the auditors' report) and quantitative financial statements. It is the most useful source of financial information issued by a limited liability entity.

In Chapter 1 we noted that limited liability entities can be divided into LLPs, *public limited companies* (which are sometimes referred to as listed or quoted companies) and *private limited companies* (which are always unlisted companies). Many public limited companies are well-known high street names, such as Boots, Marks & Spencer, J Sainsbury, Tesco and WHSmith, or banks such as Barclays, Lloyds TSB, Halifax, HSBC and NatWest. Because of the importance of public limited companies to the economy in terms of the numbers they employ and their products and services, information on them is by far the easiest to obtain. If you look in the business pages of newspapers such as the *Independent*, the *Guardian*, *The Times* or the *Financial Times*, you will find the names and share prices of the major public limited companies and other news about them.

All incorporated bodies (except some unlimited companies) have a legal obligation to file a copy of their annual report and accounts with the Registrar of Companies, which is part of the Department of Trade and Industry (DTI). Thus, the statutory accounts of limited companies, regardless of size, are public documents. For a small fee, anyone can inspect the annual report and accounts of a limited liability entity once it has been filed with the Registrar of Companies. If you do not want to pay to see a copy of an annual report and accounts, the easiest to obtain are those of a public limited company. You might start by looking on the company's website, telephoning or writing to the company. Alternatively, you can use the service offered by the *Financial Times* or look in the reference section of your library. Of course, if you are a shareholder, the company is legally required to send you a copy.

activity

Obtain a copy of the annual report and accounts for three public limited companies and compare the information they disclose and the wording they use.

In addition to the information that a company is obliged to disclose, additional material is often provided voluntarily. This may be information about its products, its employees, the environment or any charitable or community work it is involved in. Because companies differ in their activities and the amount of information they volunteer, no two annual reports and accounts are exactly the same. However, the following list shows the type of information you are likely to find:

- Chairman's statement
- Highlights of the main financial results
- Operating and financial review
- Corporate governance statement
- Environmental and community issues
- Financial statements
    - Profit and loss account (called an income statement under International GAAP)
    - Balance sheet
    - Cash flow statement (not required for qualifying small companies)
- Directors' report
- Auditors' report (not required for qualifying small companies)
- Statement of accounting policies
- Notes to the accounts.

In some cases you may find that the financial statements are headed 'consolidated'. *Consolidated accounts* are the financial statements of a group of companies. To allow shareholders to appreciate the activities of the entire group, financial information from the individual financial statements of the parent company and its subsidiaries is adjusted and combined to form these consolidated accounts. The consolidated financial statements must give a *true and fair view* of the profit or loss for the period and the state of affairs as at the last day of the period of the companies included in the consolidation.

Financial reporting is a dynamic and expensive activity. As new issues are raised as areas of public interest (for example environmental issues, directors' remuneration and corporate governance), so companies must attempt to address them in their annual report and accounts, either voluntarily or as required by the regulations. This has resulted in the annual report and accounts of major companies expanding greatly; some now exceed 100 pages. In addition to publishing printed copies of their annual report and accounts, some companies provide Braille, audio and video versions and may also put them on their websites. The publishing costs of all these activities, plus the postage costs incurred in sending a copy to every shareholder, means that financial reporting is a very expensive exercise.

2.3 accounting principles

Financial accounting is a complex activity and accountants are guided in their work by certain *accounting principles*. An accounting principle is a fundamental *concept* or *convention* that forms the basis for the work done by financial accountants in identifying, measuring, recording and communicating economic transactions. It is important that all accountants use the same principles; if they did not do so, different accountants would view similar economic transactions in different ways. Some of the main principles that underpin financial accounting cannot be properly understood until we have looked at financial statements in detail in Part II, but at this stage we can introduce some of the most important basic principles.

The *accruals concept* is the principle that revenue and costs are recognized as they are earned and incurred and they are matched with one another and dealt with in the profit and loss account of the period to which they relate, irrespective of when cash (or its equivalent) is received or paid. It lies at the heart of all financial statements and you will find that the early part of your studies will be concerned with this assumption.

activity

> During the month of August your friend sold a car for £750 that he had purchased at the beginning of the month for only £600. He paid cash for the car, but has not yet received the cash from the buyer. What is his financial position at the end of August?

Using the accruals concept we can calculate that the profit he has made as follows:

		£
	Sales	750
Less	Purchases	600
	Profit	150

However, that is only part of the story. At the end of the month he has £600 less than he had at the start of the month because he has paid for the car, but has not yet received the cash from the buyer. We can show his cash position as follows:

		£
	Cash at the start of the month	600
Less	Purchases	600
	Cash at the end of the month	0

It is because of the accruals concept that we need to use more than one financial statement to give a complete picture of the financial performance and wealth of a business.

The *going concern concept* is the principle that financial statements are normally prepared on the basis that the entity is a going concern and will continue in operation for the foreseeable future as far as it is known. Thus, unless it is known otherwise, it is assumed that the entity is not intending to close down or cut back its activities.

A business bought a machine for the production department at the beginning of the year for £1,500. It is estimated that the machine will generate profits for the next 10 years. Six months later the chief accountant finds out that if the machine had to be sold it would be worth only £1,000. Using the going concern concept, which of these two figures should be shown in the accounts?

You may have found this question quite difficult to answer. The clue lies in understanding what we mean by a going concern. As we have already seen, a going concern is a business that will continue to operate for the foreseeable future. This means that there is no intention to close the business or significantly reduce any of its activities. In other words, the business does not have to sell its machine and therefore the machine would be shown in the accounts at £1,500, as it is anticipated that it will continue to generate profits.

Next we consider what situation a business might be in if it were not a going concern. You are probably aware of the consequences of a business closing or going into liquidation. The activities of the business cease, the workforce is made redundant and any assets the business owns, such as buildings, vehicles, office equipment and so on are liquidated. This means that they are sold and the proceeds used to pay any outstanding debts. If the business is a going concern, the correct figure for the machine is the price which was paid for it: £1,500. If the business is not a going concern, the figure would be the estimated market value of the machine: £1,000. However, if there was no going concern concept, either of these figures might be used and this would be very confusing to the users of accounting information.

In addition to the accruals concept and the going concern concepts, there are six other fundamental accounting principles:

- The *materiality concept* is the principle that only items of information that are material (significant) are included in the financial statements. An item of information is material if its omission or misstatement could influence the economic decisions of those using the financial statements. Materiality depends on the size of the item or error and the circumstances of its omission or misstatement. Therefore, the materiality test provides a threshold (cut-off point) rather than being a primary qualitative characteristic that information must have to be useful (ASB, 1999).
- The *money measurement concept* is the principle that only items that are capable of being measured in monetary terms are included in the financial statements. For example, rather than recording the number of haircuts in a year, Cut Above Hairdressing must record the value of the haircuts. Thus, 1,500 haircuts at £30 each becomes a sales figure of £45,000. Related to this concept is the assumption that currency is stable and holds its value over time (for example there is no inflation or deflation and no fluctuation in foreign exchange rates).
- The *historical cost concept* is the principle that the values of assets are based on their original acquisition cost, unadjusted for subsequent changes in price or value. This presents some problems. For example, four years ago a business may have had to pay £50 for 500 sheets of printed stationery, but due to advances in technology the printed paper would only cost £45 today. On the other hand, the business may have paid £250 for a desk four years ago, but today a similar desk may cost £350 due to the higher cost of the

wood used. Some assets, such as property in a prime location, increase in value over time. There is much debate over whether historical cost, replacement cost, net realizable value (selling price less costs of selling), fair value (amount at which an asset could be exchanged between knowledgeable and willing parties in an arms-length transaction) or some other method is the most appropriate basis for considering the values of assets.

- The *consistency concept* is the principle that there is uniformity of accounting treatment of items of a similar nature within each accounting period and from one period to the next. This allows financial information to be compared easily.
- The *prudence concept* is the principle that revenue and profits are not anticipated, but are included in the profit and loss account only if there is reasonable certainty that they will be received. On the other hand, provision for all known expenses and losses must be made, whether the amount is known with certainty or is only a best estimate in the light of the information available.
- The *business entity concept* is the principle that information in the financial statements relates only to the activities of the entity and not to the activities of its owner(s). This means that a business like Cut Above Hairdressing is considered to exist separately from its owner, Roberto Garibaldi.

It can be helpful to group accounting principles into three categories (Dyson, 2004):

- *Boundary concepts* are principles that place limits on what data should be recorded and communicated.
- *Measurement concepts* are principles that guide how the data should be recorded.
- *Ethical concepts* require the accountant to follow not just the letter of the principle but also the spirit of the principle.

Figure 2.1 summarizes the eight accounting principles we have described in this chapter according to this classification system.

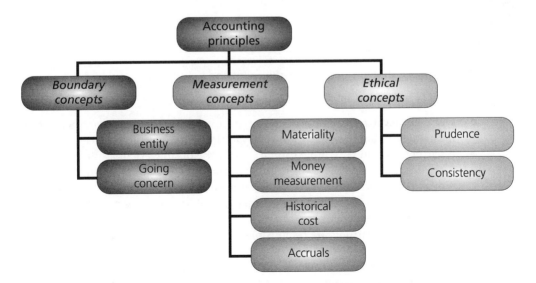

FIGURE 2.1 **Classification of main accounting principles**

In recent years the regulation of accounting has changed dramatically and over time our opinions of the importance and meaning of the accounting principles have changed, and will continue to do so. At this stage you may find the individual accounting principles fairly difficult to understand, but as they are fundamental to the preparation of financial statements, it is important to know of their existence. We will show how they are applied in later chapters.

2.4 regulation of partnerships

You will remember from Chapter 1 that a partnership is an entity in which two or more people join together in business with a view to making a profit. The Business Names Act 1985 requires the names of the partners to be shown on business stationery, but they need not be used in the business name. The partners must keep accounting records and in the absence of a written or verbal *partnership agreement*, the Partnership Act 1890 applies. Amongst its provisions are the following important rules:

- Profits and losses – All partners are entitled to share equally in the capital gains and profits, and must contribute equally towards the losses, whether capital losses or otherwise, incurred by the firm.
- Interest on capital – Partners are not entitled to any interest on capital and therefore such interest cannot be deducted in ascertaining the profits of the business.
- Interest on loans – Partners are entitled to interest at 5% per annum on any loan capital contributed in excess of the agreed capital subscribed.
- Salaries – All partners are entitled to take part in the management of the business, but no partner is entitled to any remuneration for acting in the business of the partnership.

---

activity

What are the main differences between a partnership and a sole trader?

You may have thought of some of the following points, some of which we introduced in Chapter 1:

- There are legal requirements that apply to partnerships, whereas there are no legal formalities for a sole trader who wishes to start a business.
- A partnership can raise more capital to start the business than a sole trader.
- A greater range of skills is likely to be available to run a partnership business than is available in a sole trader business because partnerships have more than one owner.
- The pressures of managing the business are shared in a partnership, whereas a sole trader must bear them alone.
- The individual partners are responsible for the actions of the others, whilst a sole trader has none of these worries.
- In a partnership no one has sole control and one partner's wishes may be overruled by the other partners; a sole trader has total control over the business.

- It can be more difficult to transfer interest in a partnership than in a sole trader business.
- In a general partnership, any loss made is shared among the partners, whereas a sole trader suffers the whole of any loss the business incurs.

One of the major disadvantages of a general partnership is the financial risk to individual partners due to the actions of other partners carried out in the normal course of business. In other words, if you are a partner and one of the other partners is totally incompetent and incurs large debts, you will have a responsibility for these even if it means bankruptcy. If the partnership has only two or three partners it may be possible to monitor the activities of all partners. With big partnerships, such as accounting firms, there can be many hundreds of partners spread throughout the world and it would be impossible to monitor all their activities. Moreover, it would not be very agreeable to accept personal liability for their actions.

To resolve this issue the Limited Liability Partnership Act 2000 was introduced. This allows a *limited liability partnership (LLP)* to enter into agreements and contracts, to be sued and to sue in the name of the partnership, as it is considered a separate legal entity from its members (the partners). Partners are only liable up to the amount of their capital in the LLP. There are some exceptions to this rule and it is essential that there is a partnership agreement for an LLP. The main advantage of an LLP is that the members' liability is limited up to the amount of their capital in the LLP, whereas partners in a simple partnership have unlimited liability. There are two main exceptions to this restriction on liability:

- Where the member of an LLP was personally at fault they may have unlimited liability if they accepted a personal duty of care or a personal contractual obligation.
- If an LLP becomes insolvent, members can be required to repay any property withdrawn from the LLP, including profits and interest, in the two years prior to insolvency. This is only applicable where it is reasonable that the member could not have concluded that insolvency was likely.

2.5 company law

All businesses with limited liability, whether they are LLPs or limited companies, are governed by *company law* and a number of other rules and regulations. It can be argued that this high level of regulation is the price they pay for having limited liability. The key elements of UK GAAP that apply to limited liability entities are:

- The *Companies Act 1985 (CA85)*, as amended by the Companies Act 1989 and subsequent statutory instruments.
- *Accounting standards* and other pronouncements issued by the Accounting Standards Board (ASB) or the International Accounting Standards Board (IASB), as applicable (we will be looking at these in the next two sections).
- *Stock exchange rules* which apply only to listed companies.

Originally, UK GAAP was based solely on company law, which provided a broad framework only. However, the 1980s saw a significant increase in the regulatory burden resulting from the obligation to incorporate the requirements of legal directives from the EU. The main directives relating to financial reporting were:

- The Fourth Directive (1978) which covered single entity accounts
- The Seventh Directive (1983) which covered consolidated (group) accounts
- The Eighth Directive (1984) which covered the statutory audit.

In the UK, the requirements of these directives were incorporated in CA85; other members of the EU share the same obligation to introduce the regulations in their national GAAP.

CA85 lays down the broad requirements and format of the financial information that must be disclosed by both public and private limited companies and LLPs. The details of how and what should be disclosed are contained in the accounting standards issued by the ASB or the IASB. The main requirements placed on every limited liability entity by CA85 are as follows:

- They must register with the Registrar of Companies at Companies House.
- They must file a memorandum of association, which defines the company's constitution and objects, and articles of association, which contain the internal regulations of the company, with the Registrar of Companies.
- They must keep accounting records which show and explain the company's transactions.
- They must prepare final accounts comprising a profit and loss account and balance sheet (there are options that offer some concessions to qualifying small entities), directors' report and auditors' report (optional for qualifying small entities) in respect of each financial year of the company and lay them before the members (shareholders) in a general meeting. This forms the basis of the annual report and accounts, which must also be delivered to the Registrar of Companies where it is available to the public.

Unless the company qualifies for exemption from statutory audit, external auditors must be appointed to audit the accounts and their report consists of an opinion on whether the accounts show a *true and fair view* of the financial performance and position of the business. Although there is no legal definition of the term, the true and fair view concept is important in the UK and may be used as an override to depart from legal requirements.

To help reduce the complexity of the annual report and accounts for individual personal shareholders in listed companies (as opposed to institutional shareholders), since 1990 they have been given the option of receiving *summary financial statements* instead, providing certain conditions are met. A summary financial statement need only contain a minimum amount of financial information, taking up some three or four pages, but many companies have chosen to incorporate it in a larger document often referred to as an *annual review*. The annual review also contains voluntarily provided information, usually concerning the company's products, progress and activities, in an attractive and easily read format. However, the company must still file the full report and accounts with the Registrar of Companies.

As we mentioned in Chapter 1, 99% of companies are private limited companies, and under CA85 one person alone may form a private company. Therefore, some private companies are very small with few employees. It is an offence for a private limited company to offer its shares to the public and private companies (and public limited companies not listed on a stock exchange) do not have to comply with stock exchange rules. In addition, there are a number of concessions for small private companies relating to the financial information they have to publish, which means they can choose to file *abbreviated accounts* with the Registrar of Companies. However, they must still provide full accounts for shareholders.

activity

> What are the main differences between private and public limited companies?

The most obvious differences are their names and the fact that public limited companies can offer their shares to the public, but there are other dissimilarities, some of which we mentioned in Chapter 1. It is usually easier for public companies to raise large amounts of finance because they can offer their shares for sale in the capital markets via a stock exchange. Large companies require considerable amounts of capital to fund their activities and therefore the company needs to be able to offer its shares to the public in this way. Public limited companies also have a higher public profile and are often, but not always, familiar names and have a good reputation. They can often pay high salaries to attract the best staff and negotiate favourable terms for many of their transactions because of their size and status.

Private limited companies have some advantages over public limited companies. They are not obliged to comply with stock exchange regulations and most small private companies do not have to disclose as much financial information as a public company. In addition, the formalities for setting up a private limited company are somewhat easier than for a public company. As discussed in Chapter 1, most companies are started as a private limited company and if they are successful and grow large, the owners may decide to re-register as a public company. This is known as *going public* or *flotation* because the company can then seek a listing on a stock exchange. Part of the proceeds from the new issue of shares goes to the original members, who inevitably lose some control of the company as the ownership widens. However, they are often well paid for the interests they are relinquishing.

2.6 UK accounting standards

Although company law is important in setting out a general framework, financial accounting is driven by *accounting standards*, which makes them a very important element of GAAP. Prior to 1970, financial reporting in the UK was governed solely by company law (and stock exchange rules for listed companies only). This basic framework was insufficient for the complexities of business and there were a number of highly publicized cases of companies reporting misleading profits. The main problems concerned the amount of flexibility permitted in the way companies could account for transactions and the minimum amount of information they could disclose. To address these problems, the accounting profession set up the Accounting Standards Committee (ASC), the first standard-setting body in the UK. The objective was to reduce flexibility by requiring all members of the accountancy bodies to apply accounting standards or face disciplinary action. The ASC issued 25 accounting standards in its lifetime known as *Statements of Standard Accounting Practice (SSAPs)*.

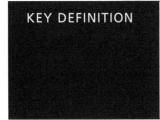

KEY DEFINITION | An accounting standard is an authoritative statement of how a particular type of transaction or other event should be reflected in the financial statements. Compliance with accounting standards is normally necessary for the financial statements to give a true and fair view.

Although the ASC did much to improve the quality of financial reporting, it never had sufficient authority or resources to deal with all the problems arising. Therefore, in 1990 an independent regulator for corporate reporting and governance, the Financial Reporting Council (FRC), was set up and the ASC was replaced by the Accounting Standards Board (ASB) with an Urgent Issues Task Force to deal with urgent matters. Other boards under the FRC include the Auditing Practices Board, which issues standards on auditing practice, and the Professional Oversight Board, which is responsible for the independent oversight of the regulation of the accountancy profession by the accountancy bodies. Figure 2.2 shows the structure of the Financial Reporting Council.

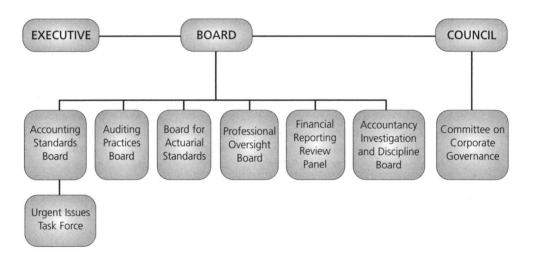

FIGURE 2.2 **Structure of the Financial Reporting Council**
Source: www.frc.org.uk/about/chart.cfm.

The ASB issues accounting standards known as Financial Reporting Standards (FRSs). Accounting standards apply to financial statements that are intended to give a true and fair view. Because of the complex structure and activities of large companies, all the accounting standards are important for them. However, some accounting standards are concerned with events and transactions that are not likely to apply to small companies. Prompted by a concern to reduce financial reporting burdens on the many small private companies and unincorporated businesses, in 1997 the ASB issued the first Financial Reporting Standard for

Smaller Entities (FRSSE). The measurement bases in the FRSSE are the same as, or a simplification of, those in existing accounting standards, and the definitions and accounting treatments are consistent with the requirements of CA85. The FRSSE is updated on a regular basis and was significantly extended in 2005. It now draws together conveniently in one document all the financial reporting requirements that apply to smaller entities under UK GAAP, including those contained in CA85.

activity

> What are the advantages and disadvantages of having accounting standards?

Looking first at the *advantages*, accounting standards offer a number of benefits to the users and preparers of accounts. The preparers have an authoritative guide to the most appropriate method for accounting for many of the important activities undertaken by companies. The users have additional financial information to that required by legislation alone, as well as information about the basis on which the accounts have been drawn up. This allows comparison of a company's results with other companies and between one year and another.

The main *disadvantage* of accounting standards is that they impose additional work and, therefore, the business incurs additional costs, which can be a considerable burden on smaller entities. However, to some extent this is offset by the sophisticated software that has been developed for the accountancy profession. Therefore, the main difficulty is faced by the standard-setters in deciding which accounting methods are appropriate for all businesses in all industries and in all circumstances.

2.7 international accounting standards

As companies have become larger and increasingly global in their ownership and activities, there has been growing pressure for *international accounting standards*. We have already mentioned that many countries have developed their own regulatory frameworks and, not surprisingly, this has led to some significant differences in corporate financial reporting. For example, differences in the accounting treatments allowed mean that a company can show one figure of profit when the financial statements are drawn up under one country's rules and a different profit when another country's rules are used. Differences in national GAAP are important when a company seeks a listing on a stock exchange in another country. For example, if a UK company wants its shares to be traded on the New York Stock Exchange as well as on the London Stock Exchange, it must prepare two sets of accounts (one complying with US requirements, the other complying with UK requirements) or a reconciliation statement. The main reasons for differences in accounting practices are shown in Figure 2.3.

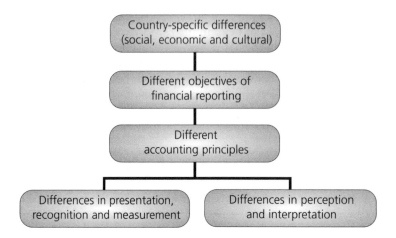

FIGURE 2.3 **Reasons for national differences in GAAP**
Source: Adapted from Haller and Walton, 1998, p. 2.

Some countries in the developing world have minimal regulation, whilst other countries have a highly developed and prescriptive system. This state of affairs is not satisfactory in today's increasingly global marketplace and has led to the development of international GAAP. In 1973, the International Accounting Standards Committee (IASC) was set up to produce basic International Accounting Standards (IAS) that could be followed by all countries. However, a major drawback was that the IASC had no power to impose the standards they issued. Another problem was that, understandably, countries are reluctant to change their own standards which have been developed in the context of their own accounting practices. The IASC also found it difficult to agree regulations that would be appropriate for all companies, in all countries and in all circumstances, because by the time it was dissolved in 2001, it had grown from 10 members to 153 members in 112 countries.

An important step in reaching international standards that are acceptable to the different stock exchanges around the world took place in 1987 when the International Organization for Securities Commissions (IOSCO) was formed. By 1995 it had been agreed that the IASC should develop a basic set of accounting standards that IOSCO would endorse as internationally acceptable. A working party was set up and after extensive consultation the IASC handed over responsibility and a new structure came into effect in 2001.

The new structure is headed by an independent oversight organization, the International Accounting Standards Committee Foundation (the IASC Foundation). Governance of the IASC Foundation rests with 19 trustees, who are responsible for appointing the members of:

- the *International Accounting Standards Board (IASB)*,which issues International Financial Reporting Standards (IFRSs)
- the *International Financial Reporting Interpretations Committee (IFRIC)*, which deals with issues in connection with the interpretation of IFRSs
- the *Standards Advisory Council (SAC)*, which advises the IASB on agenda decisions and priorities, and puts forward the views of the organization and individuals on SAC.

Figure 2.4 shows the reporting structure of the IASC Foundation.

FIGURE 2.4 **Structure of the International Accounting Standards Committee Foundation**

Source: Adapted from www.iasb.org.about/structure.asp.

One crucial element in establishing the IASB was that it would have sufficient resources to carry out the responsibilities placed upon it. The task of securing those funds rests with the 19 trustees of the Foundation. According to Article 2 of the constitution, the objectives of the Foundation are:

(a) to develop, in the public interest, a single set of high quality, understandable and enforceable global accounting standards … to help participants in the world's capital markets and other users make economic decisions by having access to high quality, transparent, and comparable information;

(b) to promote the use and vigorous application of those standards;

(c) to bring about convergence of national accounting standards and International Accounting Standards and International Financial Reporting Standards to high quality solutions.

After initially adopting the 25 IASs issued by the old IASC, the IASB has now issued some 40 new IFRSs, some of which have replaced certain IASs. In many respects, the process of standard setting by the IASB differs little from that of many national bodies. Having established an accounting issue, there is a lengthy procedure to ensure wide consultation and full consideration of problems and alternative solutions. After all comments have been examined and field tests have been conducted, the IASB publishes an *exposure draft* for public comment. The exposure draft takes the same form and content as the proposed standard. After considering all comments and making any amendments, the IASB issues the standard.

So far, the IASB has been concentrating on accounting standards for large, listed companies, but it is now developing an IFRS for SMEs, based on the same measurement rules and principles as full IFRSs. This will take the form of a stand-alone, self-contained standard, with fallbacks to full IFRSs (IASB, 2006). The aim is to:

● provide greater consistency with full IFRSs
● improve comparability for users
● reduce burdens for preparers.

The European Commission supports the work of the IASB and since 2005 all public limited companies that are listed on an EU stock exchange are obliged to use IFRSs for preparing consolidated (group) accounts. This is a big step forward in the harmonization of the regulation of financial reporting in the 25 members of the EU. However, as mentioned earlier in this chapter, this move towards convergence goes further than the EU and in total more than 100 countries are committed to adopting IFRSs. Some countries, such as the UK, have their own standard setters and have amended their standards to conform with IFRSs or have adapted IFRSs to suit their needs. Some countries with no standard setters have adopted IFRSs as their national standards. The development of the IFRS for SMEs will mean that over the next few years international accounting standards will have a major impact on the financial statements of a wider range of entities.

activity

What are the advantages and disadvantages of having an IFRS for SMEs?

Apart from contributing to international convergence, some of the specific *advantages* of the IFRS for SMEs are:

- It will reduce the financial reporting burden on SMEs wanting to adopt international standards.
- It will aid comparison if it is applied consistently.
- It reduces the risk of many different national GAAPs for SMES, all loosely based on full IFRSs.
- It will reduce information costs and information risk to users.
- It will allow easy transition to full IFRSs if the business grows.

The main *disadvantages* are:

- It is hard to agree a definition of an SME that is appropriate and acceptable throughout the developed and developing world, in both market economies and in transition economies (those that have only recently moved to market economies).
- It is based on full IFRSs, which have been designed for large, listed companies, rather than on the needs of small, private companies.
- The unique features of the national GAAP for SMEs in a particular jurisdiction may be lost.

adoption of international accounting standards

'The endorsement of IASB standards by the EU in 2005 will be an important achievement, but it will be only the first step in an important international development. Whatever the difficulties, there is undoubtedly a strong demand for international accounting standards, and basic economics tells us that, in a well-functioning market, what is demanded is usually supplied. Ultimately, markets need full, transparent information, untainted by concessions to vested interests. The IASB is attempting to meet this need by following the ultimate objective "tell it the way it is". In doing that, it hopes to avoid the accounting surprises that have so disrupted the capital markets in recent months and years. Distorting accounting information to favour particular groups may seem to be convenient in the short term, but in the longer term it will lead to further unpleasant surprises, uncertainty and lack of confidence in business, which will be damaging to future economic prosperity.'

Source: Whittington, 2005, p. 152.

2.8 conceptual frameworks

Prior to 1970, the regulatory framework in the UK was modest, and the way in which the profession attempted to achieve consistency in financial reporting was based on rationalizing what happened in practice. However, this system was criticized on the grounds that the interests of the professional regulators differed from the interests of preparers and users. This highlighted the need for a *conceptual framework* to provide a set of coherent underlying principles on which to base financial reporting and to answer such questions as:

- What are the objectives of the financial statements that are being reported?
- Who are the users of the financial statements?
- What information does each group of users need?
- What type of financial statements would best satisfy their needs?

KEY DEFINITION A conceptual framework is a statement of theoretical principles that provides guidance for financial accounting and reporting.

In the USA, the Financial Accounting Standards Board (FASB) published *Concept Statements* between 1978 and 2000. These were a strong influence on developments at the international level, and in 1989 the former IASC issued the *Framework for the Preparation and Presentation of Financial Statements*, which was subsequently adopted by the IASB. Both the US and the IASB frameworks form the basis of the UK's *Statement of Principles for Financial Reporting* (the SoP), which was published by the ASB in 1999. Our discussion will focus on the IASB Framework, which is divided into the following sections:

- The objectives of financial statements

- Underlying assumptions
- Qualitative characteristics of financial statements
- The elements of financial statements
- Recognition of the elements of financial statements
- Measurement of the elements of financial statements
- Concepts of capital and capital maintenance.

The document is relatively short, with approximately 100 paragraphs. Although it is beyond the scope of this book to examine the contents in detail, you will find it easier to understand the importance of GAAP if you know something about what the IASB Framework contains.

The objective of financial statements is 'to provide information about the financial position, performance and changes in financial position of an enterprise that is useful to a wide range of users in making economic decisions' (IASB, 1989, paras. 22–3). This objective applies to *general purpose* financial statements, which are those intended to meet the needs of users who are not in a position to demand *special purpose* reports that meet their specific information needs. The UK's SoP and the IASB Framework identify the seven groups shown in Figure 2.5 as the main users of general purpose financial statements.

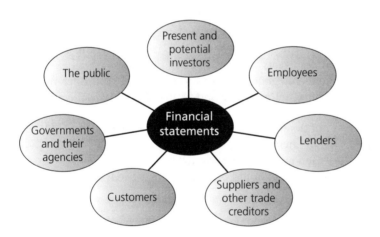

FIGURE 2.5 **Users of published financial statements**

- *Present and potential investors* need to assess the financial performance of the business (how profitable it is), its financial position (what it owns and what it owes) and the amount of dividend they will receive on their shares. They use the financial statements for economic decision making in connection with buying or selling shares and for stewardship purposes (assessing the way in which the directors are managing the business on behalf of the shareholders and whether to reappoint or replace them).
- *Employees* are interested in information that helps them assess job security, the possibility of an increase in remuneration, employment opportunities, retirement and other benefits.

- *Lenders* need information for risk assessment purposes and deciding the terms of the loan, and monitoring that risk once the loan has been given (assessing whether the interest will be paid and the loan repaid when due).
- *Suppliers and other trade creditors* need information for similar purposes to lenders, as they need to assess whether to provide goods or services to the business on credit and to assess whether the amounts owed to them by the business will be repaid.
- *Customers* are interested in information about the continued existence of the business and its ability to supply goods or services, especially if there are product warranties or specialized replacement parts involved.
- *Governments and their agencies* are interested in the allocation of resources and the effect of their economic and fiscal policies. Therefore, they need information for regulatory purposes, assessing taxation and compiling national statistics.
- *The public* are interested in information that is relevant to how they are affected by the organization. For example, the contribution the entity makes to the local economy by providing employment or using local suppliers; its involvement in the community; its contributions to political and charitable groups; the range of its activities.

All these user groups are interested in the financial performance of the entity, but investors, employees, lenders and creditors have a vested interest in the financial health of the business and whether it is a going concern. Therefore, the published financial statements are of particular importance to them.

activity

What do you think would be the effect on users if a large business with limited liability did not supply full information about its financial position, performance and changes in financial position?

You may have thought of some of the following factors:

- Investors will be suspicious that the directors have something to hide and are not running the business in the best interests of the shareholders but in order to benefit themselves. Therefore, investors would be unwilling to invest in the business.
- Employees would be unwilling to work for the business, as they would find it difficult to assess job security, future prospects, retirement benefits and so on.
- Lenders would be unable to assess risk and would not make loans to such a business.
- Suppliers would also be unable to assess risk and would refuse to sell their goods and services on credit to such a business.
- Customers would be unsure about the future prospects of the business and would refuse to enter into long-term contracts.
- Governments and their agencies would be unable to monitor the effect of their economic and fiscal policies, compile detailed national statistics and so on.
- The public would be unable to assess the impact the business has on them with any confidence.

The IASB Framework contends that general purpose financial statements that meet the information needs of investors (who are the providers of risk capital) will also satisfy most of the needs of the other user groups (para. 11). We will be looking at some of the limitations of the information contained in financial statements in Chapter 10. At this stage it is important to note that users would be unwise to rely solely on the financial statements and will also need to obtain information from other sources.

Two underlying assumptions are identified: that the financial statements will be prepared on an accruals basis and a going concern basis (paras. 22–3). These are the same as the concepts we described earlier in the chapter, although the IASB Framework uses different words.

The IASB Framework also identifies four principal *qualitative characteristics* of financial statements that make the information they contain useful to users (para. 25):

- *Understandability* – it should be readily understandable (users are assumed to have reasonable knowledge of business and accounting, and a willingness to study the information).
- *Relevance* – it should be capable of making a difference to users' decisions and materiality provides a threshold point below which relevance does not exist.
- *Reliability* – it is a complete and faithful representation, neutral and prudent.
- *Comparability* – it should be timely and prepared on a consistent basis so users can make comparisons with other periods or other entities.

Although you may find some words difficult to understand at this stage, the importance and meaning of the terms will become clearer as you progress through this book. We will return to the contents of the IASB Framework in Chapter 10, when we consider the elements of financial statements and some of the key definitions provided.

2.9 conclusions

Financial accounting is primarily concerned with providing a true and fair view of the activities of a business to external parties. In this chapter we have seen that accountants prepare financial statements in accordance with a regulatory framework of accounting principles and rules that is underpinned by a conceptual framework.

Accounting principles apply to sole proprietorships, partnerships and limited liability entities. However, the mandatory rules of financial reporting only apply to LLPs, private limited companies and public limited companies. The most stringently regulated businesses are those where there is a public interest in their financial statements, such as public limited companies that are listed on a stock exchange. Listed companies are important because they make a substantial contribution to the economy and because the accounting practices they follow are often used by the regulators to shape accounting practices followed by all businesses.

This chapter has provided an overview of the way in which accounting standards are set in the UK and the move towards international convergence. This is a very important development and we have described some of the main events leading up to the adoption of IFRSs. We will be looking at some of the individual IFRSs in Chapter 10. The impact of all these principles and rules can be seen most clearly in the annual report and accounts of public limited companies. In subsequent chapters we will be looking at how the accountant prepares different types of financial statement and how users can analyse and interpret them.

1. Describe the advantages and disadvantages of accountants using the money measurement concept when preparing financial statements.
2. Explain what is meant by financial reporting and describe the key elements of the regulatory framework for limited liability entities in the UK.
3. Obtain a copy of the annual report and accounts of a public limited company from the library and draw up a table analysing the contents according to the number of pages devoted to each section, the number of photos in each section and the number of diagrams or graphs in each section. Write brief conclusions about the differences between the presentation of the financial statements and the other sections.
4. Describe the range of economic decisions likely to be made by the different user groups identified in the conceptual framework, based on information in the published financial statements.
5. Explain the qualitative characteristics of financial information that make it useful to users.

references

ASB (1999) *Statement of Principles for Financial Reporting*, December, London: Accounting Standards Board.

Dyson, J. (2004) *Accounting for Non-accounting Students*, (6th edn), Harlow: FT Prentice Hall, Pearson Education.

Haller, A. and Walton, P. (1998) 'Country differences and harmonization', in *International Accounting*, Walton, P., Haller, A. and Raffournier, B. (eds), London: International Thomson Business Press.

IASB (1989) *Framework for the Preparation and Presentation of Financial Statements*, September, London: International Accounting Standards Board.

IASB (2006) 'Accounting standards for small and medium-sized entities (SMEs)', *Update*, February, London: International Accounting Standards Board, www.iasb.org.

Whittington, G. (2005) 'Adoption of International Accounting Standards in the European Union', *European Accounting Review*, **14**(1): 125–53.

chapter 3

importance of cash

When you have studied this chapter, you should be able to:

- Explain the theory of a finance gap for small and medium-sized enterprises

- Describe and classify potential sources of business finance

- Explain the need for cash flow information

- Construct and interpret a cash flow forecast and a cash flow statement

- Describe the principles for monitoring and controlling cash.

3.1 introduction

In Chapter 1 we referred to business as being concerned with moneymaking, but before the owners can start making money, they need to have enough cash to run the business. This is something an owner needs to consider when planning a new enterprise or buying an existing business. Once the business has started, irrespective of whether it has been set up as a sole proprietorship, partnership or as a limited liability entity, the cash position needs to be monitored closely. There are many reasons why a business may close and they are not all associated with failure. Nevertheless, the main reason for failure is that the business does not have sufficient cash or credit. Typically, the business will have fallen behind with payments for goods or services received, leading to supplies being cut off. Insufficient cash also means that employees cannot be paid and must be laid off. Thus, cash is crucial if a business is to survive and start making money for the owner(s).

Because of the importance of cash, would-be entrepreneurs and the owners and managers of existing businesses need information about the current and future cash position. This will allow them to ensure that there will be sufficient finance in terms of cash or credit facilities to meet the needs of the business and to plan the investment of any surplus cash. In this chapter we describe the main sources of finance in the UK for small and medium-sized enterprises (SMEs) and discuss the difficulties entrepreneurs may face in seeking finance to start and develop a business. We also introduce you to two simple financial statements that provide information about the cash position of a business: the cash flow forecast, which predicts the future position, and the cash flow statement, which looks at the past position. There is no legal requirement for small firms with unlimited liability to prepare these particular statements, but the majority of well-managed enterprises do so because they are an essential source of information for running the business.

3.2 the finance gap

Business is about trying to make money and you will remember that in Chapter 1 we explained that in general terms finance refers to the management of money and therefore in this sense it is a subject that can be studied. However, there are two further ways in which the term can be used and we are now ready to look at all three definitions:

KEY DEFINITION	Finance is: 1. The practice of manipulating and managing money. 2. The capital involved in a project, especially the capital needed to start a new business. 3. A loan of money for a particular purpose, especially by a financial institution such as a bank.

You can see from the second and third definitions of finance that the term is not used to refer to small amounts of money, such as the cost of £170 for the materials and labour used to make a set of office shelves (the example we looked at in Chapter 1, section 1.3). Instead, it refers to large sums of money, such as the amount invested in the business by the owner(s) or borrowed from the bank or other provider of finance for buying land, premises, vehicles, equipment and so on. From this we can deduce that one of the key considerations when planning a business is to ensure that the owner has sufficient finance in place to launch the enterprise and allow it to grow to the desired size.

It may surprise you to know that 15% of people in the 16 to 34 age group in England are thinking of going into business (SBS, 2004), but not every entrepreneur with an idea for starting a new business, or who wants to expand an existing business, can find the necessary finance. The situation where a business has profitable opportunities but is unable to raise the finance to exploit them, can be described as a *finance gap* (Jarvis, 2000). In view of the importance of SMEs to the UK economy (see Chapter 1, section 1.5), different governments have commissioned studies to examine the extent of the problem and suggest remedies (most recently the Cruikshank Report on banking in 2000).

the finance gap

'Historically, the existence of a "finance gap" was formally recognised nearly 70 years ago. In 1931 the government-sponsored Macmillan Committee reported that the financing needs of small business were not well served by the then existing financial services institutions. The committee, consisting of such eminent academics as John Maynard Keynes and politicians such as Ernest Bevin, illustrates the importance given to the subject of financing small firms by government in the 1930s. Since then this criticism of financial institutions has been echoed by other important inquiries (Bolton Report, 1971; Wilson Committee, 1979). In response to these criticisms successive governments have introduced a number of initiatives with varying success ... In recent years financial services institutions have broadened their scope and for commercial reasons have introduced new products that have made access to funds easier for smaller firms. It has been argued that if a finance gap still exists, it has been substantially narrowed because of these initiatives and subsequent responses by the market since the 1930s (Deakins, 1996). However, others dispute this claim on both empirical and theoretical grounds (for example Harrison and Mason, 1995).'

Source: Jarvis, 2000, p. 339.

The main argument supporting the notion of a finance gap is that because the majority of SMEs are sole proprietors, partnerships or private limited liability entities, they cannot raise finance by selling shares to the public. In other words, there is no capital market for privately held businesses, as only public limited companies can raise capital on a stock exchange. This aspect of the finance gap is sometimes referred to as the *equity gap*, since equity refers to the funds invested by shareholders in a limited liability entity.

activity

In addition to the equity gap, there are a number of other reasons why smaller entities may have difficulty in accessing finance when they need it. Draw up a list of other possible explanations.

Some of the explanations you may have listed relate to the start-up stage when there is no evidence of:

- the quality of the business idea
- the entrepreneur's management skills
- a financial track record that demonstrates ability to service a loan (pay the interest and repay the amount borrowed) or pay suppliers for goods and services provided on credit.

At any stage there may be obstacles such as:

- the cost of borrowing when interest rates are high
- insufficient knowledge of potential sources of finance (an *information gap*)
- lack of skills to present a convincing proposal to investors or lenders
- lack of collateral to offset risk, which may be particularly relevant in the service sector.

To put the finance gap into perspective, it is useful to look at the importance of access to finance compared to other problems. Figure 3.1 shows the most important problem faced by 922 small firms that responded to a survey in the second quarter of 2003.

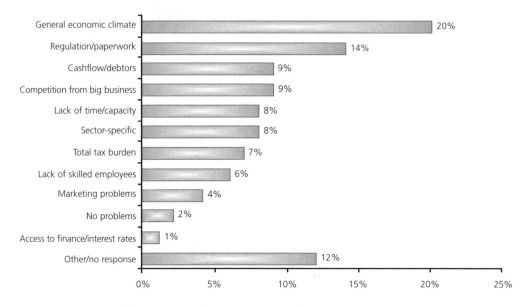

FIGURE 3.1 **Most important problem for small firms**
Source: Adapted from SBRT (Small Business Research Trust), 2003.

You can see from the figure that only 1% cited access to finance or interest rates as their most important problem. However, you need to remember that the survey was answered by the owners of existing businesses and does not include those who may be experiencing problems in obtaining start-up finance. In addition, businesses require finance for particular purposes and therefore seek finance on a contingency basis when the need arises. Consequently, it is not surprising that unremitting or regular problems or difficulties that affect a wide range of businesses, such as the state of the economy, are likely to be more important.

3.3   main sources of finance

The cash invested by the owner to start a business is known as *capital*. Sources include money from savings, redundancy, inheritance, investments, winnings and so on. Once the business is established, the capital can be increased by retaining some of the profit in the business.

KEY DEFINITION	Capital is the money invested in the entity by the owner(s) to enable it to function.

If these internal sources are not sufficient, the owner or manager may need to consider external sources of finance. These sources can be classified according to the length of time the finance is required and this, in turn, depends on the purpose for which it is required. Figure 3.2 shows this classification.

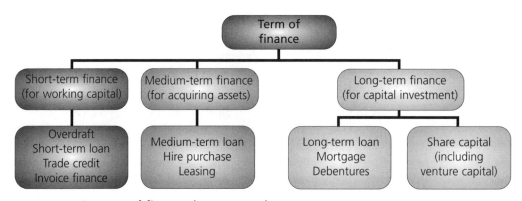

FIGURE 3.2 **Sources of finance by term and purpose**

Short-term finance is used to provide the *working capital* needed to fund the day-to-day activities of the business. For example, cash is needed to purchase stock that is sold and turned back into cash, and used to buy more stock. Thus, short-term finance is required for periods of less than a year and examples include the following:

●   An *overdraft* is a type of bank loan that is set up to be used if required to cover short periods when there is a *cash deficit* (insufficient cash coming into the bank account to cover the cash going out). If the business needs money for a fixed period of time (of less than a year), a *short-term loan* from a bank, family or friends may be more appropriate. Banks may charge a setting-up fee. Interest is charged at a rate that varies according to the risk, which is often measured by a credit rating score. Loans are repaid in instalments or at the end of the term according to the loan agreement. Lenders normally require some form of collateral or guarantee to provide security for a loan, so they can recover any amounts outstanding should the business default on the loan agreement.

- *Trade credit* is finance provided by a *trade creditor*. A trade creditor is a supplier from whom the business has purchased goods or services on credit. This means that the business does not need to pay for the goods or services until the end of the *credit period*. This is a specified length of time after they have been received (typically between 30 and 90 days) and is dependent on the purchaser's credit rating. Discounts may be offered for prompt payment on the due date. Trade credit does not provide additional cash, but allows money already in the business to be used for other purposes until it is needed to pay creditors.

- *Invoice finance* (or *factoring*) is finance raised against *trade debtors*, who are customers to whom the business has sold goods or services on credit but who have not yet paid. The *invoice financier* (usually a bank or other financial institution) assesses the credit-worthiness of the debtors and takes on the task of collecting the debts in return for a fee that represents the risk. The advantage to the business is that it receives up to 90% of the value of the invoices immediately (depending on the terms agreed) and the balance after it has been collected.

Medium-term finance is used to provide *assets* that are expected to generate cash for the business in the medium-term, such as fixtures and fittings, office equipment and vehicles. Since the finance is secured on an asset, this type of finance can be referred to as *asset-based finance*. Examples of medium-term finance include the following:

- A *medium-term loan* from a bank, government scheme, friends or family to purchase an asset over a fixed period of time that is linked to the economic life of the asset. The conditions of the loan are similar to those described above for overdrafts and short-term loans.

- A more flexible alternative to borrowing is to use *hire purchase (HP)*. HP allows the purchaser to start using the asset as soon as a deposit has been paid. The deposit represents the first of a number of instalments spread over a specified period of time. Ownership does not pass to the purchaser until the final instalment has been paid.

- Leasing is also a more flexible alternative to taking out a loan. Essentially, a *finance lease* is a financing agreement, whereas an *operating lease* is a rental agreement. Under an operating lease the lessee hires the asset for a period of time that is normally substantially shorter than the life of the asset. Therefore, ownership of the asset remains with the lessor. Operating leases are commonly used for assets where the *residual value* of the asset is uncertain. The residual value is an estimate of the amount that will be received on disposal of the asset at the end of its expected useful life. The residual value of the asset is likely to be uncertain where technological advances are rapid (such as office equipment) or there is extensive wear and tear on the asset (such as fleet vehicles). Operating leases are also used where the assets are required for a particular project (such as plant and machinery in a construction industry). Leases may be packaged with other services, such as maintenance and servicing of the asset.

Long-term finance is used to provide assets that are expected to provide economic benefits to the business in the long term. Long-term finance can be divided into *debt finance* and *equity finance*. We will start by looking at the main sources of debt finance.

- A *long-term loan* is a suitable form of finance for capital investment in fixed assets such as plant and machinery or to expand the business.
- A *mortgage* is a long-term loan for purchasing land or premises. Mortgages are usually supplied by financial institutions, such as banks and building societies, for a specified number of years (in the UK the maximum period is usually 25–30 years) at a fixed or variable rate of interest. Repayment may be in instalments or at the end of the term.
- A *debenture* (or *loan stock*) is the most common type of long-term loan taken by a limited company. Debentures are usually repayable at a fixed date, a long time in the future. The debenture holder may be a private investor or a corporate investor and normally receives a fixed rate of interest, which is lower than the rate charged for an overdraft. Debentures involve less risk to the investor than equities and can be sold on a stock exchange.

The last category is *equity finance*, which refers to finance raised from the sale of ordinary shares (preference shares are classified as non-equity shares). Therefore, this type of finance is only available to limited liability entities.

- Only public limited companies can raise capital on a stock exchange and the main UK market is the London Stock Exchange (LSE). However, small, fast-growing companies can obtain access to the market at an earlier stage in their development through a listing on the Alternative Investment Market (AIM), which was set up as a subsidiary market in 1995. This allows them to experience life as a public company, but the listing rules are less onerous (and therefore less expensive) than for the main market. For example, there is no minimum number of shares that must be issued, no trading record requirement, and no minimum market capitalization. To give you some idea of the size of these markets, in January 2003 there were 705 companies listed on AIM and 2,100 public limited companies listed on the LSE. However, there is movement in both directions between the two markets. For example, in 2005, two companies moved from AIM to the LSE, but 40 companies transferred from the LSE to AIM. One of the reasons for this is that the subsidiary market offers tax advantages for investors, as well as being less of a regulatory burden for the company.
- *Formal venture capital* from corporate investors, such as pension funds, typically provides equity finance for certain new businesses or for turnaround situations (such as a management buyout). Venture capitalists are only interested in investing in businesses that offer high returns to offset the high risks. The average size of investment is £50,000 or more.
- *Informal venture capital* from *business angels* is a valuable source of equity finance for SMEs. Business angels are wealthy individuals who wish to invest in profitable privately owned businesses (usually private limited companies). Businesses seeking angel finance often rely on firms of accountants and other professionals to introduce them to investors, but the National Business Angels Network is a recent innovation in the UK where businesses and angels can register to receive information (for a fee). It is estimated that in 2002 there were 18,000 business angels in the UK and the average size of the majority of investments was less than £50,000 (c2Ventures, 2003).

activity

Classify the following sources of finance into debt finance, asset-based finance and equity finance by ticking the appropriate box:

	Debt finance	Asset-based finance	Equity finance
(a) Share capital	☐	☐	☐
(b) Debenture	☐	☐	☐
(c) Hire purchase	☐	☐	☐
(d) Invoice finance	☐	☐	☐
(e) Leasing	☐	☐	☐
(f) Loan	☐	☐	☐
(g) Overdraft	☐	☐	☐
(h) Mortgage	☐	☐	☐
(i) Venture capital	☐	☐	☐
(j) Trade credit	☐	☐	☐

You can check your answers against Figure 3.3, which summarizes the main sources of external finance.

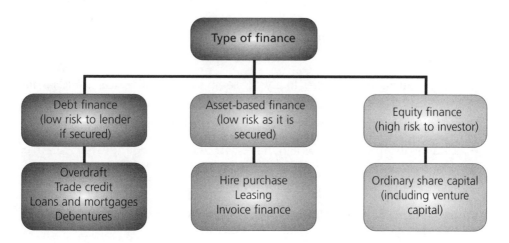

FIGURE 3.3 **Sources of finance by type**

To conclude our discussion on the sources and need for external finance, it is useful to examine some recent evidence:

external finance

The following findings are taken from a survey conducted by the University of Cambridge (Cosh and Hughes, 2003) that examined the experiences of 817 SMEs that had sought new finance in the period 2000–2002:

- The median amount of external finance was £150,000 and on average the amount of external finance was approximately equal to the level of capital expenditure. Those not seeking external finance carried out lower capital expenditure.

- Micro firms, non-innovators, firms with declining growth and the more profitable firms were less likely to seek external finance. The principal reason given for not seeking external finance was that internal cash flows were sufficient. But the cost of finance, the borrowing risk and the risk of equity dilution were also frequently cited as additional reasons.

- Older firms sought more external finance on average and were more successful in obtaining it than newer firms.

- Those that sought finance were more likely to be innovators and growing firms. Such firms also seek more finance, but are not significantly more successful in obtaining it than non-innovators and stable/declining firms.

- Larger firms were more likely to seek external finance, seek larger amounts (absolutely, but not relative to their capital expenditure) and were more likely to obtain it than smaller firms.

- Less profitable firms, which have less internally generated finance, sought more external finance, but their success in obtaining it was significantly less than their more profitable counterparts.

- Some firms obtained finance from more than one source.

Figure 3.4 summarizes the sources of SME finance used.

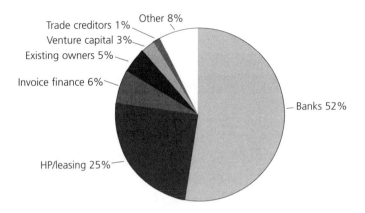

FIGURE 3.4 **Sources of SME finance used**
Source: Adapted from Cosh and Hughes, 2003, pp. 80 and 85.

3.4 need for cash flow information

Since business is about money, information about cash is very important. Without sufficient cash an individual or organization may become insolvent, which in many cases leads to a state of *bankruptcy* for an individual or *liquidation* for an organization. In business, economic transactions are based on the immediate payment of cash (a cash transaction) or payment after an agreed period (a credit transaction). The term 'cash' refers to all money, whether in the form of coins, notes, cheques or any other way of making payment that does not involve the use of credit. Businesses need to keep a careful record of all the cash receipts and payments in order to keep track of the money. These records are kept as part of the accounting system we describe in Chapter 4.

activity

Imagine you have £200 cash that you use to buy a computer from another student. You are a bit of an opportunist and see a chance to make some money. You decide to advertise the computer for sale in the newspaper, which costs £10, and you sell the computer for £300 cash. You have no other business transactions. Calculate the cash position of your business at the end of the month.

You should have found the answer by deducting all the cash outflows for the month from all the cash inflows for the month; something you might have been able to do in your head. However, you will not have arrived at the correct answer of £290 if you overlooked the recording of the capital of £200, which was the amount you invested in your business at the start. The following simple statement shows how we arrived at the correct answer.

Your Business
Cash flow statement for the month
£

Cash inflows
    Capital   200
    Sales   300
Subtotal   500

Cash outflows
    Purchases   200
    Advertising   10
Subtotal   210

---

activity

Using the same example, imagine that this time you agreed to sell the computer on credit, but a few days later you receive a letter from your telephone service provider that you will be disconnected unless you pay an overdue invoice. Which of the following actions do you think is the best one to take and which is the worst? Give your reasons.

(a) Allow the connection to be cut and have it reconnected after you have received the cash from the sale of the computer.

(b) Use your savings to pay the bill.

(c) Take out a loan to pay the bill.

(d) Ask the person who bought the computer to pay you immediately.

You may be able to think of other courses of action, but all the alternatives have advantages and disadvantages. If the connection is disconnected, it is likely to prevent you from carrying out your business activities. Although using your savings remedies the situation, you will lose any interest your investment might be earning. Borrowing money would also prevent the connection being cut, but you would incur interest charges and have to repay the loan. You may think that the best solution is to ask the buyer to pay you immediately, but he or she may not be able to do so. From this example you can appreciate that not only do we require a record of what has happened to cash in the past, but also information that will show us what is likely to happen to cash in the future.

3.5 purpose and construction of a cash flow forecast

A financial statement that shows what is likely to happen to cash in the future is known as a *cash flow forecast* and is used for the following purposes:

- to plan capital requirements at the start-up stage, where it helps establish whether the proposed capital will be sufficient to finance the activities of the new business
- to plan a forthcoming accounting period in an existing business, where it helps anticipate the need for additional finance if cash going out exceeds the cash coming in (a *cash deficit*) and the investment of cash if cash coming in exceeds the cash going out (a *cash surplus*).

A cash flow forecast shows the predicted movement of cash over a specified period of time (usually one year) and is divided into months, with a total column at the end to summarize the period covered. It predicts as accurately as possible the amount of cash that is expected to come in and go out of the business, and the expected timing of these cash transactions, which may be monthly, quarterly or annually. We will use an example to examine this in more detail.

Sarah Wick lives in the East End of London. She is planning to set up in business in January 2006 selling candles from a stall in the market square. She has £1,000 capital to invest in the business, which she is going to call Candlewick Enterprises. She will buy candles from a local supplier and sell them from the market stall and via the internet. She plans to purchase the candles for £1.50 each and sell them at £2.00 each. Her supplier will allow her one month's credit. Sales from the market stall will represent 25% of total sales and these customers will pay cash. The remaining 75% of sales will come from the mail order part of the business, where customers will be given two months' credit.

The following table shows the number of candles Sarah expects the business to purchase at £1.50 each during the first six months of trading. It also shows the amount of cash she expects to pay each month, taking into account that her supplier allows one month's credit.

	January	February	March	April	May	June	Total
Quantity	400	400	500	560	600	600	3,060
Cost of purchases	£0	£600	£600	£750	£840	£900	£3,690

Having looked at the expected purchases, we can now look at the sales Sarah hopes Candlewick Enterprises will achieve. The next table shows the number of candles Sarah expects the business to sell at £2 each during the first 6 months of trading. It also shows the anticipated amount of cash received each month, taking into account that 25% of customers will pay cash and the remaining 75% will be given two months' credit.

	January	February	March	April	May	June	Total
Quantity	400	400	500	560	600	600	3,060
Cash sales	£200	£200	£250	£280	£300	£300	£1,530
Credit sales	£0	£0	£600	£600	£750	£840	£2,790

The movements of cash are given specific names and it is important to use them to avoid confusing them with other terms you will learn in connection with other financial statements that we will be looking at in Chapters 6 and 7.

- *Cash inflows* are cash transactions that bring money into the business. They are described as *positive cash flow*. They include capital, loans, revenue and interest received.

The forecast cash inflows for Candlewick Enterprises are the capital Sarah plans to invest and the expected sales.

- *Cash outflows* are cash transactions that take money out of the business. They are described as *negative cash flow*. They include purchases of stock and overheads such as wages, rent, rates, electricity, telephone, insurance, interest payable and cash payments made in connection with loans, HP and leasing agreements. At this stage we know that the forecast cash outflows for Candlewick Enterprises are what Sarah expects to pay for purchasing candles.

- *Net cash flow* is the difference between the cash inflows and the cash outflows. If the net cash flow is a *cash deficit*, like other negative figures, it is usually shown in brackets.

- The *cumulative cash brought forward (b/f)* refers to the cash surplus or deficit at the start of the month (the first day of the month). It is the cash position that has been brought forward from the last day of the previous month. In the first month of a new business there is no cash to bring forward so this is always zero.

- The *cumulative cash carried forward (c/f)* refers to the cash surplus or deficit at the end of the month. It consists of the cumulative cash brought forward from the previous month plus the net cash flow that has taken place during the month. It shows the cash position at the end of the month, which is carried forward to become the cumulative cash brought forward at the start of the next month.

activity

The following cash flow forecast has been partially completed using the predicted figures for Candlewick Enterprises' purchases and sales which we calculated above. Calculate the subtotals for cash inflows and outflows and use them to work out the anticipated net cash flow for each month and the cumulative cash position at the start and end of each month.

Candlewick Enterprises
Draft cash flow forecast for January–June 2006

	January £	February £	March £	April £	May £	June £	Total £
Cash inflows							
Capital	1,000	0	0	0	0	0	1,000
Cash sales	200	200	250	280	300	300	1,530
Credit sales	0	0	600	600	750	840	2,790
Subtotal							
Cash outflows							
Purchases	0	600	600	750	840	900	3,690
Subtotal							
Net cash flow							
Cumulative cash b/f							
Cumulative cash c/f							

Your forecast should look like this:

	January £	February £	March £	April £	May £	June £	Total £
Candlewick Enterprises							
Draft cash flow forecast for January–June 2006							
Cash inflows							
Capital	1,000	0	0	0	0	0	1,000
Cash sales	200	200	250	280	300	300	1,530
Credit sales	0	0	600	600	750	840	2,790
Subtotal	1,200	200	850	880	1,050	1,140	5,320
Cash outflows							
Purchases	0	600	600	750	840	900	3,690
Subtotal	0	600	600	750	840	900	3,690
Net cash flow	1,200	(400)	250	130	210	240	1,630
Cumulative cash b/f	0	1,200	800	1,050	1,180	1,390	0
Cumulative cash c/f	1,200	800	1,050	1,180	1,390	1,630	1,630

You may find the following points helpful:

- The total column shows the cash receipts and cash payments for the entire six months. If we deduct the expected payments for the six months, which total £3,690, from the expected receipts, which total £5,320, you can see that there is a forecast cash surplus of £1,630.
- The figures shown in brackets in the cash flow forecast represent cash deficits. In February there will be a cumulative cash deficit.
- In a continuing business, the total column should also show any cumulative cash b/f at the beginning of the period (in a new business, such as Sarah's, this is 0).
- The cumulative cash c/f in the total column should always agree with the equivalent cumulative cash c/f at the end of the last month of the period. This acts as a crosscheck on the accuracy of the calculation of the cash position.

KEY DEFINITIONS	Cash inflows are cash transactions that bring money into the business.
	Cash outflows are cash transactions that take money out of the business.
	A cash surplus describes the net cash position where cash inflows exceed cash outflows.
	A cash deficit describes the net cash position where cash outflows exceed cash inflows.
	Cumulative cash brought forward (b/f) is the cash surplus or deficit at the start of the month that has been brought forward from the previous month.
	Cumulative cash carried forward (c/f) is the cash surplus or deficit at the end of the month that is carried forward to the next month.

It may have occurred to you that the purchase of candles is not the only cost the business will incur. This is reason why the heading refers to the forecast as a draft forecast. Accountants use the term 'purchases' to mean the purchase of goods that will be sold as part of the trading cycle. Other costs incurred are given specific names. The other costs Candlewick Enterprises is expected to incur are as follows:

- Computer equipment will be bought on 1 January, but the cost of £1,300 will not have to be paid for until February, as Sarah will make use of the one month's interest-free credit period on the business credit card.
- Rent and rates for the market stall will be £15 per month, payable at the end of the month.
- Advertising will be £25 per month, payable one month in arrears.
- Telephone and internet expenses will be £45 per quarter, payable at the end of each quarter.
- Postage and packaging is expected to cost £60 per month, commencing in February.

We now have all the information we need to complete the cash flow forecast for Candlewick Enterprises:

Candlewick Enterprises
Draft cash flow forecast for January–June 2006

	January £	February £	March £	April £	May £	June £	Total £
Cash inflows							
Capital	1,000	0	0	0	0	0	1,000
Cash sales	200	200	250	280	300	300	1,530
Credit sales	0	0	600	600	750	840	2,790
Subtotal	1,200	200	850	880	1,050	1,140	5320
Cash outflows							
Purchases	0	600	600	750	840	900	3,690
Equipment	0	1,300	0	0	0	0	1,300
Rent and rates	15	15	15	15	15	15	90
Advertising	0	25	25	25	25	25	125
Telephone and internet	0	0	45	0	0	45	90
Postage and packing	0	60	60	60	60	60	300
Subtotal	15	2,000	745	850	940	1,045	5,595
Net cash flow	1,185	(1,800)	105	30	110	95	(275)
Cumulative cash b/f	0	1,185	(615)	(510)	(480)	(370)	0
Cumulative cash c/f	1,185	(615)	(510)	(480)	(370)	(275)	(275)

Most accountants adopt the layout we have illustrated when constructing cash flow forecasts. If you have seen cash flow forecasts before, perhaps a pro forma given by a bank in a business pack, you may have noticed some differences in layout. Do not let this confuse you, because the principles are exactly the same. The main points to remember are as follows:

- The heading should state the name of the business and the accounting period to which the forecast refers.
- The columns should be labelled with the months to which they relate and the currency.
- The cash inflows (in this case the cash and credit sales) are given in the first rows and subtotalled.
- The cash outflows are itemized separately and given in the next rows and subtotalled.
- The total of the cash outflows is deducted from the total of the cash inflows to give the net cash flow. If this represents a cash deficit (a negative figure), it is shown in brackets.
- The final row calculates the cumulative cash position carried forward at the end of the month.
- The final column shows the total for the period for each item. It is calculated by adding all the rows (except the subtotals) horizontally. Once you have inserted the item totals you can calculate the subtotals by adding the appropriate groups of item totals vertically.

learn the layout

Name of the business
Cash flow forecast for the period ...

	Month 1 £	Month 2 £	Month 3 £	Total £
Cash inflows				
Subtotal				
Cash outflows				
Subtotal				
Net cash flow				
Cumulative cash b/f				
Cumulative cash c/f				

Once you have learned the layout for a cash flow forecast, you should be able to construct one manually (with the aid of a calculator or using mental arithmetic) or using a spreadsheet. The only difference is that negative figures are entered with a minus sign rather than in brackets and formulae are entered to perform the arithmetic. We used Microsoft Excel to prepare the forecast for Candlewick Enterprises and Figure 3.5 shows you the formulae we used. If you want to see the formulae in your own spreadsheet, click on Tools in the main menu, then Options. Then select the View tab and under Windows options click on Formulas (a tick will appear in the box). Simply deselect Formulas when you want to return to data view.

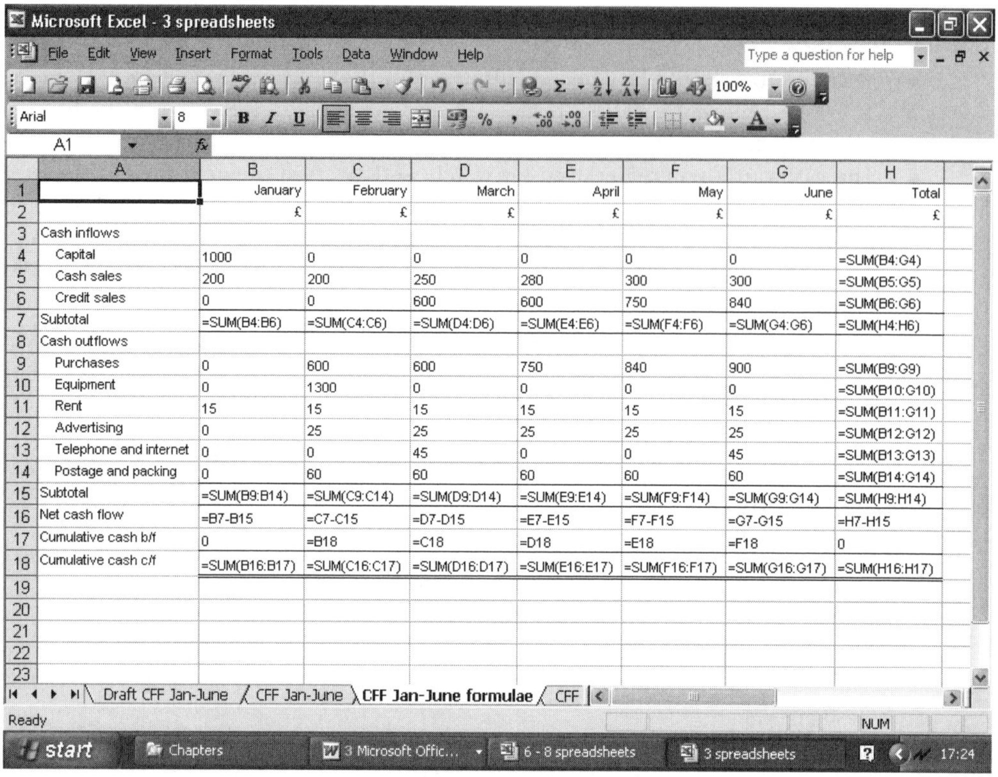

FIGURE 3.5 **Cash flow forecast formulae**

3.6 planning capital requirements

The first step for anyone thinking of starting a new business is to consider how much finance is needed and the source(s) of that finance; in other words, to plan the *capital* requirements of setting up the enterprise. We already know that Sarah is planning to invest £1,000 of her own money in Candlewick Enterprises when it starts on 1 January, but the cash flow forecast shows that by the end of February this will turn into cash deficit as the cumulative cash position is negative. Based on these predictions, Sarah would go out of business by February and it is clear that she must make some plans to avoid this before starting the business.

activity

Sarah has decided she needs to look for external finance to ensure the business is solvent for the first 6 months. How much cash does the business need to borrow to ensure there is no cash deficit in any month?

(a) £1,800   (d) £480

(b) £615   (e) £370

(c) £510

The correct answer is £615. Sarah needs at least £615 to give her sufficient cash to start the business and ensure it does not have a cash deficit during the first six months of trading. Her main choices are:

- to obtain a bank overdraft or loan
- to allow only one month's credit to the mail order customers
- to see if her supplier will allow two or three months' credit
- to lease the computer equipment or buy it on HP
- to control the cash expected to go out on telephone services, postage and packing
- to look for a cheaper market stall
- a combination of these solutions.

After discussing her cash flow forecast with the bank lending officer, Sarah takes out a bank loan for £650 over two years and arranges an overdraft for short-term deficits of up to £250. The loan has a fixed rate of interest of 7.4% which works out at £4 per month. Having made these arrangements, Sarah constructs the following revised cash flow forecast.

Candlewick Enterprises
Revised cash flow forecast for January–June 2006

	January £	February £	March £	April £	May £	June £	Total £
Cash inflows							
Capital	1,000	0	0	0	0	0	1,000
Loan	650	0	0	0	0	0	650
Cash sales	200	200	250	280	300	300	1,530
Credit sales	0	0	600	600	750	840	2,790
Subtotal	1,850	200	850	880	1,050	1,140	5,970
Cash outflows							
Purchases	0	600	600	750	840	900	3,690
Equipment	0	1,300	0	0	0	0	1,300
Rent and rates	15	15	15	15	15	15	90
Advertising	0	25	25	25	25	25	125
Telephone and internet	0	0	45	0	0	45	90
Postage and packing	0	60	60	60	60	60	300
Interest on loan	4	4	4	4	4	4	24
Subtotal	19	2,004	749	854	944	1,049	5,619
Net cash flow	1,831	(1,804)	101	26	106	91	351
Cumulative cash b/f	0	1,831	27	128	154	260	0
Cumulative cash c/f	1,831	27	128	154	260	351	351

Although it is difficult to make general rules about interpreting a cash flow forecast, because it depends on the particular business, the following checklist includes questions you should think about:

checklist for interpreting cash flow information

- Is all the cash due to the business being collected as early as possible? Although it may be necessary to give credit to customers, the credit period should not be so long as to result in cash flow problems for the business. Alternatively, can invoice finance be arranged?

- Are all payments being made by the due date and not before? To pay sooner than necessary represents poor cash management, but to pay too late runs the risk of not being allowed credit in future and/or being sued for non-payment.

- Can credit agreements be arranged with suppliers who are being paid immediately, or can longer credit periods be agreed that will further delay payments?

- Can hire purchase or leasing be arranged to spread the cost of acquiring large items, such as equipment and vehicles?

- Is there sufficient cash to ensure that the business does not become insolvent?

- Have overdraft facilities been arranged to cover relatively small amounts of cash deficit?

- Has a decision been made to invest any cash surplus where it will receive interest?

3.7 purpose and construction of a cash flow statement

A *cash flow statement* shows the actual movements of cash. The financial information provided can be used to help make decisions about whether to revise planned activities and this helps make the cash flow forecast more realistic. Having realistic plans increases the chance that the business will be successful in meeting its economic objectives, whether the business is pursuing profit maximization or satisficing strategies (see Chapter 1). Since events seldom turn out exactly as predicted, it is important to establish control of the cash on a regular basis by comparing the actual movements of cash against the predicted movements. If things are not turning out as planned, corrective action can then be taken. Without this comparison of the actual results with the plan, there will be no control.

The following cash flow statement shows the actual cash flows for Candlewick Enterprises for the first six months. The layout is exactly the same as that of the forecast, but the heading reflects the fact that it is statement of the actual cash flows rather than the planned figures:

| Cash flow statement for January–June 2006 | | | | | | | |
	January £	February £	March £	April £	May £	June £	Total £
Cash inflows							
Capital	1,000	0	0	0	0	0	1,000
Loan	650	0	0	0	0	0	650
Cash sales	160	180	200	350	410	450	1,750
Credit sales	0	0	480	540	600	780	2,400
Subtotal	1,810	180	680	890	1,010	1,230	5,800
Cash outflows							
Purchases	0	600	600	750	840	900	3,690
Equipment	0	1,300	0	0	0	0	1,300
Rent and rates	30	30	30	30	30	30	180
Advertising	25	25	25	25	25	25	150
Telephone and internet	0	0	45	0	0	61	106
Postage and packing	0	10	10	10	10	10	50
Interest on loan	4	4	4	4	4	4	24
Drawings	0	50	50	50	50	50	250
Subtotal	59	2,019	764	869	959	1,080	5,750
Net cash flow	1,751	(1,839)	(84)	21	51	150	50
Cumulative cash b/f	0	1,751	(88)	(172)	(151)	(100)	0
Cumulative cash c/f	1,751	(88)	(172)	(151)	(100)	50	50

As you can see, things have not turned out entirely as planned: the value of cash sales is slightly higher than planned, but credit sales are lower than anticipated. In addition, the rent and rates for the market stall are twice as high because none of the cheaper stalls were vacant, and it looks as though Sarah is paying the advertising costs in the month in which they are incurred, rather than taking the one month's credit allowed. You may also have noticed that the business has only paid £10 per month since February for postage and packing instead of the predicted figure of £60, as these expenses were lower than predicted. In addition, Sarah has been taking £50 cash for her own use every month since February. The withdrawal of cash (or goods and services) from the business by the owner is known as *drawings*.

Despite introducing £1,000 capital and taking out a loan for £650 you can see that the cumulative cash position at the end of February shows a cash deficit of £88 and by the end of March it has gone up to £172. This reduces over the next three months and by the end of June there is a small cash surplus of £50. Fortunately, the business has not gone into liquidation, because the cash deficits between February and May were covered by the overdraft Sarah arranged with the bank.

activity

Sarah must revise her plans for the next six months. Suggest what actions she might take.

You may think that Sarah would be in a better position if she compared her actual cash flow with her plan on a monthly basis, instead of waiting for six months. Certainly, control is improved with frequency and most businesses carry out this sort of exercise every month. Given the position Sarah is now in, you should have suggested the following:

- She introduces more capital than planned.
- She revises her planned sales figures for the next six months to reflect the level of sales she achieved in the first six months and any variations she expects during the forth-coming festive season.
- She revises the number of candles she will purchase to reduce the number she has in stock.
- She takes the one month's credit on advertising.
- She revises the planned spending on postage and packing to reflect the mail order sales more closely and reduce the build up of stocks of stamps and packaging.
- She looks for a cheaper market stall or discontinues it and concentrates solely on mail order and internet selling.

If Sarah revises the cash flow forecast, she may decide it is not worthwhile continuing the business. We have not yet allowed for the interest that must be paid on the overdraft or the increase in drawings needed to provide a living for herself. Cash flow statements sometimes show unpleasant information, but are essential to the effective running of a business.

Cash flow information is useful in a number of ways. You have seen that planned cash flow information can be used to construct what is called a cash flow forecast that predicts the monthly cash flows for the first accounting period (usually one year) for a new business. Exactly the same construction is used by existing businesses for subsequent periods, but it is usually called a *cash flow budget*. A cash flow budget is prepared in advance of the accounting period and predicts the cash flows for the following year as accurately as possible. Once that year starts, the actual figures in the cash flow statement are compared with the budgeted figures to check that the business is meeting its targets. If targets are not being met, the owner or manager can take whatever action is necessary to make sure the business meets its economic objectives. We will be looking at budgets in Chapter 18.

Constructing cash flow forecasts and statements, and making revisions to plans can be very tedious if done by hand. The task is made considerably easier and more efficient if you use a spreadsheet. Nevertheless, it is important to remember that even if it is prepared using a spreadsheet, a cash flow forecast is only as good as the quality of the predicted figures it contains.

activity

Using your own bank statement, construct a cash flow forecast for yourself for the next six months using a spreadsheet. When you have completed your statement, reflect on the decisions you need to make using the checklist given earlier in section 3.6 Planning capital requirements.

3.8 conclusions

In this chapter we have considered the importance of cash and the need all businesses have for finance. We have examined the theory of a finance gap for small and medium-sized entities, explored some of the evidence and classified the potential sources of finance. We have also looked at the need for financial information in a business and introduced you to two financial statements. The first is the cash flow forecast (or budget), which uses estimated figures to predict the cash position at the end of a future accounting period; and the second is the cash flow statement, which uses actual figures to show the actual cash position at the end of an accounting period. Cash flow information aids planning, control and decision making. In particular, it helps owners and managers to:

- ensure that the business has sufficient cash to carry out planned activities
- anticipate the need for additional finance, such as a bank overdraft or loan
- plan the investment of any cash surplus
- control cash flows by comparing actual figures against the plan or budget
- take decisions to modify activities to ensure the business remains solvent.

practice questions

1. Define finance and explain why students studying business or management should learn about the management of money.
2. Explain the theory of the finance gap.
3. Describe the potential sources of long-term finance available to a sole proprietor or traditional partnership.
4. Francesca Prada is planning to start a shoe shop called Dudes & Divas on 1 July 2006 with £25,000 she has inherited. She is going to be a sole proprietor and plans to open a small shop in the town centre. She has found suitable premises and has arranged for professional shop fitters to refurbish them. The new fixtures and fittings will cost £30,000, but will not have to be paid for until September. In addition, she estimates the following cash flows will take place during the first three months of trading:

Cash sales	£10,000 per month
Credit sales	£2,000 per month (customers will have one month's credit)
Purchases	£5,000 per month (suppliers will give two months' credit)
Overheads	£5,000 per month
Drawings	£1,500 per month

Required
(a) Construct a cash flow forecast for Dudes & Divas for the three months, 1 July to 30 September 2006.
(b) Interpret the cash flow forecast you have prepared and comment on the cumulative cash position at 30 September 2004.

5. Philip Trigg has negotiated with two manufacturers of electric circuit boards to carry out assembly work for them as a subcontractor. He will call his business Trigg Electronics. He anticipates assembling the following numbers of circuit boards for each manufacturer during 2006:

Month	Firm A	Firm B
January	120	200
February	130	200
March	130	240
April	150	240
May	140	240
June	140	220
July	160	220
August	160	270
September	170	270
October	140	270
November	140	230
December	120	210

Firm A has agreed to pay £6.60 for each board assembled and Firm B £6.50. Firm A will pay two months after the work has been done, but Firm B will pay one month after the work has been done. Philip anticipates the following expenses:

Rent and rates	£6,000 per annum, payable at the beginning of each quarter
Electricity	£120 per month, payable one month in arrears
Telephone	£50 per quarter, payable at the end of each quarter
Packaging	10% of sales, payable the month after the sale occurs
General expenses	£25 per month
Tools and equipment	£2,500 in January, £1,000 in February and £500 in March

Required
(a) Construct a cash flow forecast for Trigg Electronics for the six months, 1 January to 30 June 2006.
(b) Calculate the amount of capital Philip needs to invest in the business to prevent a cash deficit in any month.

references

Bolton, J. E. (1971) *Report of the Committee of Inquiry on Small Firms*, Cmnd. 4811, London: HMSO.

c2Ventures (2003) *Investor Pulse UK Angel Attitude Survey*.

Cosh, A. and Hughes, A. (eds) (2003) *Enterprise Challenged*, Cambridge: ESRC Centre for Business Research.

Cruikshank, D. (2000) *Review of Banking Services in the UK: Report to the Chancellor*, London: HMSO, March.

Deakins, D. (1996) *Entrepreneurs and Small Firms*, London: Butterworth.

Harrison, R. and Mason, C. (1995) 'The role of informal venture capital in financing the growing firm', in Buckland, R. and Davis, E. W. (eds), *Finance for Growing Enterprises*, London: Routledge.

Jarvis, R. (2000) 'Finance and the small firm', in Carter, S. and Jones Evans, D. (eds) *Enterprise and Small Business: Principles, Practice and Policy*, Harlow: Pearson Education.

Macmillan Committee (1931) *Report of the Committee on Finance and Industry*, Cmnd 3897, London: HMSO.

SBRT (2003) *NatWest SBRT Quarterly Survey of Small Business in Britain*, Q2, Small Business Research Trust.

SBS (2004) *SBS Household Survey of Entrepreneurship*, www.sbs.gov.uk/analytical.

Wilson Committee (1979) *The Financing of Small Firms: Interim Report of the Committee to Review the Functioning of the Financial Institutions*, Cmnd 7503, London: HMSO.

financial accounting

the accounting system

When you have studied this chapter, you should be able to:

- Describe the processes involved in an accounting system

- Explain the accounting equation

- Describe and apply the principles of double-entry bookkeeping for recording transactions involving purchases, expenses, assets, revenue, liabilities and sales.

4.1 introduction

In the preceding chapters we discussed the importance of financial information, together with the main users and uses. Although it is not necessary for students who are not specializing in the study of accounting to learn about bookkeeping, on some courses it is considered useful to give some understanding of how the economic transactions of a business are recorded. In order to generate financial information, a business needs to establish an *accounting system*. The nature of the system depends on the type of business and the size of the organization, but there are common features since procedures must be established to allow all financial transactions to be recorded. These procedures involve raising source documents, such as invoices, purchase orders and credit notes, so that those responsible in the business are made aware that a transaction has taken place and the details of the transaction can be recorded.

Some businesses keep a simple cash-based system, but many organizations record transactions in an accounting system known as *double-entry bookkeeping*. This ensures that an arithmetical check is made on the accuracy of the records. The records are used as the basis for preparing financial statements, which summarize the transactions that have taken place during any particular period of time. Large organizations carry out thousands of transactions every day and need sophisticated, tailor-made computerized accounting systems. Most small businesses use standard accounting software or spreadsheets, and a small minority keep their records manually. In this chapter we describe a simple manual system in order to explain double-entry bookkeeping, although the principles are the same when a computerized system is used.

4.2 sources of data

Some business transactions are for immediate cash, but many business transactions are credit transactions. Therefore, owners and managers need a system for recording both types of transaction and documents that give details of the transactions made. Such documents are known as *source documents* and are the foundation on which the financial records of the business are built. The main documents that provide the data recorded in the accounting system can be summarized as follows:

- sales orders, delivery notes, invoices paid by customers and credit notes issued for goods returned by customers
- purchase orders, invoices received from suppliers and credit notes received for goods returned to suppliers
- payroll records, stock records, banking records and other documents.

We will now look at the process of raising source documents in more detail. In many businesses, goods are purchased on credit and a number of external and internal documents are produced to record the activities. First, the business purchasing the goods issues a *purchase order* and sends it to the supplier. This document specifies the quantity, type and price of the goods ordered. When the purchaser receives the goods, they are examined to ensure that they match the items on the purchase order and a *goods received note* is raised. Copies of the goods received note are sent to the accounts department, the purchase department and the stores department. When the stores department receives the goods, the details are recorded on a *stores record card* so that the stores manager has a record of the goods available. Items are released by the stores department only on receipt of a properly authorized *stores requisition*, the fourth document in this chain. When the items are issued, the *stores record card* is adjusted to show the decrease in stock.

On receipt of the purchase order, the supplier sends the goods to the purchaser with an accompanying *delivery note*. The purchaser signs the delivery note and returns it to the supplier as proof of receipt. Next, the supplier issues an *invoice* showing the amount the purchaser will have to pay. If the purchaser is dissatisfied with any of the goods and returns them, the supplier issues a *credit note*. This shows the value of the goods returned, which the purchaser will not have to pay. If the supplier receives many orders from the same purchaser, rather than requiring payment of each invoice individually, the supplier may issue a monthly statement summarizing the invoices and credit notes during the month and showing the balance due.

In addition to recording transactions for goods, a business must record labour costs. In businesses in the manufacturing industry, *clock cards* may be used to record the time spent at work by employees and *job cards* to record the amount of time spent on each job. The job cards are then reconciled with the clock cards. The wages office prepares the *payroll* by calculating the wages from the clock cards for the workers paid on a time basis and from the job cards if there is an incentive scheme. In some businesses in the service industry, *time sheets* may be used to record how much time has been spent on each job so that clients can be charged for the time spent on their work.

activity

Design a flow diagram to illustrate the external and internal movement of source documents that are raised when a business purchases goods from a supplier on credit.

In constructing your diagram you will have experienced some of the difficulties in establishing and maintaining business information systems. It is necessary to ensure that each stage of the process is monitored, that the appropriate personnel are kept informed and that the records are correctly referenced and dated. The system needs to be designed so that if there is an error or a query, the appropriate source document can be traced and the problem resolved.

4.3   double-entry bookkeeping

Records need to be kept of all the economic transactions of the business. Double-entry bookkeeping is the most commonly used system of bookkeeping.

KEY DEFINITION

Double-entry bookkeeping is based on the principle that every financial transaction involves the simultaneous receiving and giving of value, and is therefore recorded twice.

If a manual system is kept, the records are kept in *ledgers*, which are the books of accounts (hence, the term 'bookkeeping'). However, in most businesses the records are computerized and transactions are recorded using spreadsheets, such as Excel or an accounting package, such as SAGE. However, whether the system is manual or computerized, it is normally based on the principles of double-entry bookkeeping. This is the most efficient and effective method for recording financial transactions in a way that allows financial statements to be prepared easily.

history of double-entry bookkeeping

'The first certain records of double-entry bookkeeping come from the early fourteenth century and relate to Italian merchant firms in Provence and in London, and to the city of Genoa. This system of double entry, which is still used in a similar manner throughout the western world, became known as the Italian method ... The Italian method was popularized by the first book to include a substantial treatise on it, which was published in Venice in 1494 by Luca Pacioli, a Franciscan friar who was a mathematics professor and good friend of Leonardo da Vinci. His influential book Summa de arithmetica, geometria, proportioni e proportionalità was copied in other countries and helped to spread double entry throughout Europe.'

Source: Nobes and Kellas, 1990, pp. 10–11 and 14–15.

In order to understand accounting and the principles of double-entry bookkeeping, you need to remember that the business is a separate entity from its owner(s) when it carries out transactions. Therefore, it can have dealings with the owner(s). All businesses need resources known as *assets*. Assets are what the business owns, such as premises, machinery, vehicles, office equipment, stock and cash. Before the business can acquire any assets, it must have finance (see Chapter 3). In a new business the most likely source of finance is the *capital* invested by the owner(s). As far as the business is concerned, capital is a liability because it is an amount that is owed to the owner(s). If this is the only source of finance, the assets of the business are equal to the capital. However, the business may have *other liabilities*; for example, it may owe money to lenders and suppliers.

KEY DEFINITIONS	An asset is 'a resource controlled by the enterprise as a result of past events and from which future economic benefits are expected to flow to the enterprise' (IASB, 1989, para. 25).
	Capital is the money invested in the entity by the owner(s) to enable it to function.
	A liability is 'a present obligation of the enterprise

resulting from past events, the settlement of which is expected to result in an outflow from the enterprise of resources embodying economic benefits' (IASB, 1989, para. 25).

The relationship between the assets, capital and other liabilities in the business forms what is known as the *accounting equation:*

Assets = Capital + Liabilities

The accounting equation states that the assets of the entity are equal to the capital and other liabilities and this reflects the dual nature of business transactions. The point about any equation is that it balances; in other words, the total of the values on each side of the equation are equal. Equations can be rearranged and you may remember from your school-days that if a positive amount is moved to the other side of the equation the sign becomes negative and vice versa. The accounting equation can be rearranged like this:

Assets – Liabilities = Capital

The accounting equation lies at the heart of double-entry booking and is the basis of an important financial statement we will be looking at in Chapter 7.

activity

A business has capital of £20,000 and assets of £20,000. It then borrows £10,000 from the bank to finance the purchase of some new office equipment. How does this affect the accounting equation?

In this case the business has assets of £20,000 which will increase by £10,000 (the new equipment), making total assets of £30,000. At the same time it will increase its liabilities by £10,000 (the bank loan) whilst the capital of £20,000 remains unchanged. The accounting equation still balances as shown below:

Assets	–	Liabilities	=	Capital
£		£		£
20,000		10,000		20,000
10,000				
30,000		10,000		20,000

In double-entry bookkeeping, every economic transaction of the business is recorded twice to keep the accounting equation balanced. This reflects the dual nature of business transactions and provides an arithmetical check on the records, which enables the business to be controlled. The bookkeeper records the business transactions in the ledgers, which are books of accounts. Accounts for each different type of transaction are kept on separate pages in the ledger. The bookkeeper records every transaction as a *debit* entry in an account that receives the value of the transaction and as a *credit* entry in an account that gives the value of the transaction. The following illustration of one page shows the layout:

		£			£
Date	Details of debit entries	Amount	Date	Details of credit entries	Amount

Table header: Name of the account

As you can see, the page is divided into two, with three columns on each side. Debit entries are shown on the left-hand side of the account and credit entries on the right. On each side there is a column for the date, details of the transaction and the amount involved. Because of their layout, ledger accounts are often referred to as T accounts.

4.4 recording assets and liabilities

The double-entry bookkeeping system provides rules for recording each different type of transaction. The rules for recording transactions concerning assets and liabilities are as follows:

- to show an increase in an asset account, debit the account
- to show a decrease in an asset account, credit the account
- to show an increase in a capital or liability account, credit the account
- to show a decrease in a capital or liability account, debit the account.

To illustrate these rules we will use an example of a business that commenced on 1 January 2005. The owner of the business is Nick Mulch and he has invested £5,000 capital in the business, which he has called Mulch Garden Design. His girlfriend, Louise, has given the business a loan of £2,000. All the money is kept in the bank. To record these transactions, we need to open three accounts: a *capital account* for the money invested by the owner; a *loan account* for the loan; and a *bank account* to show the bank transactions. There are two transactions to record: the capital invested by Nick and the loan given by Louise. Each transaction will require a debit entry to be made to one account and a corresponding credit entry of the same amount in another account:

Capital account		£			£
			1 January	Bank	5,000

Loan account		£			£
			1 January	Bank	2,000

Bank account					
		£			£
1 January	Capital	5,000			
1 January	Loan	2,000			

If you study these accounts, you can see that the rules for recording transactions have been stringently applied. The introduction of £5,000 capital by the owner has been shown as a credit in the capital account. Because the assets of the business have increased by this amount, the corresponding debit entry is in the bank account. When Louise gave the £2,000 loan to the business, its liabilities increased, so the loan account was credited with this amount. The corresponding debit entry is in the bank account, since the loan means an increase in the assets of the business. As you can see, for each transaction you need to record the date, the name of the account where the corresponding entry is made and the amount. This allows you to trace it at a later date if you have any problems with the records.

We will now extend our example by showing the transactions entered into on 2 January 2005. Using the business cheque book, Nick pays £3,000 for the premises, £1,000 for machinery and £500 for office equipment. The bank account is already open, but we need to open three new asset accounts to record these transactions:

Bank account					
		£			£
1 January	Capital	5,000	2 January	Premises	3,000
1 January	Loan	2,000	2 January	Machinery	1,000
			2 January	Equipment	500

Premises account					
		£			£
2 January	Bank	3,000			

Machinery account					
		£			£
2 January	Bank	1,000			

Office equipment account					
		£			£
2 January	Bank	500			

These records reflect the transactions that have taken place. For example, the bank account is an asset account. When the business received the capital of £5,000 from Nick and the loan from Louise, these amounts were debited to the bank account to show the increase in assets represented by the amount of money held at the bank. When the business paid for items such as the machinery, the bank account was credited. If you take the total of all the debit entries in the bank account and deduct the total of all the credit entries, the resulting figure is £2,500, which is the amount of money the business now has left at the bank.

The business repays £1,500 to Louise on 3 January and on the same day returns £250 worth of faulty equipment to the supplier and receives a refund, which is paid into the bank. Make the necessary entries in the ledger accounts.

The updated accounts should look like this:

Bank account					
		£			£
1 January	Capital	5,000	2 January	Premises	3,000
1 January	Loan	2,000	2 January	Machinery	1,000
3 January	Equipment	250	2 January	Equipment	500
			3 January	Loan	1,500

Loan account					
		£			£
3 January	Bank	1,500	1 January	Bank	2,000

Office equipment account					
		£			£
2 January	Bank	500	3 January	Bank	250

4.5   recording revenue and expenses

As well as needing accounts for its assets and liabilities, a business must have accounts for its *revenue* and *expenses*. Revenue is the income the business receives. Sales revenue is the monetary value of the sale of goods or services to customers. However, the business may receive non-sales revenue, such as interest receivable on cash invested in a savings account or rent receivable from letting part of the business premises. Expenses are the monetary value of the costs and other expenditure incurred by the business in order to obtain those revenues; in other words, the day-to-day expenses of running the business. The double-entry bookkeeping rules for recording transactions involving revenues and expenses are as follows:

● to show an increase in an expense account, debit the account
● to show a decrease in an expense account, credit the account
● to show an increase in a revenue account, credit the account
● to show a decrease in a revenue account, debit the account.

As required in double-entry bookkeeping, every transaction will involve making a credit entry to one account and a debit entry to another account. We will start by explaining what is meant by an increase in an expense account and an increase in a revenue account. On 4 January Mulch Garden Design spends £200 on printing advertisements in the form of promotional leaflets and £20 on posting them to potential customers. Prior to this date the business has not incurred any expenses, so the monetary value was nil. Now it has incurred some expenses and we need to show the increase in the appropriate accounts:

Bank account					
		£			£
1 January	Capital	5,000	2 January	Premises	3,000
1 January	Loan	2,000	2 January	Machinery	1,000
3 January	Equipment	250	2 January	Equipment	500
			3 January	Loan	1,500
			4 January	Advertising expenses	200
			4 January	Postage expenses	20

Advertising expenses account					
		£			£
4 January	Bank	200			

Postage expenses account					
		£			£
4 January	Bank	20			

As the business has paid for the advertising leaflets and postage, its cash assets at the bank must have decreased by the amount of these expenses. Therefore, these two transactions resulted in debit entries to the expense accounts and both were credited to the bank account.

On 5 January Mulch Garden Design pays £50 for the cleaning of the premises. On 6 January the business lets part of its display gardens for a wedding reception and receives £350 in rent. Make the necessary entries in the appropriate revenue and expense accounts.

You should not have had too much difficulty with this activity. The cleaning expenses were a pair of straightforward entries. The receipt of rent may have caused you to think because we have not illustrated any similar transactions. However, as long as you remembered the rule that you show an increase in revenues by crediting the revenue account (in this case, rent received), the corresponding entry had to be to debit the bank account to show an increase in cash assets of £350. The updated accounts should look like this:

Bank account					
		£			£
1 January	Capital	5,000	2 January	Premises	3,000
1 January	Loan	2,000	2 January	Machinery	1,000
3 January	Equipment	250	2 January	Equipment	500
6 January	Rent received	350	3 January	Loan	1,500
			4 January	Advertising expenses	200
			4 January	Postage expenses	20
			5 January	Cleaning expenses	50

Cleaning expenses account					
		£			£
5 January	Bank	50			

Rent received account					
		£			£
			6 January	Bank	350

4.6 recording purchases, sales and stock

In a trading business, it is not much use advertising goods unless the business has purchased a stock of goods to sell. *Purchases* of stock represent a cost to the business and it is necessary to open a purchases account, where purchases are recorded as a debit entry. However, when the business sells the goods they are not shown as a credit entry in the purchases account for two reasons. First, they will not be sold at the price for which they were purchased, as the business adds a mark-up in order to make a profit. Because we want to show the profit on a financial statement known as the profit and loss account (see Chapter 6), we do not want to lose it in the detail of the purchases account. The second reason is that at the end of a financial period it is likely there will be some unsold goods left which are known as 'stock'. Stock requires special treatment which we shall be describing at the end of this section.

Instead of crediting sales to the purchases account, a sales revenue account is opened. If the goods are sold to customers for cash, the sale is shown as a credit in the sales revenue account and the corresponding entry is a debit in the bank account. The latter entry reflects the increase in cash assets held at the bank. We need to look at a new example to shown how this is done. Katey Burton opens a boutique called Kool Kate on 1 July by investing £10,000 capital in the business. On that day she buys equipment costing £1,000, purchases stock costing £4,000 and pays £500 in advertising expenses. On 2 July she sells stock for £2,800 and buys a second-hand car for business use for £4,000. On 3 July she sells stock for £3,500 and purchases further stock for £2,000. The entries in the accounts are shown below:

Capital account		£			£
			1 July	Bank	10,000

Bank account		£			£
1 July	Capital	10,000	1 July	Equipment	1,000
2 July	Sales revenue	2,800	1 July	Purchases of stock	4,000
3 July	Sales revenue	3,500	1 July	Advertising expenses	500
			2 July	Car	4,000
			3 July	Purchases of stock	2,000

Equipment account		£			£
1 July	Bank	1,000			

Advertising expenses account		£			£
1 July	Bank	500			

Purchases account (stock)		£			£
1 July	Bank	4,000			
3 July	Bank	2,000			

Sales account		£			£
			2 July	Bank	2,800
			3 July	Bank	3,500

Car account		£			£
2 July	Bank	4,000			

In this example we have referred to the goods that the business is buying and selling as *stock*. However, we will not use a stock account until the end of the financial period, as we explain in a moment. Instead, the purchases and sales of goods have been recorded in separate accounts, named the *purchases account* and the *sales account*, respectively. Accountants use the term 'purchases' to refer only to purchases of stock for resale in a trading business or purchases of materials used to produce goods for resale in a manufacturing business. Do not confuse this with the acquisition of other assets, such as equipment and vehicles, which are not intended for resale but will stay in the business in the long term to help generate revenue.

There is one final aspect of the purchase and sale of goods that we need to consider.

Sometimes a business purchases goods, but has returned some of them to the supplier because they are faulty, or for other reasons. Alternatively, a customer sometimes returns goods to the business. The first transaction requires a *returns outward account* (also known as a *purchases returns account*) to be opened. The second transaction requires a *returns inward account* (also known as a *sales returns account*) to be opened.

The following example illustrates the returns outward account. On 1 July Kool Kate purchases goods from the usual supplier, but later a £200 suit was found to be faulty. It was returned to the supplier on 12 July and a refund of £200 was received the same day. These transactions are recorded as follows:

Bank account					
		£			£
1 July	Capital	10,000	1 July	Equipment	1,000
2 July	Sales	2,800	1 July	Purchases of stock	4,000
3 July	Sales	3,500	1 July	Advertising expenses	500
12 July	Returns outward	200	2 July	Car	4,000
			3 July	Purchases of stock	2,000

Returns outward account					
		£			£
			12 July	Bank	200

As you can see, the bank account has been debited to show the increase in cash assets due to the cash refund by the supplier, but rather than crediting the purchases account to record the goods which were returned, a returns outward account has been opened and this provides an accurate record of what has happened. This information will be used when the profit and loss account is drawn up later.

activity

The same principles are applied if one of the customers returns goods. Show how the transactions would be recorded in the ledger accounts if a customer returns £500 worth of goods to Kool Kate on 14 July and is given a refund the same day.

The transaction would be recorded as follows:

Bank account					
		£			£
1 July	Capital	10,000	1 July	Equipment	1,000
2 July	Sales	2,800	1 July	Purchases of stock	4,000
3 July	Sales	3,500	1 July	Advertising expenses	500
12 July	Returns outward	200	2 July	Car	4,000
			3 July	Purchases of stock	2,000
			14 July	Returns inward	500

Returns inward account					
		£			£
14 July	Bank	500			

4.7 credit transactions

All the receipts and payments in the examples we have used so far have been for cash. However, many economic transactions are *credit transactions* and the receipt or payment of cash does not take place until a later date. This requires accounts to be opened for *creditors* (suppliers from whom the business has bought goods or services on credit and to whom the business owes money) and *debtors* (customers who have bought goods or services on credit and who owe the business money). Thus, debtors are an asset to the business and creditors are a liability of the business. Therefore, the rules of double-entry bookkeeping for making entries into asset and liability accounts apply to debtors and creditors.

First we will consider an example where a customer of the business has not paid cash, but has obtained goods on credit. Suppose the clothes sold by Kool Kate for £2,800 on 2 July were credit sales to a customer called Philippa Merton. The entry in the sales account will still be a credit, but instead of debiting the bank account to show an increase in cash assets, we need to open an account for Philippa Merton and debit that account to show an increase in this trade debtor asset. The entries in the accounts are as follows:

Sales account					
		£			£
			2 July	Philippa Merton	2,800

Philippa Merton account (trade debtor)					
		£			£
2 July	Sales	2,800			

Because Philippa Merton is an account representing a trade debtor asset, we have followed the rules for all asset accounts. Before 2 July, Philippa owed the business nothing, but after the sales transaction on that date, she owed Kool Kate £2,800. The increase in debtor assets is shown by debiting the Philippa Merton account. The trade debtor's account has been opened in Philippa Merton's name so that a record can be kept of who owes money to Kool Kate.

activity

On 20 July Philippa Merton pays £750 of the money she owes to Kool Kate. Show how this transaction will be recorded in the accounts.

The accounts will be amended as follows:

Bank account					
		£			£
1 July	Capital	10,000	1 July	Equipment	1,000
3 July	Sales	3,500	1 July	Purchases of stock	4,000
12 July	Returns outward	200	1 July	Advertising expenses	500
20 July	Philippa Merton	750	2 July	Car	4,000
			3 July	Purchases of stock	2,000
			14 July	Returns inward	500

Philippa Merton account (trade debtor)					
		£			£
2 July	Sales	2,800	20 July	Bank	750

As you can see, cash assets have increased by £750 and debtor assets have decreased by the same amount. Note that in the bank account we have deleted the entry on 2 July for sales of £2,800 because Philippa Merton did not pay cash but took the goods on credit. Therefore, the debit entry is to the Philippa Merton account and the sales account remains unchanged.

Next we consider a case where the business has not paid cash but has obtained goods or services on credit. In such a case the business has acquired a liability and you will need to use the double-entry rules for increasing and decreasing liability accounts. On 26 July Kool Kate purchases goods on credit from her supplier, Patel & Co, for £1,500. On 28 July Kool Kate pays the amount in full. The transactions are recorded as follows:

Purchases account (stock)					
		£			£
1 July	Bank	4,000			
3 July	Bank	2,000			
26 July	Patel & Co	1,500			

Patel & Co account (trade creditor)					
		£			£
28 July	Bank	1,500	26 July	Purchases	1,500

Bank account					
		£			£
1 July	Capital	10,000	1 July	Equipment	1,000
3 July	Sales	3,500	1 July	Purchases of stock	4,000
12 July	Returns outward	200	1 July	Advertising expenses	500
20 July	Philippa Merton	750	2 July	Car	4,000
			3 July	Purchases of stock	2,000
			14 July	Returns inward	500
			28 July	Patel & Co	1,500

While working through the activities in this chapter, you may have noticed how easy it is to make a mistake and enter a transaction on the wrong side of an account. Although you may have found the process somewhat tedious, the activities help you understand the principles of double-entry bookkeeping, which can be summarized as follows:

- A transaction that represents an increase in purchases, expenses or assets is recorded as a debit entry on the left-hand side of the ledger account.
- A transaction that represents an increase in revenue, liabilities or sales is recorded as a credit entry on the right-hand side of the ledger account.

The following pearls of wisdom, passed on by students across the decades, may help you remember the rules of double-entry bookkeeping:

pearls

This mnemonic is set out as a T account and reminds you that an increase in **P**urchases, **E**xpenses or **A**ssets is a *debit* entry (on the left), whilst an increase in **R**evenue, **L**iabilities or **S**ales is a *credit* entry (on the right).

$$\text{P E A} \mid \text{R L S}$$

4.8 conclusions

Double-entry bookkeeping is an accounting system that provides a means of recording economic transactions in a way that ensures the records are mathematically accurate. The records are used as the basis for preparing financial statements, which summarize all the transactions that have taken place during any particular period.

The double-entry bookkeeping system captures the dual nature of economic transactions by making a debit entry and a corresponding credit entry for every transaction. A debit entry is recorded on the left-hand side of the ledger account and a credit entry is made on the right-hand side of the ledger account. There are separate rules for recording purchases, expenses, assets, revenue, liabilities and sales. In the next chapter we will be looking at how the accounts are balanced at the end of the financial period and the figures used to construct a trial balance.

practice questions

1. Explain the importance of the accounting equation and its relationship with the principles of double-entry bookkeeping.
2. On 1 March 2005 Jack Castle starts a business, Castle Tours, with £5,000 capital and a £5,000 loan from the bank. He keeps £300 of the loan as cash and then pays the balance of the loan and the capital into the business bank account.

   Required
   Write up the ledger accounts for Castle Tours.

3. Clive Ashley owns Ashley Kennels. On 1 August 2005 the business purchases £1,500 of dried dog food on credit from Bowin Ltd. On 2 August £50 of the food is returned to the supplier as it was beyond its sell-by date.

    Required
    Write up the ledger accounts for Ashley Kennels.

4. Rex Welling starts an agricultural fencing business called Wellworth Fencing with £50,000 capital which he has inherited. On 1 June 2005 he opens a bank account for the business and pays in the capital. On the same day he uses business cheques to buy a lorry for £16,000, to pay £1,400 to insure the lorry and to pay £4,500 for three months' rent on premises in advance. On 2 June he writes three business cheques: £5,400 to pay for equipment; £850 to pay for fencing materials from Timber Supplies; and £420 to pay for advertising expenses. On 4 June the business buys a further £120 of fencing materials from Timber Supplies on credit.

    Required
    Write up the ledger accounts for Wellworth Fencing.

5. Pamela Lawley has a gift shop called Lavender & Lace. On 4 July 2005 the cash account of the business looked like this:

Cash account					
		£			£
1 July	Opening balance	500	1 July	Postage	25
2 July	Cash sales	138	1 July	Window cleaning expenses	10
3 July	Cash sales	192	1 July	Stationery expenses	15
			1 July	Parking expenses	2
			1 July	Stationery expenses	36
			1 July	Petrol expenses	18
			2 July	Parking expenses	2
			2 July	Postage expenses	31
			2 July	Purchases of stock	104
			3 July	Parking expenses	2
			3 July	Petrol expenses	18
			3 July	Purchases of stock	89

    Required
    Write up the ledger accounts for Lavender & Lace to show the corresponding entries.

references

IASB (1989) *Framework for the Preparation and Presentation of Financial Statements*, September, London: International Accounting Standards Committee.
Nobes, C. and Kellas, J. (1990) *Accountancy Explained*, London: Penguin Books.

chapter 5

the trial balance

Learning objectives

When you have studied this chapter, you should be able to:

- Balance off accounts
- Construct a trial balance
- Describe the treatment of stock (inventory)
- Explain the limitations of a trial balance.

5.1 introduction

This chapter continues to describe an accounting system that is based on double-entry bookkeeping. As with the last chapter, on some courses it is considered useful to learn how the ledger accounts are balanced at the end of the accounting period and how the balancing figures are used to construct a trial balance.

The trial balance is a list of the balances of all the individual accounts in the accounting system. All the debit balances are entered in one column and all the credit balances in the other. The sum of these two columns should be the same. As the name implies, a trial balance is a test to see whether the double-entry bookkeeping system has been maintained accurately and the debit and credit totals balance. If they do not balance, checks must be made to identify and rectify any errors and the trial balance drawn up again. It may take a number of trials before the totals of the debit and credit columns balance. In this chapter we explain how to calculate whether individual accounts have a debit or a credit balance, how to construct a trial balance from the figures and how to identify errors if the columns do not balance.

5.2 balancing the accounts

Before you can construct a trial balance, you need to know how to determine the debit or credit balance on each of the individual accounts. The rules for balancing the accounts are very straightforward. We will continue to use the example of Kool Kate from Chapter 4 to illustrate them. At the end of an accounting period, which may be the end of the month, the end of the quarter, the end of the year, or any other period decided by the business, all the individual bookkeeping accounts are balanced using the following rules:

1. If the total amounts on each side of the account are equal, they are double underlined to close the account. This means that there is no outstanding balance on the account at the end of the accounting period. The Patel & Co account is an example of this:

Patel & Co account (trade creditor)					
		£			£
28 July	Bank	1,500	26 July	Purchases of stock	1,500

2. If the account contains only one entry, insert the figure required to make the account balance on the opposite side and label it *carried forward* (or the abbreviation c/f). Insert the same balancing figure on the same side as the original entry to start the next period, labelling it *brought forward* (or the abbreviation b/f). Kool Kate's vehicle account provides an example of this. We are still complying with the rules of double-entry bookkeeping since, as you can see, for every debit entry there is a corresponding credit entry. Therefore, to balance the account, we have credited the account with a closing balance of £4,000 and debited the account an opening balance of the same amount:

Vehicle account					
		£			£
2 July	Bank	4,000	31 July	Balance c/f	4,000
1 August	Balance b/f	4,000			

3. If the account contains a number of entries, add up both sides. If both sides are the
    same, insert the totals and double underline them. This means that there is no
    outstanding balance on the account. An extension of Kool Kate's trade debtor account
    for Philippa Merton provides an example of this:

Philippa Merton account (trade debtor)					
		£			£
2 July	Sales	2,800	20 July	Bank	750
5 July	Sales	200	28 July	Bank	2,550
12 July	Sales	300			
		3,300			3,300

4. If both sides are not the same when you add them up, use the larger figure as the total
    for both sides and then insert the balancing figure to the side that originally had the
    smaller total. Complete the entry by bringing forward the balancing figure on the oppo-
    site side to become the opening balance for the next accounting period. Kool Kate's
    bank account provides an example of this:

Bank account					
		£			£
1 July	Capital	10,000	1 July	Equipment	1,000
3 July	Sales	3,500	1 July	Purchases of stock	4,000
12 July	Returns outward	200	1 July	Advertising expenses	500
20 July	Philippa Merton	750	2 July	Car	4,000
28 July	Philippa Merton	2,550	3 July	Purchases of stock	2,000
			14 July	Returns inward	500
			28 July	Patel & Co	1,500
			31 July	Balance c/f	3,500
		17,000			17,000
1 August	Balance b/f	3,500			

You can see that the balance c/f refers to the balance at the end of the period (in this case,
at the end of July) and the balance b/f refers to the balance at the start of the next period (in
this case, the start of August.

activity

> Calculate the closing balances of the remaining accounts for Kool Kate
> from Chapter 4. These are the capital account, the sales account, the
> purchases account, the equipment account, the returns inward account,
> the returns outward account and the advertising account.

You should not have had too much difficulty with this activity if you followed the rules.
You can check your closing balances in the next section, where they are used to construct
the trial balance.

5.3 constructing a trial balance

When all the accounts have been balanced off, some of them will have been closed completely and will show no balance brought down to commence the next accounting period, whereas others will show either a debit or a credit balance. The debit balances normally represent the assets and expenses of the business and the credit balances normally represent the capital, revenue and liabilities of the business. The list of balances is drawn up in a financial statement at a particular point in time known as a *trial balance*.

KEY DEFINITION	A trial balance is a list of the balances of all the accounts in a double-entry bookkeeping system, with debit balances in the left-hand column and credit balances in the right-hand column. If the recording processes have been accurate, the totals of each column should be the same.

If you have made a debit entry for every credit entry and vice versa, the total of the debit balances should be equal to the total of the credit balances; in other words, your trial balance should balance. If they are not the same, you will need to look for the cause by checking the bookkeeping entries in the ledger accounts. It may require a number of trials to get the two columns to balance. When you have achieved this, you will have evidence of the arithmetical accuracy of the record keeping. Some last minute adjustments to the trial balance figures (for example, for closing stock, accruals, prepayments, depreciation and doubtful debts) may be necessary, after which the figures are used to draw up two important financial statements: the *profit and loss account* and the *balance sheet*. We shall be looking at these two statements in Chapters 6 and 7.

Continuing to use the example of Kool Kate, we can now calculate the closing balances for the accounts at the end of the month and construct a trial balance. You will notice that

Kool Kate
Trial balance as at 31 July 2006

	Debit	Credit
	£	£
Capital at 1 July 2006		10,000
Sales		6,800
Purchases	7,500	
Cash at bank	3,500	
Vehicles	4,000	
Equipment	1,000	
Returns inward	500	
Returns outward		200
Advertising	500	
	17,000	17,000

Note: Closing stock at 31 July 2006 was £4,000

if the balance b/f is a debit balance, the account is a debit in the trial balance; if the balance b/f is a credit balance, the account is a credit in the trial balance.

Looking at the two columns, you will see that the debit column is a list of all the expenses (for example, purchases) that will be shown in the profit and loss account, and assets (for example, premises) that will be shown in the balance sheet. The credit column is a list of the capital and the liabilities that will be shown in the balance sheet and the revenues that will be shown in the profit and loss account.

You will see that at the end of the trial balance there is a note stating that the business has closing stock of £4,000 at 31 July. As discussed earlier in this chapter, a debit is made to the purchases account when goods are purchased and a credit is made to the sales account when goods are sold. This suggests the business had some unsold stock (or *inventory* as it is now more widely known) at the end of the accounting period. This is known as *closing stock*. A business needs to have a certain amount of stock on the last day of the accounting period ready to sell on the first day of the next accounting period. Thus, closing stock at the end of one period becomes the *opening stock* at the beginning of the next period.

In order to value closing stock, at the end of the accounting period (the maximum being a year), a physical count of goods is carried out to compare the quantities counted with the records. This is referred to as *stocktaking*. The business may have to close or work overtime in order to conduct the stocktake. Once the total number of items in stock is known, the value can be calculated by multiplying the number of items by the original cost of the item. However, some items may be worth less than the price that was paid for them due to changes in taste or technological advances and other factors that may have reduced demand for them. There is an important accounting rule that requires closing stock to be valued either at the original (historic) cost or at the *net realizable value*, whichever is lower. The net realizable value is the price the business expects to get for the stock less any costs incurred in selling it.

activity

> A business purchased 100 items at £2 each with a view to selling them at £2.40 each. At the end of the year 20 items remained unsold. Due to a decline in demand, the business can now sell them for only £1.50 each. Calculate the value of the closing stock.

You may have calculated the closing stock as 20 items at £2 each (£40) but the value of the closing stock is 20 items at £1.50 each (£30) because this represents the net realizable value, which is lower than the original cost.

5.4 other transactions

You will remember that Kate started her business on 1 July and we drew up the trial balance after the end of the first month's trading on 31 July. This provides a simple example, but we can now extend this to draw up a trial balance for the first 6 months' trading. This allows us to introduce a number of new types of transaction. Instead of drawing up separate accounts using double-entry bookkeeping as we did in Chapter 4, we are going to focus on the nature of the transaction. However, the principles of double-entry bookkeeping still apply.

- Carriage – The business may have to pay delivery charges for raw materials or goods. This is sometimes referred to as *carriage inward*. It is an expense of the business and therefore appears in the debit column of the trial balance. It is regarded as part of the cost of purchasing the raw materials or goods. Sometimes the business has to bear the cost of delivery of its goods to customers, and this is known as *carriage outward*. This is also an expense and appears in the debit column of the trial balance.
- Discounts – When a business purchases goods it may be able to negotiate a trade discount and pay slightly less than the normal price. In such a case only the net price (the price after discount) is entered into the accounts. Another form of discount some-times available is a cash discount to encourage customers to pay promptly. When a busi-ness offers a cash discount to customers it is referred to in the supplier's accounts as *discounts allowed*. It is treated as an expense of the business and appears in the debit column of the trial balance. When a business receives cash discounts from its suppliers it is referred to in the customer's accounts as *discounts received* and appears in the credit column of the trial balance.
- Cash – As well as maintaining a bank account, a business may keep a very small amount of cash on the premises, known as *petty cash*. This is used to pay miscellaneous expenses, such as window cleaning, travelling expenses or the milk bill. A cash account must always appear in the debit column of the trial balance because it is an asset. The balance shown on ledger account for bank transactions appears in the debit column of the trial balance if the business has cash at the bank, as it is an asset. However, if the business has an overdraft, the balance appears in the credit column of the trial balance because it is a liability.
- Miscellaneous revenue – In addition to sales revenue, many businesses have other income, such as *rent receivable* from letting part of their business premises, or *interest receivable* on investments, or *commission* from acting as an agent for another business. As this represents revenue, it appears in the credit column of the trial balance. It is important that any miscellaneous revenue is recorded separately and is not included with sales revenue.
- Stock account – In Chapter 4 we mentioned that the stock account is somewhat special and that separate accounts are maintained for purchases and sales. When constructing a trial balance, it is usual to show the figure for *closing stock* as a footnote because it will be needed when the final accounts are drawn up.

activity

After six months' trading, a stocktake for Kool Kate on 31 December 2006 shows 180 items that cost £20 each, which can be sold for £45, and 200 items that cost £16 each, which can be sold for £14. The account balances on that date are as follows:

	£
Capital at 1 July 2006	10,000
Sales	52,400
Wages	2,400
Purchases	38,700
Cash	300
Bank (overdraft)	2,800

Vehicles	4,000
Equipment	1,000
Returns inward	900
Returns outward	800
Advertising	3,400
Carriage inward	960
Discounts allowed	1,200
Discounts received	680
Drawings	12,000
Telephone	600
Shop overheads	1,220

Draw up a trial balance for Kool Kate as at 31 December 2006.

Your completed trial balance should look like this:

Kool Kate
Trial balance as at 31 December 2006

	Debit £	Credit £
Capital at 1 July 2006		10,000
Sales		52,400
Wages	2,400	
Purchases	38,700	
Cash	300	
Bank		2,800
Vehicles	4,000	
Equipment	1,000	
Returns inward	900	
Returns outward		800
Advertising	3,400	
Carriage inward	960	
Discounts allowed	1,200	
Discounts received		680
Drawings	12,000	
Telephone	600	
Shop overheads	1,220	
	66,680	66,680

Note: Closing stock at 31 December 2006 was £6,400

If you had any difficulty with this activity, you may find it useful to think of the mnemonic PEARLS again, to remind you that balances on Purchases, Expenses or Asset accounts are *debit* balances (shown in the left-hand column), whilst the balances on Revenue, Liabilities or Sales accounts are *credit* balances (shown in the right-hand column).

5.5   limitations of a trial balance

A trial balance can only detect arithmetical errors as it is simply a list of the debit balances and credit balances on the ledger accounts at the end of the period. If the principles of double-entry bookkeeping have been followed with a debit entry for every credit entry, the sum of the debit column in the trial balance will be the same as the sum of the credit column. If they do not balance, checks must be made to identify any discrepancy. A common error is to transpose numbers; for example, writing £320 instead of £230. To find out whether this is the reason for your trial balance not balancing, calculate the difference between the total of the debit and credit columns on the trial balance. If this figure is divisible by 9, you have probably transposed a number somewhere and you should check for this error.

activity

If the trial balance balances, it does not necessarily mean that the figures are correct. What other mistakes could have been made in the recording of transactions that would not be revealed by a trial balance?

There are several types of error that might have been made:

- Omission – the transaction has not been recorded in the accounts at all.
- Wrong account – the transaction has been recorded in the wrong account (for example, in the vehicles account instead of the equipment account or in an asset account instead of a liability account).
- Wrong amount – the transaction has been recorded in the correct accounts, but the wrong amount was entered.
- Reverse entry – the transaction has been recorded in the correct accounts, but on the wrong side of both accounts.

The accuracy of the records in the accounting system is important, as they are used as the basis for preparing financial statements, which summarize the transactions that have taken place during the accounting period. This period is usually one year. Figure 5.1 summarizes the accounting process.

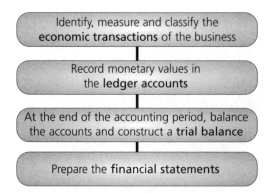

FIGURE 5.1 **Overview of the accounting process**

5.6   conclusions

On the last day of the accounting period (for example, the end of the month, end of the quarter or end of the year) all the individual ledger accounts (T accounts) are balanced. All the debit balances and all the credit balances are listed in two columns in a financial statement called a trial balance. If the sum of the debit column is equal to the sum of the credit column, we can assume that the records are mathematically accurate. However, there are some limitations to the trial balance as it does not show other errors that might have occurred during the double-entry bookkeeping process. Once all errors have been checked and corrected and the two columns agree, it is possible to draw up two important financial statements from the figures in the trial balance: the profit and loss account and the balance sheet. We shall be looking at these two important financial statements in the next three chapters.

practice questions

1. Explain the limitations of a trial balance.
2. The following bank account shows transactions for Dylan's Bookshop for the month of October:

Bank account					
		£			£
1 October	Balance b/f	6,400	2 October	Purchases	750
12 October	Sales	1,800	3 October	Advertising expenses	1,120
15 October	Rachel Jones	950	16 October	Purchases of stock	2,300
18 October	Rachel Jones	950	18 October	Laura Davies	780
30 October	Sales	1,450	25 October	Purchases	3,400

Required
Balance the account at 31 October and show the balance carried forward at 1 November.

3. The following account is that of Thomas Turner, who is a trade debtor of Dylan's Bookshop:

Thomas Turner (trade debtor)					
		£			£
2 November	Sales	850			
12 November	Sales	1,650			
18 November	Sales	260			
21 November	Sales	400			
25 November	Sales	640			

Required
On 30 November Thomas Turner pays 50% of the amount due. Show this entry and balance the account.

4. The following list of balances at 30 June 2006 is taken from the accounts of
    Harlech Health Food:

	£
Sales	26,200
Purchases	?
Returns inward	900
Returns outward	460
Discounts allowed	720
Discounts received	620
Equipment	2,000
Bank	1,500
Wages	1,600
Rent	1,400
General expenses	390
Capital at 1 July 2005	18,000

Required
Construct a trial balance at 30 June for Harlech Health Food, calculating the
figure for purchases.

5. During the financial year ending 31 December 2006 Country Furniture had sales
    that were three times the amount of its purchases and trading expenses that
    were 25% of the figure for purchases. On 31 December 2006 the business had
    £4,000 in the bank and this was half the amount it had incurred in trading
    expenses. Premises were purchased for £75,000 and one-third of this was funded
    by a bank loan. Stock at the beginning of the year was the equivalent of two
    months' sales.

Required
Construct a trial balance for Country Furniture at 31 December 2006, calculating
the figure for capital.

chapter 6

measuring financial performance

When you have studied this chapter, you should be able to:

- Explain the purpose of the trading account
- Explain the purpose of the profit and loss account
- Explain the difference between cash and profit
- Construct a simple trading and profit and loss account for a sole trader.

6.1 introduction

As well as being of interest to management, the 'financial health' of the business is of interest to the seven external groups of users we looked at in Chapter 1. This chapter focuses on financial performance and the financial statement that finds out how profitable a business has been over a particular accounting period; in other words, whether the business has made a profit or loss and the amount of this profit or loss. Not surprisingly, this financial statement is called a *profit and loss account*.

In this chapter we provide an overview of the accounting system for students who have not been required to study the more detailed examination of double-entry bookkeeping in Chapters 4 and 5. We then go on to explain the purpose of a profit and loss account and describe how to construct a simple trading and profit and loss account for a sole trader. In addition, we compare this financial statement with the cash flow statement for a sole trader described in Chapter 3; in doing so, we show how the difference between cash and profit can be analysed for a financial period.

6.2 overview of the accounting system

The economic transactions of the business are recorded in an *accounting system*. Large organizations carry out thousands of transactions every day and need sophisticated, computerized accounting systems. Most small businesses use standard accounting software or spreadsheets, and a minority keep their records manually. If a manual system is kept, the records are kept in *ledgers*, which are the books of accounts (hence, the term *bookkeeping*). However, in most businesses the records are computerized and transactions are recorded using spreadsheets, such as Excel or an accounting package, such as SAGE. Whether the system is manual or computerized, it is normally based on the principles of *double-entry bookkeeping*. This is the most efficient and effective method for recording financial transactions in a way that allows financial statements to be prepared.

KEY DEFINITION	Double-entry bookkeeping is based on the principle that every financial transaction involves the simultaneous receiving and giving of value, and is therefore recorded twice.

The data recorded in the double-entry bookkeeping system is taken from source documents, such as:

- sales orders, delivery notes, invoices paid by customers and credit notes issued for goods returned by customers
- purchase orders, invoices received from suppliers and credit notes received for goods returned to suppliers
- payroll records, stock records, cash records and so on.

At the end of an accounting period all the balances on the ledger accounts are listed in a *trial balance*, which acts as an arithmetical check on the records. The accuracy of the records in the accounting system is important, as they are used as the basis for preparing financial statements, which summarize the transactions that have taken place during the accounting period. This period is usually one year. Figure 6.1 summarizes the work of an accountant using an accounting system based on double-entry bookkeeping.

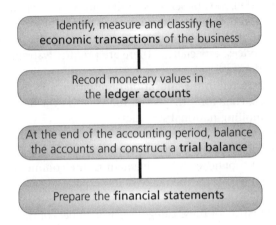

FIGURE 6.1 **Overview of the accounting system**

6.3   purpose of the profit and loss account

Account literally means 'a history of' and the purpose of the profit and loss account is therefore to show a history of the *financial performance* or *profitability* of the business over the accounting period. This means that it shows the profit or loss that the business has made over the period (usually one year). Because it is retrospective, it is sometimes referred to as a financial history book. Naturally, the financial performance of the business is of key interest to those who use the financial statements.

activity

We examined the main users of the published financial statements in Chapter 2. Test your learning by jotting down the names of the seven groups identified by the SoP (ASB, 1999) and the IASB Framework (1989).

If you have managed to remember them without referring to Chapter 2, you are making good progress. The seven groups are as follows:

- *Present and potential investors* need to assess the financial performance of the business, its financial position and the amount of dividend they will receive on their shares. They use the financial statements for economic decision making in connection with buying or selling shares and for stewardship purposes.
- *Employees* are interested in information that helps them assess job security, the possibil-

ity of an increase in remuneration, employment opportunities, retirement and other benefits.

- *Lenders* need information for risk assessment purposes and deciding the terms of the loan, and monitoring that risk once the loan has been given.
- *Suppliers and other trade creditors* need information for similar purposes to lenders, as they need to assess whether to provide goods or services to the business on credit and to assess whether the amounts owed to them by the business will be repaid.
- *Customers* are interested in information about the continued existence of the business and its ability to supply goods or services, especially if there are product warranties or specialist replacement parts involved.
- *Governments and their agencies* are interested in the allocation of resources and the effect of their economic and fiscal policies. Therefore, they need information for regulatory purposes, assessing taxation and compiling national statistics.
- *The public* is interested in information that is relevant to how they are affected by the organization. For example, the contribution the entity makes to the local economy by providing employment or using local suppliers; its involvement in the community; its contributions to political and charitable groups; the range of its activities.

Although you may not fall into the first six of these categories, as members of the public we are all potential users of published financial statements. When you have finished your course, your job may require you to read financial statements from time to time, which will necessitate understanding the purpose of the profit and loss accounts. One of the most important things to remember is that an accounting profit or loss can be made whether the transactions of the business are for cash or on credit and is the difference between revenue and the associated costs during the financial period. If this sounds familiar to you, it is because the calculation of profit is guided by the accruals concept, which we explained in Chapter 2.

| KEY DEFINITION | The accruals concept is the principle that revenue and costs are recognized as they are earned and incurred and they are matched with one another and dealt with in the profit and loss account of the period to which they relate, irrespective of when cash (or its equivalent) is received or paid. |

A profit and loss account does not show the movements of cash because, as you know from Chapter 3, that is the role of a cash flow statement.

| activity | You will remember this example from Chapter 3. Imagine you have £200 cash that you use to buy a computer from a student you meet in the bar. You are a bit of an opportunist and decide to advertise the computer for sale in the newspaper. The advertisement costs £10 and you succeed in selling the computer for £300 cash. You have no other business transactions. Calculate your cash position at the end the month and your profit for the month. |

It is likely that you have been able to work out the cash position and the profit in your head, but you may have decided to use the layout for a cash flow statement you learned in Chapter 3 where you deduct all the cash outflows from the total cash inflows to arrive at the net cash flow. To calculate the profit, you need to deduct all the costs you incurred in the month from the value of the sale. It does not matter at this stage how you calculated the figure, as long as you understand the principles involved. You may find the following layout useful, which is one accountants use:

Cash flow statement for the month	£
Cash inflows	
Capital	200
Sales	300
Subtotal	500
Cash outflows	
Purchases	200
Advertising	10
Subtotal	210
Net cash flow	290

Profit and loss account for the month	£
Sales	300
Cost of sales	
Purchases	(200)
Gross profit	100
Expenses	
Advertising	(10)
Net profit	90

As you can see, the cash position is a cash surplus of £290 and a profit of £90. You need to remember that the profit and loss account does not tell us anything about cash. For example, it does not tell us about the £200 capital or whether cash has been received for the sale of the computer; nor does it tell us whether the costs have actually been paid or merely incurred. To emphasize the difference between profit and cash we will make the example slightly more complex.

activity

The information is the same as in the previous activity. You have £200 that you use to buy a computer. You advertise the computer in the newspaper, which costs £10, and sell it for £300. You have no other business transactions. This time, the buyer is not able to pay you straight away, so you give him one month's credit. Calculate your cash position and profit now.

Cash flow statement for the month	£
Cash inflows	
Capital	200
Subtotal	200
Cash outflows	
Purchases	200
Advertising	10
Subtotal	210
Net cash flow	(10)

Profit and loss account for the month	£
Sales	300
Cost of sales	
Purchases	(200)
Gross profit	100
Expenses	
Advertising	(10)
Net profit	90

As you can see, if you have calculated the net cash flow correctly, the cash position is now a cash deficit of £10. This may have misled you into thinking that you have now made a loss of £10 (the cost you have incurred) or a loss of £300 (the amount owing to you). Neither figure is correct. The answer is still a profit of £90. It is very important to remember that profit is not the same as cash and that the profit and loss account is not a record of cash flows in and out of the business. When we calculate profit we are concerned with the intentions of the parties and the transactions they have entered into, regardless of whether any cash has changed hands. In other words, the figures for sales, cost of sales and expenses do not take into account whether you have paid the supplier for the computer, whether your customer has paid you for the computer or whether you have paid the newspaper for the advertisement. This is because you have applied the accruals concept when calculating the profit or loss for the period.

In section 3.7 of Chapter 3, we looked at Sarah Wick's business, which she started on 1 January 2006 and constructed a cash flow statement for Candlewick Enterprises for the first six months of trading. This showed that after investing £1,000 of her own money as capital in the business and borrowing £650 from the bank, she had a cash surplus of £50 at the end of June 2006.

> **activity**
>
> Do you consider that the financial performance of the business was satisfactory? Draw up a list of questions you would like to ask Sarah to find out if she thinks it is a financial success.

You may have thought of the following questions:

- Did she think the cash surplus of £50 was a satisfactory cash position, considering the money, time and effort she put into the business?
- How much profit did she hope to achieve for the first six months?
- How much profit did she actually make?
- Did she think the profit she made was satisfactory, considering the money, time and effort she put into the business?
- Were her achievements typical for her type of business?
- Would she have been better off using her money, time and effort in some other enterprise?
- Has she built up a business that is worth something in terms of the assets it has acquired (such as cash or stock) or its potential to generate profit?

This is a formidable list of questions and you may think that answering them will be very difficult. Although a cash flow statement provides some answers, others will be provided by constructing a profit and loss account to describe the financial performance.

6.4 constructing a profit and loss account

The first thing to determine when constructing a profit and loss account is the accounting period over which the profit or loss will be calculated. This will always be done on an annual basis, but even in a small business the owner-manager may want to see how profitable the business is more frequently, such as monthly or quarterly. All sources of revenue for the financial period need to be included, irrespective of whether the transactions were for cash or on credit: in other words, irrespective of whether money has been received or not. They are then matched with the revenue expenditure, which are the costs and expenses incurred during the period in order to earn the revenue, irrespective of whether money has been paid or not. Therefore, the basic calculation is:

Profit (or loss) = Revenue – Revenue expenditure

Owners and managers in trading organizations are not only interested in a single figure of profit, but also need more detailed information. Therefore, it is usual to show the profit the business makes on trading goods (buying and selling) separately. This is referred to as the *gross profit*.

Gross profit = Sales revenue – Cost of sales

It is usual to add any non-sales revenue before deducting all the revenue expenditure of the business and arriving at the final figure of *net profit* (or *net loss* if the expenses are greater than the gross profit).

Net profit (or loss) = Gross profit + Non-sales revenue – Revenue expenditure

KEY DEFINITIONS	Gross profit is the difference between the sales revenue and the cost of goods sold
	Net profit is the amount of income earned after deducting all expenses.

We are going to look at the two sections of the profit and loss account separately and then combine them. We will go on using the example of Candlewick Enterprises and see whether the business has made a profit over the first six months of trading. To find the appropriate figures, we need to look more closely at the actual sales and purchases for each month shown in the cash flow statement we constructed in section 3.7 of Chapter 3. For ease of reference this is reproduced below:

Candlewick Enterprises
Cash flow statement for January–June 2006

	January £	February £	March £	April £	May £	June £	Total £
Cash inflows							
Capital	1,000	0	0	0	0	0	1,000
Loan	650	0	0	0	0	0	650
Cash sales	160	180	200	350	410	450	1,750
Credit sales	0	0	480	540	600	780	2,400
Subtotal	1,810	180	680	890	1,010	1,230	5,800
Cash outflows							
Purchases	0	600	600	750	840	900	3,690
Equipment	0	1,300	0	0	0	0	1,300
Rent and rates	30	30	30	30	30	30	180
Advertising	25	25	25	25	25	25	150
Telephone and internet	0	0	45	0	0	61	106
Postage and packing	0	10	10	10	10	10	50
Interest on loan	4	4	4	4	4	4	24
Drawings	0	50	50	50	50	50	250
Subtotal	59	2,019	764	869	959	1,080	5,750
Net cash flow	1,751	(1,839)	(84)	21	51	150	50
Cumulative cash b/f	0	1,751	(88)	(172)	(151)	(100)	0
Cumulative cash position	1,751	(88)	(172)	(151)	(100)	50	50

When drawing up a profit and loss account, we are interested in the value of transactions that took place over the period. To calculate these figures, we need to enter them in the months when the transactions took place, rather than when the cash was received or paid. The cash flow statement shows the one month lag between the purchase of candles and the payment of cash and the two month lag between credit sales and receipt of cash.

The other point to note is that although the business purchased the same number of candles as planned, the actual sales were much lower each month. This suggests the business will have some unsold stock (or *inventory*) at the end of the accounting period. For students who have not needed to study Chapter 5, this is known as *closing stock*. A business needs to have a certain amount of stock on the last day of the accounting period ready to sell on the first day of the next accounting period. Thus, closing stock at the end of one period becomes the *opening stock* at the beginning of the next period.

In order to value closing stock, at the end of the accounting period (the maximum being a year), a physical count of goods is carried out to compare the quantities counted with the records. This is referred to as *stocktaking*. The business may have to close or work overtime in order to conduct the stocktake. Once the total number of items in stock is known, the value is calculated by multiplying the number of items by the original cost of the item.

activity

A garden centre purchased 100 plants at £2 each with a view to selling them at £2.40 each. At the end of the year 20 plants remained unsold. Because the plants are no longer in flower, the business will have to drop the price to £1.50 each. Calculate the value of the closing stock.

You may have calculated the closing stock as £40 (20 × £2), but the value the business must use is £30 (20 × £1.50) because these plants were worth less than the price that was paid for them. Apart from seasonal factors, other factors that may reduce demand for goods and services include changes in taste and fashion or advances in technology. The valuation of closing stock is guided by the principles of the historical cost concept and the prudence concept. These principles are embodied in the accounting standard, SSAP 9 Stocks and long-term contracts, which requires stock to be stated in the financial statements at the lower of historical cost or *net realizable value*.

KEY DEFINITION   Net realizable value (NRV) is the sales value of the stock minus the additional costs likely to be incurred in getting the stock into the hands of the customer.

Returning to the example of Candlewick Enterprises, the following table summarizes the quantities and values of the purchases and sales over the six month period:

	Purchases		Cash sales		Credit sales	
	Quantity	£	Quantity	£	Quantity	£
January	400	600	80	160	240	480
February	400	600	90	180	270	540
March	500	750	100	200	300	600
April	560	840	175	350	390	780
May	600	900	205	410	410	820
June	600	900	225	450	425	850
Total	3,060	4,590	875	1,750	2,035	4,070

activity

How much stock (quantity of unsold candles) did Candlewick Enterprises have at the end of June and what was its total cost?

There are a number of ways you could have calculated the answer. At this stage, it does not matter how you calculated the figure as long as you understand the principles involved. You may find the following layout useful:

	Quantity	
Purchases		3,060
Less Sales		
Cash sales	875	
Credit sales	2,035	(2,910)
Closing stock at 30 June 2006		150

The closing stock consisted of 150 candles, which cost £1.50 each. Therefore, the value of closing stock is £225. We can now construct the trading section of the profit and loss account for Candlewick Enterprises for the six months ending 30 June 2006. In this section we will calculate the *gross profit* and we will use the convention of showing deductions in brackets.

Candlewick Enterprises
Profit and loss account for 6 months ending 30 June 2006

	£	£
Sales		5,820
Less Cost of sales		
Purchases	4,590	
Less Closing stock	(225)	(4,365)
Gross profit		1,455

The business has made a gross profit of £1,455 over the six months ending 30 June 2006. We can crosscheck this by doing a small calculation. We know that the business buys each candle for £1.50 and sells it for £2.00, thus making a gross profit of 50p on each candle. As 2,910 candles have been sold in the period, the total gross profit must be 2,910 × 50p = £1,455. In a more complex business, you could not carry out these simple calculations.

Under the heading of 'cost of sales' we have calculated the cost of the goods sold. In this case we have deducted the cost of the closing stock from the cost of the stock purchased during the period. This is because we are applying the accruals concept and we are matching the sales revenue to the cost of purchasing the candles actually sold during the period and we are ignoring the movement of cash.

Cost of sales = Opening stock + Purchases – Closing stock

The figure for closing stock at the end of one period becomes the figure for *opening stock* at the beginning of the next. Therefore, in subsequent years the calculation becomes opening stock plus purchases less closing stock. If the business had any other income, such as interest received on investments or rent received from lettings, it would be shown as an addition to the gross profit.

Closing stock = Opening stock + Purchases – Sales

The cost of sales is not the only cost incurred by the business. The term *gross* is used to describe the profit at this stage because this is the larger figure of profit before the expenses of the business are deducted. We will now complete the remainder of the trading and profit and loss account by deducting these expenses.

```
                        Candlewick Enterprises
        Profit and loss account for 6 months ending 30 June 2006
                                        £           £
        Sales                                     5,820
Less  Cost of sales
          Purchases                   4,590
Less        Closing stock             (225)      (4,365)
        Gross profit                              1,455
Less  Expenses
          Rent and rates               180
          Advertising                  150
          Telephone and internet       106
          Postage and packing           50
          Interest on loan              24        (510)
        Net profit                                 945
```

You can now see that the business has made a *net profit* of £945 after the deduction of all the expenses. If the expenses were greater than the gross profit, this would be a negative figure that we would label as *net loss*.

Common mistakes students make when drawing up the profit and loss account are:

- not heading the profit and loss account with the name of the business and the period that it covers
- forgetting to include the currency symbols
- confusing opening stock with closing stock in the calculation of the cost of sales
- confusing gross profit with net profit (gross profit is a larger figure, as the expenses have not yet been deducted)
- forgetting to double underline the final figure (the net profit or net loss).

learn the layout

```
                          Name of business
             Profit and loss account for the year ending ...
                                        £           £
        Sales                                       X
Less  Cost of sales
          Opening stock                 X
Add       Purchases                     X
                                        X
Less        Closing stock              (x)          X
        Gross profit                                X
Add   Other income                                  X
                                                    X
Less  Expenses
          (List)                        X          (x)
        Net profit/(loss)                           X
```

6.5 difference between cash and profit

To review the difference between cash and profit we need to look at the events that took place during the year. On 1 January 2006 Sarah invested £1,000 capital in Candlewick Enterprises and borrowed £650 from the bank. After six months' trading, the cash flow statement shows that the business has a cash surplus of £50 and the profit and loss account for the same period shows a profit of £945. There seems to be a discrepancy of £895.

> **activity**
>
> List the items that you think caused the difference between the cash and the profit by comparing the items in the cash flow statement with the items in the profit and loss account.

The items causing the apparent discrepancy are as follows:

- Sarah has allowed two months' credit to her credit customers. From the cash flow statement we can see that cash received from credit sales totalled £2,400, but that does not include the credit sales of £820 for May and £850 for June (which represents £1,670 owed by trade debtors). This brings the value of credit sales to £4,070, to which we then add the cash sales of £1,750 to give us the sales figure shown in the profit and loss account of £5,820. Therefore, the difference in sales revenue stated in the two financial statements is £1,670.
- On the other hand, Sarah has negotiated one month's credit from the supplier from whom she buys her candles. From the cash flow statement we can see that the cash paid for purchases totalled £3,690, but to calculate profit we need to include the purchases of £900 incurred in June (which represents £900 owed to trade creditors). This brings the value of purchases to £4,590, which is the figure shown in the profit and loss account.
- At 30 June the business had 150 candles in stock. These cost £1.50 each and this is how they have been valued in the trading and profit and loss account; whether they have been paid for or not is a separate issue. Therefore, the total value of stock is £225, which is not included in the cash flow statement.
- Sarah did not take up the offer of credit for the advertising expenses and none was available for the telephone and internet expenses or the rent and rates on the market stall, so there is no discrepancy between cash and profit here.
- The cash flow statement shows all cash revenue and all cash expenditure. It includes cash inflows from the capital Sarah invested in the business and the loan made by the bank and the cash outflows on buying the equipment and Sarah's drawings. None of these items are shown in the profit and loss account, so here is another difference between the two financial statements.

In order to make the position clear, we will divide the information into good news and bad news. The good news is where Candlewick Enterprises has assets and the bad news is where the business has incurred liabilities.

	£	£
Good news (assets)		
Equipment (at cost)	1,300	
Cash owed by trade debtors	1,670	
Closing stock (at cost)	225	3,195
Bad news (liabilities)		
Capital owed to owner less drawings	750	
Loan owed to the bank	650	
Cash owed to trade creditor for purchases	900	2,300
Difference		895

As you can see, this analysis shows a difference between the assets and the liabilities of £895, which explains the apparent discrepancy between the net profit of £945 and the cash surplus of £50 (£945 – £50 = £895).

There are a number of important lessons to be learned from the principle that cash is not the same as profit and these can be used to run a business more efficiently:

- Giving credit to customers may have the advantage of increasing sales and thus poten-tial profit, but results in a delay before the sales value is realized in the cash flow. In extreme cases this means that an organization can make a good profit, but at the same time risks failure due to lack of liquidity (insufficient cash for its activities).
- Building up stock to an unnecessarily high level can have an adverse effect on cash flow. Managers who take advantage of bargains, such as special discounts, often forget this; perhaps because they consider that cash flow is the concern of the accountant and not of the organization as a whole.
- Taking credit from suppliers is one way of improving cash flow and is a form of free finance. However, if an organization takes more time than the agreed credit period, it runs the risk of losing this advantage, the supplier refusing to provide any more goods or services and difficulty in obtaining credit in future.

Both the cash flow statement and the profit and loss account analyse financial informa-tion retrospectively over the accounting period. However, the past is not an accurate guide to the future. From a management point of view, planned or budgeted financial informa-tion should be compared frequently with actual information to ensure that the business is meeting its economic objectives.

6.6 conclusions

The profit and loss account is one of the main financial statements drawn up from the accounting records at the end of the accounting period. Its main purpose is to measure the financial performance of the business over the period, which is usually one year. If the busi-ness uses a double-entry bookkeeping system, the figures are taken from the trial balance, which checks the mathematical accuracy of the records at the end of the period. If the busi-ness keeps only cash records, after some adjustments these figures can also be used as the basis of a profit and loss account.

In this chapter we have described how to construct a simple profit and loss account for a sole trader. We have examined the relationship between purchases, stock and cost of sales and noted that in the first accounting period for a new business there is no opening stock. In the next and subsequent accounting periods, the cost of opening stock is first added to the cost of purchases; then the cost of closing stock is deducted to arrive at the cost of sales (also referred to as the cost of goods sold). In the trading section, revenue from sales is matched to the cost of sales to arrive at the gross profit and then any other income is added. Then the expenses incurred during the period are deducted to arrive at the net profit or loss for the accounting period.

We have compared the cash flow statement that we introduced in Chapter 3 with the profit and loss account and examined the relationship between cash and profit. The application of the accruals concept lies at the heart of the difference:

- The cash flow statement only recognizes transactions when cash is actually received or paid and shows the actual cash position at the end of the financial period.
- The profit and loss account recognizes transactions when they occur, regardless of when cash changes hands, and shows the profit or loss achieved over the financial period.

practice questions

1. Describe the general purpose of the profit and loss account and explain the difference between this financial statement and the cash flow statement for a sole trader.
2. Explain the purpose of the cost of sales adjustment in the profit and loss account. Include a simple example in your explanation.
3. Insert the missing figures in the following examples, remembering that some items will be added and others will be subtracted:

	(a)	(b)	(c)	(d)	(e)
	£	£	£	£	£
Opening stock	100	?	1,020	?	14,960
Purchases	?	680	?	1,924	?
	500	730	?	2,156	?
Closing stock	50	?	1,550	150	18,815
Cost of sales	?	520	9,680	?	159,715

	(f)	(g)	(h)	(i)	(j)
	£	£	£	£	£
Sales	10,000	?	17,000	18,150	?
Cost of sales	6,000	450	?	?	24,590
Gross profit	?	150	3,500	17,470	3,160
Expenses	3,500	?	?	?	?
Net profit	?	50	250	2,100	740

4. Kavita Patel is a sole trader who opened a lighting shop called Uplights on 1 January 2005. Her brother is studying for his accountancy exams and is employed on a part-time basis to keep the accounts and help out in the shop on Saturdays. At the end of the first year of trading, he draws up the following trial balance from the accounting records:

Uplights Trial balance as at 31 December 2005	Debit £	Credit £
Sales		66,600
Purchases	24,500	
Fixtures and fittings (at cost)	16,000	
Trade debtors	2,000	
Trade creditors		8,000
Bank	12,800	
Cash	100	
Interest received		200
Rent and rates	25,000	
Wages	3,000	
Insurance	2,000	
Electricity	500	
Telephone	300	
General expenses	100	
Drawings	18,500	
Capital at 1 January 2005		30,000
	104,800	104,800

Note: Stocktaking took place on 31 December 2005. The stock held in the store room was valued at £750 and the goods on display in the shop at £1,750.

Required
Use the relevant figures in the above information to construct a trading and profit and loss account for Uplights for the year ending 31 December 2005.

5. George Alexandrou owns a retail business called Mega Mobiles, which sells mobile telephones. At the end of the second year of trading, his accountant draws up the following trial balance:

```
                        Mega Mobiles
              Trial balance as at 30 June 2006
                                        £              £
        Sales                                       106,900
        Purchases                    39,700
        Stock at 1 July 2005         10,000
        Fixtures and fittings (at cost)  20,000
        Trade debtors                 8,000
        Trade creditors                              13,000
        Bank                         10,000
        Cash                            300
        Interest received                               100
        Wages                        20,000
        Rent and rates               15,000
        Insurance                     3,000
        Electricity                   1,500
        Telephone/internet            2,000
        General expenses                500
        Drawings                     10,000
        Capital and reserves at 1 July 2005          20,000
                                    _____         _____
                                     140,000         140,000
```

Note: At 30 June 2006, stock was valued at £12,000.

Required

Use the relevant figures in the above information to construct a trading and profit and loss account for Mega Mobiles for the year ending 30 June 2006.

references

ASB (1999) *Statement of Principles for Financial Reporting*, December, London: Accounting Standards Board.

IASB (1989) *Framework for the Preparation and Presentation of Financial Statements*, September, London: International Accounting Standards Board.

chapter 7

measuring financial position

When you have studied this chapter, you should be able to:

- Explain the purpose of the balance sheet

- Describe how the accounting equation is reflected in the balance sheet

- Construct a simple balance sheet for a sole trader

- Explain the relationship between the cash flow statement, profit and loss account and balance sheet.

7.1 introduction

In the last chapter we explained that management and the seven main groups that use the financial statements are interested the profit and loss account because it shows the financial performance of the business over the accounting period. However, this is not the only aspect of the 'financial health' of the business that is of interest to them. In this chapter we look at a financial statement called the balance sheet, which shows the financial position of the business. It does this by summarizing what the business owns and what it owes on the last day of the accounting period.

For the benefit of students who have not been required to study Chapters 4 and 5, we start by examining the accounting equation, which describes the relationship between the assets, capital and other liabilities of the business. We then go on to explain the purpose of the balance sheet and how to construct a simple balance sheet for a sole trader, using the vertical format, which is the layout most commonly adopted. At the end of the chapter we explain the relationship between the three main financial statements for a sole trader: the cash flow statement, profit and loss account, and balance sheet.

7.2 the accounting equation

If you have already studied Chapters 4 and 5, you will be familiar with this explanation of the accounting equation. In order to understand accounting, you need to remember that the business is a separate entity from its owner(s) when it carries out transactions. Therefore, it can have dealings with the owner(s). All businesses need resources known as *assets*. Assets are what the business owns, such as premises, machinery, vehicles, equipment, stock, debtors and cash. A *debtor* is a person or entity owing money. Before the business can acquire any assets, it must have the necessary finance (see Chapter 3). In a new business the most likely source of finance is the *capital* invested by the owner(s). As far as the business is concerned, capital is a liability because it is an amount that is owed to the owner(s). If this is the only source of finance, the assets of the business are equal to the capital. However, the business may have other *liabilities*; for example it may owe money to lenders and creditors. A *creditor* is a person or entity to whom money is owed as a consequence of the receipt of goods or services.

KEY DEFINITIONS	An asset is 'a resource controlled by the enterprise as a result of past events and from which future economic benefits are expected to flow to the enterprise' (IASB, 1989, para. 25).
	Capital is the money invested in the entity by the owner(s) to enable it to function.
	A liability is 'a present obligation of the enterprise resulting from past events, the settlement of which is expected to result in an outflow from the enterprise of resources embodying economic benefits' (IASB, 1989, para. 25).

A debtor is a person or entity owing money.

A creditor is a person or entity to whom money is owed as a consequence of the receipt of goods or services.

The relationship between the assets, capital and other liabilities in the business forms what is known as the *accounting equation:*

Assets = Capital + Liabilities

The accounting equation states that the assets of the entity are equal to the capital and other liabilities and this reflects the dual nature of business transactions. The point about any equation is that it balances; in other words, the total of the values on each side of the equation are equal. Equations can be rearranged and you may remember from your school-days that if a positive amount is moved to the other side of the equation the sign becomes negative and vice versa. The accounting equation can be rearranged like this:

Assets – Liabilities = Capital

activity

A business has capital of £20,000 and assets of £20,000. It then borrows £10,000 from the bank to finance expenditure on some new office equipment. Using this second version of the accounting equation, show how this affects the accounting equation.

When the business borrows £10,000 it increases its assets by £10,000 (the new equipment), but at the same time it increases its liabilities by £10,000 (the bank loan). Thus, the accounting equation becomes:

Assets	–	Liabilities	=	Capital
£		£		£
20,000		10,000		20,000
10,000				
30,000		10,000		20,000

7.3 purpose of the balance sheet

The *balance sheet* is a financial statement that reflects the accounting equation by showing the *financial position* of the business. This means that it shows the assets, liabilities and capital of the business on the last day of the accounting period for which the profit and loss account and cash flow statement were prepared. The published balance sheet is prepared for the seven user groups we examined in Chapter 2. Because it looks at what the business owns and what it owes at one particular point in time, it is sometimes referred to as a 'financial snapshot'.

The balance sheet is divided into two parts. The first part shows the assets and liabilities of the business. The assets of the business are classified into fixed assets and current assets and the liabilities of the business are classified into amounts due to creditors within one year (current liabilities) and amounts due to creditors after more than one year (long-term liabilities).

- *Fixed assets* are assets the business owns and plans to keep in the long term, such as land and buildings, machinery, equipment, fixtures and fittings and delivery vehicles. The term 'fixed assets' is the one that has been traditionally used in the UK, but due to the move towards international convergence in financial accounting other terms, such as 'long-lived assets' or 'non-current assets', are also coming into use.
- *Current assets* are cash or other assets, such as stock and trade debtors, held for conversion into cash in the normal course of trading. The current assets that the business owns are constantly circulating from cash to stock to cash again. For this reason they are sometimes referred to as 'circulating assets'.
- *Creditors: amounts due within one year* are current liabilities owed by the business that should be paid during the next accounting period, such as trade creditors.
- *Net current assets* (or *working capital*) represent the difference between current assets and amounts due to creditors within one year. They are also referred to as the 'working capital' of the entity.
- *Creditors: amounts due after more than one year* are long-term liabilities owed by the business that do not have to be repaid within the next accounting period, such as a loan or a mortgage.
- *Total net assets* represent fixed assets plus net current assets minus creditors: amounts due after more than one year. They are also known as the 'capital employed' in the entity.

KEY DEFINITIONS	Net current assets are the difference between current assets and creditors: amounts due within one year.
	Total net assets are fixed assets plus net current assets less creditors: amounts due after more than one year.

The second part of the balance sheet shows the *capital* and *reserves*.

- *Capital* is the amount invested in the business by the owner(s) at the start of the year. In the first year of a new business the figure for capital will be the original amount of money the owner(s) invested, but in subsequent years it will include *reserves of profit* that have been retained in the business in previous years to help it grow.
- The next figure is the *net profit* earned for the year which is added to the capital at the start of the year (if the business had suffered a net loss, the amount would be deducted).
- In a sole proprietorship, the owner may take personal *drawings* from the business in the form of cash, goods or services. Therefore, drawings are deducted next to arrive at a final figure for capital and reserves.

The two halves of the balance sheet should be equal to one another. In other words, on the last day of the accounting period, the total net assets calculated in the first part will be equal to the capital and reserves calculated in the second part.

It is important to note that accountants divide expenditure into *capital expenditure,* which refers to the cost of fixed assets that are capitalized in the balance sheet, and *revenue expenditure,* which refers to the period costs and overheads that are written off in the profit and loss account for the period to which they relate (Figure 7.1).

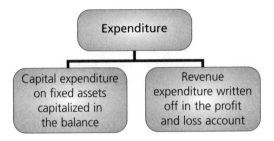

FIGURE 7.1 **Classifying expenditure**

7.4 constructing a balance sheet

In the last chapter we constructed a profit and loss account for Candlewick Enterprises for the first six months of trading, 1 January to 30 June 2006. We will continue to use this example and will start by looking at the transactions that took place on the first day of business. On 1 January, Sarah opened a business bank account with her savings of £1,000 and took out a loan of £650, which was also put into the business account. On behalf of the business, Sarah bought computer equipment for £1,300 on the business credit card, which would not need to be paid until February.

It is important to remember that the accountant preparing the financial statements is guided by the business entity concept (see Chapter 2, Accounting principles). Therefore, Candlewick Enterprises is considered to exist separately from its owner, Sarah Wick. This separation is crucial when we look at the balance sheet because this statement shows the financial position of the business and not the financial position of the owner. The most widely used presentation of the balance sheet in the UK is the vertical format. Using that format, at the end of the first day of business on 1 January 2006, the balance sheet for Candlewick Enterprises looked like this:

		£	£
	Candlewick Enterprises		
	Balance sheet as at 1 January 2006		
	Fixed assets		
	Equipment (at cost)		1,300
	Current assets		
	Bank	1,650	
Less	Creditors: amounts due within one year		
	Creditors	(1,300)	
	Net current assets		350
			1,650

Less	Creditors: amounts due after more than one year	
	Loan	(650)
	Total net assets	1,000
	Capital and reserves	
	Capital at 1 January 2006	1,000

As you can see, the name of the business and the date at which the balance sheet is drawn up is given at the top of the statement. The assets and liabilities are listed in the first half of the statement. Net current assets (the difference between current assets and amounts due to creditors within one year) are calculated and added to the fixed assets. Then amounts due to creditors after more than one year are subtracted to arrive at the total net assets. The total net assets should be equal to the capital and reserves section that forms the second half of the statement (no profit or drawings are shown yet).

In the UK, fixed and current assets are listed in order of permanence, with the most permanent first and the most liquid last. Creditors due within one year and after more than one year are listed in order of immediacy, with the most immediate first and the longest term last.

examples of assets and liabilities of a sole trader

Fixed assets	*Current assets*
Premises	Stock
Fixtures and fittings	Trade debtors
Delivery vehicles	Prepayments (expenses
Equipment	paid in advance)
	Bank
	Cash

Creditors: amounts due within one year	*Creditors: amounts due after more than one year*
Overdraft	Medium-term loan
Short-term loan	Long-term loan
Trade creditors	Mortgage
Accruals (estimates of	
accrued expenses)	

If you look closely at the above examples of current assets, you can see that they represent capital used in the day-to-day trading cycle. They are *circulating assets* that are constantly changing from cash to stock and eventually back to cash again, and the faster they circulate the better. Amounts due to creditors within one year are also an important part of the trading cycle because they reduce the amount of capital needed to be invested in current assets. We have called the difference between current assets and amounts due to creditors within one year *net current assets*. Since this capital works so hard for the business, an alternative term is *working capital* (see Figure 7.2).

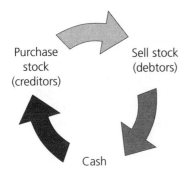

FIGURE 7.2 **Working capital and the trading cycle**

A balance sheet can be prepared at any moment in time, so we will move forward to 2 January by which time Sarah has started trading by buying 100 candles at £1.50 each, which the business will not need to pay for until February.

Candlewick Enterprises Balance sheet as at 2 January 2006		
	£	£
Fixed assets		
Equipment (at cost)		1,300
Current assets		
Stock	150	
Bank	1,650	
	1,800	
Less Creditors: amounts due within one year		
Creditors (1,300 + 150)	(1,450)	
Net current assets		350
		1,650
Less Creditors: amounts due after more than one year		
Loan		(650)
Total net assets		1,000
Capital and reserves		
Capital at 1 January 2006		1,000

As you can see, although the figures have changed, the balance sheet still balances. This is significant. The business has £1,390 worth of fixed assets and £1,800 of current assets. These assets have been financed by a combination of Sarah's capital and creditors. Amounts due within one year are £1,300 owing on the business credit card for the computer equipment and £150 owing to the supplier of the candles bought in January (totalling £1,450). Credit cards and credit agreed with suppliers are useful sources of finance, as it is normally possible to obtain interest-free credit as long as the debt is paid in full within the agreed period.

activity

We will now move on to 7 January, which is the end of the first week of trading. The business has made cash sales of 10 candles at £2 each and credit sales of 20 candles at £2 each. Using the following pro forma, construct the balance sheet as at 7 January. Any profit the business has made should be shown beneath the figure for capital. Like the capital, profit is a liability because it is owed by the business to the owner. At this stage in trading you can ignore the fact that a proportion of business operating expenses should be deducted from the profit and simply calculate the gross profit.

Candlewick Enterprises
Balance sheet as at ...

	£	£
Fixed assets		
Equipment (at cost)		
Current assets		
Stock		
Trade debtors		
Bank		
Cash		
Less Creditors: amounts due within one year		
Trade creditors		
Net current assets		
Less Creditors: amounts due after more than one year		
Loan		
Total net assets		
Capital and reserves		
Capital at 1 January 2006		
Net profit		

There are a number of calculations you need to make before you can complete the balance sheet. One of these calculations is to find out what profit the business has made over the period. For this reason it is usual to construct a profit and loss account for the period before drawing up the balance sheet.

- We know that Candlewick Enterprises sold a total of 30 candles at £2 each, so the sales revenue is £60.
- The business purchased 100 candles at £1.50 each (£150), less the 30 sold means that the closing stock is 70 candles at £1.50 (£105).

- You will remember from Chapter 6 that the cost of sales is the difference between the cost of opening stock plus purchases, less the cost of closing stock. This allows us to calculate the cost of the goods sold during the period and we are applying the accruals concept (see Chapter 2) by matching it with the sales revenue.
- As you can see from the following extract from the profit and loss account, the cost of the candles sold was £45, which is subtracted from the sales revenue of £60 to give a gross profit of £15:

Candlewick Enterprises
Profit and loss account for week ending 7 January 2006
(extract)

		£	£
	Sales		60
Less	Cost of sales		
	Purchases (100 at £1.50)	150	
Less	Closing stock (70 at £1.50)	(105)	(45)
	Gross profit		15

Strictly speaking we should now deduct a proportion of the expenses for the period and calculate the net profit, but since trading has barely commenced we are going to use the gross profit figure.

The business still has fixed assets (the computer equipment) which cost £1,300, but the current assets have changed since the balance sheet on 2 January. The above trading account shows that closing stock cost £105, but now Candlewick Enterprises has begun trading we need to consider the effect on the other current assets. The business now has trade debtors, who have not yet paid for 20 candles sold on credit at £2 each (£40), and cash from the sale of 10 candles at £2 each (£20). So the new balance sheet looks like this:

Candlewick Enterprises
Balance sheet as at 7 January 2006

		£	£
	Fixed assets		
	Equipment (at cost)		1,300
	Current assets		
	Stock	105	
	Trade debtors	40	
	Bank	1,650	
	Cash	20	
		1,815	
Less	Creditors: amounts due within one year		
	Trade creditors (1,300 + 150)	(1,450)	
	Net current assets		365
			1,665
Less	Creditors: amounts due after more than one year		
	Loan		(650)
	Total net assets		1,015
	Capital and reserves		
	Capital at 1 January 2006	1,000	
	Net profit	15	1,015

We could continue to construct a series of balance sheets covering Sarah's business on a day-to-day basis, but this would be somewhat tedious. So we will move on to the end of the first six months and construct the balance sheet as at 30 June 2006. Before we do so, it is useful to review the information we already have from reconciling the cash flow statement and the profit and loss account for the period (see section 6.4 in Chapter 6):

- Candlewick Enterprises bought computer equipment for use in the business for £1,300.
- Closing stock at 30 June is valued at £225 (150 candles at £1.50).
- Since Candlewick Enterprises allows credit customers two months to pay, customers buying in May and June have yet to pay. The amount owed by these trade debtors is £1,670 (total credit sales for the period of £4,070 – £2,400 cash received from credit sales).
- We know from the cash flow statement for the period that there was a cash surplus of £50 at 30 June. Unless you are told otherwise, you can assume that all cash is held at the bank.
- Suppliers give one month's credit, which means that stock purchased in June has yet to be paid for. The amount owed to these creditors is £900 (total purchases of £4,590 – £3,690 cash paid to suppliers).
- The business has a medium-term bank loan of £650.
- Sarah has invested £1,000 of her own money as capital in the business.
- We know from the profit and loss account we drew up in Chapter 6 that the business made a net profit of £945 over the six months ending 30 June 2006.
- Sarah has taken £250 from the business as drawings.

activity

Using the above information and the following pro forma, construct a balance sheet for Candlewick Enterprises as at 30 June 2006.

Candlewick Enterprises
Balance sheet as at ...

	£	£
Fixed assets		
Fixtures and fittings (at cost)		
Current assets		
Stock		
Trade debtors		
Bank		
Less Creditors: amounts due within one year		
Trade creditors		
Net current assets		
Less Creditors: amounts due after more than one year		
Loan		
Total net assets		
Capital and reserves		
Capital at 1 January 2006		
Net profit		
Less Drawings		

Your completed balance sheet should look like this:

Candlewick Enterprises Balance sheet as at 30 June 2006	£	£
Fixed assets		
Fixtures and fittings (at cost)		1,300
Current assets		
Stock	225	
Trade debtors	1,670	
Bank	50	
	1,945	
Less Creditors: amounts due within one year		
Trade creditors	(900)	
Net current assets		1,045
		2,345
Less Creditors: amounts due after more than one year		
Loan		(650)
Total net assets		1,695
Capital and reserves		
Capital at 1 January 2006	1,000	
Net profit	945	
	1,945	
Less Drawings	(250)	1,695

An important point to note is that it if Sarah takes cash out of the business for her own use or gives Candlewick Enterprises candles as Christmas presents to her friends without paying the business for them, these transactions are drawings. The owner's drawings are always shown as a deduction from profit in the balance sheet. Since the capital and any profit retained in the business are owed by the business to the owner, drawings reduce this liability. By keeping Sarah's personal transactions separate from the economic transactions of the business in this way, the balance sheet demonstrates compliance with the business entity concept and shows the financial position of the business and not that of the owner.

Common mistakes students make when drawing up the balance sheet are:

● not heading the balance sheet with the name of the business and date at which it is constructed
● forgetting to include the currency symbols
● not classifying assets and liabilities correctly
● forgetting to order fixed assets and current assets by permanence and liabilities by immediacy
● using the figure for opening stock instead of closing stock under current assets
● confusing net current assets with total net assets
● confusing drawings with expenses and deducting them in the profit and loss account instead of the balance sheet

- forgetting to double underline the two balancing figures in the balance sheet (total net assets calculated in the first part and capital and reserves calculated in the second part).

learn the layout

Name of business
Balance sheet as at ...

		£	£
	Fixed assets		X
	Current assets	X	
Less	Creditors: amounts due within one year	(x)	
	Net current assets		X
Less	Creditors: amounts due after more than one year		(x)
	Total net assets		X
	Capital and reserves		
	Capital at start of year	X	
	Net profit/(loss)	X	X
Less	Drawings		(x)
			X

7.5 relationship between the three financial statements

We have now looked at three financial statements for Candlewick Enterprises: the cash flow statement in Chapter 3, the profit and loss account in Chapter 6 and the balance sheet in this chapter. You may have noticed that when we constructed the balance sheet, some of the figures from the other two statements were needed. One of the obvious items was the cash position from the cash flow statement. Candlewick Enterprises had a cash surplus (if it had been a cash deficit, it would mean that the business had an overdraft). The closing stock shown in the profit and loss account also appeared in the balance sheet. In addition, you will recall that the difference between the sales figure shown in the cash flow statement (cash received from cash and credit sales) and the sales figure in the profit and loss account (total sales revenue irrespective of when cash is received) is shown as trade debtors in the balance sheet. Similarly, the difference between the purchases figure shown in the cash flow statement (cash paid for purchases of stock) and the purchases figure in the profit and loss account (total purchases irrespective of when cash is paid) is shown as trade creditors in the balance sheet. You are now beginning to see the relationship between the three financial statements.

So far, we have only looked at the financial statements for Candlewick Enterprises for the first six months of trading and we are now going to look the next six months:

- The business is still able to buy candles at £1.50 each and suppliers continue to give one month's credit. This means Sarah does not have to pay until the month after the purchases have been made.

- As the business is doing well, she has increased the selling price of each candle to £2.50 and continues to give credit customers two months' credit. This means she does not receive cash from these customers until two months after the sale has been made.

The following table shows when transactions for purchases and sales took place (not when cash was received or paid) during the year ending 31 December 2006:

Month	Purchases £	Cash sales £	Credit sales £
January	600	160	480
February	600	180	540
March	750	200	600
April	840	350	780
May	900	410	820
June	900	450	850
Subtotal	4,590	1,750	4,070
July	900	625	1,000
August	900	625	1,000
September	1,050	500	1,000
October	1,125	750	1,125
November	1,275	875	1,250
December	1,500	1,250	1,500
Subtotal	6,750	4,625	6,875

The following information is also available for the second six months:

- From 1 July, Sarah increased her drawings to £200 per month.
- Rent and rates for the market stall continued to be £30, payable on the last day of each month.
- The business paid £25 per month for advertising and has not taken up the offer of one month's credit.
- Telephone and internet expenses of £45 were paid in September and December.
- Postage and packaging expenses continued to be £10 per month during the period.
- Due to a rise in interest rates, monthly interest paid on the loan went up to £5 from 1 July.
- We know from the cash flow statement for January to June that on 30 June, the business had a cumulative cash surplus of £50. This money was held at the bank.

Using the above information, construct a cash flow statement for Candlewick Enterprises for the six months July to December 2006. If you have learned the layout, you should be able to do it without referring to a previous example. The following notes may be useful:

- The cumulative cash position at the end of one period is carried forward to the next period and becomes the cumulative cash brought forward (b/f) on 1 July.
- The cash received for credit sales in July and August was for credit sales which took place in May and June.
- Purchases are paid for one month in arrears, so purchases made in June are paid for in July.
- Sarah's monthly drawings must be shown.

Your completed cash flow statement should look like this:

Candlewick Enterprises
Cash flow statement for 6 months July–December 2006

	July £	Aug £	Sept £	Oct £	Nov £	Dec £	Total £
Cash inflows							
Cash sales	625	625	500	750	875	1,250	4,625
Credit sales	820	850	1,000	1,000	1,000	1,125	5,795
Subtotal	1,445	1,475	1,500	1,750	1,875	2,375	10,420
Cash outflows							
Purchases	900	900	900	1,050	1,125	1,275	6,150
Rent and rates	30	30	30	30	30	30	180
Advertising	25	25	25	25	25	25	150
Telephone and internet	0	0	45	0	0	45	90
Postage and packing	10	10	10	10	10	10	60
Interest on loan	5	5	5	5	5	5	30
Drawings	200	200	200	200	200	200	1,200
Subtotal	1,170	1,170	1,215	1,320	1,395	1,590	7,860
Net cash flow	275	305	285	430	480	785	2,560
Cumulative cash b/f	50	325	630	915	1,345	1,825	50
Cumulative cash c/f	325	630	915	1,345	1,825	2,610	2,610

activity

Draw up a profit and loss account for Candlewick Enterprises for the six months ending December 31 2006. If you have learned the layout, you should be able to do it without referring to a previous example. The following notes may be useful:

- From the profit and loss account for the first six months we know that at the end of June the figure for closing stock was £225 (150 candles at £1.50 each). This becomes the figure for opening stock on 1 July.
- On 31 December the value of stock was £75 (50 candles at £1.50 each). This is the closing stock for the period and will be used in the

profit and loss account and the balance sheet.

- Sarah's drawings are not shown on the profit and loss account, but will be shown in the balance sheet.

Your completed profit and loss account should look like this:

Candlewick Enterprises
Profit and loss account for 6 months ending
31 December 2006

		£	£
Sales			11,500
Less	Cost of sales		
	Opening stock	225	
	Purchases	6,750	
		6,975	
Less	Closing stock	(75)	(6,900)
Gross profit			4,600
Less	Expenses		
	Rent and rates	180	
	Advertising	150	
	Telephone and internet	90	
	Postage and packing	60	
	Interest on loan	30	(510)
Net profit			4,090

Construct a balance sheet for Candlewick Enterprises as at 31 December 2006. You will need to refer to the balance sheet as at 30 June that you drew up in section 7.4 and the cash flow statement and the profit and loss account you have just drawn up for the six month period July to December. The following notes may be useful:

- The business owns computer equipment which cost £1,300.

- Cash has not yet been received from customers for credit sales made in November and December. The amount owed by trade debtors can be calculated as follows:

		£
	Trade debtors at 30 June (from balance sheet on page 123)	1,670
Add	Total cash and credit sales July – December (from schedule on page 125)	11,500
		13,170
Less	Cash received July – December (from cash flow statement on page 126)	(10,420)
	Trade debtors at 31 December	2,750

activity

- Purchases are paid for one month in arrears, so the purchases of £1,500 made in December (see the schedule on page 125) are paid for in January. This means that the business has creditors amounting to £1,500 at 31 December.

- Sarah invested £1,000 capital in the business in January and retained £695 of the profit made in the first six months in the business (the business made a net profit of £945 during the first six months and Sarah took out £250 in drawings).

- Profit is added to capital and then drawings are deducted.

Your completed balance sheet should look like this:

Candlewick Enterprises Balance sheet as at 31 December 2006		
	£	£
Fixed assets		
Equipment (at cost)		1,300
Current assets		
Stock	75	
Trade debtors	2,750	
Bank	2,610	____
	5,435	
Less Creditors: amounts due within one year		
Trade creditors	(1,500)	
Net current assets		3,935
		5,235
Less Creditors: amounts due after more than one year		
Loan		(650)
Total net assets		4,585
Capital and reserves		
Capital at 1 July 2006	1,695	
Net profit	4,090	____
	5,785	
Less Drawings	(1,200)	4,585

7.6 conclusions

The balance sheet is one of the main financial statements drawn up from the accounting records at the end of the accounting period. Its main purpose is to measure the financial position of the business, not of its owner, at one particular point in time. This date is the last day of the period to which the trading and profit and loss account relates. If the business uses a double-entry bookkeeping system, the figures are taken from the trial balance, which checks the mathematical accuracy of the records at the end of the period. The trading and profit and loss account for the period provides the figure of net profit or net loss for the year that is shown on the balance sheet. If the business keeps only cash records, after some adjustments these figures can also be used as the basis of a trading and profit and loss account and balance sheet. In a continuing business, some figures from previous periods are also needed.

The balance sheet reflects the accounting equation by showing what the business owns in the way of assets less what it owes to creditors (assets – liabilities). This is equal to what it owes to the owner (capital + retained profit). In this chapter we have described how to construct a simple balance sheet in vertical format for a new sole trader business and for a continuing business. We have also investigated the relationship between the cash flow statement, the trading and profit and loss account and the balance sheet. Each of these financial statements shows a different aspect of the business:

- The cash flow statement is based on actual cash flows and shows the cumulative cash position at the end of the accounting period.
- The trading and profit and loss account is based on the accruals concept and measures the financial performance over the accounting period.
- The balance sheet is based on the accounting equation and measures the financial position at the end of the accounting period.

practice questions

1. Describe the general purpose of the balance sheet and explain the difference between this financial statement and the profit and loss account for a sole trader.
2. Explain how the accounting equation is reflected in the vertical presentation of the balance sheet. Include a simple example in your explanation.
3. Insert the missing figures in the following examples:

	(a) £	(b) £	(c) £	(d) £	(e) £
Fixed assets	10,000	12,000	?	20,000	25,000
Current assets	?	3,700	4,000	8,200	11,800
Creditors: amounts due within one year	1,000	1,200	1,500	?	3,300
Net current assets	2,400	?	?	6,200	?
Creditors: amounts due after more than one year	5,000	?	5,000	?	15,000
Total net assets	?	8,500	15,500	16,200	?
Capital and reserves					
Capital at start of year	5,000	?	10,000	15,000	?
Net profit for the year	3,600	4,900	?	6,000	18,100
Drawings	?	2,400	3,600	?	9,600
	?	?	?	?	?

4. Kavita Patel is a sole trader who opened a lighting shop called Uplights on 1
    January 2005. Her younger brother, who is studying for his accountancy exams, is
    employed on a part-time basis to keep the accounts and help out in the shop on
    Saturdays. At the end of the first year of trading, he drew up a trial balance and
    following table shows an extract:

Uplights Trial balance as at 31 December 2005	Debit £	Credit £
Sales		66,600
Purchases	24,500	
Fixtures and fittings (at cost)	16,000	
Trade debtors	2,000	
Trade creditors		8,000
Bank	12,800	
Cash	100	
Interest received		200
Rent and rates	25,000	
Wages	3,000	
Insurance	2,000	
Electricity	500	
Telephone	300	
General expenses	100	
Drawings	18,500	
Capital at 1 January 2005		30,000
	104,800	104,800

Note: A stocktake carried out on 31 December 2005 valued the cost of stock held
in the store room at £750 and the cost of goods on display in the shop at £1,750.

Required
Use the relevant figures to construct a balance sheet for Uplights as at 31
December 2005.

5. George Alexandrou owns a retail business called Mega Mobiles, which sells
    mobile telephones. At the end of the second year of trading, his accountant
    draws up the following trial balance:

```
                        Mega Mobiles
              Trial balance as at 30 June 2006
                                          £              £
    Sales                                             106,900
    Purchases                          39,700
    Stock at 1 July 2005               10,000
    Fixtures and fittings at cost      20,000
    Trade debtors                       8,000
    Trade creditors                                    13,000
    Bank                               10,000
    Cash                                  300
    Interest received                                     100
    Wages                              20,000
    Rent and rates                     15,000
    Insurance                           3,000
    Electricity                         1,500
    Telephone/internet                  2,000
    General expenses                      500
    Drawings                           10,000
    Capital and reserves at 1 July 2005                20,000
                                      _____          _____
                                      140,000          140,000
```

Notes: At 30 June 2006 the business had stock which had cost £12,000.
Net profit for the year ending 30 June 2006 is £27,300 (calculated in practice question 5 of Chapter 6).

Required
Use the relevant figures in the above information to construct a balance sheet for Mega Mobiles as at 30 June 2006.

references

ASB (1999) *Statement of Principles for Financial Reporting*, December, London: Accounting Standards Board.

IASB (1989) *Framework for the Preparation and Presentation of Financial Statements*, September, London: International Accounting Standards Board.

financial statements of a sole trader

Learning objectives

When you have studied this chapter, you should be able to:

- Differentiate between accruals and prepayments

- Explain what is meant by the depreciation of tangible fixed assets

- Calculate depreciation using the straight-line method or the reducing balance method

- Differentiate between bad debts and doubtful debts

- Construct financial statements for a sole trader with post trial balance adjustments.

8.1 introduction

In this chapter we bring together some the knowledge you have gained from earlier chapters. In Chapters 3, 6 and 7 we looked at the basic format and contents of the main financial statements that are commonly drawn up for a sole trader at the end of an accounting period. These are the cash flow statement, which shows the cumulative cash position of the business at the end of the accounting period; the profit and loss account, which measures the financial performance over the accounting period; and the balance sheet, which measures the financial position on the last day of the accounting period. The profit and loss account is always drawn up before the balance sheet as the net profit or loss is needed for the second half of the balance sheet where capital and reserves are shown.

The financial statements are drawn up from the records kept in the accounting system, which is sometimes a simple cash-based system or, more commonly, a computerized system based on double-entry bookkeeping. If the latter is used, a trial balance containing the balances on all the ledger accounts is drawn up to check the mathematical accuracy of the bookkeeping and these figures are used as the basis of the financial statements. However, before they can be used, certain adjustments are needed to ensure that the financial statements conform to accounting principles. These adjustments are known as post trial balance adjustments because they make use of information that was not taken into account when compiling the trial balance. The four main adjustments are concerned with stock, accruals and prepayments, depreciation, and bad and doubtful debts. In this chapter we explain the adjustments and the effect they have on the profit (or loss) reported in the profit and loss account and the financial position reported in the balance sheet.

8.2 post trial balance adjustments

When a business reaches the end of the accounting period, which may be a month, a quarter, six months or a year, there is considerable interest in knowing the final results. However, the profit and loss account and balance sheet cannot be prepared until all the accounts are balanced and the trial balance drawn up. Even in a small business this can be a lengthy process, so the accountant must start the work as soon as possible. Although the records in the accounting system may be fully up to date, it is always necessary to deal with a number of matters that crop up at the end of the accounting period. These matters are written into the ledger accounts, which means that some of the figures in the trial balance we have used so far to construct the basic profit and loss account and balance sheet for a sole trader require adjustment before these important financial statements can be finalized. These are referred to as post trial balance adjustments. The use of the Latin word 'post' (meaning 'after') refers to the fact that the accountant makes the adjustments after the trial balance has been constructed. Figure 8.1 summarizes the accounting process, including this important step.

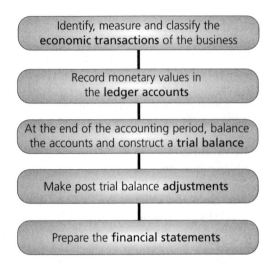

FIGURE 8.1 **Overview of the accounting process**

The post trial balance adjustments are needed to ensure that the financial statements are prepared in accordance with the accounting principles and rules we examined in Chapter 2.

activity

Name four accounting principles that are used in the preparation of financial statements.

If you did not have to refer to Chapter 2 to answer this question, you are doing very well. If you had difficulty, you should revise all the main accounting principles now. The eight principles we introduced were:

Boundary concepts
● business entity concept
● going concern concept

Measurement concepts
● materiality concept
● money measurement concept
● historical cost concept
● accruals concept

Ethical concepts
● prudence concept
● consistency concept

The last four of these principles, in particular, guide the accountant when making post trial balance adjustments. We will now look at each of the adjustments in turn, using the following trial balance for Candlewick Enterprises at 31 December 2006. This marks the end of the first year of trading and Sarah has sought the help of an external accountant in preparing the figures for the year end.

Candlewick Enterprises Trial balance at 31 December 2006		
	£	£
Sales revenue		17,320
Purchases	11,340	
Equipment (at cost)	1,300	
Trade debtors	2,750	
Trade creditors		1,500
Bank	2,610	
Rent and rates	360	
Advertising	300	
Telephone and internet	196	
Postage and packing	110	
Interest on loan	54	
Loan		650
Capital at 1 January		1,000
Drawings	1,450	
	20,470	20,470

8.3 stock

We introduced the adjustments for stock (also known as inventory) when we drew up the basic financial statements in Chapters 6 and 7. In a trading business, stock consists of unsold goods; in a manufacturing business, it consists of raw materials, work in progress and finished goods. At the end of an accounting period all unsold stock is counted to confirm that the actual quantities support the figures in the ledger accounts. This process is known as *stocktaking*. You will remember from Chapter 6 that the valuation of closing stock is guided by the principles of the historical cost concept and the prudence concept. These principles are embodied in the accounting standard, *SSAP 9 Stocks and long-term contracts*, which requires stock to be stated in the financial statements at the lower of historical cost or net realizable value (NRV).

An important point to note is that the value of closing stock for the previous period becomes the figure for opening stock at the beginning of the next period. The adjustments for opening and closing stock are incorporated in the cost of sales calculation in the profit and loss account to comply with the accruals concept. The value of closing stock is also listed as a current asset in the balance sheet.

activity

On 31 December 2006, Sarah carried out a stocktake and found that Candlewick Enterprises had 50 candles in stock which cost £1.50 each. What is the value of closing stock at 31 December 2006?

You should have found this very straightforward. The value of closing stock is £75 (50 × £1.50). This means that Sarah needs to make an adjustment to take account of the value of closing stock at 31 December. In the profit and loss account for the first year of trading ending 31 December 2006, £75 will be deducted from the cost of purchases and in the balance sheet as at that date, stock of £75 will be shown under current assets.

Imagine that during the course of the year £50 of stock was stolen from the market stall, so that the figure for closing stock is overstated on the profit and loss account. What impact would it have if the true figure were substituted?

The greatest impact would be on the profit because the gross profit would decrease by £50. If a business has stock stolen or it has deteriorated so that the value is less, it should be noticed during stocktaking. The reduced figure of stock is shown in the profit and loss account, so that the loss is borne by the business.

		Overstated closing stock		Correct closing stock	
		£	£	£	£
	Sales revenue		17,320		17,320
Less	Cost of sales				
	Purchases	11,340		11,340	
Less	Closing stock	(75)	(11,265)	(25)	(11,315)
	Gross profit		6,055		6,005

Because of the impact of closing stock values on profit, this is one area where fraud can be perpetrated if the value of stock is enhanced by ignoring lost or damaged stock and thus increasing profit.

8.4 accruals and prepayments

When the ledger accounts are closed at the end of the accounting year, some expenses incurred for goods and services used during the period may not have been recorded because the business has not yet received an invoice from the suppliers. For example, although the business has had the use of its telephone and internet connection, the service provider has not yet sent the bill for the final quarter of the year. This estimated liability is known as an *accrual*. It would not be consistent with the prudence concept or the accruals concept to report a profit that did not take this accrual into account. Therefore, the accountant needs to make an estimate of what is owed and add it to the trial balance figure for that expense.

KEY DEFINITION   An accrual is an estimate of a liability that is not supported by an invoice or a request for payment at the time when the accounts are prepared.

Candlewick Enterprises has two accruals:

- Sarah has recorded telephone expenses of £196 for the business, but these only cover the first 11 months and she estimates that a further £20 is owed for December. This means that the expense shown in the profit and loss account should be £216 (£196 + £20 accrued because it was incurred in the period).
- Sarah knows from the invoices the business has received that advertising costs were £300, but during December she took out extra advertisements to promote the stall in the Christmas market. She will not be invoiced for this until January, but she estimates the amount will be £10. Therefore, the amount that should be shown for this expense in the profit and loss account should £310 (£300 + £10 accrued because it was incurred in the period).

In the balance sheet, accruals of £30 will be shown under creditors: amounts due within one year (£20 for telephone expenses and £10 for advertising).

Another situation that commonly arises is where part of the amount paid for an expense in the current accounting period covers goods or services that relate to the next accounting period. For example, the business may have paid an insurance premium for the year to 31 December but its accounting year ends on 30 September). It would not conform to the accruals concept to include this *prepayment* when reporting the profit, because the expense belongs to the next financial period. Therefore, the accountant needs to deduct the prepaid amount from the trial balance figure for that expense.

KEY DEFINITION	A prepayment is revenue expenditure made in advance of the accounting period in which the goods or services will be received.

Candlewick Enterprises has one prepayment:

- Sarah has recorded postage and packing expenses of £110 in the accounts, but at the end of December she realizes that she has accumulated a small surplus of these items that the business will not use until January. The cost of these items was £10. Sarah needs to adjust the figures to take account of the prepayment, as it would be misleading to include the full amount if the business will not have the benefit of some of the stamps and packing materials until the next financial period.
- Therefore, £100 (£110 – £10) is charged as an expense in the profit and loss account and £10 is shown as a current asset in the balance sheet. It is a current asset because the amount was recorded in the books in the current period, but the business will enjoy the benefits in the next period.

In this chapter we will show accruals and prepayments as notes at the end of the trial balance as this is the way you are likely to encounter them in assessments.

8.5   depreciation

Depreciation is an accounting technique that spreads the cost of a *tangible fixed asset* on an arbitrary basis over the accounting periods in which the business benefits from the use of the asset. UK GAAP requires all tangible fixed assets that have a limited useful economic life to be depreciated. Guided by the accruals concept, the accountant makes a *provision for depreciation* for each tangible fixed asset, to match the revenue the asset has helped generate during the accounting year to an estimate of the cost that has been consumed during the year. The cost of acquiring or producing a fixed asset (for example buying components and building a new computer system), or enhancing an existing fixed asset (for example extending or reburbishing the premises) is classified as *capital expenditure*. Traditionally, this has been guided by the historical cost concept. As you will remember from the previous chapter, a fixed asset is an asset that is non-monetary in nature and is bought for long-term use in the business (in other words, for more than a year). Fixed assets can be classified as *tangible fixed assets* (for example premises, machinery, fixtures and fittings, and equipment) and *intangible fixed assets* (for example goodwill, concessions, patents, licences and trademarks).

Useful limited life refers to the period over which the asset is expected to be used by the entity. Some assets, such as fixtures and fittings or vehicles, will be worn out after a period of time; others, such as machinery or equipment, are likely to become obsolete through advances in technology after a certain number of years.

KEY DEFINITIONS	Depreciation is the systematic allocation of the cost (or revalued amount) of a tangible fixed asset, less any residual value, over its useful economic life.
	Tangible fixed assets are fixed assets that are non-monetary in nature and have a physical form.
	Intangible fixed assets are fixed assets that do not have a physical form.

Candlewick Enterprises has one tangible fixed asset, which is the computer equipment that was bought on 1 January at a cost of £1,300. Sarah needs a method that will measure the proportion of the benefits that have been used up during the accounting period so that she can make a provision for depreciation on equipment. Sarah estimates that the equipment has about 4 years of useful life before technological advances mean it will become redundant. Nevertheless, at the end of 4 years she thinks the business will be able to sell it in the second-hand market for £100.

activity

> What do you consider it would be fair to charge to the profit and loss account for the use of the computer equipment for the year ending 31 December 2006?

The clue to the correct figure is the word 'fair'. You might argue that the equipment has a historical cost of £1,300 and this is the figure that should be used. Alternatively, you might think that the equipment has a residual value of £100 and therefore the answer should be £1,200. However that cost is for four years' use and it would not be fair to charge the full amount against only 12 months' trading. Therefore, you may have argued that £300 is the correct figure as this takes all these factors into consideration and an accountant would agree with you that this is a fair figure to use. It would certainly not be fair to charge £100 as an expense for the year, as this is the estimated second-hand value of the asset at the end of four years. If it is sold then, the £100 will represent non-sales revenue, which is added to the gross profit in the profit and loss account.

There are two main methods for calculating a provision for depreciation. The first is known as the *straight-line* method of depreciation because it spreads the cost (or revalued amount) evenly over the life of the asset. It is calculated using the following formula:

$$\frac{\text{Cost} - \text{Residual value}}{\text{Useful economic life}}$$

The residual value is an estimate of expected net proceeds from the sale of the asset (disposal value less any costs of sale) at the end of its estimated useful economic life. All you need to do is insert the figures for Candlewick Enterprises. The first step is to deduct the esti-mated residual value from the cost and then divide the result by the estimated useful economic life:

$$\frac{£1,300 - £100}{4 \text{ years}} = \frac{£1,200}{4 \text{ years}} = £300 \text{ per annum}$$

Sarah can now add £300 for depreciation on equipment to the list of expenses in the profit and loss account for the year ending 31 December 2006. Since part of the cost of the asset has been apportioned as an expense for the period, an adjustment is also made to the value of the fixed asset in the balance sheet. Instead of only showing the fixed asset at cost as Sarah has done so far, the accountant tells her the balance sheet will show the *accumu-lated depreciation* and the *net book value*.

KEY DEFINITIONS	A provision for depreciation is an amount charged against profit and deducted from the net book value of the asset.
	Accumulated depreciation is the total depreciation charged to date.
	Net book value is the cost of a fixed asset less the accumulated depreciation.

We already know the cost of the asset was £1,300 and the equipment was bought on the first day of the financial period (which for convenience we will call Year 0). At the end of the first year (Year 1) this figure will be reduced by the annual depreciation charged to the profit and loss account. In this case, the cost of £1,300 will reduce by £300 each year for four years, and at the end of this time only the residual value of £100 will remain. The net book value (NBV) is the depreciated value of the asset at the end of the year. This is summarized below:

Year		£
0	Cost	1,300
1	Depreciation (1,200 ÷ 4)	(300)
	NBV	1,000
2	Depreciation (1,200 ÷ 4)	(300)
	NBV	700
3	Depreciation (1,200 ÷ 4)	(300)
	NBV	400
4	Depreciation (1,200 ÷ 4)	(300)
	Residual value	100

Candlewick Enterprises will use the straight-line method for depreciating the computer equipment, but for some types of assets a second method is used. This is known as the *reducing balance* method of depreciation because the cost reduces over the life of the asset. This is also based on the cost of the asset, an estimate of any residual value and the length of its useful economic life. However, with this method a depreciation rate (a percentage) is used. In the first year, any residual value is deducted from the original cost of the asset and then the depreciation rate is applied. In subsequent years, the depreciation rate is applied to the net book value of the asset in the preceding year. Therefore, the formula is:

NBV × Depreciation rate (%)

The following table illustrates how the reducing balance method would be applied to the computer equipment if Candlewick Enterprises were to choose a depreciation rate of 25%.

Year		£
0	Cost	1,300
1	Depreciation (1,200 × 25%)	(300)
	NBV	1,000
2	Depreciation (1,000 × 25%)	(250)
	NBV	750
3	Depreciation (750 × 25%)	(188)
	NBV	562
4	Depreciation (562 × 25%)	(141)
	NBV	421
	... until only the residual value remains	

To comply with the *consistency concept*, once chosen the same method of depreciation will be used every year, unless there is good cause to change it. Accountants choose the method that will provide the fairest measure of depreciation, which is the aim of the accruals concept in its requirement that revenues and costs are matched to each other and the period to which they relate.

- The straight-line method is simple and easy to use, and apportions the cost of the asset evenly over the period in which it is used.
- This is not the case with the reducing balance method, where the annual depreciation charge is higher in the early years and lower in later years. For some assets, such as vehicles and machinery, the lower depreciation charges in later years offset the higher maintenance costs that are likely as the asset ages. Thus, the reducing balance method allows the overall cost of such assets to be spread evenly.

8.6 doubtful debts

Candlewick Enterprises has a combination of cash sales and credit sales and Sarah may not realize that some customers she has allowed to buy on credit may not pay because they have died, gone bankrupt, gone into liquidation or cannot be traced; in other words, the money cannot be recovered. If during the course of an accounting period a debt is considered to be irrecoverable, the *bad debt* becomes an expense the business has to bear and will be listed in the trial balance and treated like other expenses in the profit and loss account. Since debtors who cannot pay are no longer assets of the business, such amounts would not be included in the figure for debtors shown in the trial balance. However, occasionally news of a bad debt is not received until after the trial balance has been constructed, which means that the accountant might sometimes have to make a last-minute adjustment.

Fortunately, Candlewick Enterprises has not had any bad debts, but Sarah has been giving customers two months' credit and so far she has entered all credit sales for the year in the records. Her accountant advises her that to conform to the requirements of the prudence concept she should make some allowance for the fact that not all credit customers will pay. If she does not do this, her profit may be overstated. To reduce the profit figure to a more prudent amount, Sarah should make a *provision for doubtful debts*.

KEY DEFINITIONS	A provision for doubtful debts is an amount charged against profit and deducted from debtors to allow for the estimated non-recovery of a proportion of debts.
	Bad debts are an amount owed by debtors that is considered to be irrecoverable. It is written off as a charge against profit or against an existing provision for doubtful debts.

As the provision for doubtful debts is an estimate, Sarah and her accountant can use their experience to decide what provision to make. For example, they might base the provision on the age of specific debts or on the assumption that a certain percentage of amounts due from debtors will not be received.

activity

The trial balance at 31 December 2006 shows that sales revenue for the year was £17,320, which is made up of cash sales of £6,375 and credit sales of £10,945. Trade debtors were £2,750. Which of the following figures is correct if Candlewick Enterprises makes a provision for doubtful debts of 10%?

(a) £1,732

(b) £637.50

(c) £1,094.50

(d) £275

The first amount is 10% of the total sales revenue, but as this includes cash sales this answer is wrong because these have been paid for. The figure of £637.50 is 10% of the cash sales and this is wrong because they too have been paid for. The amount of £1,094.50 is 10% of credit sales for the year, but the business has received payments for the first ten months of the year and it is only the last two months credit sales that are outstanding. This is the amount of £2,750 that is owed by trade debtors at the year end and it is against this figure that Sarah should make the provision of £275 for doubtful debts.

To comply with the consistency concept, the same method of providing for doubtful debts will be used every year, unless there is good cause to change it. The provision for doubtful debts is shown as an expense in the profit and loss account, where it ensures this financial statement complies with the accruals concept and reduces profit to a more prudent amount. The provision for doubtful debts is also shown as a deduction from debtors in the balance sheet, where it reduces current assets to a more prudent amount.

If Candlewick Enterprises has trade debtors of £2,000 next year and Sarah continues to make a 10% provision for doubtful debts, the provision will be:

$$£2,000 \times 10\% = £200$$

This is a decrease of £75 (£200 in Year 2 *less* £275 in Year 1). The provision for doubtful debts in Year 2 will be shown as decreasing expenses by £75, but the whole provision of £200 will be deducted from trade debtors in the balance sheet.

8.7 the final accounts

We are now ready to construct the financial statements for Candlewick Enterprises based on the following trial balance drawn up from the records and the additional information available at the end of the year that allows us to make the post trial balance adjustments we have looked at in this chapter.

```
                        Candlewick Enterprises
                    Trial balance at 31 December 2006
                                            £              £
        Sales                                          17,320
        Purchases                       11,340
        Equipment (at cost)              1,300
        Trade debtors                    2,750
        Trade creditors                                 1,500
        Bank                             2,610
        Rent and rates                     360
        Advertising                        300
        Telephone and internet             196
        Postage and packing                110
        Interest payable                    54
        Loan                                              650
        Capital at 1 January 2006                       1,000
        Drawings                         1,450
                                        20,470         20,470
```

Additional information available at 31 December 2006:

- Sarah conducted a stocktake and the stock was valued at £75.
- Sarah estimates accrued expenses of £10 for advertising and £20 for telephone.
- The amounts recorded for postage and packing include a prepayment of £10.
- The computer equipment is expected to have a useful economic life of four years, at which time it is expected to have a residual value of £100.
- A provision for doubtful debts will be made based on 10% of trade debtors.

activity

Using the above information and the following pro forma, construct a profit and loss account for Candlewick Enterprises for the year ending 31 December 2006 and a balance sheet as at that date.

```
                        Candlewick Enterprises
        Profit and loss account for the year ending 31 December 2006
                                                £          £
                Sales
        Less    Cost of sales
                    Purchases
        Less        Closing stock
                Gross profit
```

Less   Expenses
                Rent and rates
                Advertising
                Telephone and internet
                Postage and packing
                Interest payable
                Provision for depreciation on equipment
                Provision for doubtful debts
        Net profit

Candlewick Enterprises
Balance sheet as at 31 December 2006

	£ Cost	£ Accumulated depreciation	£ NBV
Fixed assets			
Equipment	___	___	
Current assets			
Stock			
Trade debtors			
Less Provision for doubtful debts	___		
Prepayments			
Bank		___	
Less Creditors: amounts due within one year			
Trade creditors			
Accruals		___	
Net current assets			___
Creditors: amounts due after more than one year			
Less Loan			___
Total net assets			═══
Capital and reserves			
Capital at 1 January 2006			
Net profit		___	
Less Drawings		___	═══

You will find it helpful to tick each figure every time you use it. By the time you have completed the profit and loss account and balance sheet, all the figures in the trial balance will be ticked once and all the adjustments in the additional information will be ticked twice. The first step is to look at the additional information and make the adjustments, using the information once in the profit and loss account and once in the balance sheet:

- Stock of £75 at 31 December 2006 means this is the value of closing stock, which you will show in the profit and loss account under cost of sales (1 tick) and in the balance sheet under current assets (1 tick).
- Accrued advertising expenses of £10 means this expense will become £300 + £10 = £310 in the profit and loss account (1 tick) and the aggregate figure for accruals (£10 + any other amounts accrued for expenses) will be shown in the balance sheet (1 tick).
- Accrued telephone expense of £20 means this expense will become £196 + £20 = £216 in the profit and loss account (1 tick) and the aggregate figure for accruals (£10 + £20 = £30) will be shown in the balance sheet under creditors: amounts due within one year (1 tick).
- The amounts recorded for postage and packing include a prepayment of £10, which means that this expenses will become £110 – £10 = £100 in the profit and loss account (1 tick) and the aggregate figure for prepayments (in this case, the one prepayment of £10) will be shown in the balance sheet under current assets (1 tick).
- The annual charge for depreciation on equipment is calculated as £1,300 – £100 ÷ 4 years = £300 and this is shown as an expense in the profit and loss account (1 tick), whilst the cost (£1,300), depreciation (£300) and net book value (£1,000) is recorded in the balance sheet under fixed assets (1 tick).
- The provision for doubtful debts is calculated as £2,750 × 10% = £275 and this is shown as an expense in the profit and loss account (1 tick) and as a deduction from trade debtors in the balance sheet under current assets (1 tick).

Your completed financial statements should look like this:

Candlewick Enterprises
Profit and loss account for the year ending 31 December 2006

		£	£
Sales			17,320
Less Cost of sales			
Purchases		11,340	
Less Closing stock		(75)	(11,265)
Gross profit			6,055
Less Expenses			
Rent and rates		360	
Advertising (300 + 10)		310	
Telephone and internet (196 + 20)		216	
Postage and packing (110 – 10)		100	
Interest payable		54	
Provision for depreciation on equipment (1,300 – 100 ÷ 4)		300	
Provision for doubtful debts (2,750 × 10%)		275	(1,615)
Net profit			4,440

Candlewick Enterprises
Balance sheet as at 31 December 2006

		£ Cost	£ Accumulated depreciation	£ NBV
Fixed assets				
	Equipment	1,300	300	1,000
Current assets				
	Stock		75	
	Trade debtors	2,750		
Less	Provision for doubtful debts (2,750 × 10%)	(275)	2,475	
	Prepayments		10	
	Bank		2,610	
			5,170	
Less	Creditors: amounts due within one year			
	Trade creditors		1,500	
	Accruals (10 + 20)		30	
			(1,530)	
	Net current assets			3,640
				4,640
Less	Creditors: amounts due after more than one year			
	Loan			(650)
	Total net assets			3,990
	Capital and reserves			
	Capital at 1 January 2006		1,000	
	Net profit		4,440	
			5,440	
Less	Drawings		(1,450)	3,990

By now you should be thoroughly familiar with the basic layout of these two important financial statements and the pro forma should have helped you see where the adjustments are shown. The points to note are:

- When constructing financial statements for a subsequent year, you need to remember to include the value of opening stock when calculating the cost of sales in the profit and loss account in accordance with the accruals concept. The opening stock figure is the same as the closing stock figure shown in the financial statements for the previous year.
- In accordance with the historic cost concept and the prudence concept, stock is valued at the lower of cost or net realizable value.
- Accruals are estimated figures that are included to conform to the prudence concept and the accruals concept. We have shown the accruals and prepayments as separate items in the balance sheet because this keeps them apart from transactions that have been documented. However, if they are only small amounts, many accountants add them to creditors and debtors respectively, following the principles of the materiality concept.

- If you are constructing financial statements for a subsequent year, you need to remember that the provision for doubtful debts, which is an estimated expense in the profit and loss account, is the difference between the provision for the current year and the provision for the previous year. The whole provision for the current year is shown as a deduction from debtors under current assets in the balance sheet. These adjustments ensure that the financial statements comply with the prudence concept and the accruals concept.

- Guided by the accruals concept, methods for depreciating fixed assets are based on estimates of the length of the economic life of the asset and any residual value. In sole trader accounts it is usual to show the cost of tangible fixed assets, the depreciation to date and the net book value on the face of the balance sheet. As the amount shown for depreciation is a cumulative figure, each year it increases by the annual amount charged in the profit and loss account. On the other hand, the net book value is a diminishing figure that decreases by the amount of the annual amount charged in the profit and loss account until the asset reaches the end of its economic life or the estimated residual value. The net book value is used when calculating the total net assets of the business. The choice of depreciation method has an impact on profit and on the balance sheet total and therefore the accountant follows the principles of the consistency concept to avoid misleading users.

- The post trial balance adjustments relating to depreciation, doubtful debts and accruals are based on estimates. Therefore, the financial performance shown in the profit and loss account and the financial position shown in the balance sheet are based on approximation as well as depending on the accuracy of the books and records. Moreover, because they are based on the money measurement concept, they do not show other qualitative factors that may be very important. For example, they do not show how many hours Sarah has had to put into the business during the first year to get it established or the fact that there are rumours that Wax Lyrical, a much bigger business, may be opening a branch nearby.

If you were the owner of Candlewick Enterprises or the bank manager who had lent the business £650, do you think you would be satisfied with the financial performance and the financial position shown in the results for the first year? If you look at the results you can see that although the business made a profit of £4,440, Sarah only drew out £1,450 for her own use. This is certainly not enough to live on and if she intends to increase her drawings next year, the business must increase its profits. In addition, the balance sheet shows that there is £2,610 in the bank, but current liabilities in the form of creditors totalling £1,530. If the bank called in the loan at this stage, Sarah could still pay off these creditors and have £430 cash left in the bank. If the business sold its only asset (the computer equipment) to help pay off the loan, it could force Candlewick Enterprises to close, as it relies on credit sales made through the business's website. Perhaps the results for the next year will be better and Sarah will be able to pay off the loan and increase her drawings.

However, if you had invested a large amount of money in a business or lent money to a business, you would want to keep an eye on it. The profit and loss account and balance sheet allow you to do this. We have demonstrated that even at a superficial level it is possible to draw some conclusions about the business from these financial statements. In Chapter 11 we will explain how you can use ratio analysis to make a more complete interpretation.

8.8   conclusions

A trial balance is constructed at the end of the financial period to check the mathematical accuracy of the accounting records. If the correct procedures have been followed, the totals of the debit and credit columns in the trial balance will balance. The trial balance is useful because it summarizes the economic transactions that have been identified, measured and recorded in the accounting system and these figures form the basis of the financial statements. The two main financial statements are the profit and loss account and the balance sheet. Before they are prepared, it is usually necessary to make a number of adjustments to the records to ensure the financial statements comply with the accounting principles. In the exercises in this book, these adjustments are shown as additional information below the trial balance. If you adopt a ticking system when using the information to construct the financial statements, you will find that you tick every item in the trial balance once and every adjustment twice.

practice questions

1. Explain what is meant by an accrued expense and a prepaid expense and how they affect the figures in the trial balance.
2. Explain why accountants depreciate tangible fixed assets and compare the straight-line method with the reducing balance method in terms of their different effects on the financial statements.
3. Explain the difference between a bad debt and a provision for doubtful debts, using examples to illustrate your answer.
4. On 1 July 2004 Naomi Cameron opened a health and beauty salon called Top-to-Toe, offering a range of treatments. She is renting the property and sublets one of the rooms two days a week to a reflexologist. The trial balance for the first year of business is as shown opposite.

    Additional information at 30 June 2005:

    ● Stock is valued at £790.
    ● Advertising paid in advance is £260.
    ● Accrued expenses are electricity £540, telephone £290 and administration expenses £160.

    Required
    (a) Using a spreadsheet, construct a profit and loss account for Top-to-Toe for the year ending 30 June 2005 and a balance sheet as at that date.
    (b) After taking advice from her accountant, Naomi has decided to depreciate the fixtures and fittings and the equipment using the straight-line method. She estimates that neither of these assets will have any residual value at the end of their useful economic life of four years. In the light of this new information, prepare the profit and loss account for Top-to-Toe for the year ending 30 June 2005 and the balance sheet as at that date again.
    (c) Naomi has forgotten that she should make a provision for trade debtors who may not pay and she has now decided to make a provision for doubtful debts

Top-to-Toe
Trial balance at 30 June 2005

	Debit £	Credit £
Sales		72,100
Purchases	11,160	
Wages	18,000	
Rent and rates payable	12,000	
Insurance	7,400	
Advertising	3,860	
Electricity	1,840	
Telephone	1,450	
Administration expenses	1,250	
Rental income received		1,500
Fixtures and fittings (at cost)	10,000	
Equipment (at cost)	5,000	
Trade debtors	1,200	
Trade creditors		1,620
Bank	1,060	
Capital at 1 July 2004		15,000
Drawings	16,000	
	90,220	90,220

representing 20% of trade debtors. Construct a profit and loss account for Top-to-Toe for the year ending 30 June 2005 and a balance sheet as at that date for the final time, taking this final adjustment into consideration. Examine the three sets of accounts you have prepared, and comment briefly on the overall effect of post trial balance adjustments on the financial results of the business and the main accounting principles you have been using.

5. Oil & Water is an art shop that occupies a niche market with its exclusive range of materials. It is owned by Peter Drew, who employs two part-time assistants to help in the shop at the weekend. The trial balance for the second year of business is as shown on the following page.

Additional information at 31 December 2005:

- Stock is valued at £11,400.
- Commission income due but not yet invoiced amounts to £360.
- The amount shown for business rates includes £2,000 paid in advance.
- Insurance includes a prepayment of £580 for next year.
- Estimated telephone charges for the final quarter are £250.
- Estimated cost of electricity used in the final quarter is £150.
- Fixtures and fittings are expected to have a life of three years, after which they will have no residual value. They will continue to be depreciated using the straight-line method.
- Equipment has an estimated economic life of four years and a residual value

of £1,000. It will also continue to be depreciated using the straight-line method.

● The provision for doubtful debts this year will be 10% of trade debtors.

Required

Construct a profit and loss account for Oil & Water for the year ending 31 December 2005 and a balance sheet as at that date.

Oil & Water
· Trial balance at 31 December 2005

	Debit £	Credit, £
Sales		114,740
Purchases	62,680	
Stock at 1 January 2005	18,600	
Commission income		4,030
Premises (at cost)	120,000	
Fixtures and fittings (at cost)	15,000	
Equipment (at cost)	5,000	
Trade debtors	6,100	
Trade creditors		8,050
Cash in hand	2,500	
Bank overdraft		1,380
Wages	10,550	
Business rates	8,000	
Insurance	2,580	
Advertising	2,200	
Telephone	830	
Electricity	800	
Miscellaneous expenses	160	
Provisions for depreciation at 1 January 2005:		
Fixtures and fittings		5,000
Equipment		1,000
Provision for doubtful debts at 1 January 2005		800
Long-term loan		20,000
Capital		120,000
Drawings	20,000	
	275,000	275,000

chapter 9

financial statements of a partnership

When you have studied this chapter, you should be able to:

- Construct a profit and loss account for a partnership
- Construct a balance sheet for a partnership
- Account for the admission of a new partner
- Account for the cessation of a partnership.

9.1 introduction

A *partnership* is an entity in which two or more people join together in business with a view to making a profit. It is a type of business commonly adopted by those offering professional services, such as solicitors, accountants, doctors and dentists. Limited liability partnerships (LLPs) tend to be much larger firms than general partnerships and you may wish to remind yourself of the differences between these two types of partnership (see Chapter 1) and how they are regulated (see Chapter 2).

In this chapter we are going to describe the financial statements of general partnerships rather than those of LLPs, as we will looking at the financial statements of limited liability entities in Chapter 10. We start by looking at the profit and loss account which has an additional section known as an appropriation account showing how the net profit is allocated between the partners. We then demonstrate how a capital account and a current account are opened for each partner in the double-entry bookkeeping system (see Chapter 4) to record their regular transactions with the business. This allows the net profit to be adjusted for any agreed benefits each partner may receive and both accounts are shown in the balance sheet.

Sometimes the existing partners decide to expand the business by admitting a new partner and in the next section we describe the accounting procedures this entails. If one of the partners wishes to leave the business or dies, the partnership agreement ceases, and we also explain how the accountant opens a *realization account* in the double-entry bookkeeping system to calculate the final profit or loss before closing all the accounts.

9.2 main features

The financial statements of a general partnership are similar to those we looked at for a sole trader in Chapter 8. However, some of the features of a partnership have a direct effect on the accounting records, the profit and loss account and the balance sheet. These are:

- The partners may not contribute equal amounts of capital to the business and may wish this to be recognized in some way.
- Partners can make loans to the business over and above the capital they have invested and may wish to receive interest on their loan.
- As with a sole trader, partners can make drawings during the course of the financial year in anticipation of profits. However, they may agree that drawings should be kept to a minimum and in order to encourage this, they may charge interest on drawings.
- Some of the partners may work full time in the business and wish to receive a regular salary for this work.

The partners must keep accounting records and in the absence of a written or verbal *partnership agreement*, the Partnership Act 1890 applies (see Chapter 2, section 2.4). The objective of a partnership is to make a profit and it is up to the partners to decide how they will share the profits. The following are some of the methods commonly used:

- *A fixed ratio* – Partners may agree to share the profits equally. However, if one partner has contributed more capital or spends more time working for the partnership, they may decide an alternative basis. For example, if there are three partners, it may be agreed that one partner receives 50% of the profits and the others receive 25% each.

- *A ratio based on capital balances* – If the partners have contributed unequal amounts of capital, they may agree to share the profits in the same ratio to reflect this.
- *Making allocations to partners and sharing the balance* – The partners may agree that interest will be paid on the capital contributed by the partners; that partners who spend a certain amount of time working in the business will receive a salary; or that interest will be charged on any drawings. All these transactions will be allocations of the net profit earned by the business. Once these allocations have been made, any balance (whether a profit or a loss) will be shared among the partners in an agreed ratio.

We are now ready to look at the profit and loss account for a partnership.

9.3 profit and loss account

All the basic rules that apply to the preparation of the profit and loss account for a sole trader that we have looked at so far in this book also apply to the profit and loss account for a general partnership. However, a partnership profit and loss account includes an additional section known as an *appropriation account*.

KEY DEFINITION   An appropriation account is a record of how the net profit/(loss) for the period has been distributed.

The appropriation account shows the following transactions between the business and the partners:

- *Salaries* of partners are not classified as an expense when arriving at the figure of profit. Instead their salaries are shown in the appropriation account before calculating the profit division between the partners.
- *Interest on capital* is normally paid where partners have contributed different amounts of capital, or their profit-sharing ratio is unequal. Interest paid on capital is a charge against the profits available for appropriation and therefore, like salaries, it reduces the amount of profit shared among the partners.
- *Interest on drawings* may be charged to the partners in order to avoid cash flow problems which might be caused if they draw substantial amounts from the business in anticipation of profits. This encourages partners to keep drawings to a minimum or not to make drawings until profits are calculated. Where interest is charged, the amounts received by the business are credited to the profit and loss appropriation account as income to the business and charged to the partners through their current accounts.
- *Interest on loans* provided by the partners in excess of their agreed capitals, unlike interest on partners' capitals, represents a normal business expense. The fact that the loans are provided by the partners is incidental; loans could equally be provided by outsiders to the partnership, in which case the interest paid would be deductible from the normal trading profits.

We can demonstrate these transactions with an example. Rob and John Rennie are a father and son, who are in partnership. Their business Hearth & Home involves selling and installing fireplaces and wood-burning stoves. Their net profit for the year ending 31 December 2005 was £228,000 and they received annual salaries of: Rob £44,000; John £40,000. Interest paid on capital was: Rob £27,000; John £13,000. Rob was charged interest of £4,000 on drawings for the year. The remaining profit is to be shared equally. We will now construct the profit and loss appropriation account.

Hearth & Home
Profit and loss appropriation account for
the year ending 31 December 2005

			£000	£000	£000
	Net profit available for appropriation				228
Add	Interest on drawings				4
					232
Less	Interest on capital	Rob	27		
		John	13	40	
Less	Salaries	Rob	44		
		John	40	84	(124)
	Balance of profits to be shared				108
		Rob 50%		54	
		John 50%		54	108

As you can see, interest on drawings is added to profit because it is a source of income for the business.

Jenny, Sally and Patrick are in partnership and own a fitness studio called Upbeat. They each receive a salary of £8,000 per annum and are each paid interest of 10% on the capital they have invested in the business. They share profits as follows: Jenny 60%; Sally and Patrick 20% each. Their capital balances are: Jenny £10,000; Sally £6,000; Patrick £2,000. The net profit for the year ending 31 December 2006 was £28,300. Using this information, draw up the appropriation account for the partnership.

The main difference in this activity compared with the Hearth & Home example in the text is that the profit is shared between three partners, with Jenny taking 60%. Your completed answer should look like this:

Upbeat
Profit and loss appropriation account for the year ending 31 December 2006

			£	£	£
Net profit available for appropriation					28,300
Less Interest on capital					
	Jenny	1,000			
	Sally	600			
	Patrick	200		1,800	
Less Salaries					
	Jenny	8,000			
	Sally	8,000			
	Patrick	8,000		24,000	(25,800)
Balance of profits to be shared					2,500
	Jenny	60%		1,500	
	Sally	20%		500	
	Patrick	20%		500	2,500

9.4 balance sheet

All the basic rules that apply to the preparation of the balance sheet for a sole trader that we have looked at so far in this book also apply to the *balance sheet* for a simple partnership. However, the entries made to the appropriation account that is shown in the profit and loss account for a partnership require a corresponding entry to be made to the capital accounts of the partners. This can be slightly confusing, particularly where interest is paid on capital invested by the partners. Therefore, the usual system is to maintain a *capital account* for each partner that shows any capital subscribed and withdrawn. In addition, a *current account* is opened for each partner that shows salaries, interest on capital, interest on drawings, share of profit and any drawings made. The capital accounts for each partner are shown in the balance sheet. The balance on each capital account represents the agreed fixed capital invested in the business by the partner. The fixed capital changes only when additional capital is introduced or some capital is withdrawn by agreement.

In sole trader accounts, profits or losses for the period adjust the capital invested by the owner. However, in partnership accounts, the profits or losses for the period adjust each partner's current account. You can see this in the current accounts of Rob and John Rennie.

Current accounts

		Rob	John
		£	£
	Opening balance	7,000	6,000
Add	Interest on capital	27,000	13,000
	Salary	44,000	40,000
	Share of profits	54,000	54,000
		132,000	113,000
Less	Drawings	(40,000)	(27,000)
	Interest on drawings	(4,000)	0
	Closing balance	88,000	86,000

The closing balance on each partner's current account is shown in the balance sheet and this balance represents the amount due to (or from) the partner at the date of the balance sheet.

Linda, Alan and David are partners in a family business called LAD Renovations. The total capital invested in the business is £240,000, of which Linda has invested 30%, Alan 60% and David 10%. Their partnership agreement states that they will share profits in the same ratios and that Linda and David are each entitled to a salary of £5,000 per annum. In addition, all partners are entitled to receive interest on the capital they have invested at 10% per annum and that 10% per annum interest will be charged on drawings. At 1 January 2006, the agreed balances on the capital and current accounts were as follows:

	Capital account £	Current account £
Linda	78,000	2,000
Alan	156,000	13,000
David	6,000	1,000

The net profit for appropriation for the year ending 31 December 2006 was £150,000 and the partners' drawings for the year were: Linda £10,000; Alan £10,000; David £60,000. Using this information, construct the profit and loss appropriation account for LAD Renovations for the year ending 31 December 2006, the entries in the current accounts of the three partners and how they would appear on the balance sheet.

If you followed the correct procedures, your answer should be as follows:

LAD Renovations
Profit and loss appropriation account for
the year ended 31 December 2006

		£	£	£
Net profit available for appropriation				146,000
Add Interest on drawings Linda		1,000		
Alan		1,000		
David		6,000		8,000
				154,000
Less Interest on capital				
Linda		7,800		
Alan		15,600		
David		600	(24,000)	

Less Salaries				
	Linda	5,000		
	David	5,000	(10,000)	(34,000)
Balance of profits to be shared				120,000
	Linda 30%		36,000	
	Alan 60%		72,000	
	David 10%		12,000	120,000

Current accounts

		Linda	Alan	David
		£	£	£
	Opening balance	2,000	13,000	1,000
Add	Interest on capital	7,800	15,600	600
	Salary	5,000	0	5,000
	Share of profits	36,000	72,000	12,000
		52,000	100,000	19,000
Less	Drawings	(10,000)	(10,000)	(60,000)
	Interest on drawings	(1,000)	(1,000)	(6,000)
	Closing balance	39,800	89,600	(47,400)

LAD Renovations
Balance sheet as at 31 December 2006 (extract)

		£	£
Capital accounts	Linda	78,000	
	Alan	156,000	
	David	6,000	
			240,000
Current accounts	Linda	39,800	
	Alan	89,600	
	David	(47,400)	82,000
			322,000

It is clear from this that David is in a very poor position. He has a debit balance of £47,400 on his current account. This means that he owes this amount to the business. Unfortunately, his debt is not covered by the balance in his capital account. Later on in this chapter we will see what effect this has on David and the business.

Having looked at the separate elements making up the appropriation account and the balance sheet, we can now put these together to do the final accounts for a partnership using the trial balance. To do this we will return to our example of Rob and John's business, Hearth & Home, as we have already calculated some of the figures we need. The trial balance drawn up from the partnership books is as follows:

```
                        Hearth & Home
              Trial balance as at 31 December 2005
                                      £              £
Premises                          300,000
Fixtures and fittings              60,000
Debtors                           198,000
Creditors                                          37,000
Stock at 1 January 2005            96,000
Purchases                         245,000
Sales                                             532,000
Administration expenses            43,000
Wages                              67,000
Provision for doubtful debts                        1,000
Capital accounts      Rob                         270,000
                      John                        130,000
Current accounts      Rob                           7,000
                      John                           6,000
Drawings              Rob           40,000
                      John          27,000

Bank                                               93,000
                                  ─────────      ─────────
                                  1,076,000      1,076,000
                                  ═════════      ═════════
```

At 31 December 2005, the following information is also available:

- Stock is valued at £148,000.
- The provision for doubtful debts is to be set at £2,000.
- Rob receives a salary of £44,000 and John receives a salary of £40,000.
- Interest on capital is allowed at 10% per annum.
- Interest on drawings charged to Rob is £4,000.
- Remaining profits are shared equally.

We can now prepare the partnership's profit and loss account, including an appropriation section, for the year ending 31 December 2005 and the balance sheet as at that date. We can also show the movements in the partners' current accounts for the year and the balances outstanding at the end of the financial year:

```
                        Hearth & Home
                    Profit and loss account for
                 the year ending 31 December 2005
                              £000          £000          £000
Sales                                                     532
Cost of sales
    Opening stock                            96
    Purchases                               245
                                            ────
                                            341
    Closing stock                          (148)         (193)
                                                        ────
Gross profit                                             339
```

Expenses				
Administration			43	
Wages			67	
Provision for doubtful debts			1	111
Net profit available for appropriation				228
Interest on drawings				4
				232
Interest on capital				
	Rob	27		
	John	13	(40)	
Salaries				
	Rob	44		
	John	40	(84)	(124)
Balance of profits to be shared				108
	Rob	50%	54	
	John	50%	54	108

Current accounts		
	Rob	John
	£000	£000
Opening balance	7	6
Interest on capital	27	13
Salaries	44	40
Share of profits	54	54
	132	113
Drawings	(40)	(27)
Interest on drawings	(4)	
Closing balance	88	86

```
                          Hearth & Home
              Balance sheet as at 31 December 2005
                                    £000     £000      £000
      Fixed assets
        Premises                              300
        Fixtures and fittings                  60       360
      Current assets
        Stock                                 148
        Debtors                     198
        Provision for doubtful debts  (2)     196
                                              344
      Creditors: amounts due within one year
        Creditors                     37
        Bank overdraft                93     (130)
      Net current assets                                214
      Total net assets                                  574
      Capital accounts:      Rob                270
                            John                130      400

      Current accounts:      Rob                 88
                            John                 86      174
                                                        574
```

9.5   admission of a new partner

If a business is expanding and requires additional capital or new management skills, the existing partners may decide to admit a *new partner*, who could be a member of the family or a professional colleague. Even if it is a family business, the original partners will expect the new partner to invest in the partnership. The amount of capital the new partner invests will reflect his or her share in the worth of the business.

From an accounting point of view, the admission of a new partner is relatively simple, but we need to consider how it affects the *intangible asset* known as *goodwill* that the business may have developed over the years. Goodwill can be difficult to define and measure, but is made up of such things as the business' name and reputation, the loyalty of its workforce, its customer base and its links with suppliers. The existing partners will consider the goodwill of the business as an asset and expect the new partner to recompense them for acquiring a share of it.

KEY DEFINITION	Goodwill is the difference between the value of the separable net assets of an entity and the total value.

We will illustrate this with an example. Charlie Wye and Helen Knott are partners in the Wye Knott Café and share profits equally. Each partner's existing capital account shows a balance of £60,000. Therefore, the net assets of the old partnership are £60,000 × 2 = £120,000. They have decided to allow Jonathan Letts to join the partnership and he will invest capital of £100,000 in the business and receive a one-third interest in return. They agree that goodwill will be recorded as an asset of the business. As Jonathan Letts has agreed to invest £100,000 for a one-third interest in the partnership the new capital will be £100,000 × 3 = £300,000. Using the accounting equation, if the capital is £300,000 then the net assets must be the same amount. Therefore, the amount for goodwill is as follows:

	£
Total net assets of the new partnership	300,000
Net assets of old partnership + capital invested by new partner (120,000 + 100,000)	(220,000)
Goodwill	80,000

The goodwill of £80,000 will increase Wye and Knott's capital accounts by £40,000 each, so that all three partners will have £100,000 invested in the business:

Capital accounts			
	Wye	Knott	Letts
	£	£	£
Opening balance	60,000	60,000	100,000
Goodwill	40,000	40,000	
Closing balance	100,000	100,000	100,000

Goodwill can either be written off immediately in the partners' agreed profit-sharing ratios and their capital accounts debited, or it can be written off over a number of years in the profit and loss account.

9.6 cessation of a partnership

There are a number of reasons for the *cessation* or dissolution of a partnership; for example, one of the partners might want to retire or move away, or one of them might die. Of course, if there are two or more partners remaining and they wish to carry on in business, they simply make a new partnership agreement. The accounting steps involved when a partnership closes are as follows:

- Cash from debtors and the proceeds from the sale of the assets of the business are paid into the bank account.
- Creditors are paid, including any expenses associated with dissolving the partnership.
- The profit or loss realized on the dissolution of the partnership is divided among the partners according to the agreed ratios, and the bank account is closed.

If you are required to study double-entry bookkeeping (see Chapters 4 and 5), you will need to know the detailed accounting steps that are taken. We will illustrate the process using Rob and John's business, Hearth & Home. At the end of section 9.3, we drew up the balance sheet as at 31 December 2005. However, Rob and John decided to dissolve the partnership and on 1 January 2006 the premises were sold for £260,000 and the equipment was sold for £54,000. In addition, debtors paid £193,000, the stock was sold for £141,000 and the creditors were paid in full. Before we proceed, we will revise the steps we need to take:

- We need to open an account for all the items shown on the balance sheet and enter the balances.
- Next we close off the fixed assets, stock and debtor accounts by crediting them and entering the corresponding entries on the debit side of the realization account.
- We then record the proceeds from selling the fixed assets in the realization account and the bank account.
- Then we pay off the creditors, credit the bank account and debit the creditors' accounts.
- At this stage, the only accounts that have balances on them are the realization account, the bank account and the partners' capital accounts. We need to total both sides of the realization account. If the balancing figure has to be added on the debit side, we will know that there is a profit on realization. In our example, the balancing figure has to go on the credit side, so there is a loss, which must be shared equally among the partners. Therefore we will debit their capital accounts with this amount.
- The next step is to calculate the balancing figures on the partners' capital accounts. In both cases we have debit balances and these are the proceeds the partners are due. We then debit the partners' capital accounts to close them and credit the bank account.
- Finally, we total both sides of the bank account. If they do not agree, it will be necessary to work through the example again to find the error.

We will now carry out these steps using the data in the example:

Goodwill account			
	£		£
Opening balance	300,000	Realization account	300,000

Equipment account			
	£		£
Opening balance	60,000	Realization account	60,000

Stock account			
	£		£
Opening balance	148,000	Realization account	148,000

Debtors' account			
	£		£
Opening balance	196,000	Realization account	196,000

Creditors' account			
	£		£
Bank 37,000		Opening balance	37,000

Realization account			
	£		£
Premises	300,000	Bank: Sale of premises	260,000
Equipment	60,000	Bank: Sale of equipment	54,000
Stock	148,000	Bank: Sale of stock	141,000
Debtors	196,000	Bank: Debtors realized	193,000
		Loss on realization: Rob	28,000
		John	28,000
	704,000		704,000

Bank account			
	£		£
Realization: premises	260,000	Opening balance	93,000
Realization: equipment	54,000	Creditors	37,000
Realization: stock	141,000	Capital accounts: Rob	330,000
Realization: debtors	193,000	John	188,000
	648,000		648,000

Capital account: Rob			
	£		£
Loss on realization	28,000	Opening balance	270,000
Bank	330,000	Current accounts	88,000
	358,000		358,000

Capital account: John			
	£		£
Loss on realization	28,000	Opening balance	130,000
Bank	188,000	Current accounts	86,000
	216,000		216,000

In this example, the liabilities of the business (the creditors) were paid off in full. If this had not been the case, the entries would have been put through the realization account. First, the creditors' account would have been closed by debiting with the final balance and crediting the realization account. When the agreed amount was paid, the bank account would have been credited and the realization account would have been debited.

The realization account shows that a loss has been made of £56,000 and this has been shared equally between the two partners by crediting the realization account and debiting their capital accounts. Their current accounts are then closed by transferring the outstanding balances to their respective capital accounts. The capital accounts are closed by entering the difference between the debit and credit entries. In both cases this is a debit entry which represents the amount of money owed by the business to the partner. The corresponding credit entries are entered into the bank account to represent the money paid to the partners. The two sides of the bank account should now agree. If they do not balance, you have made an error and need to work through the procedures again until you find it.

There is one occasion when the above procedures are not used. This is when one (or more) of the partners becomes insolvent. In this case, there will be a debit balance on the relevant partner's account. If the partner had money and paid this into the partnership, you would debit the bank account and close the partner's account by crediting it. However, if the partner has no cash, the capital account will show a deficit which must be shared among the other partners in the ratio of their capital accounts. This provision was set out in a famous legal case, *Garner* v. *Murray* (1904). We will illustrate this by returning to the example of LAD Renovations, the business owned by Linda, Alan and David. This illustration does not require any knowledge of bookkeeping and you should be able to follow it, regardless of whether you have studied Chapters 4 and 5. Here is the balance sheet for LAD Renovations as at 31 December 2006.

LAD Renovations
Balance Sheet as at 31 December 2006

		£	£	£
Fixed assets				
Premises			166,000	
Plant and equipment			84,500	250,500
Current assets				
Stock		44,800		
Debtors		84,300		
			129,100	
Creditors: amounts due within one year				
Creditors		38,100		
Bank overdraft		19,500	(57,600)	71,500
				322,000
Capital accounts:	Linda		78,000	
	Alan		156,000	
	David		6,000	240,000
Current accounts:	Linda		39,800	
	Alan		89,600	
	David		(47,400)	82,000
				322,000

The partnership was dissolved on 1 January 2007. The premises were sold for £156,000, the plant and equipment for £80,900 and the stock for £42,600. Debtors realized £72,100 and creditors were settled for £37,100. David was unable to make any contribution to the dissolution of the partnership. The accountant records these transactions in the books of accounts and the following summarizes the entries in the realization account, which calculates the profit or loss realized on the dissolution of the partnership and distributes it among the partners.

Realization account			£	£
	Premises at 31 December 2006		166,000	
Less	Proceeds from sale of premises		(156,000)	
	Loss on disposal			10,000
	Plant and equipment at 31 December 2006		84,500	
Less	Proceeds from sale of plant and equipment		(80,900)	
	Loss on disposal			3,600
	Stock at 31 December 2006		44,800	
Less	Proceeds from sale of stock		(42,600)	
	Loss on disposal			2,200
	Debtors at 31 December 2006		84,300	
Less	Cash received from debtors		(72,100)	
	Bad debts on dissolution			12,200
	Cash paid to creditors on dissolution		37,100	
Less	Creditors at 31 December 2006		(38,100)	
	Unpaid creditors			(1,000)
				27,000
	Loss on realization	Linda 30%	8,100	
		Alan 60%	16,200	
		David 10%	2,700	27,000

For those of you who are studying double-entry bookkeeping, the accountant would open a realization account and make the following records in the accounting system:

Realization account			
	£		£
Premises	166,000	Bank: Sale of premises	156,000
Plant and equipment	84,500	Bank: Sale of plant and equipment	80,900
Stock	44,800	Bank: Sale of stock	42,600
Debtors	84,300	Bank: Debtors realized	72,100
Payment of creditors	37,100	Creditors	38,100
		Loss on realization: Linda (30%)	8,100
		Alan (60%)	16,200
		David (10%)	2,700
	416,700		416,700

Bank account			
	£		£
Realization: Premises	156,000	Opening balance	19,500
Realization: Plant and equipment	80,900	Creditors	37,100
Realization: Stock	42,600	Capital accounts: Linda	95,000
Realization: Debtors	72,100	Alan	200,000
	351,600		351,600

Capital accounts							
	Linda	Alan	David		Linda	Alan	David
	£	£	£		£	£	£
Current account			47,400	Opening balances	78,000	156,000	6,000
Loss on realization	8,100	16,200	2,700	Current accounts	39,800	89,600	
David*	14,700	29,400		Linda*			14,700
Bank	95,000	200,000		Alan*			29,400
	117,800	245,600	50,100		117,800	245,600	50,100
* *Garner* v. *Murray* (1904)							

David's deficit is £44,100 (£47,400 deficit in his current account + £2,700 share of the loss on realization – £6,000 in his capital account). This must be shared by Linda and Alan in the same proportions as their share of capital (30% and 60% respectively) which is a ratio of 1:2. Therefore, Linda bears £14,700 and Alan bears £29,400. The balances outstanding on Linda and Alan's capital accounts are settled by payments from the bank which closes that account. This example not only demonstrates the cessation of the partnership but also the financial risk the other partners bear when one of the partners is insolvent.

9.7   conclusions

The profit and loss account for a partnership is similar to that of a sole trader, except that the figure for net profit is transferred to an additional section known as the appropriation account. This shows the financial transactions of each partner separately and is part of the double-entry bookkeeping system. Interest on capital, salary and share of profit is shown as debit entries; interest on drawings is shown as a credit entry. Corresponding entries appear in the partnership balance sheet, which shows the closing balances of each partner's capital and current accounts.

When a new partner is admitted, a goodwill account is opened so that the existing partners can benefit from the goodwill they have generated. This can be written off immediately or over a period of time. When a partnership is dissolved, a realization account is opened which allows the profit to be calculated and shared among the partners in their agreed profit-sharing ratios. However, if the cause of the cessation of the business is due to the insolvency of one of the partners, the rules of *Garner* v. *Murray* (1904) require the other partners to bear the loss in the ratio of their capital accounts.

practice questions

1. Two brothers, Harry and George Cobb, are in partnership trading as H&G Tool Hire. The following information is available for the year ending 31 December 2006:

	Harry	George
Capital accounts	£20,000	£60,000
Drawings	£35,000	£32,000
Interest on drawings	£1,500	£1,000
Salaries	£15,000	£10,000
Profit share	60%	40%

The net profit available for appropriation is £95,000 and the partners receive 5% interest on their capital.

Required
Prepare the appropriation account for H&G Tool Hire for the year ending 31 December 2006.

2. Using the information from question 1 above, show the current accounts for Harry and George Cobb for the year ending 31 December 2006.

3. Jarvis and Berry are in partnership and call their business J&B Services. Their capital accounts each show a balance of £120,000. They agree to let Archer join if he agrees to pay £200,000. For this he will receive a one-third interest in the business.

Required
Draw up a goodwill account and the partners' capital accounts.

4. On 1 January 2006 the capital and current accounts of the partners in Page & Partners were as follows:

	Capital account £	Current account £
Page	50,000	4,500
Jones	75,000	2,000
Beattie	85,000	5,000

During the year the following transactions took place:

	Salaries £	Drawings £
Page	15,000	55,000
Jones	10,000	20,000
Beattie	10,000	28,000

The net profit for the year was £131,950. Interest on capital is paid at 10% and interest on drawings is charged at 5%. The partners share the profits equally.

Required
Prepare the appropriation account for Page & Partners for the year ending 31 December 2006 and show the partners' current accounts.

5. Mourne, Noonan and Knight are in partnership, sharing profits equally. The partnership balance sheet as at 30 June 2007 is as follows:

Mourne, Noonan & Knight
Balance sheet as at 30 June 2007

	£	£	£
Fixed assets			
Premises			50,000
Current assets			
Stock	48,600		
Debtors	28,200		
		76,800	
Creditors: amounts due within one year			
Creditors	78,300		
Bank overdraft	28,700	(107,000)	(30,200)
			19,800
Capital accounts:	Mourne	8,000	
	Noonan	6,000	
	Knight	2,000	16,000
Current accounts:	Mourne	2,000	
	Noonan	1,400	
	Knight	400	3,800
			19,800

The partnership was dissolved on 1 July 2007 and the fixed assets were sold for £47,500 and the stock was sold for £41,100. On the same date, debtors realized £26,800 and creditors were paid in full. However, Knight is insolvent.

Required
Draw up the accounts in the double-entry bookkeeping system to close the partnership.

chapter 10

financial statements of a limited company

When you have studied this chapter, you should be able to:

- Explain the terms used in the financial statements of limited companies

- Understand the construction of a profit and loss account for a limited company under UK GAAP

- Understand the construction of a balance sheet for a limited company under UK GAAP

- Describe the main features of a set of financial statements under international GAAP.

10.1 introduction

Under *UK GAAP*, reporting entities (limited companies and limited liability partnerships) must comply with the requirements of the Companies Act 1985 (CA85) and the Financial Reporting Standards (FRS) issued by the Accounting Standards Board (ASB). However, as the UK moves towards convergence with *international GAAP*, some entities are required to prepare their financial statements in accordance with International Financial Reporting Standards (IFRS) issued by the International Accounting Standards Board (IASB). In addition, public limited companies with a listing on a stock exchange must also comply with the rules of that particular stock exchange. Before you continue, you may wish to refresh your knowledge of the regulatory and conceptual frameworks we discussed in Chapter 2.

This chapter focuses on the financial statements of large limited companies. We start by looking at the main features of the financial statements and introduce some of the new terminology you will need to know. We then provide an overview of the different financial statements that are required under UK GAAP and those that are required for certain entities under international GAAP. This is followed by an examination of the financial statements that measure financial performance and financial position under UK and international GAAP. Some of the differences are of a technical nature and not important at this level of study. Nevertheless, you need to develop an awareness of the terminology and layouts used in both in order to examine the financial statements of different entities with confidence.

10.2 main features

The conceptual framework for financial reporting identifies the objective of financial statements as being to provide information that is useful to users for making economic decisions, with investors and potential investors as the defining user group (IASB, 1989). The larger the entity, the more likely it is that the investors will not be involved in the management of the business and will not have access to internal financial information. Consequently, regulation of financial reporting is needed to ensure that they receive high quality, reliable information. In addition, the larger the company, the greater the range of financial transactions and events that need to be accounted for and reported. Regulation provides an accounting framework that guides the form, content and structure of financial statements and the accounting policies to be applied in their preparation.

Of the 4.3 million businesses in the UK at the start of 2004, only 24% were limited companies and the remaining 76% were sole proprietorships and general partnerships (SBS, 2005). One of the ways in which limited liability entities differ from other types of business is in their financial structure (see Chapter 3). This leads to certain differences in the items shown in the financial statements and the terminology used. Table 10.1 summarizes the main similarities and differences in terms of sources of finance.

As you can see, the range of asset-based finance is similar but the first difference to note is the way in which capital can be raised. Whilst sole proprietorships and partnerships are limited to the amount the proprietor or partners have to invest, limited liability entities can raise capital by selling shares. A public limited company can sell its shares in the capital markets by obtaining a listing on a stock exchange; a private limited company can only sell its shares privately. In both cases, the shareholders may be individuals or institutions. If the business is profitable, some of the profit will be distributed to shareholders in the form of a *dividend*. The remainder will be retained to help the business grow and is shown as a *reserve* in the balance sheet. (It is not part of share capital).

TABLE 10.1 **Similarities and differences in sources of finance**

	Sole proprietorships and general partnerships	Limited liability entities
Capital	Owner's capital Increased by retained profit (Owner can draw on capital)	Share capital (including venture capital) Reserves (Shareholders receive dividends)
Debt finance	Medium/long-term loans (eg mortgages and loans from banks, business angels, family and friends)	Medium/long-term loans (eg mortgages and loans from banks) Debentures (loan stock)
Asset-based finance	Hire purchase, leasing, invoice finance (factoring)	Hire purchase, leasing, invoice finance (factoring)

Preference shares entitle the shareholder to a specified rate of dividend. *Ordinary shares* are the most common form of share capital and ordinary shareholders receive their dividend after the preference shareholders have been paid. In Chapter 3 we explained that the term *equity finance* is used to describe the finance raised from shareholders in the form of ordinary shares and reserves. Share capital can be categorized as:

- *Authorized share capital* refers to the amount of share capital the company is allowed to issue (as stated in the memorandum of association).
- *Issued share capital* refers to the amount of share capital that the company has issued.
- *Called-up share capital* refers to the proportion of issued shares for which payment has been demanded and paid (part of the payment may have been deferred).

The following activity will help you become familiar with this terminology:

---

activity

E-messaging Ltd was formed with authorized share capital of 500,000 ordinary shares of £1 each. So far, only 300,000 shares have been issued and none has been fully paid, as only 60p per share has been demanded and paid. Calculate the following:

(a) The authorized share capital

(b) The issued share capital

(c) The called-up share capital.

You should have found this very easy. Check your answers against the following:

(a) Authorized share capital (500,000 shares × £1) = £500,000
(b) Issued share capital (300,000 shares × £1) = £300,000
(c) Called-up share capital (300,000 shares × 60p) = £180,000

A second difference in the way sole proprietorships, general partnerships and limited liability entities are financed is in the way they can raise debt finance. In addition to the usual forms of debt finance, limited liability entities can sell *debentures* (also known as *loan stock*). A debenture is a long-term loan in the form of a bond and is usually secured on the assets of the company. In common with interest paid on other forms of debt finance, the interest paid to debenture holders is charged as an expense in the profit and loss account.

In addition to the financial structure of the entity being reflected in the financial statements, there is the influence of the regulatory framework. The Companies Act 1985 (CA85) requires limited liability entities to publish audited financial statements that include a profit and loss account and balance sheet (there are options for qualifying smaller entities offering exemption from the statutory audit and simplifications in terms of disclosures). The financial statements of all entities, irrespective of legal form or size, are prepared in accordance with the accounting principles. However, the financial statements of limited liability entities differ significantly from those of sole traders in terms of format and content. This is mainly because these reporting entities must comply with the requirements of CA85 and accounting standards.

It is important to remember that the regulation of financial reporting in the UK is going through a transition period as we move towards convergence with international accounting standards. In Chapter 2 we explained that international accounting standards consist of a number of IASs that were adopted by the IASB and are still in force, plus all the IFRSs that have been issued since the IASB took over in 2001. The process of developing IFRSs is underpinned by a conceptual framework (see Chapter 2) called the *Framework for the Preparation and Presentation of Financial Statements* (usually referred to as the IASB Framework). It is important to remember that national and international financial reporting standards may be amended or replaced. Therefore, if you are doing detailed work, it is essential that you refer to the most recent standard.

Since 2005 international GAAP has been adopted as the basis for financial reporting by listed group companies in all 25 member states of the EU. In total, nearly 100 countries are committed to adopting international GAAP, including Australia, China and Hong Kong, Norway, South Africa and Switzerland. This means that you will notice some differences when you compare the financial statements of group companies that have been published before 2005 with those that have been published since. This is because before 2005 they would have been prepared in accordance with Financial Reporting Standards (FRSs) issued by the ASB, but now they are prepared using International Financial Reporting Standards (IFRSs) issued by the IASB.

To allow shareholders to appreciate the activities of the entire group, financial information from the individual financial statements of the parent company and its subsidiaries is adjusted and combined to form *consolidated financial statements*.

KEY DEFINITION   Consolidation is the process of adjusting and combining financial information from the individual financial statements of a parent undertaking and its

 subsidiary undertakings to prepare consolidated financial statements that present financial information for the group as a single economic entity.

Over the next few years it is likely that IFRS will have a major impact on the financial statements of a wider range of entities. Therefore, it is important that you can understand and interpret a set of financial statements prepared under international GAAP. *IAS 1, Presentation of Financial Statements* requires a complete set of financial statements to be presented at least annually. These are the *general purpose financial statements* that are intended to meet the needs of users who are not in a position to demand specially prepared reports that meet their precise information needs. In addition to information about the reporting period, they must provide information about the preceding reporting period. Table 10.2 compares a set of financial statements under UK GAAP with those required under international GAAP.

TABLE 10.2 **Financial statements under UK and international GAAP compared**

UK GAAP	International GAAP
Balance sheet	Balance sheet
Profit and loss account	Income statement
Statement of total recognized gains and losses	Statement of changes in equity
Cash flow statement	Cash flow statement
Notes (providing a summary of significant accounting policies and other explanatory notes)	Notes (providing a summary of significant accounting policies and other explanatory notes)

International GAAP emphasizes the measurement of financial position. This is reflected in the IASB's *objective* of financial statements, which is 'to provide information about the financial position [the balance sheet], performance [the income statement] and changes in financial position [the statement of changes in equity and the cash flow statement] of an enterprise that is useful to a wide range of users in making economic decisions' (IASB,1989, paras. 22–3). There are also some changes in terminology: the financial statement that measures financial performance is known as the profit and loss account under UK GAAP, but under international GAAP it is known as an *income statement*. Under UK GAAP a statement of total recognized gains and losses (STRGL) is required, whereas international GAAP requires a statement of changes in equity showing all changes in equity or those changes that arise from transactions with equity holders.

A statement of total recognized gains and losses not only shows the profit or loss for the period, but also all other recognized gains and losses that may have occurred during the reporting period that are normally transferred directly to the reserves on the balance sheet. For example, a company decides that the property it owns has increased in value over the years. The property is currently shown in the balance sheet at its historic cost, but the company wants to show it at its new value so that shareholders can appreciate the value of what they own. To show this increased value or gain, the company increases the assets in the balance sheet. However, it must make a corresponding entry to make the balance sheet balance. It cannot put the surplus through the profit and loss account because, although the increase has been recognized, the company has not sold the property and therefore no profit has been realized. Instead, the company creates a *revaluation reserve* which is placed under the 'capital and reserves' heading in the balance sheet.

Although the *statement of total recognized gains and losses* required under UK GAAP is not significant for most companies in terms of the number of items it contains, the amounts involved may be highly significant and can be larger than the realized profit for the period. For this reason it must be given the same prominence as the profit and loss account, the balance sheet and the cash flow statement. If a company does not have any recognized gains or losses other than the profit or loss for the period, no statement need be provided, but a note to this effect must be given immediately after the profit and loss account.

The *statement of changes in equity* required under international GAAP shows changes in equity that are attributable to the increase or decrease in net assets during the period, with the exception of transactions that have taken place directly with a shareholder. Net assets can change for a variety of reasons, such as changes in income and expenses reported in the income statement and changes in the amount of equity through the introduction of new capital or the return of capital to shareholders. *IAS 1, Presentation of Financial Statements*, requires the statement of changes in equity to present the following information:

- the profit or loss for the period
- each item of income and expense for the period that has been reported directly in equity rather than in the income statement
- total income and expense for the period (this is the sum of the first two items with any allocation to minority shareholders clearly separated)
- the effects of changes in accounting policies or the correction of errors for each component of equity.

The types of transactions that are taken directly to equity are:

- reversal of impairment losses previously taken to equity *(IAS 36, Impairment of Assets)*
- foreign exchange differences arising on consolidation *(IAS 21, The Effects of Changes in Foreign Exchange Rates)*
- revaluation surpluses on non-current assets *(IAS 16, Property, Plant and Equipment)*.

IAS 1 requires a full reconciliation of each reserve to be presented and the amount of any transaction that has taken place with shareholders to be separately identified. IAS 1 provides an example of a statement of changes in equity, but the main features we have described provide sufficient knowledge at this level of study.

The fourth financial statement under both UK GAAP and international GAAP is the *cash flow statement*. Cash flow information can be used to assess changes in net assets and the financial structure of an entity in the context of the other financial statements. It can also be used to assess the control an entity has over the amounts and timings of cash flows for adapting to changing circumstances and opportunities. Later on in the chapter we will be looking at the requirements of *IAS 7, Cash Flow Statements*.

IAS 1 requires notes to the financial statements that provide information on:

- the basis upon which the financial statements have been prepared and the accounting policies used
- disclosure of information required by IFRS that is not shown on the face of the financial statements
- additional information that is not shown on the face of the financial statements but is relevant to an understanding of any of them.

The following general principles with regard to accounting policies are given in IAS 1:

- *fair presentation* and compliance with accounting standards
- *going concern* (the business will continue to operate for the foreseeable future)
- the *accrual* basis of accounting (except for the cash flow statement)
- *consistency* (the presentation and classification of items in the financial statements will be consistent from one reporting period to the next)
- *materiality* (each material class of similar items is presented separately in the financial statements) and *aggregation* (dissimilar items are presented separately unless they are immaterial)
- *offsetting* (no offsetting of assets and liabilities, or income and expenses, is allowed unless this is covered by a standard)
- *profit or loss* for the period.

The fair presentation principle requires that the financial statements present fairly the financial position, financial performance and cash flows of an entity. This is consistent with the objective of financial statements. By complying with IFRSs, and providing any additional information necessary, it is presumed that financial statements give a fair presentation. Where financial statements comply with IFRSs, an explicit and unreserved statement must be made in the notes to that effect.

10.3 reporting financial performance under UK GAAP

As you know, the profit and loss account measures the financial performance of an entity over the reporting period. The published profit and loss account of a limited company prepared under UK GAAP differs in many ways from that of a sole trader or general partnership. One major difference is that you do not find detailed information on costs. This is because limited liability entities are not obliged to disclose this information. Because of the different types and sizes of limited companies and the diverse nature of their transactions, their profit and loss accounts look different. However, there are always a considerable number of similarities because of the requirements of the regulatory framework. The following example shows a relatively simple profit and loss account prepared under UK GAAP.

	Notes	2004 £000	2004 £000	2003 £000	2003 £000
RWJ Group plc Consolidated profit and loss account for the year ending 30 June 2004					
Turnover			11,275		10,010
Cost of sales			(6,519)		(5,537)
Gross profit			4,756		4,473
Administration expenses		(1,880)		(1,730)	
Sales and distribution costs		(1,530)		(1,450)	
Other operating income and expenditure		(500)	(3,910)	(475)	(3,655)
Operating profit			846		818
Net interest payable			(142)		(139)
Profit on ordinary activities before taxation			704		679
Taxation			(282)		(272)
Profit after taxation			422		407
Minority interests			(60)		(55)
Profit attributable to shareholders			362		352
Dividends			(172)		(122)
Retained profit for the financial year			190		230
Earnings per share	1		15.5p		15.2p

One of the first things to note is that the published profit and loss account not only gives the current year's figures, but also the figures for the previous year. This is a requirement of CA85. Although we have not shown all the numbered references to notes in our example, you will see a large number of notes in the published financial statements. These notes are shown on the pages following the financial statements in the annual report and accounts and provide additional information about accounting policies as required by *FRS 18, Accounting Policies*, as well as other notes.

We will now examine the main items shown in the above example:

- *Turnover* is the term used in CA85 for sales revenue.
- Because it is important to appreciate how a limited company is financed and the cost of borrowing money, the *operating profit* tells us the profit before any interest payable on borrowings is charged (in other words, profit before interest and tax are deducted).
- You will then see that the *profit before taxation* is shown (in other words, profit after interest payable has been deducted but before tax).
- Then, since companies are subject to tax, the *profit after taxation* (in other words, profit after interest and tax has been deducted).
- The next unusual term is *minority interests*, which represent the interests of shareholders in subsidiary companies who are entitled to receive a share of the profits of the holding company in the form of dividends. These minority interests are deducted next.
- *Profit attributable to shareholders* refers to the profit that remains after interest, tax and any minority interests have been deducted and belongs to the shareholders. Some is paid to them in the form of dividends.

- *Retained profit for the financial year* is the balance of profit remaining after dividends have been deducted. This balance is reinvested in the company to help it grow.

The *earnings per share (EPS)* is a measure on which many shareholders place considerable weight. As we showed in our example, normally a company pays out only a proportion of the profit on ordinary activities to shareholders in the form of a dividend and the remainder is retained to help the company grow. The retained profit still belongs to the shareholders and, therefore, the dividend they receive is only part of the return on their investment. The EPS figure shows the total return and is normally measured in pence. It is not required by law, but *FRS 22, Earnings per Share*, specifies the way in which earnings per share data should be calculated, presented and disclosed. Because there are a number of different ways of calculating EPS, in addition to the calculation required under FRS 22, some companies give additional figures that are relevant to their circumstances. The calculation of basic EPS for RWJ Group plc in 2004 was as follows:

$$\frac{\text{Profit attributable to ordinary shareholders}}{\text{Average number of ordinary shares issued}} \times 100 \text{ (to give an answer in pence)}$$

$$= \frac{£362,000}{2,332,000} \times 100$$

$$= 15.5p$$

Some companies provide a detailed analysis of certain figures as a result of complying with *FRS 3, Reporting Financial Performance*, which requires them to provide a breakdown of turnover and operating profit by continuing operations, acquisitions and discontinued operations in the profit and loss account. This information helps investors appreciate the underlying trend of the company's financial performance and any significant changes in its operation. A similar analysis must be made for the items between turnover and operating profit, but this can be shown either in the profit and loss account or as a note to the accounts. If the company has disposed of a significant part of its activities during the year, this allows investors to see what contribution to financial performance was made by operations that will be continued. Conversely, if the company has made any acquisitions during the year, investors can see what contribution they have made to financial performance.

activity

Obtain a copy of the annual report and accounts for a company that has been prepared under UK GAAP and identify the items described in this section in the profit and loss account.

10.4 reporting financial position under UK GAAP

The *balance sheet* measures the *financial position* of an entity at the end of the reporting period. A typical vertical presentation of a published balance sheet for a limited company prepared under UK GAAP looks very similar to that of a sole trader and represents the accounting equation:

Assets – Liabilities = Capital

The following example shows a relatively simple consolidated balance sheet for a public limited company prepared under UK GAAP:

RWJ Group plc
Consolidated balance sheet as at 30 June 2004

	Notes	2004 £000	2004 £000	2003 £000	2003 £000
Fixed assets					
Intangible assets			795		795
Tangible assets			1,590		1,236
Investments			56		76
			2,441		2,107
Current assets					
Stock		1,908		1,779	
Debtors	2	2,031		1,509	
Cash at bank and in hand		196		244	
		4,135		3,532	
Creditors: amounts due within one year		(2,334)		(2,026)	
Net current assets			1,801		1,506
Total assets less current liabilities			4,242		3,613
Creditors: amounts due after more than one year	3		(719)		(449)
Provisions for liabilities and charges			(164)		(17)
Total net assets			3,359		3,147
Capital and reserves					
Called-up share capital			583		580
Share premium account			144		120
Reserves			177		177
Profit and loss account			2,455		2,270
Total shareholders' funds			3,359		3,147

Notes	2004	2003
1 Number of shares issued (000)	2,332	2,320
2 Of which trade debtors (£000)	1,143	1,097
3 Of which trade creditors (£000)	1,590	1,350

You should be familiar with most of the items shown in the first half of the balance sheet:

- *Fixed assets* are assets which are held in the business on a continuing basis. They include tangible assets (such as land, factories and machines) and intangible assets (such as goodwill and investment in research and development).
- *Current assets* are cash and other assets that are expected to be converted into cash within one year (such as stock and debtors).
- *Creditors: amounts due within one year* are current liabilities. These are debts where repayment is due within the next financial year, such as overdrafts or trade creditors. Current

liabilities are subtracted from current assets to give *net current assets,* which is also known as *working capital*. This is added to fixed assets to give *total assets less current liabilities* (this is used to describe the *capital employed* in the business).

- *Creditors: amounts due after more than one year* are long-term liabilities. These loans, debentures and other long-term debts are deducted next to give *total net assets. Debentures* are long-term loans to the company, usually made by financial institutions. As explained earlier in the chapter, they are not part of share capital and debenture holders receive interest rather than a dividend.

The main difference between the balance sheet of a sole trader and that of a limited company is in the second half, which is headed 'Capital and reserves' and contains the following items:

- *Called-up share capital* is the capital invested by the owners of the business. Most shares are in denominations of 25p. This is the nominal or face value of the share. For example, a company may have issued 4 million 25p shares. The amount shown on the balance sheet will be £1 million (4 million × 25p). However, if you wanted to buy or sell one of the company's shares, you would need to know the market price, which is likely to be very different and depends on a number of factors.
- The *share premium account* shows the difference between the nominal value of the shares issued and the amount the company has received from the shareholders.
- *Reserves* may have arisen for a variety of reasons; for example, retained profit may have been transferred to a named reserve account. The largest reserve is usually retained profit and this is shown separately and labelled 'profit and loss account' in this part of the balance sheet.
- The items of capital and reserves are added together to give *total shareholders' funds*, which should balance with the figure for total net assets.

activity

Examine your copy of the annual report and accounts prepared for a company under UK GAAP and identify the items described in this section in the balance sheet.

10.5 reporting financial position under international GAAP

The balance sheet prepared under international GAAP measures the financial position of an entity at the end of the reporting period in terms of assets, capital (or equity) and other liabilities. The IASB Framework provides definitions of what is meant by an 'asset', a 'liability' and 'equity'. These terms should be familiar to you, but these are the IASB's technical definitions.

KEY DEFINITIONS

An asset is a resource controlled by the enterprise as a result of past events and from which future economic benefits are expected to flow to the enterprise.

A liability is a present obligation of the enterprise resulting from past events, the settlement of which is expected to result in an outflow from the enterprise of resources embodying economic benefits.

Equity is the residual interest in the assets of the enterprise after deducting all its liabilities.

Source: IASB, 1989, para. 25.

IAS 1 does not stipulate a particular format for the balance sheet and a wide variety of presentations are acceptable. However, certain information must be shown on the face of the balance sheet, providing the items are sufficiently different in nature or function to be shown separately. Additional headings, line items and subtotals are required if they are relevant to an understanding of the entity's financial position. This additional information can be on the face of the balance sheet or in the notes, depending on:

- the nature and liquidity of assets
- the function of assets within the entity
- the amounts, nature and timing of liabilities.

The following example of a balance sheet is taken from IAS 1 and illustrates a format that distinguishes between current and non-current items. It represents the accounting equation:

Assets = Capital + Other liabilities

XYZ Group Balance sheet as at 31 December 2005	2005 €000	2004 €000
ASSETS		
Non-current assets		
Property, plant and equipment	X	X
Goodwill	X	X
Other intangible assets	X	X
Investments in associates	X	X
Available-for-sale investments	X	X
	X	X
Current assets		
Inventories	X	X
Trade receivables	X	X
Other current assets	X	X
Cash and cash equivalents	X	X
	X	X
Total assets	X	X

EQUITY AND LIABILITIES		
Equity attributable to equity holders of the parent		
Share capital	X	X
Other reserves	X	X
Retained earnings	X	X
	X	X
Minority interest	X	X
Total equity	X	X
Non-current liabilities		
Long-term borrowings	X	X
Deferred tax	X	X
Long-term provisions	X	X
Total non-current liabilities	X	X
Current liabilities		
Trade and other payables	X	X
Short-term borrowings	X	X
Current portion of long-term borrowings	X	X
Current tax payable	X	X
Short-term provisions	X	X
Total current liabilities	X	X
Total liabilities	X	X
Total equity and liabilities	X	X

activity

Obtain a copy of an annual report and accounts for an EU listed company that prepares consolidated accounts under international GAAP and identify the items described in this section in the published balance sheet.

10.6 reporting financial performance under international GAAP

The *income statement* prepared under international GAAP measures the *financial performance* of the entity over the reporting period. The IASB Framework defines what is meant by 'income' and 'expenses'. Again, these terms should be familiar to you, but these are the IASB's technical definitions.

KEY DEFINITIONS

Income is increases in economic benefits during the accounting period in the form of inflows or enhancements of assets or decreases in liabilities that result in increases in equity, other than those relating to contributions from equity participants.

Expenses are decreases in economic benefits during the accounting period in the form of outflows or

depletions of assets or occurrences of liabilities that result in decreases in equity, other than those relating to distributions to equity participants.

Source: IASB, 1989, para. 70.

IAS 1 takes a similarly permissive approach to the presentation and format of the income statement as it does with the balance sheet: some analysis of how the net profit or loss is arrived at is required, but a variety of presentations are acceptable. Certain items must be shown on the face of the income statement and other disclosures can be made either on the face or in the notes. All items of income and expense recognized in the financial period must be included in the profit or loss unless a standard or an interpretation requires otherwise. The income statement can present an analysis of expenses either by *nature* or by *function*. The following example from IAS 1 provides an illustration of an income statement where expenses are aggregated according to their nature (for example purchases of material, depreciation, employee benefits).

XYZ Group plc
Income statement for the year ended 31 December 2005

	2005 €000	2004 €000
Revenue	x	x
Other income	x	x
Changes in inventories of finished goods and work in progress	(x)	x
Work performed by the entity and capitalized	x	x
Raw material and consumables used	(x)	(x)
Employee benefits expense	(x)	(x)
Depreciation and amortization expense	(x)	(x)
Impairment of property, plant and equipment	(x)	(x)
Other expenses	(x)	(x)
Finance costs	(x)	(x)
Share of profit of associates	x	x
Profit before tax	x	x
Income tax expense	(x)	(x)
Profit for the period	x	x
Attributable to:		
Equity holders of the parent	x	x
Minority interests	x	x
	x	x

The next example is also given in IAS 1 and classifies expenses according to their function (as the cost of sales or as the cost of other administrative activities). The main difference between the two methods is that this method provides a figure for gross profit.

XYZ Group plc		
Income statement for the year ended 31 December 2005		
	2005	2004
	€000	€000
Revenue	X	X
Cost of sales	(x)	(x)
Gross profit	X	X
Other income	X	X
Distribution costs	(x)	(x)
Administrative expenses	(x)	(x)
Other expenses	(x)	(x)
Finance costs	(x)	(x)
Share of profit of associates	X	X
Profit before tax	X	X
Income tax expense	(x)	(x)
Profit for the period	X	X
Attributable to:		
Equity holders of the parent	X	X
Minority interests	X	X
	X	X

activity

Examine your copy of an annual report and accounts for an EU listed
company that prepares consolidated accounts under international
GAAP and identify the items described in this section in the published
income statement.

10.7 cash flow statement under international GAAP

The purpose of the cash flow statement prepared under international GAAP is to analyse
changes in cash and cash equivalents during a financial period. *IAS 7, Cash Flow Statements*
requires cash flows to be classified into operating, investing and financing activities. This
enables users to assess the entity's ability to generate *cash and cash equivalents* and to use
those cash flows. The cash flow statement can be drawn up using the direct method or the
indirect method.

- The *direct method* is encouraged by the IASB and discloses each major class of gross cash
  receipts and gross cash payments.
- The *indirect method* is accepted by the IASB and adjusts the net profit or loss for the
  effects of non-cash transactions.

Both methods provide a figure for the cash flow from operating activities. However, the
direct method gives details of the cash flows that make up the total cash flows from oper-

ating activities. On the other hand, the indirect method makes adjustments to the net profit or loss for the period (for example adding back depreciation) to arrive at the total cash flow figure.

Cash and cash equivalents are:

- cash in hand and deposits that can be withdrawn immediately in cash without suffering any penalties
- short-term, highly liquid investments that are readily convertible to a known amount of cash and that are subject to an insignificant risk of changes in value
- bank overdrafts that are repayable on demand and are an integral part of cash
- equity investments, if they are in substance a cash equivalent (for example preferred shares acquired within three months of their specified redemption date).

The cash flow statement must classify the information under three main headings:

- *Operating activities* – the main revenue-producing activities of the enterprise, for example cash received from customers and cash paid to suppliers and employees.
- *Investing activities* – the acquisition and disposal of long-term assets and other investments that are not considered to be cash equivalents (for example acquisition of property, plant and equipment).
- *Financing activities* – activities that alter the equity capital and borrowing structure of the enterprise (for example cash from issuing shares).

IAS 7 also explains the treatment of certain items. The main ones are:

- interest and dividends received and paid may be classified as operating, investing or financing cash flows, but must be treated consistently
- tax cash flows on income are normally classified as operating unless they can be specifically identified under another heading
- extraordinary items should be disclosed separately under the most appropriate heading
- foreign currency cash flows arising from transactions should be recorded at the rate of exchange applying on the date of the cash flow
- cash flows of foreign subsidiaries should be included in the group cash flow statement translated at the exchange rate on the dates of the cash flows.

Examples of cash flow statements for financial institutions and for entities other than financial institutions are provided in IAS 7, but knowledge of the main features we have described is sufficient at this level of study.

10.8 conclusions

This chapter has examined the financial statements of limited companies in the context of considerable change in the regulatory framework for financial reporting and you may have needed to revisit Chapter 2 to remind yourself of the details. The UK is going through a period of transition in the way reporting entities are regulated as we move towards convergence with international GAAP. Listed group companies are now required to comply with IFRSs. A complete set of financial statements required under UK GAAP comprises:

- a profit and loss account
- a statement of total recognized gains and losses
- a balance sheet
- a cash flow statement
- notes providing a summary of significant accounting policies and other explanatory notes.

This differs from the complete set of financial statements required under international GAAP, which consists of:

- a balance sheet
- an income statement
- a statement of changes in equity showing either all changes in equity or those changes that arise from transactions with equity holders
- a cash flow statement
- notes providing a summary of significant accounting policies and other explanatory notes.

At introductory level, most students do not need a detailed knowledge of the statement of changes in equity and the cash flow statement required under international GAAP. Therefore, we have only provided an overview of these two statements and instead have focused on the content and presentation of the financial statements that measure financial performance and financial position. This should allow you to examine the financial statements of UK companies with confidence, regardless of whether they have been prepared under UK GAAP or international GAAP.

practice questions

1. Explain the difference between ordinary shares, preference shares and debentures.
2. Describe the main items you would expect to find in the consolidated profit and loss account and consolidated balance sheet of a limited company that are not present in the profit and loss account of a sole trader.
3. Describe the disclosure requirements of FRS 3 in respect of the profit and loss account.
4. Describe the main differences between the profit and loss account prepared under UK GAAP and the two presentations of the income statement permitted under international GAAP that we used as illustrations in this chapter.
5. Describe the main differences between the balance sheet prepared under UK GAAP and the balance sheet prepared under international GAAP that we have used as illustrations in this chapter.

references

FRS 3, *Reporting Financial Performance* (ASB, October 1992, amended June 1993).
FRS 14, *Earnings per Share* (ASB, October 1998).

FRS 18, Accounting Policies (ASB, December 2000).

IAS 1, Presentation of Financial Statements (IASB, December 2003, amended March 2004).

IAS 7, Cash Flow Statements (IASB, December 1992, amended March 2004).

IAS 16, Property, Plant and Equipment (IASB, December 2003, amended March 2004).

IAS 21, The Effects of Changes in Foreign Exchange Rates (IASB, December 2003).

IAS 36, Impairment of Assets (IASB, March 2004).

IASB (1989) *Framework for the Preparation and Presentation of Financial Statements*, September, London: International Accounting Standards Board.

SBS (2005) *Small and Medium Enterprises (SME) Statistics for the UK 2004*, URN 05/92, www.sbs.gov.uk/content/statistics.

chapter 11

analysing financial statements

Learning objectives

When you have studied this chapter, you should be able to:

- Explain the purpose of ratio analysis
- Calculate the main performance and liquidity ratios
- Calculate the main gearing and investment ratios
- Interpret the meaning of these ratios and recognize their limitations.

11.1 introduction

Regardless of the size and type of organization you work in now or in the future, being able to read and understand the financial statements of different entities is an achievement worth striving for. This skill becomes even more valuable if you can also analyse and interpret them, because you can then identify the financial strengths and weaknesses of the business you work for, and compare them with previous periods, similar businesses or industry benchmarks. In this last chapter of the financial accounting section of this book, we are going to introduce a technique that is used by management and the other main user groups for *analysing financial statements*. We should add that it is also used by investment analysts and financial journalists. The technique is known as ratio analysis.

In this chapter we are going to show you how different types of ratio can be calculated and used to assess the operating performance, solvency and efficiency in the management of the working capital of a business. We will also be looking at ratios that are used to examine the financial structure of the business, assess financial risk and evaluate shareholders' return. Although we will be illustrating the analysis by applying ratios to the financial statements of a limited company, you should be aware that some of these ratios can also be applied to the financial statements of a sole proprietorship, partnership and other organizations.

11.2 ratio analysis

A *ratio* describes a quantitative relationship between values and is usually presented as x:1 or x%. *Ratio analysis* is a technique that helps management and external users of the published financial statements interpret the financial information by examining relationships between certain data. Once a ratio has been calculated, it is compared with:

- the predetermined budget or target (internal users only)
- previous periods for the same business
- other businesses in the same sector (known as inter-firm comparison)
- industry benchmarks or norms (published averages for the industrial sector).

KEY DEFINITION	Ratio analysis is a technique for evaluating the financial performance and stability of an entity, with a view to making comparisons with previous periods, other entities and industry averages over a period of time.

It is important to remember that there are no standard definitions of the terms used in ratios. Therefore, you need to find out what definitions have been used in any ratios you are interpreting in order to understand fully what is being referred to and whether comparisons are appropriate. Obviously, you cannot compare ratios if they have not been calculated on the same basis. When calculating ratios yourself, you need to state the precise meaning of the terms you are using.

There are four main types of ratio and each has a different purpose:

- Profitability ratios are used for assessing the operating performance of the business.
- Liquidity ratios are used for evaluating the solvency, financial stability and management of working capital of the business.
- Gearing ratios are used for examining the financial structure of the business and assessing financial risk.
- Investment ratios are used for evaluating shareholders' return.

We will examine a selection of the main ratios in each of the above categories, but ultimately the choice of ratios depends on the needs of the user and the availability of the data required for the analysis. Figure 11.1 summarizes the main types of ratios and those that we will be describing in this chapter.

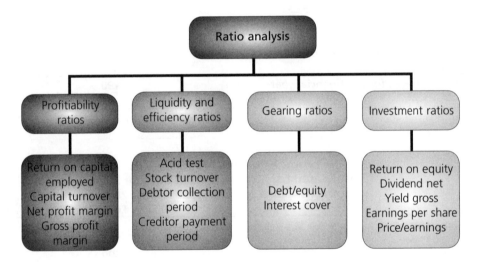

FIGURE 11.1 **Examples of main types of ratio**

Ratios can be applied to the financial statements of any size and type of business. We are going to apply them to the profit and loss account and balance sheet of RWJ Group plc, whose consolidated financial statements we examined in the previous chapter.

RWJ Group plc
Consolidated profit and loss account for the year ending 30 June 2004

	Notes	£000	2004 £000	£000	2003 £000
Turnover			11,275		10,010
Cost of sales			(6,519)		(5,537)
Gross profit			4,756		4,473
Administration expenses		(1,880)		(1,730)	
Sales and distribution costs		(1,530)		(1,450)	
Other operating income and expenditure		(500)	(3,910)	(475)	(3,655)
Operating profit			846		818
Net interest payable			(142)		(139)
Profit on ordinary activities before taxation			704		679
Taxation			(282)		(272)
Profit after taxation			422		407
Minority interests			(60)		(55)
Profit attributable to shareholders			362		352
Dividends			(172)		(122)
Retained profit for the financial year			190		230
Earnings per share	1		15.5p		15.2p

RWJ Group plc
Consolidated balance sheet as at 30 June 2004

	Notes	£000	2004 £000	£000	2003 £000
Fixed assets					
Intangible assets			795		795
Tangible assets			1,590		1,236
Investments			56		76
			2,441		2,107
Current assets					
Stock		1,908		1,779	
Debtors	2	2,031		1,509	
Cash at bank and in hand		196		244	
		4,135		3,532	
Creditors: amounts due within one year		(2,334)		(2,026)	
Net current assets			1,801		1,506
Total assets less current liabilities			4,242		3,613
Creditors: amounts due after more than one year	3		(719)		(449)
Provisions for liabilities and charges			(164)		(17)
Total net assets			3,359		3,147
Capital and reserves					
Called-up share capital			583		580
Share premium account			144		120
Reserves			177		177
Profit and loss account			2,455		2,270
Total shareholders' funds			3,359		3,147

Notes		
1 Number of shares issued ('000)	**2,332**	2,320
2 Of which trade debtors (£'000)	**1,143**	1,097
3 Of which trade creditors (£'000)	**1,590**	1,350

11.3 profitability ratios

Profitability ratios are used to assess the operating performance of a business. We are going to look at the following widely used ratios in this category:

- return on capital employed
- net profit margin
- capital turnover
- gross profit margin.

It is important to note that there are no standard definitions of the terms used in ratios. Therefore, it is important to find out what definitions have been used in any ratios you are interpreting in order to understand fully what is being referred to and whether comparisons are appropriate. Obviously, you cannot compare ratios if they have not been calculated on the same basis. When calculating ratios yourself, you need to state the precise meaning of the terms you are using. For example, we are going to define the term *return* as profit before interest and tax and we will define *capital employed* as total assets less current liabilities.

The first ratio we are going to look at is the *return on capital employed (ROCE)*. It is also known as the *prime ratio* because it is related to two subsidiary ratios: capital turnover and net profit margin. ROCE measures the percentage return on the total investment of funds in the business. This provides useful information about management's effectiveness in generating revenue from resources and their ability to control costs. The formula is:

$$\frac{\text{Profit before interest and tax}}{\text{Capital employed}} \times 100$$

We will now calculate ROCE for the RWJ Group. The first step is to find the figure for profit before interest and tax (PBIT) in the profit and loss account. In this company it is labelled the *operating profit*. We know that this is the correct figure because this is the net profit on operations before the deduction of interest payable on debt finance and taxation. Next, we need the figure for capital employed, which we defined as total assets less current liabilities. You should be able to identify this easily in the balance sheet. Substituting the figures in the formula, the answer is:

ROCE	2004	2003
$\frac{\text{PBIT}}{\text{Capital employed}} \times 100$	$\frac{846}{4,242} \times 100 = 19.94\%$	$\frac{818}{3,613} \times 100 = 22.64\%$

ROCE should reflect the element of risk in the investment and can be compared with interest rates for other investments where there is barely any risk, such as building society inter-est rates. In this case, the return is well above interest rates payable on low risk investments, such as bank deposits. However, the ratio is lower in 2004 than in 2003, which is not a welcome sign. This downward movement reflects the fact that the increased investment of capital employed in the business in 2004 did not result in proportionately higher profits. If we want to know how this profitability has been achieved or how it can be improved, we need to look at the next two ratios.

The *net profit margin* measures the percentage return on sales. The formula is:

$$\frac{\text{Profit before interest and tax}}{\text{Turnover}} \times 100$$

You have already found the figure for profit before interest and tax in the profit and loss account, so all you need to do is to identify the figures for turnover to calculate this ratio for the RWJ Group.

Net profit margin	2004	2003
$\frac{\text{PBIT}}{\text{Turnover}} \times 100$	$\frac{846}{11,275} \times 100 = 7.5\%$	$\frac{818}{10,010} \times 100 = 8.17\%$

The results show that the net profit margin was similar in both years, with the business making a net profit of approximately £8 on every £100 of sales. The net profit margin can be improved by increasing selling prices (if the market permits) or finding ways to reduce costs.

Capital turnover measures the number of times capital employed has been used during the year to achieve the sales revenue we refer to as turnover. It is usually expressed as the number of times rather than a percentage and the formula is:

$$\frac{\text{Turnover}}{\text{Capital employed}}$$

You have already found both these figures, so all we have to do is insert them in the formula to calculate the capital turnover for the RWJ Group.

Capital turnover	2004	2003
$\frac{\text{Turnover}}{\text{Capital employed}}$	$\frac{11,275}{4,242} = 2.66$ times	$\frac{10,010}{3,613} = 2.77$ times

The level of activity should be as high as possible for the lowest level of investment. In this case, the capital employed in the business was turned over nearly three times in both years to achieve the sales revenue.

These first three ratios we have looked at are interrelated:

Capital turnover × Net profit margin = Return on capital employed

We can test this with the data for the RWJ Group (the slight differences are due to rounding when presenting the answers to the ratios):

2004	2003
2.66 × 7.5% = 19.95%	2.77 × 8.17% = 22.63%

A business can improve its prime ratio by reducing costs and/or raising prices (if feasible), which will improve its profit margin. Alternatively, it can increase its sales volume and/or reduce its capital employed, which will improve its capital turnover.

activity

Which of the following methods would you suggest the directors of the RWJ Group use to try to improve the capital turnover?

(a) Decrease the sales volume

(b) Increase the sales volume

(c) Reduce the capital invested in the business

(d) Keep the capital invested in the business at the same level.

What the directors need to do is to increase the sales volume and at the same time keep the capital invested at the same level or, if possible, reduce it. Therefore, all the answers are correct except (a). In some profit and loss accounts the figure for gross profit may be disclosed, as in the RWJ Group example. In businesses in the retail sector in particular, the gross profit figure is considered to be an essential feature of management control and a guide to pricing and purchasing policies.

The *gross profit margin* measures the gross profit as a percentage of sales. The formula is:

$$\frac{\text{Gross profit}}{\text{Turnover}} \times 100$$

Both these figures are given in the profit and loss account of the RWJ Group, so we can now calculate the gross profit margin.

Gross profit margin $\frac{\text{Gross profit}}{\text{Turnover}} \times 100$	2004 $\frac{4{,}756}{11{,}275} \times 100 = 42.18\%$	2003 $\frac{4{,}473}{10{,}010} \times 100 = 44.69\%$

As you can see, the gross profit margin is much higher than the net profit margin because it is calculated before the overhead expenses have been deducted.

If we had the data, we could compare all the profitability ratios for the RWJ Group discussed in this section with similar companies and industry benchmarks. It would be useful to analyse them over a longer period of time to identify the trend. For example, supposing we had calculated the net profit margin for the RWJ Group for the four-year period 2001–2004. We could show this as a table or a graph as follows:

2001	2002	2003	2004
8.5%	8.31%	8.17%	7.5%

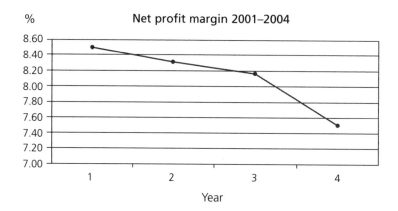

You can see from the table that there has been a decline in net profit margin of 1% over the period and the graph clearly illustrates this downward trend. This gradual fall in net profit margin suggests that selling prices are not keeping pace with rising costs.

11.4 liquidity and efficiency ratios

Liquidity and *efficiency ratios* are used to evaluate the solvency and financial stability of a business and to assess how effectively it has managed its working capital. We will examine the following widely used ratios in this category:

- acid test
- stock turnover
- debtor collection period
- creditor payment period.

The *acid test* is a liquidity ratio that shows the relationship between the business's liquid assets (all current assets except stock, which takes longer to convert into cash) and its current liabilities. The ratio is usually expressed as a ratio of x:1 rather than x% and the formula is:

$$\frac{\text{Current assets} - \text{Stock}}{\text{Creditors: amounts due within one year}}$$

The figures for current assets and stock are both shown in the balance sheet and you will remember that the figure for creditors: amounts due within one year is labelled as current liabilities when the financial statements are prepared under international GAAP. Using the RWJ Group data, we will now calculate the acid test ratio.

Acid test

	2004	2003
$\dfrac{\text{Current assets} - \text{Stock}}{\text{Creditors due within 1 year}}$	$\dfrac{4,135 - 1,901}{2,334} = 0.95{:}1$	$\dfrac{3,532 - 1,779}{2,026} = 0.87{:}1$

It is useful to consider what the acid test ratio means. In simple terms we are saying that in 2004 the business had £0.95 of liquid assets for every £1 of current liabilities. Therefore, if all the creditors had to be paid immediately, the business would not be able to do so (without having to obtain a loan). However, you need to remember that the accounts are prepared on a prudent basis and that the amounts owed to current creditors at the end of the financial year will be due at different times in the next financial year. Generally, the ratio should not fall below 1. However, this would not be true of all businesses. For example, some businesses give their customers 30 days' credit, but receive 90 days' credit from their suppliers. This results in a low level of debtors and higher level of creditors, varying according to the time of the year. It is difficult to generalize about ideal levels of liquidity, but in many industries there are benchmarks of what is considered to be a good ratio. In the case of the RWJ Group, we can say that the acid test ratio for 2004 shows some improvement over 2003.

Stock turnover is an efficiency ratio that measures the average number of times stock has been sold and replaced during the year. The formula is:

$$\dfrac{\text{Cost of sales}}{\text{Average stock}}$$

You need to look at the profit and loss account to obtain the figures for the average stock. If they are disclosed, you can use the following formula:

$$\dfrac{\text{Opening stock} + \text{Closing stock}}{2}$$

However, if a figure for opening stock is not provided, you can use closing stock as a proxy, which is what we have done for the RWJ Group.

Stock turnover

	2004	2003
$\dfrac{\text{Cost of sales}}{\text{Stock}}$	$\dfrac{6,519}{1,908} = 3.42 \text{ times}$	$\dfrac{5,537}{1,779} = 3.11 \text{ times}$

In general, the more frequently stock is turned over the better and the results show a slight improvement in 2004 compared to 2003.

The *debtor collection period* is an efficiency ratio that gives an indication of the effectiveness of the management of working capital. It measures the average time trade debtors (customers) have taken to pay the business for goods and services bought on credit over the year. The debtor collection period in days is calculated using the following formula:

$$\frac{\text{Trade debtors}}{\text{Turnover}} \times 365$$

If a breakdown of debtors is not given in the balance sheet, it is likely that the figure for trade debtors is given in the notes to the accounts, as in our example. We will now calculate the ratio for the RWJ Group.

Debtor collection period	2004	2003
$\frac{\text{Trade debtors}}{\text{Turnover}} \times 365$	$\frac{1,143}{11,275} \times 365 = 37$ days	$\frac{1,097}{10,010} \times 365 = 40$ days

The results show that trade debts have been collected in an average of 37 days in 2004, compared to 40 days in 2003. If the company's policy is to give customers 30 days' credit, then 45 days is the average length of the credit period. Therefore, a ratio of more than 45 days would indicate bad management. In this case, 37 days indicates good credit control and suggests that management is very efficient in collecting the money owed by trade debtors, although we would want to confirm these assumptions and make industry comparisons to ensure that we are drawing the correct conclusions.

The *creditor payment period* is an efficiency ratio that measures the average time that the business has taken to pay its trade creditors. The creditor payment period in days is calculated using the following formula:

$$\frac{\text{Trade creditors}}{\text{Purchases}} \times 365$$

If the figure for purchases is not disclosed, you can use the cost of sales figure, as we are going to do for the RWJ Group. This is not quite such a good measure because it is affected by changes in the level of stock. However, as long as we are consistent, it is possible to draw conclusions from it.

Creditor payment period	2004	2003
$\frac{\text{Trade creditors}}{\text{Purchases}} \times 376$	$\frac{1,590}{6,519} \times 365 = 89$ days	$\frac{1,350}{5,537} \times 365 = 89$ days

The interpretation of the results depends on the length of credit period agreed with trade creditors.

activity

It would appear that the directors of the RWJ Group have taken more than twice as long to pay the money owed to suppliers than they do to collect their debts from customers. Does this indicate efficient or inefficient cash management?

Although some people do not like debts and prefer to pay invoices and statements soon as they receive them rather than wait until they are due, this is not a good way of managing cash. Receiving goods on credit is the equivalent of having an interest-free loan. If the supplier does not give credit, the business may have to go into overdraft to pay cash for the goods. This does not mean that a business should wait until it receives a solicitor's letter or risk supplies being cut off, but from a business point of view, management should take the maximum time allowed to pay trade creditors, whilst collecting payment from trade debtors as quickly as possible. This is what the RWJ Group appears to be doing and shows efficient financial management.

If we had the data, it would be useful to analyse all the liquidity and efficiency ratios for the RWJ Group discussed in this section over a longer period of time to identify the trend. We could also compare them with similar businesses and industry benchmarks.

11.5 gearing ratios

One impact on the financial performance of a business is its financial structure. By this we mean the relationship between equity and long-term debt, which is known as *gearing* or *leverage*. *Gearing ratios* are used by investors and lenders to assess financial risk when a business has an obligation to service and repay long-term debt(s). The following are two of the main ratios used:

- Debt/equity
- Interest cover.

The *debt/equity ratio* describes the financial structure of the business in terms of the proportion of debt to equity. There are a number of different ways that debt and equity can be defined. We will define *debt* as creditors due after more than one year and *equity* as capital plus reserves. The ratio is shown as a percentage and the formula is:

$$\frac{\text{Creditors: amounts due after more than one year}}{\text{Capital} + \text{Reserves}} \times 100$$

We will now calculate the debt/equity ratio for the RWJ Group.

Debt/equity	2004	2003
$\frac{\text{Creditors due after} > 1 \text{ year}}{\text{Capital} + \text{Reserves}} \times 100$	$\frac{719}{3,359} \times 100 = 21.41\%$	$\frac{449}{3,147} \times 100 = 14.27\%$

The results show that the business was more highly geared in 2004 than in 2003 because it has borrowed more. The general interpretation is that the higher the gearing, the higher the risk that the business will be unable to pay the interest on its loans or make repayments in times of economic recession. This makes it a risky investment for shareholders. On the other hand, the higher the gearing, the higher the returns to shareholders will be in strong economic conditions.

The second ratio is *interest cover*, which assesses the relative safety of interest payments by measuring the number of times interest payable on long-term debt is covered by the available profits. This avoids problems related to differences in the definition of debt and equity. The formula is:

$$\frac{\text{Profit before interest and tax}}{\text{Interest payable}}$$

We will now calculate the interest cover for the RWJ Group.

Interest cover	2004	2003
$\dfrac{\text{PBIT}}{\text{Interest payable}}$	$\dfrac{846}{142} = 5.96$ times	$\dfrac{818}{139} = 5.88$ times

The results show that interest payable on debt finance was covered by profit before interest and tax nearly six times in both years, which seems very safe. We can also make a positive comment on the very small increase in cover in 2004, despite the company becoming more highly geared in 2004 compared to 2003 by increasing its long-term debts.

If the data were available it would be useful to analyse the gearing ratios for the RWJ Group discussed in this section over a longer period of time to identify the trend. We could also compare them with similar firms and industry benchmarks.

activity

Recalculate the ROCE, net profit margin and capital turnover for RWJ Group plc for 2004 using profit after interest instead of profit before interest and tax, and comment on the differences.

Check your calculations against the following:

2004 data	£000	£000
Return	846	704
Capital employed	4,242	4,242
Ratios	Using profit before interest	Using profit after interest
ROCE	19.94%	16.60%
Net profit margin	7.50%	6.24%
Capital turnover	2.66 times	2.66 times

In this activity, return has been defined as profit after interest, which is lower than when it is defined as profit before interest. Therefore, it is no surprise that ROCE has decreased from 19.94% to 16.6%. Net profit margin is also slightly lower but capital turnover is unaffected. If you consider the relationship of the figures, you will see that there is a good argument for not using capital employed when return is defined as profit after interest. This is because RWJ Group plc has long-term debts of £719,000 on which interest is paid. If return is defined as profit after interest, it is more logical to use the owner's investment only, and exclude the loan. This illustrates why there is no standard definition of the terms used in ratios, as this leaves users free to choose the most appropriate definition for the particular circumstances.

11.6 investment ratios

Investment ratios are used by investors, analysts and financial journalists to evaluate the shareholders' return and aid investment decisions. We are going to look at the following commonly used ratios:

- Return on equity
- Dividend net
- Yield gross
- Earnings per share
- Price/earnings.

The definitions we used to calculate the profitability ratio ROCE reflect our desire to evaluate management's ability to generate profits from capital employed. We defined capital employed as total assets less current liabilities. In order to make the balance sheet balance, this must be equal to capital and reserves (total shareholders' funds) plus long-term debt. We can demonstrate this with the RWJ Group data:

$$£4,242,000 = £3,359,000 + [£719,000 + £164,000]$$

From this you can see that ROCE does not take account of the gearing of the company because it includes both equity and debt. However, the investment ratio *return on equity (ROE)* excludes debt finance and focuses solely on the return generated on the investment of the shareholders' funds. Consequently, for ROE, we will define *return* as profit after tax (PAT) and *equity* as capital and reserves in the following formula:

$$\frac{PAT}{Capital + Reserves} \times 100$$

We are now ready to calculate ROE for the RWJ Group and compare it with our earlier results for ROCE.

	2004	2003
ROE		
$\dfrac{PAT}{Capital + Reserves} \times 100$	$\dfrac{422}{3,359} \times 100 = 12.58\%$	$\dfrac{407}{3,147} \times 100 = 12.95\%$
ROCE		
$\dfrac{PBIT}{Capital\ employed} \times 100$	$\dfrac{846}{4,242} \times 100 = 19.94\%$	$\dfrac{818}{3,613} \times 100 = 22.64\%$

You can see from this comparison that ROE shows a more modest return than ROCE.

The *dividend net* calculates the amount of dividend per share for the financial year and is also known as the *dividend per share*. The ratio is shown in pence and the formula is:

$$\frac{\text{Total dividends}}{\text{Number of ordinary shares}}$$

Substituting the figures for the RWJ Group in the formula, we obtain the following results:

Dividend net	2004	2003
$\dfrac{\text{Total dividends}}{\text{No. of ordinary shares}}$	$\dfrac{172}{2,332}$ = £0.0738 or 7.38p	$\dfrac{122}{2,320}$ = £0.0526 or 5.26p

The results show a low dividend per share, but you need to remember that in both years only a proportion of the profit was paid out in dividends, whilst the remainder was retained to help the business grow. The good news for investors is that the dividend net increased by slightly over 2p per share in 2004 compared to 2003, reflecting the increase in the proportion of total dividends to the number of called-up shares.

The *yield gross* builds on the above ratio and measures the dividend yielded on a share in relation to the current market price of the share. For this reason, it is also known as the *dividend yield*. The answer is shown as a percentage and the formula is:

$$\frac{\text{Dividend net}}{\text{Share price}} \times 100$$

If the share price of RWJ Group plc on the last day of the financial year was 227p in 2004 and 202p in 2003, the yield gross for the two years was as shown below.

Yield gross	2004	2003
$\dfrac{\text{Dividend net}}{\text{Share price}} \times 100$	$\dfrac{7.38}{277} \times 100 = 2.66\%$	$\dfrac{5.26}{202} \times 100 = 2.60\%$

These results show a low yield gross for both years. There is little difference between the two years because the higher dividend net in 2004 is balanced by a higher share price.

The next ratio we are going to illustrate is the *earnings per share (EPS)*, which we referred to in Chapter 10. Profit retained in the company to help it grow still belongs to the shareholders and therefore the dividend they receive is only part of the return on their investment. The EPS figure shows the total return, as it is based on the total profit available to ordinary shareholders. Like the dividend net, it is shown in pence per share and the formula is:

$$\frac{\text{Profit attributable to ordinary shareholders}}{\text{Number of ordinary shares}}$$

We will now insert the figures for the RWJ Group into the formula:

EPS	2004	2003
Profit for ordinary shareholders / No. of ordinary shares	$\frac{362}{2,332}$ = £0.1552 or 15.5p	$\frac{352}{2,320}$ = £0.1517 or 15.2p

The EPS is a measure on which many shareholders place considerable weight. In the case of the RWJ Group, there was a very small increase in 2004, but in both years the total return was just over 15p per share, which indicates a similar profit performance for shareholders in both years.

The final ratio is based on the EPS and is called the *price/earnings (P/E) ratio*. This compares the amount invested in one share with the EPS and reflects the stock market's view on how long the current level of earnings per share will be sustained. It is measured in years and the formula is:

$$\frac{\text{Share price}}{\text{Earnings per share}}$$

activity

Using the above formula, calculate the P/E ratio for the RWJ Group and interpret your results.

Calculating the ratios should be straightforward. Check your answer against the following:

P/E	2004	2003
Share price / Earnings per share	$\frac{277}{15.5}$ = 18 years	$\frac{202}{15.2}$ = 13 years

The higher the P/E ratio the better, as it reflects the stock market's confidence in the company's financial prospects. In this case, the higher P/E ratio in 2004 is a positive sign and indicates that the market believes that the RWJ Group has a bright future and is therefore willing to pay more for its shares than the current level of earnings would justify.

As we have noted at the end of our discussion of each group of ratios in this chapter, if the data were available, it would be useful to analyse the investment ratios we have looked at for the RWJ Group over a longer period of time to identify the trend. We could also compare them with similar firms and industry benchmarks. This would allow us to comment further.

11.7 limitations of ratio analysis

Ultimately the choice of analysis depends on the needs of the user and the availability of the data. The possibility that the data required for a particular ratio may not be available leads us to consider the limitations of ratio analysis, as like any other technique there are always a number of drawbacks. The main limitations are as follows:

- There are no agreed definitions of the terms used, so ratios based on different definitions will not be comparable.
- The figures needed to calculate the ratios may not be disclosed and less precise alternatives may have to be used.
- Comparative data may not be available for previous periods (for example trend analysis is not possible for a new business).
- Comparative data may not be available for similar companies in the same industry (for example if the business operates in a niche market and there are no industry benchmarks).
- Figures in financial statements may be misleading if there is high inflation, window dressing (any creative accounting practice that attempts to make a situation look better than it really is. For example, changes in short-term funding have the effect of disguising or improving the reported liquidity position) unscrupulous manipulation, or if an unusual accounting treatment has been used (normally figures for earlier years are adjusted in published trends if a significant change has taken place).
- The financial statements do not take account of non-financial factors. Therefore, not all aspects of a business that should be taken into account are captured by ratio analysis. For example, does the business have sound plans for the future, a good reputation, a strong customer base, reliable suppliers, loyal employees? Does it have obsolete assets, strong competitors or poor industrial relations? Does it have activities in a high risk industry?

Despite these drawbacks, ratio analysis is an invaluable method for interpreting the financial statements of an organization. Users should not treat ratios as absolute answers, but as an indication of where further investigation might be directed to find out the underlying reasons for the financial performance or position.

11.8 conclusions

In this chapter we have examined a technique for analysing the financial statements of a business known as ratio analysis. This type of analysis is widely used by management, investors and the other user groups we described in Chapter 2. There is a wide range of ratios that can be calculated and we have described some of the main ones. We have looked at a number of profitability ratios, considered the relationship between them and identified the role of management in bringing about improvements in the operating performance of a business. We have also examined some of the most widely used liquidity and efficiency ratios, gearing ratios and investment ratios.

In order to interpret ratios effectively, there needs to be some basis of comparison. This can be between businesses in the same industrial sector or a particular business and the industry benchmark. Comparison of ratios between the current period and the preceding period for a particular business and trend analysis is also useful. Ultimately the choice of analysis depends on the needs of the user and the availability of the data. In this chapter we have considered the main limitations of ratio analysis, but despite some drawbacks, you need to remember that this method of interpreting financial statements is one of the most useful and commonly used techniques in the financial world.

practice questions

1. Explain the purpose of ratio analysis and describe the main limitations of the technique as a tool for evaluating the financial statements of a business.

2. The following extracts are taken from the financial statements of Adams Ltd and Evelyn Ltd.

	Adams Ltd £	Evelyn Ltd £
Capital employed	281,000	596,000
Profit before interest and tax	29,500	41,500
Gross profit	71,400	156,200
Turnover	354,900	706,260

Required

(a) Calculate the main profitability ratios for both companies.

(b) Suggest reasons for any differences you find.

3. The following financial statements are for Orchard Fruits plc, which has gone through a period of expansion.

Orchard Fruits plc
Profit and loss account for the year ending 31 December 2004

	2004 £000	2004 £000	2003 £000	2003 £000
Turnover		560		350
Cost of sales		462		280
Gross profit		98		70
Administration expenses	11		11	
Sales and distribution costs	16	27	10	21
Operating profit		71		49
Net interest payable		5		5
Profit on ordinary activities before taxation		66		44
Taxation		22		14
Profit attributable to shareholders		44		30
Proposed dividends		14		5
Retained profit		30		25

Orchard Fruits plc
Balance sheet as at 31 December 2004

	2004 £000	2004 £000	2003 £000	2003 £000
Fixed assets				
Land and buildings		155		85
Equipment		120		70
		275		155
Current assets				
Stock	98		56	
Trade debtors	84		35	
Cash at bank and in hand	63		84	
	245		175	
Creditors: amounts due within one year				
Trade creditors	(28)		(35)	
Taxation	(22)		(14)	
Proposed dividends	(14)		(5)	
Net current assets		181		121
Total assets less current liabilities		456		276
Creditors: amounts due after more than one year				
10% debentures		(50)		(50)
Total net assets		406		226
Capital and reserves				
Called-up share capital (ordinary shares of £1 each)		300		150
General reserve		26		19
Profit and loss account		80		57
Total shareholders' funds		406		226
Note				
Share price		150p		200p

Required

Analyse the financial statements for Orchard Fruits plc by calculating the following ratios for both years:

(a) Return on capital employed
(b) Net profit margin
(c) Capital turnover
(d) Gross profit margin
(e) Acid test
(f) Stock turnover
(g) Debtor collection period
(h) Creditor payment period.

For each ratio, include the formula in words, your workings and append brief comments that explain and interpret your results.

4. Analyse the financial statements for Orchard Fruits plc given in the previous question by calculating the following ratios:

(a) Debt/equity

(b) Interest cover
(c) Return on equity
(d) Dividend net
(e) Yield gross
(f) Earnings per share
(g) Price/earnings.

For each ratio, include the formula in words, your workings and append brief comments that explain and interpret your results.

5. The annual financial statements for Toni's Takeaway plc for the year ending 31 December 2004 are set out below.

Toni's Takeaway plc
Profit and loss account for the year ending 31 December 2004

	2004 £000	£000	£000	2003 £000
Turnover		53,109		43,825
Cost of sales		(28,054)		(23,132)
Gross profit		25,055		20,693
Administration expenses	(11,813)		(10,230)	
Sales and distribution costs	(8,663)		(7,150)	
Other operating income and expenditure	(16)	(20,492)	(99)	(17,479)
Profit on ordinary activities before interest and taxation		4,563		3,214
Net interest payable		(324)		(352)
Profit on ordinary activities before taxation		4,239		2,862
Taxation		(1,404)		(858)
Profit attributable to shareholders		2,835		2,004
Dividends		(1,018)		(668)
Retained profit		1,817		1,336

Toni's Takeaway plc
Balance sheet as at 31 December 2004

	2004 £000	£000	£000	2003 £000
Fixed assets				
Intangible assets		2,386		2,484
Tangible assets		13,685		12,181
Investments in joint venture		307		277
		16,378		14,942
Current assets				
Stock	1,411		1,260	
Debtors (See Note 1)	10,702		8,421	
Cash at bank and in hand	3,885		3,231	
	15,998		12,912	
Creditors: amounts falling due within one year	(12,919)		(10,203)	

Net current assets	3,079	2,709
Total assets less current liabilities	19,457	17,651
Creditors: amounts falling due after more than one year	(7,756)	(8,053)
Total net assets	11,701	9,598
Capital and reserves		
Called up share capital	2,546	2,518
Share premium account	2,395	2,192
Reserves	4,943	3,552
Profit and loss account	1,817	1,336
Total shareholders' funds	11,701	9,598

Notes		
1 Of which trade debtors (£000)	2,533	2,621
2 Number of shares issued (000)	50,920	50,360

Required

(a) Analyse the financial statements for Toni's Takeaway plc by calculating and comparing the following ratios for the two years 2004 and 2003.

- Net profit margin
- Debtor collection period
- Stock turnover
- Interest cover
- Earnings per share.

For each ratio, include the formula in words, your workings and append brief comments that explain and interpret your results.

(b) Give five limitations of the analysis you have conducted.

management
accounting

importance of cost information

Learning objectives

When you have studied this chapter, you should be able to:

- Explain why it is important to know the cost of making a product or providing a service

- Distinguish between direct costs and indirect costs

- Construct a simple statement to calculate the total cost per unit

- Calculate the selling price based on the total cost per unit.

12.1 introduction

As you will remember from earlier chapters in this book, the purpose of financial accounting is to give information about the entire organization primarily to external users, and the format and content of the financial statements are guided by accounting principles and, in the case of limited liability entities, rules. In this third part of the book, we focus on management accounting, which has evolved from financial accounting and is concerned with techniques that provide information to internal users.

In this and the next five chapters we are going to look at a particular aspect of management accounting known as cost accounting, which is concerned with providing timely and detailed information to management about the cost of manufacturing goods or providing services. In this chapter we start by looking at why management needs systems for supplying detailed information about costs and clarifying what we mean by cost. We also explain what is meant by a cost unit and a cost centre and the various ways in which cost can be classified. We then demonstrate how the elements of cost are built up to calculate the total cost per unit and how this cost information can be used to establish the selling price per unit.

12.2 management's need for information

Research suggests that accounting systems and the information they provide develop according to management's needs; in other words, on a contingency basis (Gordon and Miller, 1976; Chapman, 1997). During the early stages of the development of the business, the owner-manager obtains information using informal methods and relies on tacit knowledge. As the number of business transactions increase, this informal personal control by the owner-manager becomes stretched and is replaced by formal delegated methods. This does not mean that formerly information and control had been poor, but that they are no longer appropriate to the size and complexity of the business (Perren, Berry and Partridge, 1999).

Table 12.1 summarizes the key characteristics of small firms and compares them with those of their larger counterparts, where it is likely that the need for more detailed and timely information will have led to the development of formal systems of control.

TABLE 12.1 **Typical characteristics of small and large firms**

Small firms	Large firms
Typically 1–2 owners	Many owners
Likely to be owner-managed	Managed by managers/directors
Little delegation of control	Control is delegated
Operations are relatively simple	Operations are complex and divided into functional areas
Multitasking is common	Need for functional specialists
Systems tend to be informal	Systems tend to be formal
Reliance on tacit knowledge	Reliance on explicit information

In order to run a business successfully, those responsible for management need to know the *cost* of running the business. Costs include:

- the cost of goods sold in a trading business, the cost of goods manufactured in a manufacturing business or the cost of services sold in a business in the service sector
- the overhead expenses and other expenditure.

There are a number of different ways of defining cost, but we will start with a general definition.

KEY DEFINITION Cost is the amount of expenditure incurred on goods and services required to carry out the economic activities of the entity.

The calculation of the cost of sales for a sole trader is:

Opening stock + Purchases – Closing stock

You will remember from Chapter 8 that the accounting principles guide the accountant to value opening stock and purchases at the historical cost, and to value closing stock prudently at the lower of cost or net realizable value. Therefore, calculating the cost of goods sold for a trading business is relatively straightforward. However, calculating of the cost of goods manufactured (for an entity in the manufacturing sector) or calculating the cost of services (for an entity in the service sector) is more complex. This is made even more difficult if more than one type of product or service is produced, because the cost of each one must be built up from the individual elements of cost that can be identified.

activity To understand the importance of cost information, it is useful to consider why managers need such information. Why do you think managers of a business in the manufacturing sector need to know the cost of making a product or supplying a service?

Business is about making money and those responsible for managing the business are charged with the responsibility for making sure that the business makes a profit. Therefore, the main reasons why managers need to have cost information are:

- To *value stock* – In a manufacturing business, managers need cost information to help them value stocks of raw materials, work-in-progress and unsold finished goods.
- To *plan production* – It would be very difficult to determine the best way to plan production without knowing the relevant costs. It is necessary to know the cost of all the elements making up the production process and the funds required to support them. Such costs are not confined to materials and labour, but also include machinery, buildings, transport, administration, maintenance and many other items.

- To *maintain control* – Managers have no control if they do not know the costs incurred and are unable to compare them with the original plan. This would lead to the organization's resources being employed inefficiently, resulting in waste and, in the worst circumstances, the complete failure of the organization.
- To *aid decision making* – It is imperative that managers have knowledge of costs for the correct decisions to be taken. For example, managers need information about costs to decide whether it would be worthwhile investing in new manufacturing machinery, to evaluate alternative ways of carrying out activities and to determine the selling prices of products and services.

Although we have used an example of a manufacturing business, many of the above reasons apply to businesses in other sectors.

activity

Having stressed the importance of knowing the costs involved in making a product or providing a service, they are not always easy to identify. Imagine that you buy a box of 10 computer disks for £15 on Friday. On Sunday a friend asks you to sell him one for some urgent work he is doing. You know that if you were to replace that single disk on Monday it would cost you £2.00. What is the cost of the disk?

(a) £1.50

(b) £2.00

(c) Both these figures

(d) Neither of these figures

You may have answered this by taking the original cost of 10 disks (£15) and dividing it by the number of disks to reach the answer of £1.50, or you may have decided that the cost is Monday's price of £2.00. You may be surprised to know that in some senses all the answers are correct. However, to decide the most appropriate answer, we need to define what we mean by cost precisely and put it in a context. As you can see, one difficulty we have is that our view of cost is determined by:

- whether we are buyers or sellers
- the context in which we are making our calculations
- our reasons for wanting the information.

12.3 cost accounting

To meet managers' needs for precise information about costs, a branch of management accounting known as *cost accounting* has developed, which is based on analysing the costs relating to cost units and cost centres.

KEY DEFINITION | Cost accounting is the process of collecting, processing and presenting financial and quantitative data within an entity to ascertain the cost of the cost centres and cost units.

All organizations provide an identifiable output which may be in the form of a service, a product or both. The output of a business can be measured by devising some form of *cost unit*. A cost unit is a quantitative unit of the product or service to which costs are allocated. The type of cost unit depends on the type of industry. In a manufacturing industry there may be a large number of identical products. For example, a brick manufacturer may have a cost unit of 1,000 bricks, because the cost of one brick is so small that it would be difficult to measure. In the service sector the cost unit may be of a more abstract nature. For example, in a hotel the cost unit may be a room occupied.

activity

Suggest appropriate cost units for the following businesses:

(a) A car manufacturer

(b) A carrier bag manufacturer

(c) A transport business

(d) A plumber

(e) A sports and leisure centre

(f) A hairdresser

Some of these businesses may have been more difficult than others to find suitable cost units for, particularly if you are not familiar with the industries. However, you may have identified some of the following types of cost unit:

- A car manufacturer producing a range of different models could use each model as a cost unit. If the same organization manufactures the engine, gearbox, body and electrical system, these could also be treated as separate cost units.
- A carrier bag manufacturer has the same problems as a brick manufacturer: the costs identified with manufacturing one carrier bag are so small that they cannot be measured. Therefore, a suitable cost unit might be 1,000 bags of each type produced.
- A transport business is a bit more difficult. You need to consider what information management would find useful. This might be the costs associated with moving 1 tonne of goods over one mile. Therefore, the cost unit will be 1 tonne/mile.
- Plumbers often work on a number of small jobs, which may vary from fitting a bathroom suite to replacing a tap washer. The plumber needs to know the cost of each job and so a suitable cost unit would be each job.
- In the case of a sports and leisure centre, the management needs to know the separate cost of supplying badminton, squash, swimming, table tennis, keep fit and so on for a period of time. Therefore, a suitable cost unit would be each activity for an hour.

- A hairdresser is likely to offer a number of standard services, such as cut and blow dry, restyling, colouring and so on. Therefore, a suitable cost unit would be each standard service.

As you can see from these examples, many businesses offer a range of different products or services. Before the cost of each product or service can be calculated, a quantitative unit must be identified to which costs can be allocated.

KEY DEFINITION	A cost unit is a unit of production for which costs are collected.

The cost unit can be:

- the final product (for example a chair or a table in a furniture factory)
- a subassembly of a more complex product (for example a car chassis in the motor industry)
- a batch of products where the unit cost of an individual product is very small (for example a batch of 120 light bulbs in a light bulb factory).

In a manufacturing organization it should be fairly easy to identify the cost units as being the products made. In a service organization there may not be any identifiable cost units. In a hotel, the cost unit used might be the room occupancy; in a distribution company a cost unit might be a tonne/mile (the cost involved in moving 1 tonne of goods one mile); in a dating agency it may be the cost of matching one couple.

As well as calculating the costs for each cost unit, an organization will probably also need to know the costs for particular *cost centres*. A cost centre is an identifiable part of an organization for which costs can be collected. It may be based on a function, a department, section, individual, or any group of these.

activity

Indicate which of the following could be cost centres in the following two businesses:

Toy manufacturer	Hotel
Assembly department	Kitchen
Stores department	Cost of drinks sold
Sales team	Reception area
Specialized moulding machine	Laundry
Clerical salaries	Restaurant

You may not know anything about the manufacture of toys, but the definition of a cost centre given above should have helped you to identify the first four of these as possible cost centres. Clerical salaries are usually an expense, not a cost centre. The specialized moulding machine may be a cost centre if it is sufficiently important and complex to allow a number of costs to be identified with that particular activity. Of course, not all toy manufacturers would use the above cost centres, but they are all areas of activity where managers may need to know the costs. As far as the hotel is concerned, the cost of drinks sold is an item of expense, but all the others are potential cost centres.

KEY DEFINITION	A cost centre is a designated location, function, activity or item of equipment for which costs are collected.

Cost centres are of two main types:

- *production cost centres* are those concerned with making a product
- *service cost centres* provide a service to other parts of the organization.

Identifying cost centres is relatively easy as they are usually clearly defined. One example is that of a factory canteen or a college refectory. In a manufacturing business, departments may be referred to as shops (for example the machine shop). The sort of financial information that would be available for a canteen includes employees' wages, the cost of electricity used for cooking, lighting and heating, the cost of food and beverages and so on, and the meals may be used as the cost units.

Figure 12.1 shows typical cost centres in a light bulb factory where costs are collected for a cost unit consisting of a batch of 120 light bulbs.

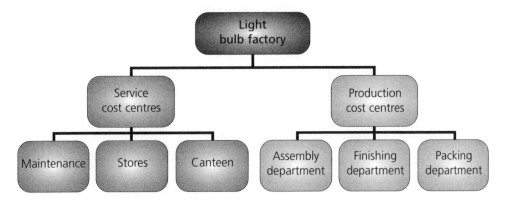

FIGURE 12.1 **Typical cost centres in a factory**

Some organizations do not formally identify their cost centres or cost units, but answering the following questions should help you to identify them:

- What can be regarded as the cost centres and cost units in the organization?
- What financial information is generated in respect of potential cost centres and cost units?
- Is someone directly responsible for any of them or able to influence them?

12.4 classifying costs and expenses

Expenditure can be divided into *capital expenditure*, which is spending on fixed assets that are capitalized in the balance sheet and *revenue expenditure*, which is spending that is written off to the profit and loss account in the period in which it is incurred. Although it is useful to know the total revenue expenditure for an accounting period, it is even more useful if revenue expenditure is broken down into individual costs and expenses. By classifying costs, we can obtain more detailed information and use it in a variety of ways for planning, controlling and decision making. In addition, classifying costs helps us to understand better what is meant by the term cost.

Costs can be classified by:

- Nature of the cost, such as those that can be identified for materials, labour and expenses, and those for materials that can be divided into the different types of raw materials, maintenance materials, cleaning materials and so on.
- Function of costs, such as production costs, administration costs, selling and distribution costs.
- Whether they are *product costs*, which can be identified with the cost unit and are part of the value of stock, or *period costs*, such as selling and administration costs, which are deducted as expenses in the current period.
- Whether they are *direct costs*, which can be identified with a specific cost unit, or *indirect costs*, which cannot be identified with a specific cost unit, although they may be traced directly to a particular cost centre. Indirect costs must be shared by the cost units. Examples of direct costs are the cost of materials used to make a product; the cost of labour if employees are paid according to the number of products made or services provided; the cost of expenses, such as subcontract work. Examples of indirect costs are expenses such as rent and managers' salaries.
- Behaviour of the cost and whether they are *variable costs*, which in total change in proportion with the level of production activity or *fixed costs*, which are not changed by fluctuations in production levels. Direct costs are usually variable and indirect costs are usually fixed. Examples of direct costs that are fixed are patents, licences and copyright relating to a particular product and some direct expenses such as the hire of a particular piece of equipment to produce a specific order.

Figure 12.2 summarizes this typology.

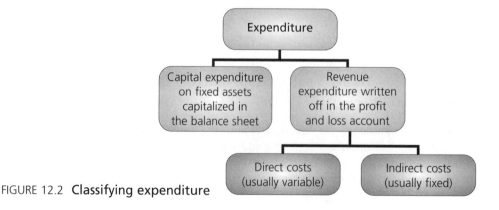

FIGURE 12.2 **Classifying expenditure**

Classify the following costs into direct costs, indirect costs, variable costs and fixed costs:

Materials used in the product   Canteen
Cost of renting the factory   Supervisors' salaries
Insurance of the factory   Production workers' wages
Depreciation   Accountants' salaries
Maintenance of machinery

Even if you do not have any experience of working in a manufacturing environment, you should have been able to work out the answers from the definitions of direct and indirect costs. Materials can be identified with the product and are therefore direct costs; so too are the production workers' wages, if they are paid according to the number of units produced rather than a flat rate irrespective of the level of production. Rent, insurance, maintenance of machinery, canteen and the salaries cannot be identified with a single product, but must be shared over a number of products, therefore these are indirect costs. In a service industry, the same principles apply.

You may have had more difficulty in distinguishing between fixed and variable costs. One thing you may have noticed is that direct costs in our example are also variable costs and the indirect costs are also fixed costs. For example, the materials used in the product can be identified directly with the product, and the more items produced, the higher the total cost of materials used. Therefore, these product direct costs are variable costs. On the other hand, rent and insurance for the period remain the same, regardless of the quantity of products produced, therefore these are classified as fixed costs.

We will now look more closely at the difference between fixed and variable costs using an example. Sam Reeves has a taxi business. The average mileage by a taxi for three months is 15,000 miles and the following table shows the quarterly costs, analysed by nature:

Expense	Cost per quarter £
Driver's salary	2,670
Petrol and oil	1,050
Annual service	450
Tax and insurance	1,110
Depreciation	870

We can use the details of Sam's business expenses as the basis for calculating further cost information. For example, we can add up the costs so that Sam can find out that the total costs per quarter for one taxi are £6,150. From this we can calculate the total cost per mile:

$$\frac{\text{Total costs}}{\text{Total mileage}} = \frac{£6,150}{15,000 \text{ miles}} = 41\text{p per mile}$$

We can now calculate the cost per mile for each of the expenses:

Expense	Cost per quarter	Cost per mile
	£	Pence
Driver's salary	2,670	17.8
Petrol and oil	1,050	7.0
Annual service	450	3.0
Tax and insurance	1,110	7.4
Depreciation	870	5.8
Total	6,150	41.0

Sam now has a considerable amount of information, including the total cost per mile, which is further analysed by the nature of the expense. However, there are some problems if Sam tries to use this cost information without understanding the difference between fixed and variable costs. For example, he may want to know what the cost is per mile if the taxi travelled 30,000 miles in one quarter. Your immediate response may be to say that the cost per mile would remain at 41p. However, on consideration, you may have seen that the cost per mile is likely to be lower. This is because the total fixed costs (the cost of the driver's salary, taxation, insurance and depreciation) will remain the same, even though the mileage has doubled. On the other hand, the total variable costs (the cost of petrol and oil) will change in direct proportion to the change in the level of activity. This means that if activity doubles (in our example, if mileage doubles), the variable costs will double. We shall be looking at the importance of fixed and variable costs again in Chapter 16, but for the moment you need to remember that calculating the average total cost per unit can be misleading if there are significant changes in the activity level of the business.

12.5 elements of total cost

The *total cost* of a product or cost unit is built up from a number of different elements. In order to identify these elements, costs are classified according to their nature, function, whether they are product or period costs and whether they are direct costs or indirect costs, as we described in the previous section. The following cost statement shows the elements of total cost in a typical manufacturing business.

Total cost statement

	£	£
Product direct costs		
Direct materials	X	
Direct labour	X	
Direct expenses	X	
Prime cost		X
Production overheads		X
Production cost		X
Indirect costs		
Administration overheads	X	
Selling and distribution overheads	X	
Research and development overheads	X	X
Total cost		X

The elements of total cost consist of direct costs (such as the cost of direct materials, direct labour and direct expenses) that can be traced directly to the cost unit. When added together, these give what is known as the *prime cost*. The production overheads (the indirect production costs that cannot easily be traced to the cost unit) are then added to give the *production cost*. Finally, the non-production overheads are added to arrive at the total cost.

KEY DEFINITIONS	A direct cost is expenditure that can be directly traced to a cost unit.
	An indirect cost is revenue expenditure that cannot be traced directly to a cost unit and is therefore an overhead cost.

Direct costs can be classified as:

- *direct materials*, which are the cost of materials and components used to make the product
- *direct labour*, which are the costs of employing the workforce that converts the direct materials into the finished product
- *direct expenses*, which are not always incurred but include such costs as subcontract work or special tools and equipment bought for a particular order.

Indirect costs can be classified as:

- *administration overheads*, which are the non-production costs of operating the business
- *selling and distribution overheads*, which are the costs of promoting, selling and delivering the products (and any after-sales services)
- *research and development overheads*, which are not always present but are the costs associated with developing or improving products and production processes.

activity

Jon Hazel is the owner-manager of a small business called Hazelwood Products Ltd that makes 10 traditionally crafted bookcases per week. The costs for week ending 7 January are:

Direct materials	£440
Direct labour	£660
Production overheads	£200
Administration overheads	£80
Selling and distribution overheads	£60

The business has no direct expenses or research and development overheads. Using the following pro forma, calculate the total cost for the week.

```
                    Hazelwood Products Ltd
              Total cost w/e 7 January (10 bookcases)
                                              £           £
        Direct costs
           Direct materials
           Direct labour                   _____
        Prime cost
        Production overheads                            _____
        Production cost
        Indirect costs
           Administration overheads
           Selling and distribution overheads  _____   _____
        Total cost
                                                        ══════
```

Your answer should look like this:

```
                    Hazelwood Products Ltd
              Total cost w/e 7 January (10 bookcases)
                                              £           £
        Direct costs
           Direct materials                  440
           Direct labour                     660
        Prime cost                                     1,100
        Production overheads                             200
        Production cost                                1,300
        Indirect costs
           Administration overheads           80
           Selling and distribution overheads 60         140
        Total cost                                     1,440
                                                       ══════
```

Now he knows the total cost per week, Jon can ensure that the business has sufficient funds to support these costs. The most important source of funds will be the sales revenue generated from selling the bookcases and further analysis of the above cost information will help Jon decide on an appropriate selling price for the bookcases.

activity

Using the same layout as before, construct a statement showing the total cost per unit (in this case, one bookcase). As this is a very simple business, you can apportion the overheads by dividing them by the number of units produced. In addition, calculate the selling price if Hazelwood Products Ltd wants to make a profit that represents a mark up of 40% on the production cost.

You should have found this fairly straightforward and the answer is given below.

```
┌─────────────────────────────────────────────────────────┐
│                Hazelwood Products Ltd                     │
│                  Total cost (1 unit)                      │
│                                        £           £      │
│    Direct costs                                           │
│        Direct materials                44                 │
│        Direct labour                   66                 │
│    Prime cost                                     110     │
│    Production overheads                            20     │
│    Production cost                                130     │
│    Indirect costs                                         │
│        Administration overheads         8                 │
│        Selling and distribution overheads   6      14     │
│    Total cost                                     144     │
│    Add Profit (130 x 40%)                          52     │
│    Selling price                                  196     │
└─────────────────────────────────────────────────────────┘
```

The total cost per unit is £144 and all you need to do is add the profit element based on 40% of the production cost (£130 × 40% = £52) to arrive at a selling price of £196. In other words, if each bookcase is sold for £196, the total cost per unit of £144 will be covered and the business will make a profit of £52.

12.6 conclusions

In this chapter we have looked the importance of cost information to those responsible for the management of a business, particularly those in the manufacturing and service sectors. Cost accounting techniques require costs to be classified so that the cost of all the designated cost centres and cost units can be ascertained. Production cost centres are those concerned with making a product, while service costs centres provide a service to other parts of the organization. A cost unit can be the final product, a subassembly or a batch of products.

The classification of costs involves distinguishing between direct and indirect costs, variable and fixed costs, the nature of costs and the function of costs. The cost per unit is calculated by identifying the different elements of cost: the direct costs plus a fair share of the indirect costs. A percentage mark-up representing profit can be added to the cost of per unit to establish the selling price per unit.

practice questions

1. Explain the purpose of cost accounting and why it is important for managers to have cost information.
2. Describe the main classifications of cost.
3. Classify the following costs incurred in a manufacturing business into production costs, selling costs, distribution costs and administration costs:

Factory rent	Delivery drivers' salaries
Insurance of office buildings	Factory security guards' salaries
Electricity for powering machinery	Piecework wages paid to factory
Electricity for office lighting and	operatives
heating	Salary paid to managing director's
Tax and insurance of delivery	secretary
vehicles	Salaries paid to factory canteen staff
Depreciation of factory machinery	Fees paid to advertising agency
Depreciation of office equipment	Maintenance of machinery
Commission paid to sales team	Accounting software
Salaries paid to accounts office staff	Bonuses for factory staff
Factory manager's salary	Training course for clerical staff

4. Petra is the owner-manager of Petra Pots, which makes plant pots. The business plans to produce 2,000 units over the next month and each unit requires the same amount of materials and takes the same time to produce. The expected costs for next month are as follows:

	£
Rent	
Factory	1,000
Office	400
Lighting and heating	
Factory	2,000
Office	800
Power	700
Factory wages	
Operators (piecework)	10,000
Maintenance staff (fixed)	1,500
Canteen staff (fixed)	2,500
Sand, cement and clay	6,000
Depreciation	
Moulds	2,200
Factory fixtures and fittings	800
Office equipment	200
Office salaries	1,800
Sales team's salaries and commission	2,200
Sales team's car expenses	1,600
Delivery expenses	500
Cement mixer repairs	900
Finishing paint	200
Packing	800

Required

(a) Construct a costing statement for Petra Pots that shows the elements of cost and calculates the total cost of producing 2,000 pots.

(b) Interpret your statement by explaining the following terms:
- (i) Direct costs
- (ii) Prime cost
- (iii) Production cost
- (iv) Indirect costs
- (v) Total cost.

5. Using the information for Petra Pots in Question 4, construct a statement that shows the elements of total cost for one unit (as this is a very simple business, you can apportion the overheads by dividing them by the number of units produced). In addition, calculate the selling price of one unit if the business requires a profit margin based on 50% of the production cost.

references

Chapman, C. S. (1997) 'Reflections on a contingent view of accounting', *Accounting Organizations and Society*, pp. 189–205.

Gordon, L. A. and Miller, D. (1976) 'A contingency framework for the design of accounting information systems', *Accounting Organizations and Society*, **1**(1): 59–69.

Perren, L., Berry, A. and Partridge, M. (1999) 'The evolution of management information, control and decision-making processes in small growth-orientated service sector businesses: Exploratory lessons from four cases of success', *Journal of Small Business and Enterprise Development*, **5**(4): 351–61.

costing for product direct costs

Learning objectives

When you have studied this chapter, you should be able to:

- Describe the main stages in controlling direct materials

- Calculate the cost of direct materials and closing stock using different costing methods

- Describe the advantages and disadvantages of different costing methods

- Describe and apply methods for costing direct labour and direct expenses.

13.1 introduction

In Chapter 12 we identified the prime cost as one of the key components of the total cost of a cost unit. In this chapter we are going to examine the individual elements of the prime cost, which are the product direct costs relating to direct materials, direct labour and direct expenses.

Even in the smallest business, the minimum information required is the total for each of these different elements of cost that are incurred in producing the cost units. However, management usually needs more detailed information and a breakdown of the cost of each product or service helps them in their responsibility for planning, controlling and decision making. For example, managers need to know the cost of all the different materials used in making a product, the cost of the different types of labour in the factory, maintenance department, stores and canteen and any direct expenses. Once systems have been established to collect this detailed information, the total cost of direct materials, the total cost of direct labour and the total cost of any direct expenses can be calculated for each product or service. For example, a car manufacturer can establish the prime cost of making a particular model; a civil engineering company can establish the prime cost of constructing a particular building; and a plumber can establish the prime cost for a particular job.

In this chapter we start by describing the procedures and documents used to record and control the purchase and receipt of materials used to produce a product or cost unit. We go on to examine two methods that are used for pricing issues of direct materials from stores and valuing the remaining stock. We also describe the procedures and documents used to record the direct labour costs associated with each cost unit, which are related to the methods of remuneration for employees involved in production process. Finally, we discuss the difficulty of identifying direct expenses.

13.2 material control

In a manufacturing business the control of materials used in the production process is essential. *Material control* is necessary to ensure that production is not delayed due to shortages of materials and it is equally important that the business does not tie up capital by storing excess quantities of stock. In a well-managed business, materials are available in the right place, at the right time and in the right quantities, and all materials are properly accounted for.

KEY DEFINITION	Materials are the supplies of raw materials, components or subassemblies used to make a product.

The cost of materials purchased from a supplier is classified as revenue expenditure. Materials can be divided into direct materials, which feature in the final product produced (such as wood and metal in furniture), or indirect materials, which are necessary to carry out production but do not feature in the final product (such as maintenance and cleaning materials). Initially, deliveries of materials are taken to the place where they will be stored (the stores) and records are kept of quantities received and prices paid. Depending on the amount of space needed to house the materials, the stores may consist of anything from a small stockroom to a large warehouse or secure yard from which they can be issued conveniently to production when they are required.

Some organizations have just-in-time (JIT) manufacturing systems in which products are produced in time to meet demand, rather than producing products in case they are needed. This greatly reduces or eliminates the need for large stocks of materials. In some organizations the value of materials in stores is very high, for example precious metals or other scarce resources used in the production process. Records should be maintained of the quantity of goods in store and it is essential that a physical count is made because of the possibility of errors and theft. This is known as *stocktaking* and should be done at least annually. It requires a substantial amount of work and can be very disruptive. Some organizations use continuous stocktaking, where employees check a few items every day so that all stock is checked at least once a year.

The stores often carry many hundreds of different types of materials. Therefore the business requires an efficient and accurate system for recording and controlling the cost of materials. This can be either a manual or a computerized system. Although managers devise material control systems and procedures to suit their particular needs, there are a number of different prime documents used at each stage and each of these forms must be properly completed and authorized. The main stages in material control are as follows:

- The stores or production department sends a *purchase requisition* to the purchasing department, giving details of the quantity and type of materials required.
- The buyer in the purchasing department sends a *purchase order* to the supplier.
- The supplier sends the materials with a *goods received note*, which is checked against the materials received and the purchase order.
- The materials are added to the existing stock in the stores and the quantity is added to the stock level shown on the *bin card*.
- When materials are required, the production department sends a *materials requisition* to the stores and the stores issues the materials and deducts the quantity from the stock level shown on the bin card. Periodic stocktaking ensures that a physical count of all stock is made to confirm that the actual quantities support the levels shown on the bin cards.

Copies of all prime documents are sent to the accountant so that he or she can check that materials have been properly ordered and received before paying the supplier's invoice. The accountant also records all stock movements (the quantity and value of receipts and issues of materials) and the quantity and value of stock balances for each type of material are recorded in a *stock account*. This allows the cost of materials used in each cost unit to be calculated.

activity

Draw a diagram showing the flow of documents used to control the movement of materials.

The design of your diagram will depend on your creative abilities and the assumptions you have made, but you should have shown a logical flow of information that relates to the main stages in material control we have outlined in this section.

13.3 costing direct materials

The purchase of direct materials used in the production process represents a substantial cost and managers require information to establish what these costs are. Having looked at the procedures for purchasing, storing and issuing materials, we now need to consider the methods used for *costing direct materials* issued to production. These focus on the price at which materials are issued from stores to production and an effective system ensures that:

- the correct materials are delivered
- materials are stored and issued only with proper authorization
- production is charged with the cost of materials used
- the stock of materials in the stores is correctly valued.

Calculating the cost of direct materials can be a problem. For example, it may not be possible to identify each issue of materials with the corresponding receipt into stores or it may be complicated by the fact that materials have been received on different dates and at a number of different purchase prices. Fluctuating prices may be due to a number of reasons, such as:

- a general rise in the price of goods or services due to inflation or a general lowering of prices due to deflation
- variations in exchange rates if materials are purchased overseas
- shortages in the supply of materials
- temporary reductions due to special offers, discounts and so on.

There are a number of methods used for costing materials issued to production. The method chosen not only has implications for the cost of the units produced, but also for the closing stock of materials remaining in the stores. Although some of the methods that might be used are acceptable for internal use, they are not acceptable for valuing stock in the annual financial statements, as the method chosen must meet the requirements of *SSAP 9, Stocks and long-term contracts* or *IAS2, Inventories*; nor are all methods acceptable for taxation purposes. You may remember from Chapter 6 that this accounting standard provides the rule that stock should be valued at the lower of cost or net realizable value. In a manufacturing business, cost refers to the total cost incurred in bringing the product to its present location and condition, including an appropriate proportion of production overhead costs. Therefore, to avoid having to use one method for management accounting purposes and another for financial accounting purposes, most businesses choose the method that is suitable for both. There are four main methods:

- The *standard cost* method uses predetermined planned costs known as standard costs. The standard cost is derived from a standard quantity of materials allowed for the production of a specific cost unit at standard direct materials price. This method of standard costing is closely associated with a system of budgetary control and we will be looking at these topics in Chapters 18 and 19.

- The *unit cost* method is the simplest method as far as actual costs are concerned, but it can only be used in a relatively small business where the cost of purchasing the specific direct materials used to produce the cost unit can be identified. As a business grows in terms of production volume and range of products, this is clearly no longer possible.
- The *first in, first out (FIFO)* method uses the price of the earliest consignment of materials for all issues to production until the quantity received at that price has been issued, then the price of the next consignment is used.
- The *continuous weighted average (CWA)* method uses the weighted average price, which is calculated each time a consignment of materials is received. The weighted average price is calculated as:

$$\frac{\text{Total stock value}}{\text{Total quantity of stock}}$$

We will now look at the last two methods in some detail.

activity

Hazelwood Products Ltd started making bookshelves on 1 January. The goods received notes and the materials requisitions show the following receipts and issues of wood during the first three days. As you can see, Jon Hazel, the owner-manager, was able to negotiate a lower introductory price for the first delivery and then paid the regular price for the second delivery.

1 January	Received 50 units at £3.00 per unit
2 January	Received a further 50 units at £4.00 per unit
3 January	Issued 50 units to production

Complete the following record in the stock account and calculate the cost of the 50 units issued to production on 3 January and 50 units remaining in stock using FIFO and CWA.

FIFO	Receipts			Issues			Stock balance	
	Quantity	Price £	Value £	Quantity	Price £	Value £	Quantity	Value £
January								
1								
2								
3								
Total								

CWA	Receipts			Issues			Stock balance	
	Quantity	Price £	Value £	Quantity	Price £	Value £	Quantity	Value £
January								
1								
2								
3								
Total								

Check your answer against the one given below:

FIFO	Receipts			Issues			Stock balance	
	Quantity	*Price*	*Value*	*Quantity*	*Price*	*Value*	*Quantity*	*Value*
January		£	£		£	£		£
1	50	3.00	150.00				50	150.00
2	50	4.00	200.00				100	350.00
3				50	3.00	150.00	50	200.00
Total						150.00		

CWA	Receipts			Issues			Stock balance	
	Quantity	*Price*	*Value*	*Quantity*	*Price*	*Value*	*Quantity*	*Value*
January		£	£		£	£		£
1	50	3.00	150.00				50	150.00
2	50	4.00	200.00				100	350.00
3				50	3.50	175.00	50	175.00
Total						175.00		

If you compare the results, you can see that the total cost of materials issued to production (and hence the cost of direct materials used in the product) and the value of the stock remaining in stores vary according to the method used.

KEY DEFINITIONS	First in, first out (FIFO) is a method of costing for direct materials that uses the price of the earliest consignment received for all issues to production until the quantity received at that price has been issued, then the price of the next consignment is used.
	Continuous weighted average (CWA) is a method of costing for direct materials based on the weighted average price, which is recalculated every time a consignment is received.

To make certain you fully understand the two methods, we will extend the illustration by adding further information. As the number of receipts and issues increase, Jon Hazel may find it is more efficient to use a spreadsheet to record the movement of stock and calculate a continuous stock balance, and you may wish to do so for the next activity.

activity

Unfortunately, the wood Jon wanted was not available on 4 January and he had to purchase a more expensive type. However, he kept his order as small as possible and his supplier was able to meet his next order on 6 January. Using the following information, calculate the quantity and value of materials issued to production during the first week and the quantity and value of closing stock at 7 January using FIFO and CWA.

Date	Transaction
1 January	Received 50 units at £3.00 per unit
2 January	Received 50 units at £4.00 per unit
3 January	Issued 50 units to production
4 January	Received 10 units at £5.00 per unit
5 January	Issued 40 units to production
6 January	Received 40 units at £4.00 per unit
7 January	Issued 30 units to production

The answer is as follows. If you have used a spreadsheet to construct the two different stock accounts, you may find the accompanying illustrations that show the formulae for the two methods useful.

FIFO	Receipts			Issues			Stock balance	
	Quantity	Price	Value	Quantity	Price	Value	Quantity	Value
January		£	£		£	£		£
1	50	3.00	150.00				50	150.00
2	50	4.00	200.00				100	350.00
3				50	3.00	150.00	50	200.00
4	10	5.00	50.00				60	250.00
5				40	4.00	160.00	20	90.00
6	40	4.00	160.00				60	250.00
7				10	4.00	40.00	50	210.00
7				10	5.00	50.00	40	160.00
7				10	4.00	40.00	30	120.00
Total						440.00		

Microsoft Excel - 12 - 13 spreadsheets

File   Edit   View   Insert   Format   Tools   Data   Window   Help   Type a question for help

Arial   10   B I U

A1   fx FIFO

	A	B	C	D	E	F	G	H	I
1	FIFO		Receipts				Issues		Stock balance
2		Quantity	Price	Value	Quantity	Price	Value	Quantity	Value
3	January		£	£		£	£		£
4	1	50	3	=B4*C4				=B4	=D4
5	2	50	4	=B5*C5				=H4+B5	=I4+D5
6	3				50	=C4	=E6*F6	=H5-E6	=I5-G6
7	4	10	5	=B7*C7				=H6+B7	=I6+D7
8	5				40	=C5	=E8*F8	=H7-E8	=I7-G8
9	6	40	4	=B9*C9				=H8+B9	=I8+D9
10	7				10	=C5	=E10*F10	=H9-E10	=I9-G10
11	7				10	=C7	=E11*F11	=H10-E11	=I10-G11
12	7				10	=C9	=E12*F12	=H11-E12	=I11-G12
13	Total						=SUM(G4:G12)		
14									
15									
16									
17									
18									
19									
20									
21									
22									
23									

Hazelwood FIFO formulae / Hazelwood AVCO formulae / Perfect I

Ready   NUM

start   Chapters   13 Product direct cos...   Microsoft Excel - 12 - ...   21:04

CWA	Receipts			Issues			Stock balance	
	Quantity	Price	Value	Quantity	Price	Value	Quantity	Value
January		£	£		£	£		£
1	50	3.00	150.00				50	150.00
2	50	4.00	200.00				100	350.00
3				50	3.50	175.00	50	175.00
4	10	5.00	50.00				60	225.00
5				40	3.75	150.00	20	75.00
6	40	4.00	160.00				60	235.00
7				30	3.92	117.50	30	117.50
Total						442.50		

	A	B	C		E	F	G	H	I
						Issues		Stock balance	
1	CWA		Receipts						
2		Quantity	Price	Value	Quantity	Price	Value	Quantity	Value
3	January		£	£		£	£		£
4	1	50	3	=B4*C4				=B4	=D4
5	2	50	4	=B5*C5				=H4+B5	=I4+D5
6	3				50	=I5/H5	=E6*F6	=H5-E6	=I5-G6
7	4	10	5	=B7*C7				=H6+B7	=I6+D7
8	5				40	=I7/H7	=E8*F8	=H7-E8	=I7-G8
9	6	40	4	=B9*C9				=H8+B9	=I8+D9
10	7				30	=I9/H9	=E10*F10	=H9-E10	=I9-G10
11	Total						=SUM(G4:G10)		

The main thing to remember about using CWA is that you need to recalculate the average price at which stock will be issued if a new consignment of that particular material has been received by the stores. This means calculating the new total value of the material in stock and dividing it by the new total quantity of stock at that date. To find the cost of materials issued on 3 January, you should have divided the stock value of £350 by the quantity in stock (100 units) to arrive at £3.50 per unit. Another consignment is received on 4 January, so the cost of materials issued on 5 January is the new stock value of £225 divided by the quantity that is now in stock (60 units), which is £3.75 per unit. Since further stock is delivered on 6 January, you need to divide the new stock value of £235 by the quantity in stock (60 units), which is £3.92 per unit (rounded to the nearest 1p). This is the new weighted average price used for the materials issued on 7 January.

In Chapter 12 we looked at the total costs for Hazelwood Products Ltd for week ending 7 January, when 10 bookcases were produced, in the context of describing the different elements of cost. In the above activity we have been focusing on how the cost of direct materials is calculated. You can see from the total cost statement, which we have reproduced below, that Jon used a figure of £440 as the cost of the direct materials issued to production during week ending 7 January.

Hazelwood Products Ltd
Total cost (10 bookcases)

	£	£
Direct costs		
Direct materials	440	
Direct labour	660	
Prime cost		1,100
Production overheads		200
Production cost		1,300
Indirect costs		
Administration overheads	80	
Selling and distribution overheads	60	140
Total cost		1,440

If you look at the same figure in the two sets of stock accounts you have drawn up for the above activity, you will see that Jon must have been using the FIFO method, as the CWA method results in the higher figure of £442.50. Both figures are correct and this is another example of why business owners and managers need to have some understanding of the techniques used by accountants in order to make informed decisions about their accounting policies.

13.4 advantages and disadvantages

There are a number of advantages and disadvantages associated with the different methods for costing direct materials. Since this information is likely to be used for financial accounting purposes, which is guided by the consistency concept, it is important that the business chooses the most appropriate method and then uses it consistently, unless there is a good reason for changing it.

> **activity**
>
> Compare FIFO and CWA by drawing up lists of the advantages and disadvantages of each method.

Your list may include some of the following.

Advantages of FIFO:

- It is acceptable to financial accountants in the UK and also to HM Revenue and Customs. This means that in addition to being used for management accounting purposes, it can be used for financial reporting and computing profits for taxation purposes.
- It is a logical choice if it coincides with the order in which stock is physically issued to production. For example, if the stock consists of perishable materials or materials that have a finite life for some other reason, it makes sense to issue those that have been stored the longest first. This avoids the possibility of deterioration, obsolescence and waste.

- It charges the cost of direct materials against profits in the same order as costs are incurred.
- The value of stock at end of period is close to current prices.

Disadvantages of FIFO:

- It is complex and an arithmetical burden, even when a spreadsheet is used.
- The cost of direct materials issued to production is based on historical prices.

Advantages of CWA:

- It is acceptable to financial accountants in the UK and also to HM Revenue and Customs. This means that in addition to being used for management accounting purposes, it can be used for financial reporting and computing profits for taxation purposes.
- It is a logical choice if it coincides with way in which stock is physically issued to production. For example, if stock consists of volume and liquid materials (for example building materials or chemicals), an averaging method makes sense as it may not be possible to differentiate between old and new stock held in bulk storage containers.
- It smoothes out the impact of price changes in the profit and loss account.
- It takes account of quantities purchased and changing prices.
- It takes account of prices relating to previous periods.
- It can be relatively simple to calculate by entering the quantity and pricing information from the goods received notes and purchase orders (or stores requisitions) into a spreadsheet or specialist software package.

Disadvantages of CWA:

- Prices of materials issued to production must be recalculated every time a new consignment is received.
- Prices of materials issued may not match any of the prices actually paid.
- Value of closing stock lags behind current prices if prices are rising.

13.5 costing direct labour

Apart from materials, a second element of direct costs is expenditure on the wages paid to the workforce who are directly employed in producing the products or cost units. The methods for *costing direct labour* are closely related to the different methods of remuneration. The main types of pay schemes are:

- piecework schemes, which are used when workers are paid an agreed amount for each unit produced or piecework time is paid for each unit produced
- time-based schemes, which are used when workers are paid a basic rate per time period
- incentive schemes, which are used when a time allowance is given for each job and a bonus is paid for any time saved.

The documents used in labour costing depend largely on the method of payment used. The main documents used in a manual system are as follows, but many businesses now use computerized *direct data entry* from individual department terminals:

- *piecework tickets*, which refer to each stage of manufacture
- *clock cards*, which record attendance time
- daily or weekly *time sheets*, which record how workers have spent their time, and are usually required to be countersigned by a supervisor or manager
- *job cards*, which refer to a single job or a batch of small jobs, and record how long each activity takes to pass through the production process.

You should not be misled into thinking that costing for labour is used only in manufacturing businesses. For example, professionals such as solicitors and accountants usually complete time sheets so that individual clients can be properly billed for the services they receive. In all organizations it is necessary to have a system to ensure that employees are properly remunerated for their contribution. In many service organizations, some form of bonus or profit-sharing scheme is likely to exist and this requires more detailed information to be kept.

In *piecework schemes*, wages can be calculated using the following formula:

Units produced × Rate of pay per cost unit

For example, if an employee is paid £1.50 per cost unit and produces 240 units in a week, his or her weekly pay will be £360. This method works only where all units are identical and if the employee produces a number of units a conversion factor must be applied. As a piecework system is based on time spent on production, a standard time allowance is given for each unit to arrive at a total of piecework hours. Perhaps the same employee is allowed 15 minutes to produce one unit of product A (a simple electronic circuit board) and 30 minutes to produce one unit of product B (a more complex electronic circuit board). If the employee produces 40 units of product A and 60 units of product B and is paid £7.50 per hour, his or her pay can be calculated as:

Product	Number of units	Time allowance per unit	Total piecework hours
A	40	0.25 hours	10
B	60	0.50 hours	30
			40
		Pay (40 × £7.50)	£300

Calculating pay for *time-based schemes* is straightforward. A system is required to ensure that the employee is properly appointed and, if necessary, a procedure is in place to record the employee's attendance at the workplace. In many jobs it is assumed that the employee is present unless absence is specifically reported. The records from the clock cards and/or time sheets are then used as the basis for calculating pay.

Incentive schemes are usually introduced where workers are paid under a time-based scheme. There are various types of scheme in operation, but most are based on setting a target for output and actual performance is compared with the target. If actual performance exceeds the target, employees receive a payment for their efficiency. This payment is a proportion of the savings made by the business because of the increased efficiency and therefore the labour cost per unit should be lower. It is important to remember that a performance-based scheme cannot be used if the output cannot be measured reliably. Even though output might be easy to measure, it would be preferable to adopt a time-based method of remuneration where the quality of output is important. This would avoid the danger of quality deteriorating as workers strive to achieve higher levels of output that bring them increased monetary rewards.

activity

Jon Hazel employs Chris, Mike and Adam in the workshop of Hazelwood Products Ltd. As Chris and Mike are apprentices, they are paid £5 per hour, but Adam has qualifications and experience and is paid £10 per hour. Their time sheets for week ending 7 January show that Chris spent 35 hours, Mike spent 35 hours and Adam spent 25 hours on making the 10 bookcases they produced. Jon's accountant, who handles the payroll, estimates that the additional costs incurred in terms of employer's national insurance, pension contributions and holiday pay amount to an additional 10% of the wages they are paid. Calculate the direct labour cost for the 10 bookcases produced.

The answer is as follows:

	Hours	Rate per hour	Total
		£	£
Chris	35	5.00	175
Mike	35	5.00	175
Adam	25	10.00	250
			600
Employer's costs (600 × 10%)			60
Total direct labour costs			660

If you look at the total cost statement for Hazelwood Products Ltd, which is reproduced below, the direct labour costs are the most significant element of the direct costs for this business and therefore a key part of the prime costs for the week. One way in which Jon Hazel controls the direct labour costs in his business is by ensuring that employees complete their time sheets accurately and differentiate between time spent on making bookshelves and time spent on general tasks, such as clearing up and maintenance. Indeed, both Chris and Adam spent half an hour each day on general tasks and Adam spent two and a half hours each day supervising the apprentices and helping Jon plan the production process. Since this time cannot be identified directly with the products, the wages bill for this part of their jobs (£50) is included with the production overheads in the costing statement:

```
┌─────────────────────────────────────────────────────────────┐
│                    Hazelwood Products Ltd                     │
│                   Total cost (10 bookcases)                   │
│                                        £              £       │
│  Direct costs                                                 │
│     Direct materials                  440                     │
│     Direct labour                     660                     │
│  Prime cost                                        1,100      │
│  Production overheads                                200      │
│  Production cost                                   1,300      │
│  Indirect costs                                               │
│     Administration overheads           80                     │
│     Selling and distribution overheads 60           140      │
│  Total cost                                        1,440      │
└─────────────────────────────────────────────────────────────┘
```

Sometimes students find it difficult to decide which costs are direct labour costs and which are indirect costs when classifying the elements of cost. The guide to remember is that direct labour costs are those which can conveniently be identified with a cost unit. To do this, a documentation system, as described in this chapter, is needed. Indirect labour costs are the wages of indirect workers, such as supervisors and maintenance staff, plus the wages of direct workers when working on indirect tasks, such as cleaning machinery and setting up production lines.

13.6 costing direct expenses

Apart from direct materials and direct labour, a business may have some *direct expenses*. Examples of direct expenses include subcontract work or hiring special equipment for a particular job. For instance, Jon Hazel might decide to continue to produce bookcases with a simple wax finish, but also make some with a paint finish as chosen by the customer. He may decide to subcontract the finishing of the painted bookcases ordered by customers to an expert. The cost of this extra work is not a direct material, as the paint is never owned by Hazelwood Products Ltd, nor is it direct labour, as the painter is not on the payroll, but the cost can be directly traced to a product. Therefore it is classified as a direct expense.

The main method for costing direct expenses to a product or cost unit is very simple and the accountant bases the cost on the amount shown in the relevant invoice. If it is not possible to do this because it is too difficult to trace the expense to a particular cost unit, the amount is simply added to the production overheads. We will be looking at these in more detail in the next chapter.

13.7 conclusions

In this chapter we have described the key documents and procedures involved in costing for product direct costs. These are the costs that can be directly traced to a cost unit. When aggregated, these make up the prime cost. They can be divided into three elements: direct materials, direct labour and direct expenses.

Goods received notes give details of the direct materials received into the stores and materials requisitions give details of the stock issued for use in the production process. If the materials are stored for a period of time before they are used, records are maintained that will ensure an adequate level of stock and periodic stocktaking ensures proper stock control. In the accounts department, the stock account records the quantity and cost of materials to be charged to the cost unit. We have examined two methods for pricing direct materials and valuing closing stock and discussed the main reasons why different methods for costing direct materials might be adopted.

Direct labour converts the direct materials into the finished goods. The time employees spend on cost units can be calculated from clock cards, time sheets, job cards, piecework tickets or direct data entry systems and the method used for costing direct labour is related to the method of remuneration. We have also examined the reasons why direct expenses are not always identifiable, but should be included if they can be traced directly to the appropriate cost unit. For example, subcontract costs can be charged by means of an invoice from the subcontractor.

In many organizations the systems for recording and controlling direct costs are computerized and part of a management information system that is capable of providing a wide range of information for different purposes. Typically, this includes accounting information that is used for both financial and management accounting purposes.

practice questions

1. Describe the main stages in controlling direct materials.
2. Compare and contrast the advantages and disadvantages of the FIFO and CWA methods.
3. Janet's wages are based on piecework and she is paid £5 per piecework hour. Calculate her pay for a 36-hour week in which she produces the following units:

Product	Number of units	Time allowance per unit
A	12	0.8 hours
B	30	0.6 hours
C	24	0.5 hours

4. Perfect Pans Ltd manufactures cooking pans. On 1 December the stock records show a stock of 500 kg of metal alloy, which is valued at £2.00 per kg. The goods received notes and materials requisitions show the following receipts and issues during the month:

2 December	Issued 450 kg to production
7 December	Received 550 kg at £2.10 per kg
8 December	Issued 500 kg to production
14 December	Received 600 kg at £2.20 per kg
15 December	Issued 600 kg to production
30 December	Received 500 kg at £2.30 per kg
31 December	Issued 100 kg to production

Required

(a) Construct the stock account for Perfect Pans Ltd and calculate the cost of metal alloy used in the production process during December and the stock balance in terms of quantity and value at the end of the month using:
   (i) FIFO
   (ii) CWA.

(b) Assuming that the business needs to choose between the two methods, recommend which method management should adopt, giving at least five reasons.

5. The following records show the movement of stock for beans, the main ingredient used by The Bean Company Ltd in its canned products, for the month of September:

| Date | Receipts | | Issues |
	Quantity (tonnes)	Price per tonne £	Quantity (tonnes)
1 September	1,000	5.00	
2 September	1,000	5.50	
3 September			750
14 September			750
15 September	1,000	6.00	
16 September			750
29 September	1,000	6.50	
30 September			750

Required

(a) Construct the stock account for The Bean Company Ltd and calculate the cost of beans used in the product during September and the stock balance in terms of quantity and value at the end of the month using:
   (i) FIFO
   (ii) CWA.

(b) Identify which of the two methods would give the higher profit for the month in this particular case, giving your reasons.

chapter 14

costing for indirect costs

Learning objectives

When you have studied this chapter, you should be able to:

- Describe the main purposes of absorption costing

- Explain the main stages in costing indirect costs

- Construct a production overhead analysis

- Calculate the total cost of a cost unit using absorption costing methods

- Describe the problems associated with apportioning and absorbing indirect costs.

14.1 introduction

In Chapter 13 we looked at the methods that allow us to calculate the product direct costs (direct materials, direct labour and direct expenses) for each cost unit. However, the direct costs are only part of the total cost of producing a product or service; there are also the indirect costs of the business that need to be considered when making management decisions. The indirect costs are the overheads incurred by the business, which can be classified as production overheads, administration overheads, selling and distribution overheads or research and development overheads. In many businesses these indirect costs are very high and it is essential to find a suitable method for charging them to the cost units. Absorption costing is the traditional costing technique used to meet this need.

In this chapter we are going to focus on how to allocate and apportion the indirect costs to the cost centres and cost units so that the total cost of a single cost unit can be calculated. To do this, we will be working out the total costs of the business. This information will be similar to that found in the financial accounts, but there are differences. In management accounting the total costs are required on a monthly basis and in some cases they may be based on forecast figures. Therefore, the figures may be less accurate than those prepared for financial accounting purposes, but because they are calculated more frequently than once a year, they are timelier. In addition, more detailed information is required in a management accounting system than is needed for financial accounting. However, at the end of the financial year, we would expect the total costs for the business shown in the annual financial statements to be very similar to the aggregated costs in the management accounts.

14.2 absorption costing

Absorption costing is a technique that analyses revenue expenditure in order to arrive at a total cost for each cost unit. You will remember from Chapter 12 that revenue expenditure refers to the costs that are written off to the profit and loss account in the period in which they incurred. Since the focus of absorption costing is on calculating the total cost per unit, it is also known as *total costing*. The production cost of a product or other cost unit is primarily needed for valuing stock and for planning and controlling production costs, whereas the total cost is needed to determine the selling price.

KEY DEFINITIONS	Absorption costing is a method of costing that, in addition to direct costs, assigns a proportion or all the production overheads to the cost units. Costs are first allocated or apportioned to the cost centres, where they are absorbed into the cost unit using one or more overhead absorption rates.
	An overhead absorption rate is a means of attributing production overheads to a product or service.

In Chapter 13 we looked at the ways in which costs can be classified and one way is to divide them into direct costs and indirect costs. The total of the product direct costs is the prime cost and if we then add the indirect costs of production (the production overheads), we arrive at the production cost. The following activity allows us to examine this in more detail.

Hazelwood Products Ltd, the business we looked at in previous chapters, is thriving. During the first year, the workshop made 1,000 bookcases with the same design and size specifications. Production overheads for the year were £20,000; direct materials for each bookcase were £50 and direct labour costs for each bookcase were £80. What is the production cost of one bookcase?

You should have had no problem in deciding that the total direct costs are £130, made up of £50 for materials and £80 for labour. However, the total cost must include a fair share of the production overheads, but what is a 'fair share'? As the business is making only one product and they are all the same, a fair method would be to divide the production overheads by the total number of units produced:

$$\frac{£20,000}{1,000} = £20$$

The following costing statement draws these calculations together:

Hazelwood Products Ltd
Production cost (one bookcase)

	£	£
Direct costs		
Direct materials	50	
Direct labour	80	
Prime cost		130
Production overheads		20
Production cost		150

As a business grows, it is likely to become more complex than Hazelwood Products Ltd was in its first year and when this happens a business may decide to organize itself into a number of functional departments. In a manufacturing business, some of these will be production departments, whilst others will be service departments providing services, such as maintenance, storage or canteen facilities, administration, selling and distribution functions and so on. In addition, the business may have a range of different products or other cost units, with each spending a different amount of time in the production department and therefore making different demands on resources. In such cases, the method we have used for Hazelwood Products Ltd is not a fair way of sharing the production overheads over the cost units. However, absorption costing helps overcome this difficulty, by apportioning these indirect (overhead) costs to the cost units using rates that are calculated for each cost centre as shown in Figure 14.1.

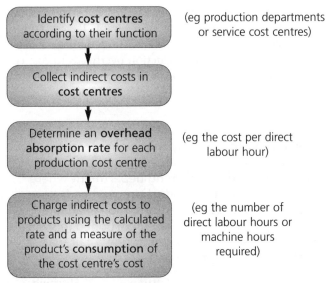

FIGURE 14.1 **Main stages in absorption costing**
Source: Adapted from Weetman, 1999, p. 751.

14.3 allocating and apportioning production overheads

Absorption costing seeks to provide answers to two practical problems:

- how to share the total overheads of the organization over the various production cost centres
- how to share the overheads for a particular production cost centre over the various products passing through it.

> **activity**
>
> In the previous example of Hazelwood Products Ltd, was the method used a solution to the first or the second of these problems?

The method used was a solution to the second problem because we were looking at a small organization with only one production department or workshop. By dividing the total overheads by the number of bookcases produced, we shared the production overheads over the products passing through the production department. Usually we have to solve the first problem before we can tackle the second.

You will remember from Chapter 13 that we can classify overheads by nature, such as rent, wages and depreciation. When overheads are classified in this way, they fall into two main groups. The first group is those that can be wholly identified with one particular cost centre, for example all the depreciation charge on machinery may be due to only one particular production department. This process of charging to one particular cost centre is called *cost allocation*. The second group of overheads is that which cannot be identified with a single cost centre, but must be shared or apportioned over all the cost centres benefiting from them. This process is known as *cost apportionment*, for example factory rent might be apportioned over the production cost centres on the basis of the proportion of space each department occupies in the factory. To charge the production overheads to cost centres by allocation and apportionment a *production overhead analysis* is prepared. This classifies the total overheads by nature and then shows how they are apportioned across the production cost centres. We will use an activity to illustrate this.

Jarvis Jackets Ltd is a medium-sized company that makes leather jackets. It has two cost centres: the cutting department where the jackets are cut out by machine, and the stitching department where they are sewn and finished. Some of the production overheads have been allocated to the two cost centres from information available within the business, but the remainder must be apportioned in some way. The following information should help you decide a fair way of sharing them between the two departments:

	Total	Cutting department	Stitching department
Production area	400 sq metres	250 sq metres	150 sq metres
Number of employees	20	5	15
Value of machinery	£120,000	£100,000	£20,0000
Value of stock	£120,000	£40,000	£80,0000

Before you can complete the following pro forma, you need to decide on the basis on which the production overheads will be apportioned and then calculate the portion that will be borne by each cost centre. The indirect materials and indirect labour used in production have already been allocated and entered in the analysis. The rent has also been apportioned to show you the method. Rent is best apportioned on the basis of the area occupied. The total area is 250 + 150 = 400 sq metres and the rent is £12,000. Therefore, the rent can be apportioned as follows:

Cutting department: $\frac{250}{400}$ sq metres × £12,000 = £7,500

Stitching department: $\frac{150}{400}$ sq metres × £12,000 = £4,500

Jarvis Jackets Ltd
Production overhead analysis

Overhead	Total	Basis of apportionment	Cutting department	Stitching department
	£		£	£
Indirect materials	40,000	Allocated	17,500	22,500
Indirect labour	17,100	Allocated	4,200	12,900
Rent and rates	12,000	Area	7,500	4,500
Electricity	4,000			
Depreciation on machinery	9,000			
Supervisors' salaries	22,000			
Stock insurance	900			
Total	105,000			

After deciding a fair way of apportioning the production overheads, the calculations should not have presented any great problems. Check your completed analysis against the following:

Jarvis Jackets Ltd Production overhead analysis				
Overhead	Total	Basis of apportionment	Cutting department	Stitching department
	£		£	£
Indirect materials	40,000	Allocated	17,500	22,500
Indirect labour	17,100	Allocated	4,200	12,900
Rent and rates	12,000	Area	7,500	4,500
Electricity	4,000	Area	2,500	1,500
Depreciation on machinery	9,000	Value of machinery	7,500	1,500
Supervisors' salaries	22,000	No. of employees	5,500	16,500
Stock insurance	900	Value of stock	300	600
Total	105,000		45,000	60,000

If your analysis differs from the above, it may be because you decided to use different bases of apportionment, so we will look at the reasons for the choices we made. Both rent and electricity would seem to be best shared on the basis of the area occupied by each cost centre. Depreciation is clearly related to the value of the machinery used in each cost centre. Deciding on the best way to apportion the supervisors' salaries is more difficult. In the absence of any other information, we have assumed that their salaries are related to the number of employees. You might argue that they could be related to floor space and in some circumstances you would be right. Finally, the stock insurance is based on the value of the stock and therefore has been allocated accordingly.

Agreeing on a fair way to apportion overheads is a major problem in many organizations and it is important to remember that the methods of apportionment are arbitrary. Nevertheless, the method chosen should be reasonable. They should be relatively easy to obtain from the records of the business and relate to the manner in which the cost is incurred by the cost centre benefiting from its use. Finally, they should reflect the use by the cost centre of the resources represented by the overhead. Later in this chapter we will be looking at the problem of service cost centres, but at this stage we will concentrate on how to allocate or apportion production overheads to our two production departments. The following table shows some commonly used bases of apportionment.

main bases for apportioning production overheads

Production overhead	Basis of apportionment
Rent and rates	Area or volume
Lighting and heating	Area or volume
Buildings insurance	Area
Insurance of machinery	Value of machinery
Depreciation of machinery	Value of machinery
Power for machinery	Machine hours, horsepower or horsepower per hour
Supervisors' salaries	Number of employees
Canteen	Number of employees

14.4 calculating the production overhead absorption rate

We now know that the total production overheads are £45,000 for the cutting department and £60,000 for the finishing department. Next we must decide on an appropriate *overhead absorption rate* to share the production overheads between all the jackets passing through the two production cost centres. The choice of absorption rate depends on the basis of apportionment and the resources used. We will examine the following methods:

●   The cost unit overhead absorption rate
●   The direct labour hour overhead absorption rate
●   The machine hour overhead absorption rate.

The *cost unit overhead absorption rate* is the simplest method and involves dividing the production overheads for each production cost centre by the number of cost units passing through them. We applied this in the Hazelwood Products Ltd example. In a more complex business there may be more than one production cost centre and a different overhead absorption rate will be needed for each. For example, Jarvis Jackets Ltd makes two styles of jacket: the classic jacket and the designer jacket. In one year, 4,000 classic jackets are made and 1,000 designer jackets, making a total of 5,000 cost units. Using the cost unit overhead absorption rate, we will now calculate the amount of the overheads that will be borne by each jacket. This requires some care, as we need to remember that each jacket must pass through both the cutting department and the stitching department. Therefore, a separate overhead absorption rate per jacket must be calculated for each cost centre and then aggregated.

Cost unit overhead absorption rate	Cutting department	Stitching department
$\dfrac{\text{Cost centre overhead costs}}{\text{Total number of cost units}}$	$\dfrac{£45,000}{5,000} = £9.00$	$\dfrac{£60,000}{5,000} = £12.00$

The absorption rate will be £21.00 (£9.00 + £12.00). This means that every jacket will absorb £21.00 of the production overheads incurred in running these two production cost centres.

Although using cost unit overhead absorption rate is the easiest method, it would be unfair to charge the same overhead to the different styles of jackets, since the more expensive designer jackets use up more of the resources. It would be fairer if the product that uses up more of the resources bears more of the overhead. For example, if you took your car to the garage merely to have the brakes adjusted and you were charged the same overhead charge as someone who had had a full service, you would be very upset. It would not help if the garage owner told you that he had worked out his overhead charge by dividing his total overheads by the number of cars repaired. So what other basis might he use for charging overheads on the work done?

You may consider that the overheads should be charged on a time basis. Garages usually charge an hourly rate for repairs, as do many other businesses, such as plumbers and electricians. The hourly rate can be calculated on the basis of the time an employee spends working on the product, the direct labour hour rate, or on how long the product is on a machine, the machine hour rate.

Returning to our example of Jarvis Jackets Ltd, now calculate the hourly overhead absorption rate for each department. You can choose to base the rate on direct labour hours or on machine hours. The following table gives details of the direct labour hours and machine hours required in each department to make 5,000 jackets.

	Cutting department	Stitching department
Direct labour hours	10,000	30,000
Machine hours	40,000	5,000

You may have found this difficult. To calculate the direct labour hours overhead absorption rate for each cost centre, you need to divide the overhead by the total direct labour hours and add them together. If you decided to calculate the machine hours overhead absorption rate, for each cost centre, you should have divided the overhead by the total number of machine hours and added them together. The following tables show these calculations.

	Cutting department	Stitching department
Direct labour hour overhead absorption rate		
$\dfrac{\text{Cost centre overhead costs}}{\text{Total direct labour hours}}$	$\dfrac{£45,000}{10,000} = £4.50$	$\dfrac{£60,000}{30,000} = £2.00$
Machine hour overhead absorption rate		
$\dfrac{\text{Cost centre overhead costs}}{\text{Total machine hours}}$	$\dfrac{£45,000}{40,000} = £1.13$	$\dfrac{£60,000}{5,000} = £12.00$

Other types of overhead absorption rates in use are often based on a percentage calculation, but we will concentrate on these three widely used methods as they illustrate the main principles. The following table summarizes the information we have so far:

	Cutting department	Stitching department
Total overheads	£45,000	£60,000
Number of cost units	5,000	5,000
Direct labour hours	10,000	30,000
Machine hours	40,000	5,000
Cost units overhead absorption rate	£9.00	£12.00
Direct labour hours overhead absorption rate	£4.50	£2.00
Machine hours overhead absorption rate	£1.13	£12.00

Although we have calculated three different types of overhead rate for Jarvis Jackets Ltd, only one rate will be used in each department, but you can see that since each produces a different absorption rate, it is important that the management accountant uses the fairest rate for each cost centre, bearing in mind that the same rate need not be used in both departments. We have already pointed out that it would be unfair to use the cost unit absorption rate because the two types of jacket use unequal amounts of resources. With the other two rates, we need to consider the main sources of expenditure in each department by examining the overhead costs. In the cutting department, you can see that the overheads have been incurred mainly in terms of machine hours, therefore this is the most appropriate basis for calculating the overhead absorption rate for that cost centre. However, in the finishing department, the work is mainly manual; therefore the direct labour hour rate is the most appropriate overhead absorption rate to use for this cost centre.

14.5 calculating the production cost per unit

We have now reached the final and most important stage of our calculations. Although we have spent some time learning how the overheads are calculated, we must not forget to charge for the product direct costs (the direct materials and direct labour used in making the jackets). The following information is available:

	Classic jacket	Designer jacket
Direct materials	£50	£80
Direct labour	£20	£40
Cutting department machine hours	7	12
Stitching department direct labour hours	5	10

We can now calculate the production cost incurred in making each type of jacket.

Production cost per unit				
	Classic jacket		Designer jacket	
	£	£	£	£
Direct costs				
Direct materials	50.00		80.00	
Direct labour	20.00		40.00	
Prime cost		70.00		120.00
Production overheads				
Cutting department (£1.13 per machine hour)	7.91		13.56	
Stitching department (£2.00 per direct labour hour)	10.00	17.91	20.00	33.56
Production cost		87.91		153.56

You may consider that calculating a different overhead absorption rate for each production department is a complex activity: it would be far simpler to calculate a factory-wide absorption rate. Thus, if a factory had total overheads of £1m and there were 250,000 direct labour hours worked during the period, the overhead absorption rate would be £4.00 per labour hour in all the separate departments. Although this method is simple and inexpensive to apply, it is likely to generate incorrect data, except in the most straightforward production systems. If there are a number of departments and products do not spend an equal time in each department, separate departmental overhead absorption rates must be calculated. If this is not done, some products will receive a higher overhead charge than they should fairly bear and others a lower charge. This will make it difficult for management to control costs and make decisions on pricing and alternative production systems.

14.6 apportioning service cost centre overheads

So far, we have considered only production cost centres. However, most businesses also have cost centres that provide services to other cost centres. Examples of service cost centres include departments associated with the production areas, such as maintenance, stores and canteen, and others which are not, such as administration, sales and distribution. The first stage is to calculate the total production cost as before, but this time we will include the service cost centres associated with the production area. We will deal with other overheads later. The same procedure is used: the different types of production overheads are allocated and apportioned, and subtotalled. Then the subtotal of the service cost centres is apportioned to the production cost centres on a fair basis.

Jon Hazel's business, Hazelwood Products Ltd, has expanded and now makes bookcases of different sizes. Instead of a single production department, Jon has found it more efficient to divide the work into separate stages and there are now three departments, each of which is a separate cost centre. The following information is available:

	Joinery department	Finishing department	Maintenance department
Area	200 sq metres	200 sq metres	100 sq metres
Number of employees	12	16	4
Value of machinery	£250,000	£100,000	£50,000

Complete the following production overhead analysis by showing the basis of apportionment and the overhead to be borne by each of the three production cost centres. The allocated overheads have been entered for you. Once you have arrived at a subtotal for all three cost centres, you must apportion the service costs for the maintenance department over the two production departments on whatever basis you consider appropriate.

Hazelwood Products Ltd
Production overhead analysis

Overhead	Total	Basis of apportionment	Joinery department	Finishing department	Maintenance department
	£		£	£	£
Indirect materials	10,000	Allocated	6,000	3,000	1,000
Indirect labour	31,500	Allocated	4,000	8,000	19,500
Rent and rates	20,000				
Electricity	5,000				
Depreciation on machinery	40,000				
Supervisors' salaries	36,000				
Subtotal	142,500				
Apportioned service costs	–				
Total	142,500				–

Your completed production overhead analysis should look like this:

Hazelwood Products Ltd
Production overhead analysis

Overhead	Total	Basis of apportionment	Joinery department	Finishing department	Maintenance department
	£		£	£	£
Indirect materials	10,000	Allocated	6,000	3,000	1,000
Indirect labour	31,500	Allocated	4,000	8,000	19,500
Rent and rates	20,000	Area	8,000	8,000	4,000
Electricity	5,000	Area	2,000	2,000	1,000
Depreciation on machinery	40,000	Value of machinery	25,000	10,000	5,000
Supervisors' salaries	36,000	No. of employees	13,500	18,000	4,500
Subtotal	142,500		58,500	49,000	35,000
Apportioned service costs	–	Value of machinery	25,000	10,000	(35,000)
Total	142,500		83,500	59,000	–

The overhead costs of £35,000, which represent the cost of running the maintenance department, have been apportioned to the two production departments on the basis of the value of the machinery in these two departments (the value of the machinery in the maintenance department itself is excluded from the calculations). The total cost of machinery is £250,000 + £100,000 = £350,000. Therefore, the maintenance department overheads can be apportioned as follows:

Joinery department: $\dfrac{£250,000}{£350,000} \times £35,000 = £25,000$

Finishing department: $\dfrac{£100,000}{£350,000} \times £35,000 = £10,000$

Continuing this example, the overhead absorption rate in the joinery department is based on 10,000 machine hours and in the finishing department on 30,000 direct labour hours. We can now calculate the two overhead absorption rates in the joinery and finishing departments. This is done by dividing the total cost centre overhead for the period by the number of units of the basis of absorption; in this case, the machine hours in the joinery department and the direct labour hours in the finishing department:

Joinery department: $\dfrac{£83,500}{10,000} = £8.35$ per machine hour

Finishing department: $\dfrac{£59,000}{30,000} = £1.97$ per direct labour hour

Supposing a customer puts in an order for a bookcase for which the direct costs are direct materials £80.00 and direct labour £50.00. It is estimated that the bookcase will require 8 machine hours in the joinery department and 10 labour hours in the finishing department. We can calculate the total production cost as follows:

Hazelwood Products Ltd Production cost (one bookcase)	£	£
Direct costs		
Direct materials	80.00	
Direct labour	50.00	
Prime cost		130.00
Production overheads		
Joinery department (8 hours @ £8.35)	66.80	
Finishing department (10 hours @ £1.97)	19.70	86.50
Production cost		216.50

What we have just calculated is the production cost for the bookcase, but you will remember from Chapter 12 that in order to find out the total cost per unit, we need to add a proportion of the non-production overheads. In this example, these consist of the administration overheads and the selling and distribution overheads. The data for the period is as follows:

	£		£
Direct costs	87,500	Administration overheads	18,250
Production overheads	142,500	Selling and distribution overheads	27,750
Total production cost	230,000	Total non-production overheads	46,000

A simple method for apportioning non-production overheads to a cost unit is to add a percentage representing the proportion of non-production costs to production costs. This is an arbitrary measure, as there is no theoretical justification for a relationship between these two costs. The formula is:

$$\frac{\text{Non-production overheads}}{\text{Production cost}} \times 100$$

Substituting the figures in the formula:

$$\frac{£46,000}{£230,000} \times 100 = 20\% \text{ of the production cost } (£216.50 \times 20\%) = £43.30$$

Now we have all the figures we need to calculate the total cost of the bookcase. This is primarily of use to management for determining the selling price, since stock valuation and controlling production costs do not require the inclusion of the non-production costs.

Production cost (one bookcase)	£	£
Direct costs		
Direct materials	80.00	
Direct labour	50.00	
Prime cost		130.00
Production overheads		
Joinery department (8 hours @ £8.35)	66.80	
Finishing department (10 hours @ £1.97)	19.70	86.50
Production cost		216.50
Non-production overheads (20% of production cost)		43.30
Total cost		259.80

14.7 predetermined overhead absorption rates

So far, we have implied that the absorption rates are based on actual costs, but in practice these costs are usually estimated, which means that the overhead absorption rates are based on predicted figures. The actual costs are not used because the collection, analysis and absorption of overheads to cost units takes a considerable time, and the actual figures may not be available until after the end of the financial period. Naturally, it would be impossible to wait until then to invoice customers, submit estimates, make decisions on production methods or carry out any other management task.

Before the start of a financial period, which may be as short as a month or as long as a year, decisions will be made on the likely level of activity and the estimated costs that will be incurred during the period. In Chapter 18 we will be looking at budgetary control, which is the process of establishing detailed financial plans for a forthcoming period, comparing them with the actual figures during the period and taking action to remedy any adverse variances. As far as absorption costing is concerned, the planned level of activity will need to be decided, the number of machine hours and labour hours estimated and forecasts made of the likely overhead costs. This will allow a *predetermined overhead absorption rate* to be calculated at the beginning of the financial period and applied throughout the period.

activity

What problems do you think might arise from using a predetermined overhead rate instead of an actual rate?

You may have thought of the following main problems:

- Actual overheads are likely to differ from those budgeted
- The actual absorption rate may differ from that used in the budget
- A combination of the above factors.

These problems can have serious consequences. If an organization has been invoicing customers on a predetermined overhead rate that is wrong, it could have a significant impact on profits. Where the overheads charged to production are higher than the actual overheads for the period, the variance is known as *overabsorption*. In other words, too much overhead has been charged to production. Where the overheads charged to production are lower than the actual overheads, the variance is known as *underabsorption*. The underabsorption or overabsorption of overheads is written off as an expense in the profit and loss account for the period in which it is incurred.

14.8 conclusions

Revenue expenditure can be classified into product direct costs, which can be traced directly to a cost unit, and indirect costs, which cannot. We looked at the methods for costing product direct costs (direct materials, direct labour and direct expenses) in Chapter 13. In this chapter we have looked at absorption costing, which is a cost accounting system that charges each cost unit with a fair share of the indirect costs or overheads. This enables the total cost (the direct and the indirect costs) of a cost unit to be calculated. The main steps in absorption costing are:

1. Using a production overhead analysis, allocate or apportion indirect costs to each cost centre on a fair basis using an appropriate method of apportionment.
2. Allocate or apportion indirect costs from service cost centres to the production cost centres.
3. Then absorb the resulting overheads from each production cost centre into the cost unit using a suitable overhead absorption rate.
4. Construct a costing statement showing the different elements of direct and indirect costs for the cost unit.

Absorption costing can be based on either predetermined or actual costs. The information thus provided can be used to aid the planning and control of costs and for establishing the selling price of products.

Although we have used the manufacture of furniture and jackets in this chapter as examples, the same principles of allocating, apportioning and absorbing overheads apply in all organizations where management wants to know the total cost of a cost unit. However, it is important to remember that absorption costing has some limitations, since it is based on a series of simple assumptions and rudimentary arithmetical apportioning. We shall be discussing an alternative technique for charging overheads in Chapter 16 when we look at activity-based costing.

practice questions

1. Describe the main stages for calculating the total cost per unit under an absorption costing system.
2. Explain what it means to allocate, apportion and absorb indirect costs.
3. Discuss the advantages and disadvantages of using an absorption costing system for calculating the total cost of a product.
4. The monthly production overheads for Toy Craft Ltd are as follows:

Production overheads	
	£
Indirect materials	24,500
Indirect labour	54,500
Rent and rates	26,000
Electricity	4,000
Depreciation on machinery	36,000
Supervisors' salaries	42,000

The business has two production cost centres and one service cost centre, details of which are given below:

	Machine department	Assembly department	Maintenance department
Allocation of indirect materials	12,000	10,000	2,500
Allocation of indirect labour costs	14,000	18,000	22,500
Area (sq metres)	500	400	100
Value of machinery (£)	300,000	100,000	50,000
Number of employees	7	21	2
Number of machine hours	42,500	–	–
Number of direct labour hours	–	15,000	–

Required

(a) Decide on a suitable basis of apportionment for each of the indirect costs that are not going to be allocated and construct a production overhead analysis for Toy Craft Ltd.

(b) Calculate the machine hour overhead absorption rate for the machine department.

(c) Calculate the direct labour hour overhead absorption rate for the assembly department.

5. West Wales Windsurfers Ltd makes two models of windsurfer: the Fun Wave and the Hot Racer. The company has two production departments. It also has a

canteen, which serves all employees. The predicted sales and costs for next year are as follows:

	Fun Wave	Hot Racer
Selling price per unit	£600	£700
Sales/production volume	2,000 units	2,500 units
Material costs per unit	£80	£50
Direct labour		
Body workshop (£3 per hour)	50 hours per unit	60 hours per unit
Finishing workshop (£2 per hour)	40 hours per unit	40 hours per unit
Machine hours		
Body workshop	30 hours per unit	80 hours per unit
Finishing workshop	10 hours per unit	

The production overheads for the cost centres are shown below, together with other relevant data.

Production overheads	Total	Body workshop	Finishing workshop	Canteen
	£	£	£	£
Variable costs	350,000	260,000	90,000	0
Fixed costs	880,000	420,000	300,000	160,000
Total	1,230,000	680,000	390,000	160,000
Number of employees		150	90	10
Floor area (sq metres)		40,000	10,000	10,000

Required

(a) Advise the company on the method of overhead absorption that should be used for each cost centre, giving reasons for your choice.

(b) Calculate an appropriate overhead absorption rate for each production department.

(c) Calculate the predicted production cost per unit for each model.

references

Weetman, P. (1999) *Financial and Management Accounting*, (2nd edn), Edinburgh: Pearson Education.

chapter 15

costing for specific orders and continuous operations

When you have studied this chapter, you should be able to:

- Differentiate between specific order costing and continuous operation costing

- Calculate the total cost of a job

- Calculate the total cost of a contract

- Calculate the average cost per unit using unit costing, service costing or process costing.

15.1 introduction

The costing methods used for establishing the cost of products and services can be divided according to the nature of their production into *specific order costing* and *continuous operation costing*. Specific order costing is used where the business produces a different product or service for each customer (for example a cabinet-maker who designs and makes furniture to meet customers' requirements, a dressmaker who makes wedding dresses for individual customers, or a builder who does different home improvements for customers). It is also used where the business provides a service (for example a plumber who repairs a washing machine or an electrician who fits additional electric sockets). Continuous operation costing is used in businesses that make products or provide services as a constant operation (for example a brewery producing and bottling beer or a utility company providing electricity, gas or water). Although the unit of analysis varies, the methods for costing specific orders and continuous operations are based on the same principles.

In this chapter we are going to start by looking at the two methods that are used for costing specific orders: job costing and contract costing. Job costing is usually combined with absorption costing (see Chapter 14) and therefore our examples are based on that assumption. We then go on to examine three methods used for costing continuous operations: output costing (which has some of the features of job and batch costing), service costing and process costing. Process costing is used where production is carried out in a series of stages (or processes) and costs are accumulated for the whole production process and average unit costs of production are computed at each stage. We will be explaining the rules that are applied to the valuation of work in progress and wastage, and how the accountant draws a distinction between the main product of the process and any by-products and joint products.

15.2 job costing

Specific order costing is the basic cost accounting method used when work consists of separately identifiable jobs, batches or contracts. We start by looking at *job costing*, where costs are attributed to individual jobs. A job is an identifiable discrete piece of work carried out to a customer's specific requirements. Another characteristic of a job is that the work is relatively small and short in duration. It can be carried out in the factory or workshop, or on the customer's premises. Job costing is used by small businesses in the service sector, where the owner-manager needs to know the cost of each service the business provides, for example landscape gardeners, electricians, plumbers, decorators and small printing firms. It is also used by businesses in other sectors, such as small builders, artisans and small manufacturers making a number of different products.

KEY DEFINITIONS	Specific order costing refers to methods of cost accounting used where a different product or service is produced for each order.
	Continuous operation costing refers to methods of cost accounting used where products or services are produced as a constant operation.

Job costing is a method of costing for specific orders in which costs are attributed to individual jobs.

It is not unusual for a business using job costing to adopt a *cost plus pricing policy*, where the selling price is calculated by adding a fixed profit margin to the cost of the job. This approach has a number of weaknesses, as there is no incentive to control the cost of the job, it ignores market conditions and the total costs are dependent on the method of overhead recovery. However, it is simple to apply and it allows the business to ensure that it recovers its costs where competitive pricing is not an issue.

To facilitate the collection of costs associated with each job, a unique reference number is usually given to each job. The costs incurred in carrying out the job are usually analysed into the different elements of cost, such as direct materials, direct labour and overheads. The type of job costing used depends on the complexity of the business and the sophistication of its recording system, but in all forms of job costing rigorous costing procedures are needed. The main stages are:

- The customer informs the company of the specific requirements.
- The estimating department prepares an estimate, quoting a selling price to the customer.
- If the customer accepts the estimate and places an order, a *works order* with an identifying number is raised.
- A *materials requisition note* is prepared so that materials can be drawn from the stores department.
- A *purchase requisition note* is sent to the purchasing department for any special materials and equipment that may be required.
- Traditionally, a *job card* is raised. This shows the written instructions for the operations to be carried out for the completion of a job. The instructions are now likely to be in the form of a computer printout.
- If workers with special skills are needed, a *labour requirement note* is sent to the human resources department.
- The job is entered into the production schedule with a starting date that will allow completion by the agreed delivery date.

Failure to maintain adequate records of all the costs relating to a specific job means that the profit or loss for the job cannot be calculated and future estimates based on past records will be inaccurate. All systems used to collect job costs concentrate on identifying the materials and labour for each job and recording them on a *job cost sheet*. Although many businesses have now adopted computerized systems, the principles remain the same.

The general procedure for collecting the costs of individual jobs in a manufacturing business is as follows:

- A *materials requisition note* is sent to the stores department identifying the materials required for the job. The materials requisition note is used to cost the materials to the job cost sheet.
- A *job card* is given to the worker who is performing the first operation. The starting and finishing times for that operation are clocked onto the ticket and the same procedure is

followed for subsequent operations. Finally, the job card is sent to the cost office where the time is costed and entered on the *job cost sheet.*

- Direct expenses are entered on the job cost sheet from the invoices or an analysis of the cash book.
- The cost of direct materials and direct labour as recorded on the job cost sheet is charged to the *job account.*
- The job account is charged with an appropriate share of the production overheads, usually on the basis of predetermined overhead absorption rates.
- If the job has not been completed at the end of an accounting period, it is valued at production cost on the balance sheet.
- If the business has a number of very small jobs, it is not practical to keep a separate job cost sheet for each job. Instead, a general jobbing account is kept to which all the costs of the jobs are charged.
- On completion of the job, an appropriate share of the administration, selling and distribution overheads are charged to the job account. This account now shows the total cost of the job.

The following activity allows you to see how job costing works in practice.

Mayo Metalwork Ltd manufactures individually designed wrought iron gates and railings to meet customers' requirements. The company uses absorption costing and the following information is available:

Department	Budgeted overheads £	Basis of absorption
Machine shop	12,000	3,000 machine hours
Press shop	7,000	2,000 labour hours
Assembly shop	6,000	2,500 labour hours

An order has been placed for Job No. 365 with a selling price of £5,200. The following information relates to the job:

Direct materials	£1,415
Direct labour	
Machine shop	50 hours @ £3.00 per hour
Press shop	180 hours @ £2.50 per hour
Assembly shop	100 hours @ £1.75 per hour
Time booked in machine shop	210 machine hours

Using the following pro forma, calculate the total cost of the job and the profit.

activity

Mayo Metalwork Ltd
Job No. 365

	£	£
Direct costs		
Direct materials		x
Add Direct labour		
Machine shop	x	
Press shop	x	
Assembly shop	x	x
Prime cost		x
Add Production overheads		
Machine shop	x	
Press shop	x	
Assembly shop	x	x
Production cost		x
Add Indirect costs		
Administration and selling overheads		x
Total cost		x
Add Profit		x
Selling price		5,200

The first step is to work out the overhead absorption rates:

Machine shop $\dfrac{£12,000}{3,000}$ = £4.00 per machine hour

Press shop $\quad\dfrac{£7,000}{2,000}$ = £3.50 per labour hour

Assembly shop $\dfrac{£6,000}{2,500}$ = £2.40 per labour hour

Your completed costing should look like this:

Mayo Metalwork Ltd
Job No. 365

	£	£
Direct costs		
Direct materials		1,415
Add Direct labour		
Machine shop	150	
Press shop	450	
Assembly shop	175	775
Prime cost		2,190

	£	£
Add Production overheads		
Machine shop (210 × £4.00)	840	
Press shop (210 × £3.50)	630	
Assembly shop (100 × £2.40)	240	1,710
Production cost		3,900
Add Indirect costs		
Administration and selling overheads		975
Total cost		4,875
Add Profit		325
Selling price		5,200

Batch costing is similar to job costing. It is used where the individual units are so small that the resulting cost per unit would be very small indeed or where a specified number of identical units can be grouped together conveniently as a batch. The batch is treated as a single job. If the average cost per unit is required, the total costs for the batch are divided by the number of good units in the batch.

KEY DEFINITION	Batch costing is a method of costing for specific orders in which costs are attributed to a group of similar items that maintains its identity throughout one or more stages of production.

15.3 contract costing

Contract costing is used where the business has large, long-term contracts, such as construction and civil engineering projects. The contract agreed with the customer will include details of what work is to be carried out, the method and timing of payments and any financial penalties that can be invoked if the work is not completed to the required standard and in the agreed time. Contract costing allows the relevant costs for each contract to be identified and collected, and the profit or loss to be calculated on a contract at the end of a financial period. Only a proportion of the total profit on the contract is transferred to the profit and loss account on incomplete contracts at the end of the financial period.

The main characteristics of contract costing are as follows:

● Each contract takes a long time to complete and may span more than one accounting period.
● Most material is ordered specifically for each contract.
● Most labour costs, including staff such as site clerks and security guards whose wages are normally regarded as indirect costs, are direct costs to the contract.
● Most expenses, such as site electricity and telephones, are direct costs to the contract.
● A method must be found to charge plant and machinery used on site to the contract and the most appropriate is usually a time basis.

- Nearly all the overhead costs can be identified as head office costs.
- An architect or surveyor inspects the work periodically and issues certificates to the contractor that detail satisfactorily completed work. Such work is valued at selling price and the contractor sends the certificate to the client with an invoice to obtain interim payments.
- The contract often states that the client can withhold a proportion of the contract value for a period after final completion. This is known as *retention monies* and until the date when this is finally settled the contractor must make good any defects appearing in the work.

KEY DEFINITION	Contract costing is a method of costing for specific orders in which costs are attributed to individual long-term contracts.

The general procedure for collecting the costs of contracts is as follows:

- A separate account is opened for each contract. This is charged with all the costs and credited with the contract price. Each contract account is regarded as a separate profit and loss account. The profit or loss on each account is transferred to the main profit and loss on contracts account.
- Materials are charged either direct from the invoice or, if drawn from stores, from a materials requisition note. Any materials returned to stores from site are credited to the contract.
- All labour must be charged to each contract. If employees are working on a number of contracts at the same time, they must complete time sheets for each contract.
- Direct expenses can be charged directly from invoices submitted to the company. In the construction industry, a significant amount of the work may be completed by subcontractors, and these are regarded as direct expenses.
- Any plant and machinery costs are charged to the contract in a number of different ways, depending on the circumstances. If it is hired, the cost is a direct expense. If it is owned but on site short term, it is charged at an hourly rate for each item. If it is owned but is on site long term, the contract is charged with the value of the plant on arrival at the site and credited with its depreciated value when it is removed.
- Overhead costs are usually added on the basis of a predetermined overhead absorption rate. If a contract is unfinished at the end of the financial period, head office general costs are not added and only production overheads are included in the value of any work in progress.
- The contract price is credited to the contract account from the architect's certificate and any profit or loss transferred to the profit and loss on contracts account. An agreed percentage should not be transferred until all defects have been remedied and retention monies received.

To illustrate contract costing we will look at Kennet Construction Ltd, which has a long-term contract to restore a terrace of period houses at Worcester Place for a housing association. At the end of the financial year, 31 December, the following information is available.

```
                     Kennet Construction Ltd
              Contract No. 590 – Worcester Place
                                                        £
Value of materials delivered to site                125,160
Materials from stores                                22,240
Net book value of plant on site at 1 January        96,420
Operating costs of plant and machinery              11,470
Wages                                               53,120
Subcontractors' charges                             20,000
Site expenses                                       16,200
Materials returned to stores                         1,230
Net book value of plant removed from site           10,640
Materials on site at 31 December                    10,020
Net book value of plant on site at 31 December      74,240
Cost of work in progress not certified at 31 December  32,580
Total contract value                               500,000
Value of work certified at 31 December             250,000
Estimated costs to complete contract               220,000
```

Using this information, a contract account is drawn up as follows:

Kennet Construction Ltd Contract No. 590 – Worcester Place			
	£		£
Materials purchased	125,160	Materials to stores	1,230
Materials from stores	22,240	Plant transferred	10,640
Plant operating costs	11,470	Materials on site c/f	10,020
Plant to site	96,420	Plant on site c/d	74,240
Wages	53,120	Work in progress c/f	32,580
Subcontractors' charges	20,000	Cost of work certified	215,900
Site expenses	16,200		
	344,610		344,610
Cost of work certified b/d	215,900	Value of work certified	250,000
Profit on contract to date	16,718		
Profit in suspense c/d	17,382		
	250,000		250,000
1 January			
Materials on site b/f	10,020	Profit in suspense b/f	17,382
Plant on site b/f	74,240		
Work in progress b/f	32,580		

There are a number of calculations in the account that need explaining. The cost of work certified (£215,900) is the net balance on the first part of the contract account. The

cost of work not certified (the work in progress of £32,580) is added to the cost of work certified (£215,900) to give the cost of all work done to date (£248,480). The profit for the period
is calculated as follows:

	£	£
Contract value		500,000
Costs to date	248,480	
Estimated future costs	220,000	468,000
Estimated total profit		31,520

As the contract is not yet finished, it would be wrong to take the full amount of estimated
profit of £31,520 and only a proportion should be recognized in the profit and loss account.
There are a number of ways in which this can be calculated and the one used in this
example uses costs as follows:

$$\text{Profit for period} = \frac{\text{Cost of work done}}{\text{Estimated total costs}} \times \text{Estimated total profit}$$

$$= \frac{£248,480}{£468,480} \times £31,520$$

$$= £16,718$$

The profit in suspense is calculated as follows:

		£
	Value of work certified	250,000
Less	Cost of work certified	(215,900)
		34,100
Less	Profit in period	(16,718)
	Profit in suspense	17,382

activity

Kennet Construction Ltd started Contract No. 591 for a building project
in Salisbury Road on 1 March and it was completed on 31 August in the
same accounting period The following information is available:

Direct materials	£65,000
Direct labour	£42,000
Direct expenses	£13,000

The book value of plant charged to the contract on 1 March was
£75,000. At the completion of the contract, the plant was removed
from site and had a written down value of £68,000. The company
charges overheads to contracts at the rate of £1,500 per month. The
contract price was £150,000 and the final certificate has been issued.
Draw up a contract account.

Your completed contract account should look like this:

Kennet Construction Ltd Contract No. 591 – Salisbury Road			
	£		£
Materials	65,000	Cost of sales	136,000
Labour	42,000		
Expenses	13,000		
Plant costs (£75,000 – £68,000)	7,000		
Overheads (£1,500 × 6 months)	9,000		
	136,000		136,000

In the company's profit and loss account, £150,000 will be included in the figure for turnover and £136,000 will be shown in the cost of sales figure. Assuming there are no retention monies and no cash has been received from the client, an amount of £150,000 is due.

This concludes our examination of the main techniques for specific order costing, which are summarized in Figure 15.1.

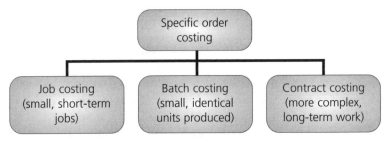

FIGURE 15.1 **Specific order costing techniques**

15.4 output costing

We will now turn our attention to the first of the methods used for costing continuous operations. *Output costing* is used when essentially only one product is being manufactured, although various types or grades of the product may be made. It is commonly used in highly mechanized industries, such as quarrying and the manufacture of cement. Costs are collected for the financial period (usually by nature) and the total is divided by the number of units produced to give an average cost per unit. Any partly completed units at the end of the financial period are usually ignored, as they are likely to be insignificant compared with the total number of whole units produced. In addition, the amount of unfinished units tends to be constant at the end of each period.

KEY DEFINITION	Output costing is a method of cost accounting used where only one product is manufactured.

The cost statements used by companies vary according to the nature of the industry and the information needs of managers. To allow some control, it is normal to show the costs classified by their nature for the period and the cost per unit. The general term for such a statement is a *unit cost statement*. It is useful if some basis of comparison is also given, such as the results for the previous period or the planned (budgeted) figures for the period (we will be looking at budgets in more detail in Chapter 18). The following example shows a unit cost statement for 1 kg of cement.

Unit cost statement for the month ending 30 April 2006			
	Total cost (10,000 kg) £	Actual unit cost (per kg) £	Planned unit cost (per kg) £
Salaries and wages	25,000	2.50	2.50
Materials	40,000	4.00	3.95
Packaging	2,000	0.20	0.25
Transport	3,500	0.35	0.35
Depreciation	4,500	0.45	0.45
Electricity	8,000	0.80	0.75
Rent and business rates	7,500	0.75	0.75
Repairs and maintenance	1,500	0.15	0.25
Total cost	92,000	9.20	9.25

You can see how the total costs for the month have been collected by the nature of the cost and that they have been divided by the number of units produced to give an average cost per unit. In this case, the comparative figures are the budgeted costs, which are the estimated figures prepared in advance of the financial period. You can see from a cursory examination of the actual and budgeted figures that although some of the actual costs were higher than the budget, others were exactly as planned or lower. However, management will be pleased that the actual average cost per unit for the month is 5p per kilogram lower than planned.

15.5 service costing

Service costing is used when specific services or functions, such as service centres, depart-ments or functions, are to be costed. The services may be offered to external parties, such as hotel accommodation or car hire, or the business may be a manufacturing organization that needs to know the cost of services provided internally, such as the canteen, stores or main-tenance department. The main problem is identifying a cost unit so that the service being provided can be measured. For example, a hotel may decide on an occupied bed night; a bus company on a passenger mile. If particular industries have agreed on common cost units, it is possible to make inter-company comparisons.

KEY DEFINITION   Service costing is a method of cost accounting used where specific services or functions are provided.

Many of the organizations using service costing are large, national businesses. Rigorous systems and procedures are therefore needed to collect and analyse the costs. Such organizations are often subject to fluctuating demands for their services (for example there are peak periods of demand during the day for electricity, water and public transport). Fluctuating demand means that managers will need information to distinguish between fixed costs and variable costs. However, not all service organizations use service costing because if the services provided do not have a high degree of homogeneity, a form of job costing must be used. This is the case with the services provided by professional practices of solicitors, accountants and architects, for example, whose services are tailored to the needs of individual clients.

There are a number of features associated with service costing. Usually the cost of direct materials is relatively small compared with direct labour and overhead costs. The service may not be a revenue earner, so the purpose of service costing is not to establish a profit or a loss, but to provide information to managers for the purpose of cost control and predicting future costs. A typical example is that of a factory canteen. The business needs to know the cost of running the canteen and the average cost per meal. A monthly statement is drawn up showing the various costs. Typically, these would include:

- *Labour costs* – Hourly paid staff need to complete time sheets to provide this information; the salaries of any supervisors and managers would be regarded as fixed costs.
- *Food and beverages* – These costs are collected from the suppliers' invoices. A separate stores may be in operation for supplies of food and beverages. If so, this will require the usual controls and procedures we described in Chapter 13.
- *Consumables* – These are items such as crockery, cutlery and cleaning materials that all require regular renewal.
- *Ovens, fixtures and fittings and equipment* – A depreciation charge is made for these fixed assets.
- *Occupancy or building costs* – Some apportionment is made so that the canteen carries a fair share of the costs incurred through the space it occupies.

All these costs are recorded for the month to give a total cost figure for running the canteen. By dividing this figure by the number of meals serviced during the period, the management accountant can calculate the average cost per meal.

---

activity

A training college has annual running costs per student of £800,000. It provides a basic training course that can be taken full time, block release or as a sandwich course. The following table gives details of the courses and the student numbers:

Mode of study	Number of students	Number of attendance days
Full time	60	125
Block release	300	34
Sandwich	180	85

Determine a suitable cost unit for the training college and calculate the cost per unit.

Although it is possible to use a student as a cost unit, this would not provide a meaningful figure because of the different modes of study. An alternative would be to use a student day as the cost unit by multiplying the number of students by the number of attendance days for each mode of study, as follows:

Mode of study	Number of students	Number of attendance days	Number of student days
Full time	60	125	7,500
Block release	300	34	10,200
Sandwich	180	85	15,300
			33,000

$$\text{Cost per student day} = \frac{£800,000}{33,000} = £24.24$$

15.6 process costing

Process costing is a method of costing used when the production process is carried out in a series of stages. In other words, the finished output at one stage of production becomes the input for the next stage in the process and so on. At the end of all the stages, the completed production is sold or transferred to finished goods stock. This type of production is often found in chemical works, oil refineries and paint manufacturers.

KEY DEFINITION — Process costing is a method of cost accounting used where the production process is carried out as a sequence of operations.

Costs are accumulated for the whole process and average unit costs of production are computed at each stage. In process costing special rules are applied to the valuation of work in progress (WIP), normal losses and abnormal losses and it is usual to distinguish between the main product of the process, by-products and joint products. For each stage in the process, both direct costs, such as materials and labour, and production overheads are charged. By dividing the costs on one process by the number of units, the average cost per unit is calculated. Cost units that are similar in nature pass through each of the production processes. It is essential that appropriate cost units are chosen. For a liquid product, the cost unit might be a litre; for a solid product, a kilogram or a tonne would be more appropriate. As cost units move from one process to another, the costs incurred accumulate and are transferred with them.

Although the actual method of process costing varies from one organization to another, the main features of such costing systems are as follows:

● There are separate processes that can be defined easily and the costs collected for each process.

- The output from one process forms the input of the next process.
- Both direct costs and overheads are charged to the processes.
- Costs are accumulated in respect of cost units as production goes through the various processes.
- The average unit cost is calculated by dividing the total cost of a process for a period of time by the number of cost units for the period.

The latter can be expressed as a formula:

$$\text{Average cost per unit} = \frac{\text{Costs incurred during the period}}{\text{Number of units produced}}$$

We will look at an example to illustrate how the formula is used to arrive at the average cost per unit for the period. Brilliant Paints plc produced 50,000 completed units in January and the following cost information is available:

Direct materials	£5,000
Direct labour	£3,500
Production overheads	£1,500

A simple calculation gives the total costs of this production of £10,000. The relevant figures can now be inserted in the formula as follows:

$$\text{Average cost per unit} = \frac{£10,000}{50,000} = £0.20$$

At the end of the financial period there are always some units that are only partly complete because they have not yet passed through the entire production process. This balance of unfinished work is known as *work in progress (WIP)*. The costs incurred for the period relate to all the units, whether completed or only partly completed. To find out the average cost per unit when there are partly completed units, we must first convert them to the equivalent of whole units known as *equivalent units*. For example, if there are 2,000 partly finished units in WIP that were 50% complete, they would be counted as 1,000 equivalent units (2,000 × 50%). We can now adjust the formula for calculating the average cost per unit for the period as follows:

$$\text{Average costs per unit} = \frac{\text{Costs incurred during the period}}{\text{Completed units produced} + \text{Equivalent units in WIP}}$$

We will now apply these principles to Brilliant Paints plc, which produced 55,000 completed units in February. WIP was 2,000 units which were 50% complete and the costs incurred for the period were as follows:

Direct materials	£5,500
Direct labour	£4,000
Production overheads	£1,500

Substituting the figures in the formula:

$$\text{Average cost per unit} = \frac{£11,000}{55,000 + (2,000 \times 50\%)} = £0.20$$

The costs incurred in production comprise the usual elements of direct materials, direct labour and production overheads. When WIP is examined at the end of a period, the degree of completion may vary for each cost element. For example, the units may be almost complete as far as materials are concerned, but further substantial labour and overhead costs may be incurred in order to complete the units. In such cases, the cost elements must be treated separately in order to find out the number of equivalent units before the average cost per unit can be calculated.

activity

Moving on to March, the following figures are available for Process 1 at Brilliant Paints plc:

Direct materials	£8,050
Direct labour	£12,375
Production overheads	£8,400

There are 5,000 completed units and 1,000 units in WIP. The units in WIP are 75% complete for materials, 50% complete for labour and 25% for production overheads. Calculate the average cost per unit.

Using the formula, you should not have had too much difficulty with this activity. First you need to calculate the value of WIP for each of the elements of cost:

$$\text{Direct materials} \left(\frac{£8,050}{5,000 + (1,000 \text{ WIP units} \times 75\%)} \right) \qquad 1.40$$

$$\text{Direct labour} \left(\frac{£12,375}{5,000 + (1,000 \text{ WIP units} \times 50\%)} \right) \qquad 2.25$$

$$\text{Production overheads} \left(\frac{£8,400}{5,000 + (1,000 \text{ WIP units} \times 25\%)} \right) \qquad 1.60$$

Total cost per unit $\underline{\underline{5.25}}$

The next step is to calculate the cost of the equivalent units:

	£	£
Direct materials (750 equivalent units × £1.40)	1,050	
Direct labour (500 equivalent units × £2.25)	1,125	
Production overheads (250 equivalent units × £1.60)	400	2,575
Value of completed units (5,000 units × £5.25)		26,250
Cost of equivalent units		28,825

You may have noticed that the value of WIP (£2,575) plus the value of the completed units (£26,250) equals the total cost incurred for Process 1 for March (£28,825). This is a check that should always be carried out.

So far we have only considered the first process. Let us take the above figure of 5,000 completed units at the end of March for Process 1 and add information concerning Process 2, which is the second stage of production. At the end of April, the following information is available:

Direct materials	£6,000
Direct labour	£3,800
Production overheads	£2,850

There were 4,500 completed units transferred to stock and 500 units in WIP that were 50% complete. With this information we can calculate the value of WIP and the completed production transferred to finished goods store at the end of April. However, there are two points to note. The first point is that Process 2 starts with the 5,000 units transferred from Process 1 at the end of March. The second point is that when calculating the number of equivalent units, there will be no further materials costs incurred, as materials were needed at the start of the process. WIP is therefore 100% complete as far as direct materials are concerned. The following table offers a suitable layout for tackling the calculations in a logical way:

Brilliant Paints plc
Process 2 – Costs for April

Cost element	Total cost	Completed units	Equivalent units in WIP	Effective units	Cost per unit	Value of WIP
	£				£	£
Previous process costs	26,250	4,500	500	5,000	5.25	2,625
Direct materials	6,000	4,500	500	5,000	1.20	600
Direct labour	3,800	4,500	250	4,750	0.80	200
Production overheads	2,850	4,500	250	4,750	0.60	150
	38,900				7.85	3,575

	£
Value of completed units (4,500 × £7.85)	35,325
Value of WIP	3,575
Total cost	38,900

This example illustrates a number of important points. The first and second columns in the table are straightforward; the third column shows the number of completed units transferred to finished goods stock. The fourth column shows the number of equivalent units in WIP. There are 500 units in WIP and for previous process costs and materials costs the units are 100% complete. By definition, previous process costs are always complete. In this example, the materials were added at the beginning of the process. This means that even when there are partly finished units in WIP at the end of the period, the units must be complete as far as the material cost element is concerned. This is a favourite examination topic and the following rules should be applied:

- If any cost elements are added at the start of the process, no further costs of this nature will be incurred.
- If any cost elements are added at the end of the process, as the units in WIP have not reached this stage, no part of the cost element can be included in WIP.
- Having calculated the number of equivalent units, this is added to the number of completed units to give the number of total effective units. The total cost for each element in the second column is divided by the number of total effective units to give the cost per unit in the sixth column. To find the value of WIP, the number of equivalent units in WIP for each element is multiplied by the cost per unit.
- The final stage is to calculate the value of the completed units at the bottom of the table and add the value of WIP. The total of these two figures must agree with the figure of total costs as shown in the second column.

Closing WIP for a process at the end of one period forms the opening WIP for the same process at the start of the next period. This raises the problem of how WIP should be valued. Certain assumptions can be made to decide the method of valuation. Management may assume that the units comprising WIP are completed during the current period and use the first in, first out (FIFO) method (see Chapter 13). Alternatively, it may be assumed that the partly finished units forming the opening WIP are mixed with the current period's production and as it is not known which units are completed at the end of the period, the average cost method can be used. We will use an example to illustrate both these methods.

Brilliant Paints plc has three production processes. For the month of December, the opening WIP for Process 2 was 300 units (50% complete) valued at £4,500. At the start of the period, there were 900 completed units transferred from Process 1 and these were valued at £2,700. The total costs for Process 2 for the month were £8,100. At the end of December, 1,000 completed units were transferred to Process 3 and the closing WIP was 200 units, which were 25% complete. We will now calculate the value of closing WIP using FIFO. The various calculations can be broken down into a number of steps as follows:

1. The number of effective units produced by Process 2 during December:

	Units
Closing WIP (200 × 25%)	50
Completed units transferred to Process 3	1,000
	1,050
Less Opening WIP (300 × 50%)	(150)
Effective units produced in the period	900

2. Costs incurred during the month to produce 900 effective units:

	£
Costs transferred from Process 1	2,700
Other costs incurred in the period	8,100
Cost of effective units produced in the period	10,800

3. Valuation of closing WIP:

$$\frac{\text{Total costs incurred in period}}{\text{Number of effective units}} = \frac{£10,800}{900} = £12 \text{ per unit}$$

Number of equivalent units in WIP (200 × 25%) = 50

Therefore, the value of closing WIP = 50 units × £12 = £600

4. Valuation of 1,000 completed units transferred to Process 3:

	£
Opening WIP	4,500
Costs transferred from Process 1	2,700
Other costs incurred in the period	8,100
	15,300
Less Closing WIP	(600)
Value of completed units transferred to Process 3	14,700

Using the *average cost method*, the opening WIP valuation plus the period costs are used to calculate the average cost per unit. The same average cost per unit is used to value both the closing WIP and the completed units. The steps are as follows:

1. The number of effective units produced by Process 2 during December:

	Units
Completed units transferred to Process 3	1,000
Closing WIP (200 × 25%)	50
	1,050

2. Total costs incurred:

	£
Opening WIP	4,500
Costs transferred from Process 1	2,700
Other costs incurred in the period	8,100
Total costs incurred in the period	15,300

3. Valuation of closing WIP:

$$\frac{\text{Total costs incurred}}{\text{Total number of effective units}} = \frac{£15,300}{1,050} = £14.5714$$

Therefore, the value of closing WIP = (200 × 25%) × £14.5714 = £728.57

4. Valuation of 1,000 completed units transferred to Process 3:

	£
Costs transferred to Process 3 (1,000 × £14,5714)	14,571.40
Closing WIP	728.57
Value of completed units transferred to Process 3	15,299.97

The above examples demonstrate the input of the different WIP valuations on the value of completed units transferred to the next process. The consequence is that under the two different methods the final profit for the business will also differ. Therefore, once a policy has been established, it is essential that the accountant uses that method consistently.

15.7 waste

One aspect that needs to be considered in process costing is how to account for *waste* (also known as *spoilage*) because even in a highly efficient production process there is likely to be an amount of material that is spoilt or otherwise wasted during the production process. An acceptable level of waste, known as *normal loss*, is included in the cost of production and allowed for in the product costs. Normal loss can take place at any point in the process. When waste occurs partway through a process, some of the loss is charged to WIP. If the loss takes place at the end of a process (for example at the final inspection stage), only those units that have been completed during the period are charged with the loss. The procedure for dealing with normal loss occurring at the end of the process is as follows:

* Complete a table for process costs as explained in the previous section.
* The third column of the table should show all the completed units, both the good units and those which have been designated as normal loss.
* Complete the table and use the cost per unit to calculate the value of the normal loss.
* Divide the value of the normal loss by the number of good completed units and add to the original cost per unit to obtain a revised cost per unit.

We will illustrate this by returning to our example of Brilliant Paints plc where the following information for the period is available:

Direct materials (added at the start of the process)	£18,000
Direct labour	£31,000
Production overheads	£15,725

There were 2,000 units of closing WIP at the end of the period, which were 50% complete as far as labour costs were concerned and 25% complete with regard to production overheads. There were 18,000 completed units, of which 1,000 units were scrapped. Using this information, we can construct a table to calculate the process costs.

Brilliant Paints plc
Normal loss process costs for the period

Cost element	Total cost	Completed units	Equivalent units in WIP	Effective units	Cost per unit	Value of WIP
	£				£	£
Direct materials	18,000	18,000	2,000	20,000	0.90	1,800
Direct labour	31,350	18,000	1,000	19,000	1.65	1,650
Production overheads	15,725	18,000	500	18,500	0.85	425
	65,075				3.40	3,875

Value of normal loss $\left(\dfrac{1{,}000 \times £3.40}{17{,}000}\right)$ 0.20

Revised cost per unit   3.60

	£
Value of completed units (17,500 x £3.60)	61,200
Value of WIP	3,875
	65,075

Having considered normal loss in a manufacturing or chemical process, we will now turn our attention to *abnormal loss*, which is the loss arising from abnormal waste, shrinkage, seepage or spoilage in excess of the normal loss. It may be expressed as a weight or volume or in other units appropriate to the process and is usually valued on the same basis as the good output. An abnormal gain is an unexpected surplus of output that may occur if the actual loss is less than the normal loss. The abnormal losses must carry their share of the costs of the normal losses. It is important to do this calculation before working out the value of the abnormal loss to be charged to the profit and loss account. The procedure is as follows:

- Complete a table for process costs, as explained earlier.
- The third column of the table should show all the completed units: the good units, those which have been designated as normal loss and the abnormal loss.
- Complete the table and use the cost per unit to calculate the value of the normal loss.
- Divide the value of the normal loss by the number of good completed units and abnormal loss units and add to the original cost per unit to obtain a revised cost per unit.
- Multiply the revised cost per unit by the number of units of abnormal loss to obtain the value of the abnormal loss to be charged to the profit and loss account.

activity

Brilliant Paints plc has provided the following information for the period:

Direct materials (added at the start of the process)	£50,000
Direct labour	£47,500
Production overheads	£18,000

There were 2,000 units of closing WIP at the end of the period, which were 75% complete as far as labour costs were concerned and 50% complete with regard to production overheads. There were 8,000 completed units. Normal loss is 500 units, but actual waste in the period was 750 units. Using this information, construct a table to calculate the process costs.

If you were able to follow the procedure for calculating normal loss, you should not have had too many problems with this activity. Check your answer against the following:

Brilliant Paints plc Abnormal loss process costs for the period					
Cost element	Total cost	Completed units	Equivalent units in WIP	Effective units	Cost per unit	Value of WIP
	£				£	£
Direct materials	50,000	8,000	2,000	10,000	5.00	10,000
Direct labour	47,500	8,000	1,500	9,500	5.00	7,500
Production overheads	18,000	8,000	1,000	9,000	2.00	2,000
	115,500				12.00	19,500

$$\text{Value of normal loss} \left(\frac{500 \times £12.00}{7,500}\right) \quad 0.80$$

Revised cost per unit   12.80

	£
Value of completed units (7,250 × £12.80)	92,800
Value of WIP	19,500
Value of abnormal loss (250 × £12.80)	3,200
	115,500

The abnormal loss of £3,200 (250 units valued at £12.80) will be written off in the profit and loss account for the period.

This concludes our examination of the main techniques for costing continuous operations, which are summarized in Figure 5.2.

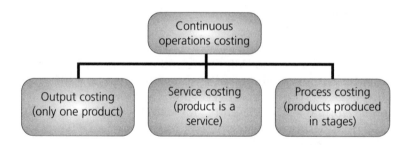

FIGURE 15.2 **Continuous operations costing techniques**

15.8 conclusions

In this chapter we have looked at a number of techniques that help provide management with information for calculating the cost of products and services. The type of technique used depends on whether those products and services represent specific orders or arise as a result of continuous operations. Although the costing methods for specific orders have much in common, each has its own requirements:

- Job costing is used when customers specify their requirements and the order is for work that is relatively small in size and short in duration.

- Batch costing is used if the cost units are very small and/or homogeneous. The costs for each batch are collected in the same way as for job costing. The total batch cost can be divided by the number of good units produced to give the average cost per unit.
- Contract costing is used where the work is large and often complex, and the contract spans more than one accounting period. A particular problem of long-term projects is how to determine the annual profits to be taken to the profit and loss account when the contract is incomplete. This requires the valuation of work in progress at the end of the financial year. When work has been done, but has not yet been certified, it is valued at cost, without any profit element.

There are three main methods for costing continuous operations:

- Output costing has some of the features of job costing insofar as the aim is to calculate the cost per unit. However, output costing is used where standardized goods or services are produced from a single operation over a period of time.
- Service costing is used for costing services provided to internal or external customers.
- Process costing is used where production is carried out as a series of processes. Costs are accumulated for the whole production process and average unit costs of production computed at each stage. Special rules are applied to the valuation of work in progress and waste.

practice questions

1. Distinguish between normal losses, abnormal losses and explain their costing treatments.
2. Imprint Ltd is a jobbing printer and the business recovers production overheads at £2.50 per direct labour hour and adds 20% for general overheads to the total production costs to arrive at the total cost of a job. A further 25% is added to the total cost to arrive at the selling price. Job 213 is an order for wedding invitations to be printed for a customer, for which the following additional information is available:

Materials	£30.00
Labour	4 hours
Wages	£5 per hour

Required
Calculate the selling price for Job 213.

3. Townday Building Ltd is undertaking Contract No. 33 where the price is £320,000 and the estimated total cost of the contract is estimated at £260,000. At the end of the financial year, the cost of work certified is £140,000 and the cost of work done but not certified is £34,000. The company intends to calculate its profit at the year end using costs as the basis of the estimated degree of completion.

Required
Calculate the share of profit at the year end on the incomplete Contract No. 33.

4. Each month Pollution Control Ltd carries out 240 standard tests for traces of hydrocarbons in its laboratory. The annual costs of running this service department are as follows:

Technician's wages	£12,000
Materials	£2,500
Overheads	£15,500

    Required
    Calculate the cost per test.

5. The following production information is available for Paul Wilkinson (Processing) Ltd for the month of August:

Number of units received from Process 1	16,000
Value of units received	£910,000
Processing costs	
Labour and overheads	£701,200
Materials introduced	£49,500

    There was no WIP at the beginning of the period, but at the end of the period there was WIP of 3,800 units, which were 100% complete for materials and 50% complete for labour and overheads.

    Required
    Construct a cost statement for Process 2 that calculates the cost per effective unit completed during the month of August, the value of the completed units and the value of WIP at the end of the month.

chapter 16

activity-based costing

When you have studied this chapter, you should be able to:

- Explain how activity-based costing can add value to the business

- Calculate product costs using activity-based costing

- Apply activity-based costing to marketing and administration functions

- Describe the advantages and disadvantages of activity-based costing.

16.1 introduction

You will remember from previous chapters that revenue expenditure can be classified into product direct costs, which can be traced directly to a cost unit, and indirect costs, which cannot. We looked at the methods for costing product direct costs (direct materials, direct labour and direct expenses) in Chapter 13 and then examined absorption costing in Chapter 14. Absorption costing is based on the allocation and apportionment of indirect costs or overheads to production cost centres and their absorption into the cost of products using predetermined rates. *Activity-based costing (ABC)* is an alternative cost accounting system for indirect costs. Its name is derived from the fact that costs are assigned first to activities and then to the cost units on the basis of the use they make of these activities.

In this chapter we start by examining the need for an alternative approach and explain how ABC developed as a reaction to perceived deficiencies in absorption costing, the traditional approach. We describe the main stages in ABC and define the terms used. We then go on to provide a worked example in order to demonstrate how the product costs are calculated before considering the advantages and disadvantages of this alternative method.

16.2 need for an alternative to absorption costing

In absorption costing (see Chapter 14), each product or cost unit is charged with a fair share of the indirect costs or overheads, thus enabling the total cost (the direct costs plus the indirect costs) of the firm's products to be calculated. Under this system, any overheads that cannot be allocated to a particular production cost centre must be apportioned on whatever is judged to be a fair basis. The resulting total production cost centre overhead is then absorbed into the cost of the product using a predetermined overhead absorption rate. In a simple business with only one product, this rate can be based on the number of cost units passing through the production cost centre. In a more complex business, it is commonly based on time, such as direct labour hours or machine hours.

Although accountants try to be as rigorous as possible in the application of absorption costing, this costing system is based on arbitrary decisions about the basis for apportionment and absorption of overheads. In addition, general overheads are spread across the product range with little regard for how the costs are actually generated. Therefore, there is always some concern that the total cost of each product is not being calculated in the most precise manner. If the business is miscalculating the cost of its products and basing its selling prices on this inaccurate information, it could have a dramatic impact on financial performance. For example, if the inaccuracies result in selling prices that are too high, the business could lose market share to competitors; if they result in selling prices that are too low, the business will not achieve its planned profit. To overcome these potential problems, some firms now use activity-based costing (ABC).

ABC was proposed by Johnson and Kaplan (1987), who questioned the relevance of traditional management accounting practices to modern business. Management accounting has its roots in the Industrial Revolution of the 19th century, when manufacturing was the major industry. However, as the century progressed, a need for financial accounting began to evolve and they suggest that this split was one of the main causes for what they describe as the fall in the relevance of management accounting. A second reason they give is that modern business is no longer dominated by the manufacturing industry and therefore management accounting techniques based on the needs of manufacturers are not relevant to businesses in non-manufacturing sectors.

Due to the increased complexity of production operations, many manufacturing businesses now use computer-controlled operations and robotic methods of production (car manufacturers, for example). Why do you think this might encourage firms to consider activity-based costing as an alternative to absorption costing?

You may have thought of several reasons, but one key reason is that advances in technology have increased overhead costs, such as power, maintenance and depreciation of machinery. Therefore, it is critical that these costs are charged to the products as accurately as possible. The increased use of technology has also been associated with a decline in the importance of direct labour and a change in its characteristics. Employees who provide direct labour are often paid on a monthly basis rather than an hourly basis as in the past. In addition, their remuneration is less closely related to the level of production and they are likely to receive additional benefits, such as pensions and sick pay, which were formally only given to managers and administrators.

A further factor that is important in some firms is the amount of stock (or inventory) they hold. You will recall from previous chapters that the correct value placed on closing stock is critical for calculating the profit or loss for a financial period. This stock value normally includes a share of indirect overheads. Increasing companies have moved to JIT techniques, where a low level of stock is held and receipts of raw materials and delivery of finished goods to customers are phased in with the production process. With low stock levels, the value of closing stock has declined in importance.

In addition to these internal developments, competition has been increasing and firms are using a variety of techniques to improve the efficiency of their manufacturing operations. These include *value-added analysis*, where operations that do not add value in converting the raw materials into the final product are examined and eliminated if possible. One of the claims made for ABC is that it enhances the value added to production for a business that has complex manufacturing processes and several different products, because it recognizes that costs are incurred by every activity in the organization and is based on the principle that the cost units should bear costs according to the activities they use.

KEY DEFINITIONS

Activity-based costing (ABC) is a method of costing in which overheads are assigned to activities and cost drivers are used to attach the activity cost pools to the cost units.

An activity cost pool is a collection of all the elements of cost associated with an activity.

A cost driver is any factor that causes a change in the cost of an activity. An activity may have multiple cost drivers associated with it.

16.3 main stages in activity-based costing

The two main stages in ABC are shown in Figure 16.1. First, the overhead costs are assigned to the different activities in the business and then cost drivers are used to attach activity costs to the cost units.

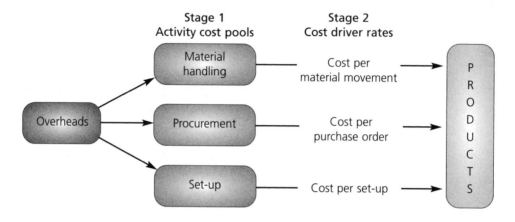

FIGURE 16.1 **Main stages in ABC**
Source: CIMA, 1996, p. 21.

This makes ABC look misleadingly simple, but each stage involves a substantial amount of research into the firm's operations and costing procedures. This can be highly beneficial, but can cause disruption to normal production. The implementation of an activity-based costing system involves four main steps:

1. Identify the main *activities* in the organization and classify them into activity centres if there are a large number of different activities. An activity centre is an identifiable unit of the organization that performs an operation that uses resources. For most organizations the first activity will be the purchase of materials. This will involve several sub-activities, such as drawing up material specifications, selecting suppliers, placing the order, receiving and inspecting the materials that have been delivered.
2. Identify the *cost drivers* associated with each activity centre. A cost driver is any factor that causes a change in the cost of an activity or series of activities that takes place in the business. For example, with the purchase of materials, it would be the number of orders placed. If we were looking at the costs of operating a customer support hotline, it might be the number of calls answered; for a quality control activity, it might be the number of hours of inspection conducted. Some activities have multiple cost drivers and it is important to note that cost drivers are not confined to a specific department.
3. Calculate the *cost driver rate*. This is the cost per unit of activity. For example, in purchasing it would be the cost per order placed.
4. Assign costs to the products by multiplying the cost driver rate by the volume of the cost driver units consumed by the product. With purchasing, the cost driver rate will be calcu-

lated on the basis of orders placed. If Product A requires 15 orders to be placed in January, the cost of purchasing activity for Product A will be 15 times the cost driver rate.

Figure 16.2 contrasts the main stages in absorption costing with those involved in ABC.

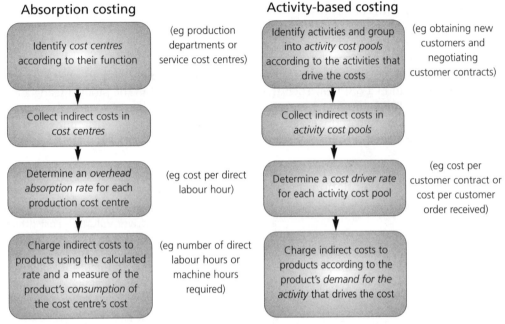

FIGURE 16.2 **Comparison of the main stages in absorption costing and ABC**
Source: Adapted from Weetman, 1999, p. 751.

16.4 activities and cost drivers

As a general rule, the more complex the production process, the greater the number of different activities and cost drivers. A business making a simple product is likely to find that any differences have little impact on overhead costs.

> **activity**
>
> List the various activities that the owner of a takeaway pizza business has to undertake in order to make and deliver pizzas to customers.

You may be surprised at the number of activities you have been able to list, even if you omit all the administration and advertising. You will probably have identified some of the following activities or more, depending on the assumptions you made about the size of the business:

- Ordering raw materials, such as flour, meat and vegetables (usually referred to as procurement)

- Preparation of raw materials and disposal of waste
- Cooking
- Cleaning and maintenance of kitchen equipment
- Employment of delivery staff
- Receiving orders from customers
- Dealing with complaints.

With complex productions and a wide range of products, there are likely to be a great many activities, but companies usually restrict their analysis to the key activities. Any major activity is likely to have several overhead costs associated with it, which are grouped together to form a *cost pool*. Then the cost pool is charged to the product using a common cost driver. The following table gives examples of activities and cost drivers and shows how the predetermined cost driver rate is calculated by dividing the predetermined overhead by the predetermined cost driver volume.

Calculating the predetermined cost driver rate

Activity	Cost driver	Predetermined annual overhead £	Predetermined cost driver volume	Predetermined cost driver rate
Purchasing	Number of orders placed	400,000	100,000 orders	£4 per order
Machine setups	Number of machine setups	300,000	300 setups	£1,000 per setup
Quality control	Number of inspection hours	500,000	5,000 hours	£100 per hour
Power	Number of machine hours	250,000	100,000 hours	£2.50 per hour
Total		1,450,000		

The above table shows that the business anticipates that the annual production overheads will total £1,450,000. You need to remember that this is in addition to the direct costs (that is, direct materials, direct labour and direct expenses). The predetermined cost driver volume has been calculated for the year and the last column shows the calculation of the predetermined cost driver rate.

activity

A business makes two products (Product A and Product B). Using the following information for the month of January, calculate the total production cost of the two products for the period:

	Product A	Product B
Direct labour costs	£ 95,000	£120,000
Direct material costs	£116,000	£145,000
Number of purchase orders placed	3,000	8,000
Number of machine setups	12	18
Total of inspection hours	350	180
Total machine hours	6,000	5,500

At this stage in your studies, you should have had little difficulty in activity-based costing procedures. Check your calculations against the following model answer:

	Product A	Product B
	£	£
Direct labour costs	95,000	120,000
Direct material costs	116,000	145,000
Purchasing	12,000	32,000
Machine setups	12,000	18,000
Quality control	35,000	18,000
Power	15,000	13,750
Total	285,000	346,750

16.5 the decision to adopt activity-based costing

Managers considering whether to adopt ABC will need to make a number of decisions. The example in the previous section simplifies the process greatly; in real life there are likely to be many problems that must be resolved.

activity

> What do you consider are the main benefits and drawbacks to adopting an activity-based costing system?

There are several benefits and drawbacks, most of which relate to the benefit of having more accurate cost information and the drawback of incurring costs in order to acquire it. You may have identified the following:

- The different basis for assigning costs to products is likely to result in a different total cost per unit. This can have important consequences for decision making and strategy in the company.
- The cost information should be more accurate and could lead to some products being eliminated and changes in the market price of other products.
- More record keeping will be involved and this may require more trained staff and new computer systems.
- Installing the system will require teamwork between accounting, production, marketing and other functions in the company.

Management must conduct a cost/benefit analysis before implementing ABC. Unless the expected benefits are greater than the costs, the firm should not go ahead with changing from absorption costing to ABC.

16.6 costing for marketing and administration overheads

Many firms that use traditional absorption costing to calculate the total cost of a product tend to concentrate on production costs. Marketing and administration overheads are often added to the total production cost using a *blanket rate* for the factory as a whole, which replaces the need to calculate a separate rate for each production cost centre.

What are the advantages and disadvantages in using a blanket rate?

A key advantage is that it is simple to calculate and apply. The accountant only needs to collect all the overheads together and then select one allocation base. The allocation base is normally related to volume so it could be number of products, direct hour rate or machine hour rate. A blanket rate may be acceptable in a very simple organization with very few products, but there are disadvantages. One main disadvantage is that if there is more than one activity, the blanket rate may distort the total cost. For example, if there are two prod- ucts and the marketing department is spending most of its time in promoting one of them, it would not be equitable to charge the other product the same overhead rate. Firms using absorption costing will attempt to achieve a better allocation of costs by identifying sepa- rate departments and different rates. It will take more time and effort to collect the informa- tion and make the calculations, but the resulting costing data will be more informative for management decision making.

In complex organizations, management may decide it is worth the additional costs to implement ABC. In such cases, this cost accounting system can be used to break down the costs involved in marketing and administration by applying the same principles as used for production costs. This enables management to make decisions about the operation of marketing and administration and determine whether it is possible to add value.

We will demonstrate this by applying the principles to Photoprint Ltd, a small company that designs and prints high quality calendars. One of the products is a wildlife calendar, which features photographs and information on endangered species. Each calendar costs £20 to print and it has been the firm's practice to add 15% to cover the cost of advertising, postage and packaging (£20 ? 15% = £3.00). Advertising has been by sending leaflets to a large customer mailing list that the company has built up over the years.

However, management is concerned that the price it charges for the calendar to make a profit is not sufficiently competitive and that its existing customer database contains a substantial amount of out-of-date information. In addition, the accountant has looked at the marketing side of the operation and has identified the following activities that give rise to costs:

- Sending out leaflets to potential customers
- Taking orders by post, telephone or through the internet
- Sending calendars to customers who have ordered them
- Dealing with customer queries (for example non-deliveries and complaints about damaged goods).

These activities are shown in the first column of the following table and the second column identifies the cost driver. The third column shows an estimate of the annual costs for each activity and the forth column gives details of the estimated annual driver volume. The final column calculates the cost driver rate by dividing the estimated annual cost of each activity by its estimated driver volume.

Activities	Cost drivers	Estimated annual costs £	Estimated driver volume	Cost driver rate £
Leaflet design and printing	Customer mailing list	80,000	100,000	0.80
Leaflet dispatch	Customer mailing list	23,000	100,000	0.23
Taking orders	Number of orders	6,000	10,000	0.60
Calendar dispatch	Number sent	4,410	9,800	0.45
Customer complaints	Customer complaints	300	200	1.50
Total cost				3.58

At first glance, the blanket marketing cost of £3.00 per calendar does not look very different from the cost driver rate of £3.58 shown in the above table. However, the reality is that the operation is costing £3.58 per calendar and this is reducing predicted profit by 58p per calendar. It also means that as the market is competitive, management needs to make decisions about the future of the operation.

With the above information, management can consider each activity and determine whether savings can be made. For example, instead of sending leaflets to an existing customer mailing list, it may be more effective and less costly to have advertisements in appropriate magazines. As far as taking orders is concerned, management may decide to accept internet orders only or to outsource the entire operation.

16.7 advantages and disadvantages

You may be wondering why every business has not adopted ABC, if it is such a good system. One of the main reasons is the question of cost and the problems associated with change. There is little inducement to undertake the substantial changes required to introduce a new system, if the business already produces product costing information that meets their needs. Even if the business is not entirely satisfied with its present system, the cost of implementing and managing a new system may seem too large to make it worthwhile.

ABC is probably best suited for businesses that operate in highly competitive markets and have many different products that require complex production processes. In such organizations the arbitrary process of traditional absorption costing does not generate sufficiently specific information to aid managers in planning, controlling and decision making. The main *advantages* of ABC are as follows:

- It provides more comprehensive detail about product costs.
- It generates data that is more specific and reliable than traditional costing.
- Because it does not distinguish between production overheads and general overheads, it overcomes the problem of finding a meaningful relationship between these non-production overheads and the production activity.

- It provides better information about the costs of activities, thus allowing managers to make more informed decisions.
- It improves cost control by identifying the costs incurred by specific activities.

The main *disadvantages* of ABC are:

- It can be costly and difficult to implement.
- Trained and experienced staff are required to operate the system.
- Substantial IT costs may be required.
- Managers may not find the information useful.
- It uses predetermined rates and therefore underabsorption or overabsorption of overheads will still occur as they do under absorption costing.

16.8 conclusions

Activity-based costing has emerged as an alternative to absorption costing because of changes in manufacturing operations. The greater use of technology, the use of techniques such as JIT and the reduction and change in the nature of direct labour have meant that traditional costing methods are not providing sufficiently accurate information for decision-making purposes.

ABC is a costing system in which costs are first assigned to activities and then to products based on each product's use of activities. The principle assumption is that products consume activities and activities consume resources. There are four stages in implementing an activity-based costing system. These appear simple, but in practice they are complex and time-consuming. One of the major problems for companies is identifying those activities that consume resources and keeping this to a workable number. Once the activities have been identified and the costs assigned to them, a cost rate can be calculated by using the cost driver.

ABC offers the advantage of more accurate information than absorption costing because it looks for a closer relationship between overheads and the cause of these indirect costs. However, it suffers from the disadvantage that it is costly to implement and operate. It is most suitable for complex organizations with a range of products where absorption costing fails to provide costing information that is useful to management.

practice questions

1. Discuss the reasons why accountants have developed ABC as an alternative to the traditional method of absorption costing for charging overheads to products or services.
2. Describe the four main stages in implementing a system of activity-based costing, defining all terms used.
3. Write a short report discussing the types of business where ABC might be appropriate and the advantages and disadvantages of implementing this type of cost accounting system.
4. Galloy Communications Ltd manufactures two types of telephone: the standard and the advanced. The budget for the next financial year is as follows:

	Standard	Advanced
Production output	100,000	50,000
	£	£
Direct labour	200,000	100,000
Direct materials	50,000	20,000

The indirect overhead costs have been identified with three cost drivers as follows:

Cost driver	Cost assigned	Activity level Standard	Activity level Advanced
Number of production runs	£150,000	40	10
Quality test performed	£40,000	8	12
Deliveries made	£20,000	80	20

Required

(a) Calculate the total cost per unit produced for each product.

(b) Prepare a presentation to be given to the board demonstrating the calculations and interpreting the results.

5. Perfect Perfumes Plc has a factory in France producing two aromatherapy oils. Sweet Dreams is intended for the mainstream market and Allure is aimed at the more sophisticated customer. The most significant costs incurred by the company relate to the packaging and advertising of the two products. The chief accountant has attended a seminar on ABC and has decided that it would be beneficial to implement it. The following information relates to the production in the current period:

	Sweet Dreams	Allure
Number of litres produced	20,000	4,000
Number of purchasing orders	150	60
Quality inspection hours	1,000	750
Number of batches of materials	2,000	1,000
	€	€
Cost of direct materials	35,000	12,000
Cost of direct labour	25,000	16,000

The budgeted cost pools and drivers for the financial year are as follows:

Activity	Cost driver	Predetermined annual overhead	Predetermined cost driver volume	Predetermined cost driver rate
		€	€	€
Purchasing	Number of orders placed	180,000	15,000 orders	12 per order
Quality control	Number of inspection hours	50,000	12,500 hours	4 per hour
Material handling	Batches of materials	20,000	10,000 hours	2 per hour

Required
(a) Calculate the cost per unit for each of the two products.
(b) Discuss the decision of the chief accountant to implement the system in the context of the available information.

references

Johnson, H. T. and Kaplan, R. S. (1987) *Relevance Lost: The Rise and Fall of Management Accounting*, Boston: Harvard Business School Press.

CIMA (1996) *Management Accounting Official Terminology*, London: Chartered Institute of Management Accountants.

Weetman, P. (1999) *Financial and Management Accounting*, (2nd edn), Edinburgh: Pearson Education.

chapter 17

marginal costing

Learning objectives

When you have studied this chapter, you should be able to:

- Describe the main purposes of marginal costing

- Construct a marginal cost statement and associated profit statement

- Conduct breakeven analysis

- Rank products using contribution analysis

- Describe the limitations of marginal costing.

17.1 introduction

We saw in Chapter 15 that absorption costing takes account of both the direct costs and a portion of the indirect costs when calculating the cost per unit. This chapter examines a costing technique known as *marginal costing*, which only takes account of the variable costs of production when calculating the cost per unit and the fixed costs for the period are written off in full, without attempting to charge them to the cost units. The advantage of this is that marginal costing recognizes that costs behave differently as activity changes. Therefore, whereas absorption costing requires costs to be classified as direct or indirect costs, marginal costing requires costs to be classified as variable or fixed costs. In view of its focus on the variable costs of production, marginal costing is also known as *variable costing*.

Although it has some limitations, marginal costing is widely used technique and the principles are simple to understand and easy to apply. In this chapter we explain how to construct a marginal cost statement to calculate the contribution made by the production and sale of a cost unit towards covering the fixed costs and, hence, profit. We also examine how breakeven analysis and other types of contribution analysis using planned or actual figures can provide useful information to management for a number of short-term decisions.

17.2 classifying costs by behaviour

Marginal costing meets the need for detailed information about costs in a business where production levels fluctuate. This costing method requires revenue expenditure to be classified into either variable costs or fixed costs according to their behaviour when the level of production or sales activity changes. The variable cost incurred in producing one unit is known as the marginal cost.

KEY DEFINITIONS	The marginal cost is the variable costs per unit of production.
	A variable cost is an item of revenue expenditure that varies directly with changes in the level of production or sales activity.
	A fixed cost is an item of revenue expenditure that is unaffected by changes in the level of production or sales activity in the short term.

The *variable costs* per unit are usually regarded as the direct costs plus any variable overheads and are assumed to be constant in the short term. Therefore, a characteristic of a variable cost is that it is incurred at a constant rate per unit, for example the cost of direct materials will tend to double if output doubles.

From these definitions we can deduce that product direct costs will always be variable costs, whilst indirect costs tend to be fixed costs. Some indirect costs can be described as *semi-variable costs*. This means that they contain a variable element and a fixed element, each of which must be identified so that the variable element can be added to the other variable costs and the fixed element can be added to the other fixed costs. For example, the cost of electricity used to power machinery in a factory may consist of a standing charge (the fixed cost) plus a charge per kilowatt used (the variable cost).

activity

Classify the following costs for a manufacturing business into variable and fixed costs.

Depreciation on machinery

Direct materials

Direct labour

Factory rent and rates

Factory manager's salary

Commission paid to the sales team

Even if you do not have any experience of working in a manufacturing environment, you should have been able to identify these from the definitions of fixed and variable costs. Depreciation, rent and rates, and salaries (unless part of pay is related to productivity levels) are all examples of fixed costs. Direct materials, direct labour and commission paid to the sales team are usually considered as variable costs, because they change in accordance with changes in the level of production or sales activity.

In Chapter 12 we looked at Sam Reeve's taxi business, where the average mileage by a taxi in one quarter of the year was 15,000 miles and the quarterly costs, analysed by nature, were as follows:

Expense	Cost per quarter
	£
Driver's salary	2,670
Petrol and oil	1,050
Annual service	450
Tax and insurance	1,110
Depreciation	870
Total	6,150

Sam wants to tender for a special job that will involve an additional 500 miles per quarter. This mileage can be done in the driver's current time allowance, so no additional salary will be incurred. Sam needs to know the cost of the additional 500 miles per quarter, so that he can submit a quotation for the job.

activity

Explain how the following figures have been calculated and identify the correct cost of the additional 500 miles.

(a) £205

(b) £116

(c) £35

The total cost per mile is calculated by dividing the total cost for the quarter by the average mileage for the quarter:

$$\frac{£1,050}{15,000} = £0.07 \text{ or } 7p$$

Answer (a) is the result of multiplying the mileage of 500 miles by the total cost per mile of 41p. However, we know that no additional wages for the driver will be incurred, so it would be incorrect to take £205 as the cost of the additional 500 miles. The driver's wages, in this example, can be considered as a fixed cost. In our example, activity is measured in miles.

Answer (b) has been calculated by multiplying the 500 miles by 23.2p, that is, the total cost per mile less the driver's element. But this is not the correct answer to the question, because if you look at the list of costs, you will see that the driver's salary is not the only fixed cost. Certain other costs will not increase because of the additional 500 miles per quarter. Taking them in the order in which they are listed, the costs for petrol and oil will obviously rise with the increased mileage, so they are not fixed. With regard to servicing and repairs, some routine servicing will be carried out regardless of the mileage and this is therefore a fixed cost. However, other servicing and repair costs depend on the mileage. Clearly, tax and insurance are fixed costs and, like the driver's salary, should be excluded from our calculations of the cost for the additional 500 miles. Depreciation, to some extent, is influenced by the amount of mileage, but in a taxi business, depreciation depends mainly on the passage of time.

The above identification of fixed costs should help you with answer (c). The answer of £35 has been calculated by multiplying the 500 miles by 7p, the cost of petrol and oil per mile. In view of the information we have available, this is the best answer. If we are to be more precise, we will need more details of the service and repair costs so that we can identify which are fixed.

activity

Circle the correct answer in the following statements:

(a) If activity increases, total fixed costs will increase/decrease/stay the same.

(b) If activity increases, the fixed costs per unit will increase/decrease/stay the same.

(c) If activity decreases, total fixed costs will increase/decrease/stay the same.

(d) If activity decreases, the fixed costs per unit will increase/decrease/stay the same.

You should have had little difficulty in deciding the answers to (a) and (c). These are drawn straight from the definition and in both cases the total fixed costs stay the same regardless of changes in the level of activity. You may have found the answers to (b) and (d) a little more difficult, and some simple figures may help. We will take as our example a factory where the rent is £8,000 per annum, a fixed cost. The output of the factory each year is 1,000 units. The cost for rent per unit is therefore £8. If the factory makes 1,500 units one year, what is the rent per unit? The total rent cost will stay the same at £8,000, so the cost per unit for rent will decrease to £5.33. Therefore, the answer to (b) is that if activity increases, the fixed cost per unit will decrease. The reasoning is similar with statement (d), if activity decreases, the fixed cost per unit will increase.

activity

Circle the correct answer in the following statements:

(a) If activity increases, total variable costs will increase/decrease/stay the same.

(b) If activity increases, the variable cost per unit will increase/decrease/stay the same.

(c) If activity decreases, total variable costs will increase/decrease/stay the same.

(d) If activity decreases, the variable cost per unit will increase/decrease/stay the same.

You should have found this activity fairly straightforward after the earlier example. The answer to statements (b) and (d) is that if activity increases or decreases, the variable cost per unit will stay the same. The answer to statement (a) is that when activity increases, the total variable cost will increase. Similarly, with statement (c), when activity decreases, the total variable cost decreases.

17.3 calculating contribution

We saw in the previous section that in total the variable costs tend to increase or decrease in line with production or sales activity, whilst the fixed costs tend to remain the same, despite changes in the level of activity. Semi-variable costs contain both variable and fixed elements and must be analysed so that the variable elements can be added to the other variable costs and the fixed elements can be added to other fixed costs. Because some costs change and others stay the same when activity changes, the total cost per unit changes and the total cost for all production changes, but not directly.

Under marginal costing, only the variable costs are charged to the units. The difference between sales and the variable costs is not the profit, since no allowance has been made for the fixed costs incurred; it is the *contribution* towards fixed costs.

KEY DEFINITION   Contribution is the sales value less the variable costs and is based on the assumption that the sales value and the variable costs will be constant.

Contribution can be calculated for one unit or for any chosen level of sales. The *contribution per unit* is the selling price less the variable costs per unit. The *total contribution* is the total sales value less the total variable costs. It can also be calculated as the contribution per unit multiplied by the number of units produced. As soon as the total fixed costs have been covered by the total contribution, the business starts making a profit.

We will examine the concept of contribution by looking at an example. Mementos Ltd manufactures ceramic models of historic buildings for the tourist trade. The selling price of each model is £2.30. Direct materials cost 60p per unit, direct labour costs are 30p per unit and each model is packed in a presentation box which costs 15p per unit. The total fixed costs are the overheads for the business, which total £850 per week. The normal weekly output is 1,000 units. With this information we can draw up a *marginal cost statement*. The following statement calculates the total contribution and the net profit or loss for the week (assuming 1,000 units are produced and sold).

Mementos Ltd		
Marginal cost statement for one week		
		1,000 units
	£	£
Sales		2,300
Variable costs		
Direct materials (60p × 1,000)	600	
Direct labour (30p × 1,000)	300	
Packaging 15p × 1,000)	150	(1,050)
Contribution		1,250
Fixed costs		(850)
Net profit/(loss)		400

Marginal costing forms the basis of a number of useful techniques for making short-term decisions and can be based on budgeted or actual costs. The theory is simple to understand and easy to apply.

17.4 breakeven analysis

Marginal costing principles are used in *breakeven analysis* to identify the *breakeven point*, which gives management further useful information.

KEY DEFINITION   The breakeven point (BEP) is the level of activity at which there is neither a profit nor a loss, as measured by volume of production or sales, percentage of production capacity or level of sales revenue.

As you can see from the above definition, the breakeven point can be measured in a number of different ways, which we will illustrate with the data for Mementos Ltd. The following marginal cost statement calculates the contribution per unit, together with the total contribution and the net profit, assuming 1,000 units are produced and sold during one week.

Mementos Ltd				
Marginal cost statement for one week				
		1 unit		1,000 units
	£	£	£	£
Sales		2.30		2,300
Variable costs				
Direct materials	0.60		600	
Direct labour	0.30		300	
Packaging	0.15	1.05	150	1,050
Contribution		1.25		1,250
Fixed costs				(850)
Net profit/(loss)				400

Perhaps the business wants to know the number of *units* it needs to produce and sell in order to break even. This can be found by applying the following formula:

$$\text{breakeven point (units)} = \frac{\text{Total fixed costs}}{\text{Contribution per unit}}$$

Substituting the appropriate data for the words in the formula:

$$\text{breakeven point (units)} = \frac{£850}{£1.25} = 680 \text{ units}$$

Management can obtain further useful information by calculating the *sales value* at the breakeven point. The formula is:

$$\text{breakeven point (sales value)} = \frac{\text{Total fixed costs} \times \text{Sales value}}{\text{Total contribution}}$$

The amounts for sales value and contribution can be at the maximum level of activity, per unit or any other level. We will now insert the data into the formula:

$$\text{breakeven point (sales value)} = \frac{£850 \times £2,300}{£1,250} = £1,564$$

If the business has set a *target profit*, the level of activity needed to achieve the target profit can be found by using the following formula:

$$\text{Level of activity to achieve target profit} = \frac{\text{Fixed costs} + \text{Target profit}}{\text{Contribution per unit}}$$

Using the formula, we can work out how many models the company needs to sell to make a target profit of £200 per week:

Level of activity to achieve target profit of £200 = $\dfrac{£850 + £200}{£1.25}$ = 840 units

The difference between the level of activity to achieve the target profit (in this case, 840 units) and the breakeven point (in this case, 680 units) is known as the *margin of safety*. This means that the company could miss its target of 840 units by 160 units before it goes below the breakeven point and starts making a loss.

All this information can be shown graphically. The procedure for constructing a *breakeven graph* is as follows:

1. Draw a horizontal axis to measure activity (in units).
2. Draw a vertical axis to measure costs and revenue (£).
3. Plot a fixed costs line that will be parallel to the horizontal axis.
4. Plot the total costs line by adding the variable costs to the fixed costs, remembering that at nil activity there will be no variable costs, but there will be total fixed costs.
5. Plot the revenue line. The breakeven point will be where the revenue line and the total costs line intercept.

activity

Using graph paper, draw a breakeven graph for Mementos Ltd. Assume that the maximum level of activity is 900 models.

If you have drawn your graph accurately, you should have obtained the same breakeven point as you calculated using the formula and your graph should look like Figure 17.1.

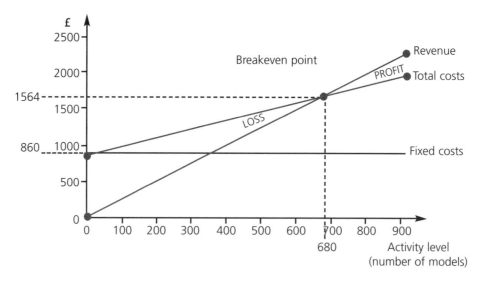

FIGURE 17.1 **Mementos Ltd, breakeven graph**

Although the breakeven point can be calculated by applying a formula or constructing a graph, the same answer would be arrived at by either method. However, the advantage of using a formula is that with more complex data it permits a greater degree of accuracy.

In this section we have concentrated on calculating the breakeven point. However, the same principles can be used for calculating the profit at different levels of activity. For this reason, accountants sometimes use the term *cost–volume–profit analysis*, as this focuses on what will happen to the financial results if the level of activity (such as the volume of products produced and sold) fluctuates.

17.5 contribution analysis

Marginal costing principles are used in *contribution analysis* to provide management with information to help with other short-term decisions, such as:

● setting the minimum selling price of a product, particularly in times when the market is depressed and when introducing new products
● evaluating the proposed closure or temporary cessation of part of the business
● assessing whether to accept a special contract or order
● comparing the cost implications of different methods of manufacture
● choosing which of a range of products to make.

Perhaps the management at Mementos Ltd wants to know the minimum selling price that could be set for its models. If you look at the marginal cost statement, you will see that the answer is £1.05, which is the variable cost per unit; any lower than this amount would mean that the company would not recover the costs incurred in making the model. However, if the selling price was set at this price, the business would not obtain any contribution towards covering the fixed costs. This can be examined further by looking at another example:

activity

Icetreats Ltd makes three types of ice lolly and shares its fixed overheads equally over the three types. A summary of the profit statement for last month is shown below.

Icetreats Ltd

	Fruit Ice	Choc Ice	Kool Ice	Total
Number of units produced	11,200	9,000	6,000	
	£	£	£	£
Sales	5,500	4,500	2,400	12,400
Variable costs	(2,400)	(1,800)	(1,300)	(5,500)
Contribution	3,100	2,700	1,100	6,900
Fixed costs	(2,000)	(2,000)	(2,000)	(6,000)
Net profit/(loss)	1,100	700	(900)	900

The sales director has suggested that as sales of all ice lollies are expected to decrease by 10% next month, production of Kool Ice should be stopped until demand picks up. Redraft the above statement, first showing what will happen if there is a 10% decrease in demand, and, second, if production of Kool Ice is halted.

Check your answer against the following figures:

	Icetreats Ltd			
	Fruit Ice	Choc Ice	Kool Ice	Total
Number of units produced	10,080	8,100	5,400	
	£	£	£	£
Sales	4,950	4,050	2,160	11,160
Variable costs	(2,160)	(1,620)	(1,170)	(4,950)
Contribution	2,790	2,430	990	6,210
Fixed costs	(2,000)	(2,000)	(2,000)	(6,000)
Net profit/(loss)	790	430	(1,010)	210

The above statement shows the impact of the 10% decrease in sales will have on profit, as well as the fact that Kool Ice is making a contribution to fixed costs. If production of Kool Ice is stopped, then the net profit would turn into a net loss as the following figures show:

	£	£
Contribution		
Fruit Ice	2,790	
Choc Ice	2,430	
Total contribution		5,220
Fixed costs		(6,000)
Net loss		(780)

The difference between the old profit of £210 and the new position (a loss of £780) is £990. This is the contribution lost if the business stops producing the Kool Ice product. The £780 loss is calculated on the basis of the assumption that the £6,000 of fixed costs will stay the same, at least in the short term, regardless of changes in activity or the cessation of one of the product lines. We can conclude from this that, in general, if a product or service makes a contribution towards fixed costs, it is financially worthwhile continuing to produce it. Of course, there may be other business reasons for dropping it, or it may be financially prefer-able to direct the activities of the organization in another direction. However, from a finan-cial point of view, in this example it is advisable to continue production of Kool Ice.

Let us assume that a large hotel has approached Icetreats Ltd and offers to place an order for 600 Kool Ices per month, as long as the price is reduced from 40p to 30p per lolly. The order would restore demand, but should the company accept it in view of the low price offered? The general rule is that, if the business has spare production capacity, it is worth-while accepting a special order, as long as it makes a contribution. The key figures for Kool Ice, calculated to the nearest penny, are as follows:

	Per unit			Per unit
	£			£
Current selling price	0.40	Proposed selling price		0.30
Variable costs (1,300 ÷ 6,000)	(0.22)	Variable costs (1,300 ÷ 6,000)		(0.22)
Contribution	0.18	Contribution		0.08

As the special price will still give a contribution of 8p, it is worthwhile accepting, but there may be other factors that must be considered before making a final decision, such as the reaction of other customers who may learn of this discounted price.

Now the production manager says he can change the production method so that up to 12,000 Fruit Ices can be produced per month for an additional fixed cost of £500 per month. He estimates that this will save variable costs of 4p per Fruit Ice. Do you think this plan should be implemented? There is no need to do a full calculation again, but look instead at the maximum possible savings in variable costs and compare them with the fixed costs. The maximum savings will be 4p × 12,000 = £480. Since this is lower than the £500 additional fixed costs incurred, the proposal is not financially worthwhile.

Even when a business occupies a very specialist market, it is unlikely to rely solely on manufacturing a single product, as there is a strong demand in the developed world for a choice of products. Therefore, it is likely that at some stage the business will have more than one product and need cost accounting information to help management make decisions about which is the most profitable. This will then lead to a decision to concentrate production on the most profitable product until demand for that product has been met, and then the next most profitable and so on. The information provided by marginal costing allows us to use contribution to *rank products* and we will explain this by turning back to the example of Mementos Ltd.

activity

So far the business has only made one model: the Westminster Abbey. Direct materials for this model cost 60p, direct labour 30p, packaging 15p per unit and it sells for £2.30. It has now been suggested that they could also make a model of Windsor Castle. Direct materials for Windsor Castle will cost 90p, direct labour 35p and packaging 20p per unit and it will have a selling price of £3.00. The fixed costs of £850 per week would be unchanged by this proposal. Construct a marginal cost statement showing the marginal cost for one unit of each model and rank the two products according to the *contribution per unit*.

You should have had no difficulty with the first part of this activity if you have remembered the correct format for a marginal cost statement. Compare your answer with the one below.

Marginal cost statement (one unit)				
	Westminster Abbey		Windsor Castle	
	£	£	£	£
Selling price		2.30		3.00
Variable costs				
Direct materials	0.60		0.90	
Direct labour	0.30		0.35	
Packaging	0.15	(1.05)	0.20	(1.45)
Contribution per unit		1.25		1.55
Ranking		2nd		1st

Interpreting the information is straightforward if you have recognized that the reason for constructing a marginal cost statement is to calculate the contribution. If you compare the contribution per unit for each model, you can see that the Windsor Castle model has the higher contribution. It contributes £1.55 towards the fixed costs compared to only £1.25 from the Westminster Abbey model. Assuming that it is just as easy to sell the Windsor Castle model as it is to sell the Westminster Abbey model and there are no limiting factors, the general rule for ranking products is to concentrate on making the product that gives the highest contribution first, in order to cover the fixed costs the fastest and start making the business a profit as quickly as possible. The fixed costs do not need to be considered in this decision because they remain unchanged by the choice of model produced.

The disadvantage of ranking products according to the contribution per unit is that we are ignoring differences in sales volume (the number of units sold) and, hence, differences in revenue generated. If 1,000 units of the Westminster Abbey model and 700 units of the Windsor Castle model can be sold in one week, the total contribution for each product will be:

Total contribution = Contribution per unit × Number of units sold

	Westminster Abbey	Windsor Castle
Total contribution	£1.25 × 1,000 = £1,250	£1.55 × 700 = £1,085
Ranking	1st	2nd

As you can see, ranking by *total contribution* reverses our earlier opinion and we can now recommend that the business concentrates on producing and selling the Westminster Abbey model.

17.6 limiting factors

So far we have assumed that there is no factor present that would prevent the business from achieving the level of activity required to break even or achieve the desired level of profit. In reality, this is rarely the case and there is nearly always some *limiting factor*, such as shortages of materials or labour, a restriction on the sales demand at a particular price or the production capacity of machinery. Therefore, limiting factors are the last aspect we will consider in making decisions using contribution analysis.

KEY DEFINITION	A limiting factor is any constraint that limits the business from achieving higher levels of performance and profitability.

The first step is to identify any limiting factor and arrange production so that the contribution per limiting factor is maximized. For example, perhaps the owner of Mementos Ltd is concerned about the supply of direct materials used in the products due to industrial action at the docks where they are imported. This could mean that the company will only be able to make a limited number of products. Management has a dilemma, since the same type of materials is used in both models, but we can see from the marginal cost statement in the previous section that the Windsor Castle model uses 50% more materials (direct materials are £0.90 per unit compared with £0.60 for the Westminster Abbey model). Under these circumstances, which model should the company make to obtain the maximum profit?

This is a slightly more difficult than the decisions we have looked at so far. When a limiting factor is present, the general rule is to maximize production of the product with the highest *contribution per unit of limiting factor*. We do not know the amount of materials, but if we did, we could calculate the contribution per kilo by dividing the contribution per unit by the number of kilos per unit. However, we do know the cost of materials for each model. Therefore, we can calculate the contribution for each £1 spent on the limiting factor. The general formula for calculating the contribution per limiting factor is as follows:

$$\text{Contribution per limiting factor} = \frac{\text{Contribution per unit}}{\text{Limiting factor per unit}}$$

Substituting the figures for the words in the formula:

	Westminster Abbey	Windsor Castle
Contribution per limiting factor	$\frac{£1.25}{£0.60} = £2.08$	$\frac{£1.55}{£0.90} = £1.72$
Ranking	1st	2nd

If there is a shortage of direct materials, the management at Mementos Ltd should select the product that gives the greatest contribution for every £1 of direct materials used. This would be the model of Westminster Abbey, since you can see that it has the higher contribution per limiting factor. The results of our analysis show that for every £1 of direct materials used for making and selling Westminster Abbey models, the company would get a contribution of £2.08, but only £1.72 from selling Windsor Castle models.

The following table draws together the results of the three different methods we have used for ranking products, starting with the basic approach and increasing in level of sophistication until we find a method that takes account of factors that may constrain profitability.

	Westminster Abbey	Windsor Castle
Contribution per unit	£1.25	£1.55
Ranking	2nd	1st
Total contribution	£1,250	£1,085
Ranking	1st	2nd
Contribution per limiting factor	£2.08	£1.72
Ranking	1st	2nd

As you can see, our subsequent analysis shows that the company will need to reverse its first decision to focus production on the Windsor Castle model based on the contribution per unit, as it needs to take account of the sales volume for each product. We have also found out that if direct materials are in short supply, the Westminster Abbey model will still be the more profitable of the two products.

17.7 limitations and the relevant range

The principles of marginal costing are based on assumptions about the behaviour of fixed and variable costs, but these rarely hold true over a complete range of activity or for any length of time. This leads to a number of limitations:

- Marginal costing is based on the assumption that variable costs will vary in direct proportion to changes in the level of activity, but they may also vary for other reasons. For example, variable costs may rise steeply in the early stages because production is not very efficient and rise again at the peak of activity due to pressure of work causing inefficiencies; a special discount on the price of direct materials for a short period may cause variable costs to fluctuate, whilst production levels remain constant.
- It is based on the assumption that fixed costs are not affected by changes in the level of activity, but they may change for other reasons. For example, the cost of electricity used to power machines used in the production process may decrease in steps as the level of consumption increases; other fixed costs may increase in steps as additional facilities such as another machine, more factory space and so on, become necessary as activity levels expand.
- Management may find it difficult to identify the variable and fixed elements of cost within semi-variable costs.
- Care must be taken when taking decisions based on contribution, since in the longer term the business will also need to recover the fixed costs.
- Like other accounting techniques, marginal costing does not take account on non-financial factors, such as changes in the motivation, skills and experience of employees that might affect activity levels.

In breakeven analysis, the limited range of activity over which the assumptions about the behaviour of costs hold true is known as the *relevant range*, and decisions should be restricted to this range unless investigations are conducted.

> **KEY DEFINITION**   The relevant range is the activity levels within which assumptions about cost behaviour in breakeven analysis remain valid.

17.8 conclusions

Marginal costing is a cost accounting technique that only takes account of the variable costs of production when calculating the cost per unit. In this chapter we have explained how a marginal cost statement is drawn up and how the contribution of various products is calculated. We have drawn a breakeven graph and used it to find the breakeven point as well as using a number of formulae. Finally, we have discussed the importance of limiting factors, which may constrain the growth of an organization and therefore affect the decision-making process. We have also explained the general rules for calculating which product will be more profitable to produce when limiting factors are present.

The principles upon which marginal costing techniques, such as breakeven analysis and contribution analysis, are based rest on the assumption that variable costs are not incurred unless production activity takes place, whilst fixed costs are incurred irrespective of the level of activity. However, the assumptions about the behaviour of variable and fixed costs in relation to changes in the level of activity are only reliable in the short term and over the relevant range of activity.

practice questions

1. Describe the purposes of marginal costing and the importance of contribution.
2. Explain the impact of limiting factors and how you would allow for them. Use a worked example to illustrate your answer.
3. Funfair Engineering Ltd manufactures fairground equipment. The company uses absorption costing and has been experiencing falling demand for its products due to the economic recession. Steve Wrench, the production manager, is worried because the total cost per unit is increasing, despite strict cost controls. Diane Flowers, the marketing manager, is complaining that selling prices will have to be reduced to maintain sales levels. At a recent meeting they found that the selling price suggested by Diane is lower than the total cost per unit calculated by Steve and they concluded that lowering the selling price to increase sales will only lead to even larger losses.

   Required
   Write a report addressed to Mr Wrench and Ms Flowers explaining:

   (a) Why the total cost per unit increases as production decreases.
   (b) Why marginal costing may be more appropriate than absorption costing for decision making in times of recession.

4. Edwards & Co Ltd manufactures teddy bears. The company's bears are in demand all year round and in the next financial year the sales manager plans to sell 12,000 teddies. The management accountant collects cost information for one unit of production (one teddy bear). Based on last year's figures, each unit will

sell for £10 and the variable costs will consist of direct materials, which will cost £1.00 per unit, and direct labour, which will cost £5.00 per unit. The fixed costs for the year are expected to be £32,000.

Required
You have been asked to provide information that will help the managing director consider the effect on profitability of changes in the level of sales activity next year.

(a) Draw up a marginal cost statement that calculates the contribution per unit.
(b) Draw up a marginal cost statement on the basis that 12,000 units will be sold and calculate the net profit or loss.
(c) Briefly explain what is meant by the breakeven point.
(d) Using the contribution per unit you have calculated in (a) calculate the following, showing the formulae in words and your workings:
   (i) The breakeven point in number of units.
   (ii) The breakeven point in terms of total sales value.
   (iii) The level of sales activity to reach a target profit of £20,000.
   (iv) Calculate the margin of safety in units at the level of sales activity you have computed in (iii).

5. Audiomax Ltd manufactures three models of audio systems: Premier, Deluxe and Superior. When planning next year's production, the management team wants to make sure the most profitable mix of models is produced. The following table shows the selling price and variable costs per unit for each model:

	Premier	Deluxe	Superior
	£	£	£
Selling price	100	150	240
Direct materials	30	40	50
Direct labour	30	50	120
Direct expenses	10	25	24

Required
(a) Construct a marginal cost statement that calculates the contribution per unit for each model.
(b) Calculate the contribution per limiting factor for each model on the assumption that the supply of direct materials is limited and rank the products accordingly. In addition, interpret your results by making a brief recommendation on the action management should take regarding prioritizing the production of these products.
(c) Calculate the contribution per limiting factor for each model on the assumption that the supply of direct labour is limited and rank them accordingly. In addition, interpret your results by making brief recommendations on the action management should take regarding prioritizing the production of these products.
(d) Point out any other relevant matters that management should consider.

budgetary control

When you have studied this chapter, you should be able to:

- Describe the main stages in budgetary control

- Differentiate between fixed and flexible budgets

- Explain the purpose of budgetary control and the requirements for an effective system

- Describe the advantages and disadvantages of budgetary control.

18.1 introduction

Unlike financial accounting, there are no rules and regulations governing the preparation of management accounting information, as it is intended for internal rather than external users. One advantage of this is that the information can be produced about future financial periods as well as past financial periods. We have already seen that cost accounting techniques may use actual (past) costs or budgeted (future) costs. In this chapter we introduce a major technique for planning and control known as budgetary control that uses budgeted figures for income and expenditure. Financial control is exercised by preparing detailed business plans for all aspects of the organization's activities, monitoring them against actual performance and taking any actions necessary to address any unfavourable deviations from the plan.

There are very few managers who do not encounter a budgetary control system during their careers. The technique of budgetary control is used in service and manufacturing businesses, as well as not-for profit organizations. Apart from governments' budgets, some of the most publicly announced budgets are those of major films, where they are so important that the credits at the end of the film show the name of the accountant.

In this chapter we explain the importance of budgetary control and the procedures for setting up the system. We also describe how it is used to generate valuable information that helps managers with the task of planning and controlling activities, and making decisions that ensure the business achieves its financial objectives.

18.2 importance of business planning

Business planning is essential if the owners and managers of a business are to make a profit. In Chapter 1 we explained that some businesses pursue profit maximization strategies, whilst small businesses may pursue satisficing strategies that will give their owner-managers sufficient profit to maintain a certain lifestyle and no more (Simon, 1960). The financial objectives of organizations in the not-for-profit sector are simply to break even. You know from Chapter 17 that this means they will be concerned with generating enough revenue to cover their total costs without making either a profit or a loss.

We will examine the importance of business planning by looking at an example. Cascade plc manufactures bathroom fittings. Based on last year's production records, the production manager believes that 15,000 shower units will be needed and buys all the materials and stores them in a warehouse. The marketing manager has heard that the water companies are considering changing their charging methods from rates based on the value of the property where the water is used to a metered system based on the amount of water used. As a result, he has launched a massive sales campaign and believes that 30,000 shower units will be sold. The financial accountant has received a letter from the bank stating that overdraft facilities will be withdrawn and has decided to stop any expenditure that is not absolutely necessary. The designer has come up with a new design that incorporates recycling waste water from the shower unit. The personnel manager believes the economic recession will get worse and has started issuing redundancy notices to the workforce. This illustrates how a lack of coordination of the various activities and managers following their own ideas can lead to resources not being matched to the demands made on them, which results in waste and inefficiency.

All this can be avoided if the business adopts a system of *budgetary control* to help them meet their financial objectives. Budgetary control is a major technique used in a wide range of organizations for planning and control. Traditionally, it took the form of a centralized and bureaucratic system of cost control, but it has evolved to meet the needs of modern business. In many organizations, it has moved to a more participative exercise that includes the involvement of managers at lower levels and the use of budgets to contribute directly to value creation (CIMA, 2004).

KEY DEFINITION

Budgetary control is the process by which financial control is exercised by managers preparing budgets for revenue and expenditure for each function of the organization in advance of an accounting period. It also involves the continuous comparison of actual performance against the budget to ensure the plan is achieved or to provide a basis for its revision.

18.3 main stages in budgetary control

The first stage in a system of budgetary control is for management to set out their *assumptions* about what is going to happen to the firm's markets and business environment.

---

activity

Make a list of the factors that management should consider when arriving at their assumptions about what is going to happen to their markets and the business environment.

Depending on the type of organization you are thinking of, the sort of factors you may have included are as follows:

- changes in the size of the organization's market and its market share
- competitors' strategies
- changes in interest rates or sources of funding
- increases in costs and availability of energy, materials and labour
- changes in legislation or social pressures that will affect the organization
- the effects of the activities of other related organizations
- changes in climate, consumer demographics, social and environmental factors and so on.

Having set out their assumptions, management can then start making predictions about what is likely to happen in the year ahead. However, if they were to leave it at that, they would not be discharging their managerial responsibilities. For example, perhaps they forecast that the business will become insolvent and unable to pay its debts when they fall due. Although this might be an accurate prediction, it would not be acceptable and they must find ways of minimizing any threats to the organization and taking advantage of any opportunities. By setting out their *financial strategies* and the actions that must be taken in view of their predictions, they are making business plans that will help them meet their financial objectives.

The next step requires detailed plans (the *budgets*) to be drawn up with specific financial plans for each designated part of the business (the *budget centres*), thus covering every aspect of the organization's activities.

KEY DEFINITIONS	A budget is a quantitative or financial statement that contains the detailed plans and policies to be pursued during a future accounting period.
	A budget centre is a designated part of an entity for which budgets are prepared and controlled by a manager.

The budget period is usually one year and the budget is normally broken down into monthly figures. Initially, it may be expressed in quantitative terms (for example the numbers of each type of product to be made and the quantity of materials to be ordered), but it will be converted into financial terms for the budgetary control system. A budget centre is typically a department or function in the business, a cost centre, an individual or any combination of these that management wishes to treat as a budget centre.

activity

Give an example of a budget using the knowledge you have gained from your studies so far.

A cash flow forecast is a good example of a budget. You will be familiar with this from Chapter 3. A cash flow forecast is a statement that shows the amount of cash expected to come in and go out during some period in the future. It is usually drawn up for each month over a 12-month period, and shows the monthly cash inflows and outflows, the net cash flows and the cumulative cash position at the end of each month. A cash flow forecast is not a tool for control because it is only a plan. In order to achieve control, comparison must be made with the actual figures. In budgetary control, responsibility for monitoring and controlling items of income and expenditure is devolved to the managers of the budget centres. The management accounting system provides information to these managers on a regular basis (often monthly) that gives details of the budgeted figures and the actual figures achieved, so that they can compare their performance against the plan and take any actions deemed necessary. The provision of information to all levels of an organization based on responsibility of the individual managers is known as *responsibility accounting*.

The next stage involves translating the detailed plans into actions for each manager to pursue.

activity

Both the production manager and the marketing manager of Cascade plc need to know how many shower units they plan to sell in the coming year, so they can ensure that the number of shower units to be made will meet the anticipated demand. What suggestions would you make if either of the following circumstances arose?

(a) Many more shower units are made than can be sold.

(b) Many more orders are received than the number of shower units made.

In situation (a) you may have decided that it is necessary to cut back severely on production. This could lead to redundancies, with machines and other resources not being used to their full capacity. Alternatively, you may have suggested that production continues at the same level and the excess production is stored, which could be very expensive. Finally, you may consider that the organization should boost sales through price reductions or increased marketing. Both these options could also be very expensive. Although you may think that situation (b) is a good position for the business to be in, it can lead to considerable problems. If the company attempts to boost production, it may need overtime working at a higher wage rate. More machines and larger premises may be required, which may require taking out a loan to pay for them. If the company fails to meet the orders, customers will become dissatisfied and the firm's reputation will be harmed; customers may go to competitors where the service is better.

Whichever of the above alternatives the company chooses, the policy will have to be communicated to all managers. This will ensure that detailed plans can be drawn up which minimize the potential damage to the company's financial performance. However, even if detailed plans are made available to all managers so that activities are coordinated, it does not mean that there is control. Because the plans are based on predictions, it is very likely that events such as the following may occur that prevent the plans from being achieved:

- prices may rise unexpectedly
- new competitors may enter the market and offer cheaper products
- machines may break down
- suppliers may not be able to deliver materials on time.

Once the period has commenced, regular financial statements are usually produced comparing actual performance with the budget. This is the final stage, where the individual managers responsible for the budget centres are expected to remedy any controllable adverse *variances* (differences) or revise the plan if necessary.

KEY DEFINITION	A variance is the difference between the predetermined cost and the actual cost, or the difference between the predetermined revenue and the actual revenue.

Assumptions and predictions about what is going to happen to the firm's markets and business environment are normally made at the highest level, following consultation throughout the organization. Collecting information to measure actual performance is part of the accounting function and accountants are also responsible for issuing financial statements that compare the actual performance with the plan. At this stage, most managers find that they have a role in explaining any variances between the planned and actual figures, and in suggesting the appropriate course to pursue. If there is no formal system of planning and control, there will probably be an informal system. In a very small business, the owner-manager may be responsible for all the stages. In larger businesses, there is likely to be a formal system, with a greater division of responsibility at each stage. Figure 18.1 summarizes the main stages in budgetary control.

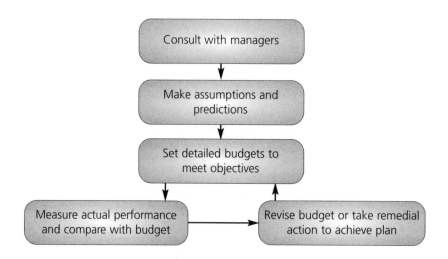

FIGURE 18.1 **Main stages in budgetary control**

18.4 purpose of budgetary control

Whilst the overall purpose of budgetary control is to help managers to plan and control the use of resources, there are a number of more specific purposes:

- A formal system of budgetary control enables an organization to carry out its planning in a systematic and logical manner.
- Control can be achieved only by setting a plan of what is to be accomplished in a specified time period and managers regularly monitoring progress against the plan, taking corrective action where necessary.
- By setting plans, the activities of the various functions and departments can be coordinated. For example, the production manager can ensure that the correct quantity is manufactured to meet the requirements of the sales team, or the accountant can obtain sufficient funding to make adequate resources available to carry out the task, whether this is looking after children in care or running a railway network.
- A budgetary control system is a communication system that informs managers of the objectives of the organization and the constraints under which it is operating. The regular monitoring of performance helps keep management informed of the progress of the organization towards its objectives.

- By communicating detailed targets to individual managers, motivation is improved. Without a clear sense of direction, managers will become demotivated.
- By setting separate plans for individual departments and functions, managers are clear about their responsibilities. This allows them to make decisions within their budget responsibilities and avoids the need for every decision to be made at the top level.
- By comparing actual activity for a particular period of time with the original plan, any variance (difference), expressed in financial terms, is identified. This enables managers to assess their performance and decide what corrective action, if any, needs to be taken.
- By predicting future events, managers are encouraged to collect all the relevant information, analyse it and make decisions in good time.
- An organization is made up of a number of individuals with their own ambitions and goals. The budgetary control process encourages consensus by modifying personal goals and integrating them with the overall objectives of the organization. Managers can see how their personal aims fit into the overall context and how they might be achieved.

There is no single model of a perfect budgetary control system and each organization needs a system that meets its own particular needs. The following list summarizes the main requirements for an effective system of budgetary control:

- A sound and clearly defined organization with the managers' responsibilities clearly indicated
- Effective accounting records and procedures which are understood and applied
- Strong support and the commitment of top managers to the system of budgetary control
- The education and training of managers in the development, interpretation and use of budgets
- The revision of the original budgets where circumstances show that amendments are required to make them appropriate and useful
- The recognition throughout the organization that budgetary control is a management activity and not an accounting exercise
- The participation of managers in the budgetary control system
- An information system that provides data for managers so that they can make realistic predictions
- The correct integration of budgets and their effective communication to managers
- The setting of reasonable and achievable budgets.

18.5 budget setting

The budgets themselves give details of the planned income and expenditure during a financial period that will achieve the given financial objective. In the first instance, the budgets may be measured in quantitative terms, such as the number of cost units to be produced or sold, the quantity of materials required or the number of employees needed. However, they will be converted into financial terms for the budgetary control system. Therefore, both *financial budgets* and *non-financial budgets* are normally prepared. Figure 18.2 shows typical budgets prepared for the sales and marketing department (a budget centre):

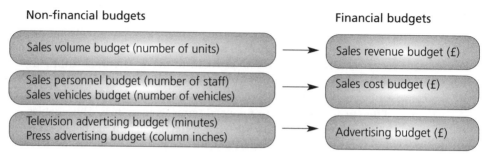

FIGURE 18.2 **Sales and marketing budgets**

There are two main methods for setting budgets:

- In *incremental budgeting* management adds a percentage to the current year's income and expenditure to take account of predicted changes in prices. However, this means that the budget will include non-recurring income or expenditure and will not be tailored to the conditions expected to prevail during the forthcoming budget period.
- In *zero-based budgeting* management starts from zero and builds in each budget figure where it can be justified from the policies and conditions that are likely to exist. This makes the budget much more relevant to the particular conditions expected in the budget period than incremental budgeting.

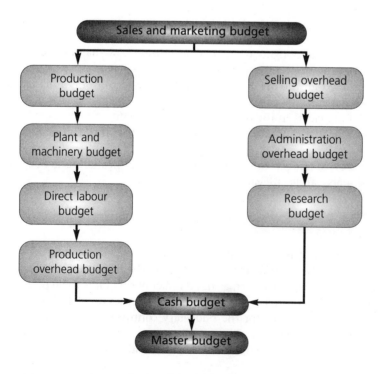

FIGURE 18.3 **Interrelationship of budgets**

Budgets are drawn up for individual departments and functions, as well as for capital expenditure, stock holding and cash flow. Therefore, both *functional budgets* and *non-functional budgets* are needed. Non-functional budgets are not the responsibility of a specific functional manager, but require contributions from various managers and the accountant. Non-functional budgets include the *capital expenditure budget*, which gives details of planned capital expenditure analysed by asset, project, functional area and budget period, the *cash flow budget*, the *budgeted profit and loss account* and the *budgeted balance sheet*. The *master budget* incorporates all the budgets and is the final coordinated overall budget for the period. Figure 18.3 shows the interrelationship of budgets in a simple business.

We can illustrate the interrelationship of budgets by looking at an example. Portalight Ltd manufactures torches. The sales director has estimated that the following quantities will be sold over the next six months:

	January	February	March	April	May	June
Forecast sales volume	1,000	1,200	1,500	1,600	1,600	1,750

The production department will manufacture the torches in the month before the sales take place and it has been agreed that a buffer stock of 200 torches will be maintained. On 1 December of the previous year there is an opening stock of 100 torches.

activity

Calculate the number of torches that must be manufactured each month.

The best way to tackle this problem is to draw up a table giving all the information.

	December	January	February	March	April	May	June
Opening stock	100	1,200	1,400	1,700	1,800	1,800	1,950
Production	1,100	1,200	1,500	1,600	1,600	1,750	
Sales		1,000	1,200	1,500	1,600	1,600	1,750
Closing stock	1,200	1,400	1,700	1,800	1,800	1,950	

We know that the opening stock on 1 December was 100 torches. To find out how many torches need to be manufactured in December, you need to consider how many are expected to be needed to cover the sales volume of 1,000 in January and ensure that there is a buffer stock of 200 torches on 31 December (1,000 + 200 = 1,200). Therefore, the December production volume needs to be the closing stock less the opening stock (1,200 – 100 = 1,100). You will remember that the closing stock at the end of one month becomes the opening stock at the beginning of the next. Therefore, on 1 January the opening stock is the same as the closing stock on 31 December (1,200 torches). We continued to use these principles to calculate the forecast production volumes for the rest of the period.

Having calculated the number of torches that must be produced, we now need to consider the decisions the production manager must take and which budgets will be affected. The most immediate decision concerns whether there is sufficient machine capacity and labour to make the torches. It may be that more machines and labour are required in the busy months and more space will be required in the factory; therefore all these budgets will be affected. The accountant will be concerned with the cash requirements for any changes and will want to ensure that the implications of these decisions are shown in the cash budget. It is because of the interrelated nature of budgets that a change in any one budget can affect the other budgets.

The process of preparing budgets for each of the functions and other activities in an organization and drawing up a master budget can take a number of months. The budgets must be communicated to managers before the start of the appropriate financial period, called the *budget period*, so they know what the plans are for their own departments and can implement them. Some organizations adopt a 'top-down' approach to budget setting, where the owners or senior management decide the individual plans for each department and function, and these plans are given to the individual managers to implement. Other organizations use a 'bottom-up' approach to budget setting, where individual managers construct their own budgets, which are given to the owners or senior managers, who then coordinate the individual budgets into a master budget. These are the two extremes, and most organizations fall somewhere between the two.

A *budget committee* may be formed, made up of the functional or departmental managers and chaired by the chief executive. The management accountant usually occupies the role of committee secretary, and he or she coordinates and assists in the preparation of the budget data provided by each manager. The budget committee reviews the budgets submitted by individual managers and ensures that each has the following characteristics:

- conforms to the policies formulated by the owners or directors
- shows how the objectives are going to be achieved, and recognizes any constraints under which the organization will be operating
- is realistic
- integrates with the other budgets
- reflects the responsibilities of the manager concerned.

If a budget does not display all these characteristics, it will need to be revised. This may affect other budgets and there may need to be negotiations between the managers concerned to introduce the necessary budget changes. When the budgets have been approved by the budget committee, they are submitted to the directors for approval prior to the commencement of the budget period. If the directors accept the budget, it is then adopted by the organization as a whole and becomes the working plans.

18.6 fixed and flexible budgets

A *fixed budget* is a budget that is not changed once it has been established, even though there may be changes in the level of activity. It may be revised if the situation so demands, but not merely because the actual activity level differs from the planned level of activity. This can be a considerable disadvantage, because a fixed budget may show an adverse variance on costs, which is simply due to an increase in variable costs because activity is higher than anticipated. As you will remember from Chapter 17, total variable costs increase or decrease in proportion with changes in activity level.

On the other hand, a *flexible budget* is designed to change with the level of activity.

Therefore, in a flexible budget, any cost variance can be assumed to be due to an increase or decrease in fixed costs. A flexible budget may be used at the planning stage to illustrate the impact of achieving different activity levels. It can also be used at the control stage at the end of a month to compare the actual results with what they should have been.

KEY DEFINITIONS	A flexible budget is a budget that changes in accordance with activity levels and reflects the different behaviours of fixed and variable costs.
	A fixed budget is a budget that is not changed merely because the actual activity level differs from the planned level of activity.

We will illustrate the importance of flexible budgeting by returning to the example of Portalight Ltd. The budget for January is based on an output of 1,000 torches. The following budget report shows the budgeted and actual figures for the month when 1,100 torches were sold:

Portalight Ltd
Budget report for January

	Fixed budget		Actual	
	£	£	£	£
Sales (£1.50 × 1,000)		1,500		1,650
Variable costs (75p × 1,000)	750		880	
Variable overheads (25p × 1,000)	250		260	
Fixed overheads	200		200	
Total costs		(1,200)		(1,340)
Profit		300		310

The managing director has been sent the above budget statement and is delighted that the actual profit is £10 above the budget.

activity	Write a brief report to the managing director explaining why he should not be so pleased with the results. Support your report with calculations.

After all the work you have done on marginal costing in Chapter 17, the words 'variable costs' should immediately have alerted you to the problem of comparing the actual results with the original budget when there has been a change in activity level. In this case the number of torches sold was 1,100 compared with the planned amount of 1,000. Although the sales department must be congratulated on achieving increased sales, the company needs to construct a flexible budget to see if they have controlled their variable costs. This is done by multiplying the planned variable costs per unit by the actual level of production.

The variable costs were originally set at £750 for 1,000 torches, which is 75p per torch. The variable overheads were originally set at £250 for 1,000 torches, which is 25p per torch. If we assume that as the number of torches manufactured increases, the total variable costs increase, the flexible budget compared with the actual results is as follows.

	Portalight Ltd Budget report for January			
	Flexible budget		Actual	
	£	£	£	£
Sales (£1.50 × 1,100)		1,650		1,650
Variable costs (75p × 1,100)	825		880	
Variable overheads (25p × 1,100)	275		260	
Fixed overheads	200		200	
Total costs		(1,300)		(1,340)
Profit		350		310

The flexible budget shows that at an output level of 1,100 torches, a profit of £350 should have been made, but the business has only made a profit of £310. A comparison of the figures shows that although variable overheads have been reduced, there is an overspend on variable costs that must be investigated. This demonstrates the advantages of using a flexible budget, where the budget is amended if the actual activity level is not the same as planned. By comparing the actual results with what should have been achieved at that level of activity, a more accurate measure is given.

Variance analysis is the investigation of the factors that have caused the differences between the actual and the budgeted figures (the differences are known as variances). Actual progress is measured from the beginning of the budget period (usually one year). At the end of each month, the actual figures for all items of revenue and cost are compared with the plan and reported to the managers responsible. If actual revenue is higher than the budgeted revenue, there will be a favourable variance. On the other hand, if actual income is lower than budgeted income, there will be an adverse variance. There may also be cost variances. If actual costs are lower than the budgeted costs, there will be a *favourable variance*. If actual costs are higher than the budgeted expenditure, the variance is known as an *adverse variance*. Unless they can be remedied, adverse variances will result in a lower profit.

activity

Richard Pillinger manages a farm that produces some crops early in the year by growing them under cover in large polythene tunnels.
Complete the following budget report for May by calculating the variances and indicating whether they are favourable or adverse.

Early crops
Budget report for May

	Budget £	Actual £	Variance £
Sales			
Cucumbers	25,000	24,500	
Peppers	18,000	17,200	
Tomatoes	19,000	19,600	
Subtotal	62,000	61,300	
Costs			
Salaries	28,400	29,000	
Expenses	12,500	12,000	
Administration	1,800	1,700	
Miscellaneous	700	300	
Subtotal	43,400	43,000	
Profit	18,600	18,300	

You should not have had too much difficulty with this, as it is simply a matter of subtracting the actual figures from the budgeted figures and deciding whether the variance is favourable or adverse. Compare your answer with the completed budget report below.

Early crops
Budget report for May

	Budget £	Actual £	Variance £	
Sales				
Cucumbers	25,000	24,500	500	Adverse
Peppers	18,000	17,200	800	Adverse
Tomatoes	19,000	19,600	600	Favourable
Subtotal	62,000	61,300	700	Adverse
Costs				
Salaries	28,400	29,000	600	Adverse
Expenses	12,500	12,000	500	Favourable
Administration	1,800	1,700	100	Favourable
Miscellaneous	700	300	400	Favourable
Subtotal	43,400	43,000	400	Favourable
Profit	18,600	18,300	300	Adverse

The budget report shows that the business made a profit in May which was £300 lower than planned. This was due to lower income from sales of cucumbers and peppers than planned, combined with higher salaries paid. Now he must decide whether these adverse variances require any action on his part. The salary increase may not have been planned but is nevertheless necessary. The lower sales income may be due to factors beyond his control, such as unexpected bad weather affecting yield. Most businesses experience peaks and troughs during the year, especially where there are seasonal factors affecting production and demand. Therefore, these variations need to be reflected in the monthly budget figures. On the other hand, Richard may discover it is due to poor marketing or distribution problems. Therefore, before he can make any decision, Richard must first investigate the causes.

18.7 advantages and disadvantages

Sometimes management implements a system of budgetary control, but becomes disillusioned with it because the disadvantages seem to outweigh the advantages.

> **activity**
>
> When an organization has a budgetary control system, internal planning and control should be improved, which must be a considerable advantage. What other advantages might there be, and what are the disadvantages of a budgetary control system?

The main *advantages* of budgetary control are:

- Coordination – all the various functions and activities of the organization are coordinated.
- Responsibility accounting – accounting information is provided to the managers responsible for items of income and expenditure.
- Utilization of resources – capital and effort are used to achieve the financial objectives of the business.
- Motivation – managers are motivated through the use of clearly defined objectives and the monitoring of achievement.
- Planning – planning ahead gives time to take corrective action, since decisions are based on the examination of future problems.
- Establishing a system of control – control is achieved if plans are reviewed regularly against performance.
- Transfer of authority – authority for decisions is devolved to the individual managers.

There are quite a number of potential drawbacks associated with budgetary control systems. How serious these drawbacks are depends on the way the system is operated. The main *disadvantages* of budgetary control are:

- Set in stone – managers may be constrained by the original budget and not take effective and sensible decisions when the circumstances warrant it (for example make no attempt to spend less than maximum or exceed target income).
- Time-consuming process and time spent on setting and controlling budgets may deflect managers from their prime responsibilities of running the organization.
- Unrealistic if fixed budgets are set and actual activity level is not as planned. This can lead to poor control.

- Disillusioning for managers if fixed budgets are set and are not achieved simply due to a change in the level of activity.
- Demotivating for managers if budgets are imposed by top management with no consultation.

The first letter of each of the advantages and disadvantages in the above lists of budgetary control form two mnemonics (CRUMPET and STUDD), which some students find useful for remembering these points.

18.8 conclusions

Budgetary control involves the preparation of detailed business plans for the forthcoming financial period. These plans take the form of budgets for income and expenditure, which are the responsibility of the managers of each budget centre. Financial control is achieved by these managers monitoring the actual performance of the budget centre against the budget on a regular basis, and taking whatever action is considered necessary to correct any adverse variances that are within their control.

In this chapter we have looked at the need for business planning and the cycle of planning and control in an organization. We have examined the way in which budgets are established for separate functions and how they are integrated into a master budget. We have seen how variance analysis is conducted and considered what organizational factors are required to operate an effective system of budgetary control. Finally, we have looked at the benefits of using flexible rather than fixed budgets in a business where activity levels are likely to fluctuate and examined the general advantages and disadvantages of budgetary control.

practice questions

1. Describe the main stages in budgetary control and the specific purposes of a system of budgetary control.
2. Describe the advantages and disadvantages associated with systems of budgetary control.
3. Explain the difference between a fixed budget and a flexible budget, using an example to illustrate your answer.
4. The managing director of Leisure Magazines Ltd has recently introduced a budgetary control system. The accountant drew up budgets for the advertising and editorial departments based on the actual results for the last three years. At the end of the first month of the new financial period, the actual total revenue was higher than planned, but the actual total advertising department costs were higher than budgeted. The actual costs for the editorial department were the same as those budgeted and the actual profit for the period was higher. On receiving the first month's results, the managing director threatened to dismiss the advertising manager for exceeding the budgeted costs. The advertising manager retaliated by saying that he would resign unless the budgetary control system was scrapped. The accountant left to join another company.

Required

You work for the firm of consultants that has been asked to advise the company. Prepare a preliminary report covering the following:

(a) An analysis of the problems, and how you think they have arisen.
(b) Guidelines for the operation of a successful and effective budgetary control system.
(c) Recommendations as to what action the director of the client company should take.

5. John Smith is starting a small business selling bicycles on 1 January 2006. He has £25,000 capital to invest in the business and has arranged bank loan of £25,000 over five years with a fixed interest rate of 6% per annum. Details of the anticipated revenue and expenditure for John's Bike Shop are as follows:

Cash sales	£30,000 per month
Credit sales	£5,000 per month (1 month's credit)
Purchases	£10,000 per month (2 months' credit)
Rent and rates	£24,000 per annum payable in full on 1 January
Insurance	£6,000 per annum payable monthly
Advertising	£1,000 quarterly, starting in January
Telephone and internet	£100 per month
Wages	£3,600 per month
Lighting and heating	£200 per month
Equipment	£12,000 payable in full on 1 January
Fixtures and fittings	£20,000 payable in full on 31 January
Drawings	£2,500 per month

Interest on the bank loan will be paid in instalments at the end of each month. The equipment will be depreciated over four years and the fixtures and fittings over five years; neither is expected to have any residual value at the end of their respective useful economic lives. At the end of the first quarter, John expects to have £10,000 worth of stock.

Required

Using a spreadsheet, construct the following budgeted financial statements for the first quarter:

(a) Cash flow budget for the three months 1 January to 31 March
(b) Budgeted profit and loss account for the three months 1 January to 31 March
(c) Budgeted balance sheet as at 31 March.

Tip: You can refresh your knowledge of the layouts of these financial statements by referring to Chapters 3 and 8.

references

CIMA (2004) *Better Budgeting*, London: Chartered Institute of Management Accountants, July.
Simon, H. (1960) *Administrative Behaviour*, (2nd edn), London: Macmillan – now Palgrave Macmillan.

chapter 19

standard costing

Learning objectives

When you have studied this chapter, you should be able to:

- Describe the technique of standard costing

- Calculate the direct materials variances

- Calculate the direct labour variances

- Describe the advantages and disadvantages of standard costing.

19.1 introduction

This chapter introduces a method of financial control known as standard costing in which predetermined standard costs and standard revenues are compared with actual costs and actual revenues. Standard costing is closely associated with budgetary control, which we looked at in Chapter 18. Although either can be used without the other, it is unusual to find a standard costing system in operation without a budgetary control system also being present.

We have already seen that budgetary control is applied to budget centres and the organization as a whole, and can be used in any type of business or not-for-profit organization, such as a charity, university, hospital, government department and so on. On the other hand, standard costing is mainly applied to products and processes. Therefore, it is a technique that is more commonly used in manufacturing organizations, although it may also be useful in service industries. As in a budgetary control system, it allows the comparison of predetermined costs and income with the actual costs and income achieved. Any variances, or differences, can then be investigated. Managers within the organization can be held responsible for these variances and, by analysing the reasons for the variances, control can be achieved.

In this chapter we explain the principles upon which the technique of standard costing is based and demonstrate how the different variances associated with total direct costs are calculated. We also discuss the typical causes of any variances and describe the general advantages and disadvantages of standard costing.

19.2 standard costs and revenues

Standard costing is a technique for controlling costs in which predetermined standard costs and revenues are compared with the actual costs and revenues to identify any variances. The predetermined costs and revenues are known as *standard costs* and *standard revenues*. Standards are set in defined working conditions and represent a benchmark of resource usage. They can be set on the following bases (CIMA, 1996, p. 47):

- an *ex ante* estimate of expected performance
- an *ex post* estimate of attainable performance
- a prior period level of performance by the same organization
- the level performance achieved by comparable organizations
- the level of performance required to meet organizational objectives.

KEY DEFINITION	Standard costing is a method of control in which standard costs and revenues are compared with actual performance to identify variances, which can be used to improve performance.

Standards can be set at an *ideal* level or an *attainable* level, depending on the philosophy of the business. Ideal standards are based on the best possible working conditions, but attainable standards are more widely used because they are based on realistic efficient performance and allow for such problems as machine breakdowns, materials wastage and so on. Although ideal standards are useful for management decision making, there is some risk that employees will be demotivated by the impossibility of achieving them.

The standard cost is the planned unit of cost that is calculated from technical specifications. These specify the quantity of materials, labour and other elements of cost required, and relate them to the prices and wages that are expected to be in place during the period when the standard cost will be used. It is usual to measure the time in which it is planned to complete a certain volume of work in standard hours or standard minutes. This means that a standard hour is a measure of production output, rather than a measure of time.

> **activity**
>
> A company has set one standard hour's production at 500 units. In a seven-hour day, 4,000 units are produced. What is this output in standard hours?

To answer this question, you will have needed to make the following calculation:

$$\frac{4{,}000 \text{ units}}{500 \text{ units per standard hour}}$$

= 8 standard hours' production

19.3 variance analysis

You will remember from Chapter 16 that variance analysis is the periodic investigation of the factors that have caused the differences between the actual and the budgeted figures. As in budgetary control, these differences are known as *variances*. At the end of each month of the budget period, the actual figures for all items of revenue and cost are compared with the plan and reported to the managers responsible. Timely reporting gives the opportunity for any adverse variances to be remedied if this is possible.

> **KEY DEFINITION**
>
> A variance is the difference between the predetermined cost and the actual cost, or the difference between the predetermined revenue and the actual revenue.

Any variances are analysed to reveal their constituent parts, so that sufficient information is available to permit investigation by management. *Favourable variances* are those which improve the predetermined profit and *adverse variances* are those which reduce the predetermined profit.

> **activity**
>
> In the stitching department of Jarvis Jackets Ltd 100 pockets can be made in one standard hour. In an eight-hour day, 950 pockets are produced. Determine whether this will give rise to a favourable or adverse variance.

The first step is to calculate how many pockets should be made in an eight-hour day:

100 units per standard hour × 8 actual hours

= 800 standard hours' production

Next you should have calculated the variance by subtracting the standard hours' production (800) from the actual production (950) to arrive at a figure of 150. This is a favourable variance because 150 more pockets are produced than the 800 planned. Now we are ready to make this part of the standard costing system, by expressing the variance in financial terms.

In a manufacturing business, the direct costs associated with each cost unit are normally direct materials and direct labour. The reasons for overspending or underspending on either of these costs are based on the following simple concept:

Total cost of direct materials/labour = Quantity used × Unit price

Any variance in the total direct costs will be due to differences in the quantity used, the price per unit or a combination of both these factors, as shown in Figure 19.1.

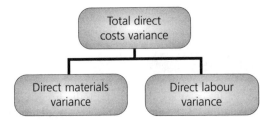

FIGURE 19.1 **Total direct costs variance**

We will now look at the direct materials variance and the direct labour variance in a little more detail.

19.4 direct materials variance

The above principles are applied to the cost of direct materials. Predetermined standards are set both for the usage level of direct materials for a given volume of production and the price allowed per unit of direct materials. The price standard is based on the price per unit expected to be paid or budgeted for the level of purchases projected over the period for which the standard is to be applied. In general, any price variance is considered to be the responsibility of the buyer or purchasing manager and any variation in the volume or quantity of materials consumed is considered to be the responsibility of the production manager. However, due to the interdependence of price and usage, it may be difficult to assign these responsibilities.

The *direct materials variance* is based on the following formula:

Total cost of direct materials = Quantity used × Price per unit

Standards are set for the quantity of materials to be used for a specific volume of production and the price to be paid per unit of direct materials. The *total direct materials variance* can be calculated using the following formula:

(standard quantity used × standard price per unit) – (actual quantity used × actual price per unit)

> **activity**
>
> Jarvis Jackets Ltd has decided to extend its range to include denim jackets. One jacket requires a standard usage of 3 metres of direct materials, which has been set at a standard price of £2.20 per metre. In the period, 80 jackets were made and 260 metres of materials consumed at a cost of £1.95 per metre. Using the above formula, calculate the total direct materials variance.

The first stage is to calculate the standard quantity of materials for the actual level of production. As 80 jackets were made and the company planned to use 3 metres of denim per jacket, the standard quantity for that level of production is 240 metres. Inserting the appropriate figures into the formula, the total direct materials variance is:

(240 metres × £2.20) – (260 metres × £1.95)

= £528 – £507

= £21 favourable

The difference of £21 between the planned cost and the actual cost is a favourable variance because we have spent less on our materials than we planned for that level of production. Although this information is useful, it needs to be more precise to enable the management to take any action required. The reason why the actual cost of materials can differ from the planned cost of materials for a given level of production is due to two factors. Either we have used more or less materials than planned and/or we have paid more or less per unit of materials than we planned.

The total direct materials variance can be divided into a usage variance and a price variance, as shown in Figure 19.2.

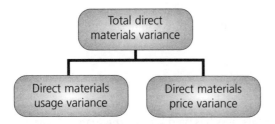

FIGURE 19.2 **Total direct materials variance**

The *direct materials usage variance* is the difference between the standard quantity specified for the actual production and the actual quantity used at standard price per unit. The formula is:

(standard quantity × standard price per unit) – (actual quantity × standard price per unit)

If the data is available, you may find it more convenient to shorten this to:

(standard quantity – actual quantity) × standard price per unit

activity

Calculate the direct materials usage variance from the data for Jarvis Jackets Ltd.

Inserting the appropriate figures into the formula, the direct materials usage variance is:

(240 metres – 260 metres) × £2.20

= (£44.00) adverse

In this instance, there is an adverse variance because the company has used more materials than planned for that level of production.

The final stage is to find out the *direct materials price variance*. This is the difference between the standard and actual purchase price per unit for the actual quantity of materials purchased or used in production. The formula is:

(standard price per unit × actual quantity) – (actual price per unit × actual quantity)

If the data is available, you can use the following shortened formula:

(standard price per unit – actual price per unit) × actual quantity

activity

Calculate the direct materials price variance from the data for Jarvis Jackets Ltd.

Inserting the appropriate figures in the formula, the direct materials price variance is:

(£2.20 – £1.95) × 260 metres

= £65.00 favourable

The variance is favourable because the business has paid less for the materials than planned for that level of production. If you deduct the adverse usage variance of £44.00 from the favourable price variance of £65.00, you will arrive at the total direct materials variance of £21 favourable. Thus, the first two variances explain the last one you have calculated.

Of course, working out the figures is not the end of the task. Managers need to investigate the reasons for the variances and determine whether any corrective action is required. There are a number of reasons for the adverse usage variance. Perhaps inferior materials were used and this led to higher wastage than planned, or the labour force was inexperienced and this led to high levels of wastage. Alternatively, some materials may have been lost or stolen. One strong possibility for the price variance is that the company has used lower quality and therefore less expensive materials. This would tie in with the possible reason for the adverse usage variance. Other reasons may be that the business is using a different supplier than originally intended or has negotiated a bulk discount.

19.5 direct labour variances

The same principles are applied to the cost of direct labour. Standards are established for the rate of pay to be paid for the production of particular products and the labour time taken for their production. The standard time taken is expressed in standard hours or standard minutes and becomes the measure of output. By comparing the standard hours allowed and the actual time taken, labour efficiency can be assessed. In practice, standard times are established by work, time and method study techniques.

The *direct labour variance* is based on the following formula:

Total labour cost = Hours worked × Rate per hour

The total direct labour variance is calculated by using the following formula:

(standard direct labour hours × standard rate per hour) – (actual direct labour hours × actual rate per hour)

activity

The management of Jarvis Jackets Ltd decides that it takes six standard hours to make one denim jacket and the standard rate paid to labour is £8.00 per hour. The actual production is 900 units and this took 5,100 hours at a rate of £8.30 per hour. Calculate the total direct labour hour variance.

With your knowledge of the calculation of materials variances, this activity should have caused you few problems. The first stage is to calculate the standard direct labour hours for this level of production:

900 jackets × 6 standard hours = 5,400 standard hours.

The total direct labour hour variance can then be calculated as follows:

(5,400 standard hours × £8.00) – (5,100 actual hours × £8.30)

= £43,200 – £42,330

= £870 favourable

The variance is favourable because the actual total labour cost is less than the planned cost for that level of production.

The total direct labour variance can be divided into an efficiency variance and a rate variance, as shown in Figure 19.3.

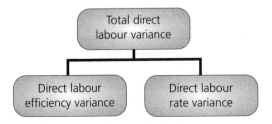

FIGURE 19.3 **Total direct labour variance**

The *direct labour efficiency variance* (sometimes referred to as the *labour productivity variance*) is the difference between the actual production achieved, measured in standard hours, and the actual hours worked, valued at the standard labour rate. The formula is:

(standard hours × standard rate per hour) – (actual hours × standard rate per hour)

If the data is available, it may be more convenient to shorten the formula to:

(standard hours – actual hours) × standard rate per hour

> **activity**
>
> Calculate the direct labour efficiency variance from the data for Jarvis Jackets Ltd.

Inserting the appropriate figures into the formula, the direct labour efficiency variance is:

(5,400 standard hours – 5,100 actual hours) × £8.00

= £2,400 favourable

The *direct labour rate variance* is the difference between the standard and actual direct labour rate per hour for the actual hours worked. The formula is:

(standard rate per hour × actual hours) – (actual rate per hour × actual hours)

If the data is available, you can use the following shortened formula:

(standard rate per hour – actual rate per hour) × actual hours

activity

Calculate the direct labour rate variance from the data for Jarvis
Jackets Ltd.

Once more, all you need to do is to insert the appropriate figures into the formula and the
direct labour rate variance is:

(£8.00 – £8.30) × 5,100 actual hours

= (£1,530) adverse

The variance is adverse because employees have been paid more than planned for that level
of production. If you deduct the adverse direct labour rate variance of £1,530 from the
favourable efficiency variance of £2,400, you arrive at the favourable total direct labour variance of £870. Therefore, the first two variances explain the last one you have calculated.

The most likely reason for the labour rate and efficiency variances is that the company
has used more highly skilled labour than originally planned. Therefore, the rate paid was
higher and in addition the output was higher than planned. There are other possible
reasons, such as the business may have given a pay rise or employees may have had to work
overtime and been paid at higher rates. Further investigation would be required to identify
the actual reasons and to determine whether any corrective action is required.

19.6 advantages and disadvantages

As with budgetary control, many of the benefits of standard costing are associated with the
processes of planning. Control is improved and it compels managers to make decisions,
coordinate activities and communicate with one another.

activity

Make a list of advantages and disadvantages of standard costing.

With your knowledge of budgetary control, you should not have had many problems with
this activity. The main *advantages* of standard costing are:

- Standard setting establishes a benchmark against which actual costs can be compared.
- The technique permits a thorough examination of the organization's production and
  operations activities.
- As the standards are based on future plans and expectations, the information provided
  to management is more accurate than that based merely on past performance.
- By examining the reasons for any variances between standard and actual costs and
  income, management needs to concentrate only on the exceptions to the planned
  performance. This leads to greater managerial efficiency.
- Variance analysis may result in cost reductions, and control of costs is improved.

The main *disadvantages* of standard costing are:

- It may be difficult to set standards, particularly in a new or dynamic organization.
- The standard costing system may be expensive to maintain and the additional record keeping may become a burden to busy managers.
- Standards will naturally become out of date and require revision. In a very dynamic organization, this may happen so quickly that managers lose confidence in the system.
- Information provided by the system is of value only if it is used by managers for control purposes. If the information has no credibility or is not understood, it has no value.

19.7 conclusions

Standard costing is a method of financial control that is often used in organizations that have a system of budgetary control. Standard costing is mainly applied to products and processes and for this reason it is more commonly used in the manufacturing sector and can also be used in the service sector. Financial control is achieved by the individual managers responsible receiving accounting information on a regular basis that allows them to monitor actual performance against the standard performance. They must then investigate the cause of any adverse variances that are considered to be excessive and take action to correct any that are within their control. This is necessary to ensure that the business achieves its financial objectives.

In this chapter we have looked at standard costing and the calculation of variances. We have described how to calculate variances for both total materials costs and total labour costs. We have also examined the calculation of the sub-variances and considered the reasons why they have occurred. Finally, we have examined the advantages and disadvantages of a standard costing system.

practice questions

1. Calculate and suggest possible reasons for the materials price variance from the following data:
   - Standard price is £4 per kilo
   - Standard usage is 5 kilos per unit
   - Actual price is £3 per kilo
   - Actual usage is 5 kilos per unit

2. Calculate and suggest possible reasons for the materials usage variance from the following data:
   - Standard price is £50 per tonne
   - Standard usage is 1,000 tonnes
   - Actual price is £50 per tonne
   - Actual usage is 995 tonnes

3. A manufacturing company has set a standard price for materials of £100 per kilo and anticipates that it will make 4 units from 1 kilo of materials. The actual production is 200 units and 52 kilos of materials are used at a price of £98 per kilo. Calculate all the materials variances and discuss the possible reasons for them.

4. A company plans to make 1 unit every 10 hours and the standard rate per hour is set at £9. In a financial period 50 units are made and this takes 460 hours. The total labour cost for the period is £5,060. Calculate all the labour variances and discuss the possible reasons for them.

5. Four years ago, your cousin Nikos set up Aphrodite Ltd, a small manufacturing company that manufactures shower screens. The business makes two models: Larnaca, the standard model and Paphos, the deluxe model. Both are made from frosted glass and have aluminium frames and fittings. Larnaca has plain glass and a silver finish to the frame and fittings, whereas Paphos has an attractive design etched on the glass and a gold finish to the frame and fittings.

    Once a year Nikos comes back to spend Christmas with the family. This year, knowing that you are studying management accounting as part of your course, he asks for your advice. He explains that despite a buoyant market and excellent sales figures, his profits have been very disappointing and he wants to embark on a cost-cutting exercise. After discussions, you find that he does not operate a standard costing system and does not seem to know what it is. However, he is very keen to learn but he is only staying a few days, so he asks you to write to him in Cyprus with full details.

    Required
    Write a letter to Nikos explaining the advantages of a standard costing system, how it can be implemented and the information he can expect to obtain.

references

CIMA (1996) *Management Accounting Official Terminology*, London: Chartered Institute of Management Accountants.

capital investment appraisal

When you have studied this chapter, you should be able to:

- Explain the purpose of capital investment appraisal

- Calculate and interpret the payback period for an investment project

- Calculate and interpret the accounting rate of return for an investment project

- Describe the advantages and disadvantages of these two techniques.

20.1 introduction*

Whilst the cost accounting techniques we have looked at in previous chapters provide detailed information to aid decisions about revenue expenditure, this chapter and the next focus on techniques that provide information to aid management decisions about capital expenditure. The process of appraising projects that involve the investment of large sums of capital is known as capital investment appraisal and a number of techniques have been developed to provide information that will help management choose between different long-term projects. For example, a business may want to invest capital in extending its premises, buying new delivery vehicles or adopting new technologies. In any major project that requires capital investment, there are a number of decisions that management needs to make. Some are important organizational and personnel decisions, but it is crucial that the financial implications of any such decisions are considered.

In this chapter and the next, we will be looking at the different approaches to capital investment appraisal and some of the commonly used techniques. We start with the payback period, which is a simple method that considers the project purely from the point of view of how long it takes to recover the initial capital invested. We then go on to examine the accounting rate of return, which focuses on profit rather than cash. In order to evaluate the usefulness of these methods, we also discuss the advantages and disadvantages of each. The next chapter examines techniques based on discounted cash flows.

20.2 purpose of capital investment appraisal

The purpose of *capital investment appraisal* is to provide information to management that will help them decide which of several proposed capital investment projects is likely to yield the highest financial return. Capital expenditure is the outlay of a considerable amount of money on a project such as the purchase of a new fixed asset (for example buying a new factory), the enhancement of an existing fixed asset (for example extending the existing factory) or investment in a new business venture. You will remember from Chapter 7 that fixed assets are assets the business owns and plans to keep in the long term in order to generate future streams of revenue.

KEY DEFINITION Capital investment appraisal is the evaluation of proposed investment projects, with a view to determining which is likely to give the highest financial return.

Capital investment decisions are among the most important decisions made by management and are critical not only for the owners and managers of the business, but at the macro-level they are also important for the country's economy. Research in innovative small, medium and large firms (Chittenden and Derregia, 2004) shows that some of these entrepreneurial businesses bypass the investment decision-making process by using operating leases, rental or hire contracts to obtain some of the fixed assets they require, such as land, buildings and capital equipment. This reduces the effect of uncertainty on decisions and increases the resources available to the business for a much lower initial outlay. However, not all fixed assets can be obtained like this and some are only available for outright purchase; hence the continuing need for methods to help management choose between different capital investment projects.

Capital investment decisions are very important to the long-term survival of the business and can be distinguished from short-term decisions. Table 20.1 compares the key characteristics of such decisions.

TABLE 20.1 **Comparison of short-term decisions and long-term capital investment decisions**

Characteristic	Short-term decisions	Capital investment decision
Time span	1–2 years	2+ years
Nature	Operational (eg whether to discontinue a product)	Strategic (eg whether to build or buy a new factory)
Level of expenditure	Low–medium	Medium–high
External factors	Generally of little importance	Very important (eg interest rates and rates of inflation)
Typical techniques	Contribution analysis Breakeven analysis	Payback period Accounting rate of return Discounted cash flow techniques

Source: Adapted from Jones, 2002, p. 452.

When a business is considering investing capital in a long-term project, management needs to be sure that the amount of money received during the life of the project will be higher than the initial amount invested; at the very least, management needs to know that the business will get its money back. The annual profit and the distinction between fixed and variable costs is therefore of less importance than the timing and amount of the cash going in and out of the business. In some cases an investment is made to make a saving on costs, rather than to generate more cash. For example, a business may be deciding whether to replace an old machine with the latest model that will be less expensive to run. The question that the managers of the business need to answer is whether the saving on costs is likely to be sufficiently high that they make the investment worthwhile. Once again, cash is the most important factor.

activity

The directors of The Cheddar Cheese Company Ltd are considering investing in a new packing machine. They have a choice of three suitable machines, each of which would cost £150,000 and each of which would have an estimated useful economic life of five years, with no residual value. However, the net cash flows over that period (the difference between the cash coming in and going out each year) are expected to vary. The following table shows the budgeted annual net cash flows.

	Machine 1	Machine 2	Machine 3
Year	£	£	£
1	60,000	20,000	10,000
2	50,000	30,000	20,000
3	40,000	40,000	30,000
4	30,000	50,000	40,000
5	20,000	60,000	150,000

Which machine would you recommend the company purchases?

One way to make the comparison is to total the annual net cash flows for each machine:

	Machine 1	Machine 2	Machine 3
Year	£	£	£
1	60,000	20,000	10,000
2	50,000	30,000	20,000
3	40,000	40,000	30,000
4	30,000	50,000	40,000
5	20,000	60,000	150,000
Total	200,000	200,000	250,000

Both machine 1 and machine 2 are expected to give a total net cash flow of £200,000 over the five-year period, which suggests that perhaps either would be a worthwhile investment. However, you may decide that machine 1 is preferable because the cash comes in more quickly. Machine 3 looks better than the other two because the total net cash flow is £50,000 more than the other two machines. However, the directors would have to wait until year 5 before the business generates most of the cash and this means increased risk. Indeed, the net cash flows are forecast figures for all three machines and the further into the future the estimate is, the more unreliable the prediction is likely to be.

As you can see, it is difficult to decide which machine would be the best to buy, but accountants have developed a number of different investment appraisal techniques that can provide useful information to aid the decision. Figure 20.1 shows the methods we will examine in this chapter.

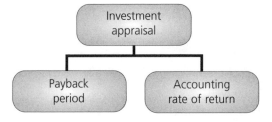

FIGURE 20.1 **Non-discounting methods for capital investment appraisal**

20.3 payback period

The *payback period* is a widely used investment appraisal technique, as it is very simple to apply and is easily understood by non-accountants. Each project is considered purely from the point of view of the cash flows and the time it takes to recover the capital that has been invested. Naturally, owners and managers will be very keen to know how long it will take to break even and the payback period of the proposed project is compared with the required payback period to determine whether the proposed project should be considered for approval.

KEY DEFINITION	The payback period is the time required for the predicted net cash flows to equal the capital invested in a proposed investment project.

The project taking the shortest possible time is the one preferred. To calculate the payback period, the following estimates are needed:

- the amount of capital required
- the annual net cash flows (the cash inflows and outflows, including repayments of capital)
- the timing of the movements of cash.

We will illustrate the method with an example. Jimmy Chang is considering investing £15,000 in a hot dog van that will have an estimated useful economic life of five years, with no residual value after that time. He would employ someone to operate it from a single site in the marketplace in the centre of town. His accountant has done some research and estimates that annual cash flows will be as follows:

	£	£
Cash receipts		
Sales		20,000
Cash payments		
Purchases of stock	5,000	
Operator's wages	8,000	
Motor expenses (petrol, tax, insurance, repairs and so on)	2,000	(15,000)
Net cash flow		5,000

With this information, we can calculate the payback period:

Year	Net cash flow £	Cumulative net cash flow £
0	(15,000)	(15,000)
1	5,000	(10,000)
2	5,000	(5,000)
3	5,000	0
4	5,000	5,000
5	5,000	10,000

As you can see, depreciation of the van is not included because depreciation is not a cash flow. The cash flow relating to the van is the cash paid when the van was bought, but there are several other things in this table which need explaining:

- Year 0 is a conventional way of referring to the start of year 1. Year 1, 2, 3 and so on means the end of year 1, 2, 3 and so on.
- It is customary to assume that cash flows during a year will be received evenly throughout the year. Of course, this is not likely to be true, but it is one way of simplifying the calculation. It is possible to estimate cash flows on a quarterly or monthly basis, but this is seldom done in payback calculations, because forecasting to this degree of refinement is rarely possible.
- Negative cash flows (cash going out) are shown in brackets.

The cumulative cash flows are shown as zero at the end of year 3. This means that at the end of year 3, the net cash flowing in from the investment has reached the figure of £15,000, which is same as the initial cash outflow in payment for the van at the start of year 1. Therefore, we can tell Jimmy that, based on his estimates, the payback period for this project will be exactly three years.

If the projected net cash flows after the initial investment are constant annual sums, as in the above scenario, then you can also use a simple formula to calculate the payback period:

$$\frac{\text{Initial capital investment}}{\text{Annual net cash flow}}$$

$$= \frac{£15,000}{£5,000}$$

$$= 3 \text{ years}$$

However, this formula cannot be used when the projected annual net cash flows vary from one year to another. We will illustrate this by continuing the example of our entrepreneur, Jimmy Chang.

activity

At the same time as considering the hot dog van project, Jimmy is also considering investing £15,000 in the purchase of a fish and chip van. The van is expected to have an economic life of five years, with no residual value after that time. The operator will drive the van around the main suburban areas of town and Jimmy's research suggests that it will take some time to build up a customer base. The following table shows how the estimated net cash flows for this project are expected to gradually build up over the period.

Year	Net cash flow £
0	(15,000)
1	3,000
2	4,000
3	5,000
4	6,000
5	7,000

Calculate the payback period for the fish and chip van project.

The first step is to work out the cumulative net cash flows over the period. Check your answer against the following table:

Year	Net cash flow £	Cumulative net cash flow £
0	(15,000)	(15,000)
1	3,000	(12,000)
2	4,000	(8,000)
3	5,000	(3,000)
4	6,000	3,000
5	7,000	10,000

The cumulative net cash flows show that the payback period lies somewhere between three years (when the cumulative position is expected to be a cash deficit of £3,000) and four years (when the cumulative position is expected to be a cash surplus of £3,000). Assuming the net cash flow is regular throughout the year, we can calculate the part year by dividing the figure for the earlier year by the sum of the two years (ignoring the negative sign on the earlier year):

$$\frac{3,000}{3,000 + 3,000} = 0.5 \text{ of a year}$$

Therefore, the payback period for the investment in the fish and chip van is 3 years and six months, compared with only three years for the hot dog van. Each project requires the same capital outlay, but on the basis of the time it will take to break even, Jimmy would be best advised to choose the hot dog van since he will recover his investment six months sooner.

20.4 advantages and disadvantages

The main *advantages* of the payback period are as follows:

● It is simple to calculate and is understood by managers who are not very numerate.
● It is useful for comparing risky projects where the prediction of cash flows after the first few years is difficult, due to possible changes in the business environment. For example, changes in technology could make a product obsolete in a year or so, although the current market seems assured.
● It is useful where short-term cash flows are more important than long-term cash flows. For example, if the business has insufficient capital to sustain long-term objectives, it is little use aiming for long-term profitability if the business becomes insolvent 6 months later.
● It is useful if borrowing or gearing is a concern.

The main *disadvantages* of the payback period are:

● It is difficult to estimate the amount and timing of future cash flows.
● It ignores net cash flows after the payback period.

- It ignores profitability, therefore the project with the shortest payback period might be chosen, even though an alternative project with a longer payback period might be more profitable.
- It ignores the size of the investment. Therefore the project with a smaller initial investment may have a shorter payback period than an alternative project that requires a larger investment but is more profitable in the long-run.
- The simple payback period ignores the time value of money because it gives net cash flows in later years the same importance as those in year 1, even though cash received this year is worth more than the same amount in five years' time.

activity

Returning to the example of The Cheddar Cheese Company Ltd at the beginning of this chapter, which packing machine would you recommend the directors purchase on the basis of the payback period method?

Your answer should be machine 1, because this has a payback period of only three years compared with more than four years for the other two machines. The calculations are as follows:

	Machine 1		Machine 2		Machine 3	
	Net cash flow	Cumulative net cash flow	Net cash flow	Cumulative net cash flow	Net cash flow	Cumulative net cash flow
Year	£	£	£	£	£	£
0	(150,000)	(150,000)	(150,000)	(150,000)	(150,000)	(150,000)
1	60,000	(90,000)	20,000	(130,000)	10,000	(140,000)
2	50,000	(40,000)	30,000	(100,000)	20,000	(120,000)
3	40,0000	0	40,000	(60,000)	30,000	(90,000)
4	30,000	30,000	50,000	(10,000)	40,000	(50,000)
5	20,000	50,000	60,000	50,000	150,000	100,000

$$\left(4 \text{ years} + \frac{10,000}{10,000 + 50,000}\right) \quad \left(4 \text{ years} + \frac{50,000}{50,000 + 100,000}\right)$$

Payback period   3 years | 4.17 years | 4.33 years

However, if the directors relied solely on the payback period and chose machine 1, they would not be taking account of the fact that machine 3 is likely to give the greatest return of cash, which is what we observed when we first looked at this example in section 20.2. This illustrates the disadvantage of the payback period method due to the fact that it ignores any cash flows that occur after the initial investment has been recovered.

20.5 accounting rate of return

Whereas the payback period method is concerned with cash flows, the focus of the *accounting rate of return (ARR)* is on profit. Not only is this a more conventional measure of success in business than cash, but it also takes account of depreciation, which spreads the capital costs of acquiring or enhancing tangible fixed assets over their useful economic life. The accounting rate of return is an accounting ratio that measures the relationship between profit and capital employed (capital plus any loans).

You will remember from previous chapters that there are a number of different ways in which profit can be defined and therefore we can only compare ratios that have been calculated on the same basis. We will define profit as the average annual profit before interest and tax that is expected to be generated over the life of the project. We will define capital employed as the average capital employed to finance the project. The formula is:

$$\frac{\text{Average profit before interest and tax}}{\text{Average capital employed}} \times 100$$

KEY DEFINITION	The accounting rate of return (ARR) measures the predicted average profit before interest and tax as a percentage of the average capital employed in a proposed investment project.

The project with the highest ARR is the one preferred. We will now illustrate the ARR with an example. The owners of Cut Above Hairdressing are considering refurbishing the salon and are trying to decide between two different projects. Project A will require an initial investment of £19,000 (year 0) but at the end of year 1 the capital employed in the project will have increased to £21,000. Project B is more ambitious and will require an initial investment of £40,000 (year 0) and by the end of year 1 the capital employed in the project will have increased to £50,000. After a good deal of careful budgeting, the accountant has produced the following table showing the annual profits before interest and tax (PBIT) that the two projects are expected to generate.

Year	Project A £	Project B £
1	5,000	12,000
2	4,500	10,000
3	4,000	8,000
4	3,500	8,000
5	3,000	6,000

Before we can work out the accounting rate of return for the two projects, we need to calculate the averages.

	Year	Project A £	Project B £
PBIT	1	5,000	12,000
	2	4,500	10,000
	3	4,000	8,000
	4	3,500	8,000
	5	3,000	6,000
Total		20,000	44,000

	Year	Project A £	Project B £
Average PBIT (÷ 5)		4,000	8,800
Capital employed	0	19,000	40,000
	1	21,000	50,000
Total		40,000	90,000
Average CE (÷ 2)		20,000	45,000
$\frac{\text{Average PBIT}}{\text{Average CE}} \times 100$		$\frac{4,000}{20,000} \times 100$	$\frac{8,800}{45,000} \times 100$
ARR		20%	20%

You can see from the results that although the average annual profit for Project B is a little more than twice as much as the average for Project A, both projects give a similar rate of return. This is because this technique also takes into account the average capital employed in the project, which for Project B is slightly more than twice the amount needed for Project A. However, both projects appear to be worthwhile and offer an ARR of 20%, which seems satisfactory when compared to an alternative, non-risky investment.

However, the ARR has not helped the owners of Cut Above Hairdressing choose between the two projects and they will need to take other factors into consideration, such as the cost of raising the larger sum of capital for Project B and the length of time that business will be disrupted by this more ambitious refurbishment. The most important thing to remember is that the calculation of the accounting rate of return is based on projected figures. Therefore the technique relies on assumptions and best estimates and, however careful the accountant is in preparing the figures, it is difficult to predict future profits with accuracy.

activity

Robbie Oliver already owns a successful restaurant in London. He is now considering opening a second restaurant in either Richmond or Hampton. Property is slightly cheaper in Hampton, but sales are likely to be lower than in Richmond. The following table shows financial estimates for the two locations.

	Richmond £	Hampton £
Average sales	872,000	500,000
Average costs and expenses	656,000	340,500
Average capital employed	1,440,000	800,000

Calculate the ARR for each restaurant, and decide which investment is the more favourable of the two.

Before you can use the formula, you need to calculate the average profit. Drawing on your knowledge of financial accounting, you should remember that profit is sales less all the costs of sales and expenses. Check your answer against the following:

	Richmond	Hampton
	£	£
Average sales	872,000	500,000
Average costs and expenses	(656,000)	(340,500)
Average PBIT	216,000	159,500
$\dfrac{\text{Average PBIT}}{\text{Average CE}} \times 100$	$\dfrac{216,000}{1,440,000} \times 100$	$\dfrac{159,500}{800,000} \times 100$
ARR	15%	20%

If we rank these projects by their ARR, the Hampton restaurant is ranked first, as the rate of return is 20% compared with 15% for the Richmond restaurant. However, Robbie would be well advised not to base his decision purely on this method of investment appraisal. For example, it would be useful to know what the payback period for each project would be. We cannot use this technique because the cash flow information is not available. Also, you can see that the Richmond restaurant requires more capital (an average of just under £1.5m compared with £800,000 for the Hampton restaurant), but the Richmond restaurant is likely to give a significantly higher average annual profit in absolute terms (£216,000 compared with £159,500 for the Hampton restaurant).

Assuming that the capital required for the Richmond restaurant is available for investment, and since the Hampton restaurant requires considerably less, what is Robbie going to do with the difference? He could deposit it in a bank or building society, but the return would be likely to be much less than the 15% for the Richmond restaurant. He might want to consider investing in a similar project, but this might not be possible.

Robbie may find it useful to calculate the ARR for each year of the project and examine the incremental effects. In the early years, a project tends to have a lower ARR (because revenues are growing and assets are new), whereas in later years, the ARR is likely to be higher (because revenues are higher but the net book value of assets is lower).

20.6 advantages and disadvantages

As you can see, the accounting rate of return is useful because it allows us to compare projects. However, it leaves many questions unanswered and is not sufficient on its own for making important capital investments decisions.

The main *advantages* of the accounting rate of return are as follows:

- The calculations are very simple and the results are easy to understand.
- The entire life of the project is taken into account.
- The technique is compatible with ROCE, a similar ratio used in financial accounting for assessing the financial performance of the business.

The main *disadvantages* of the accounting rate of return are:

- There is no standard definition of terms used in the formula, which means that comparison of ratios that have not used the same definitions are unreliable.
- Averages can be misleading as they are hypothetical values; the actual figure in any year may be higher or lower.

- It does not take into account the benefit of earning a larger proportion of the total profit in the early years of the project.
- It is based on profit, yet the crucial factor in investment decisions is cash flow.
- It takes no account of the timing of profits or cash.
- There is no guidance on what is an acceptable rate of return.
- It takes no account of the time value of money, a topic we discuss in the next chapter.

activity

The directors of The Cheddar Cheese Company Ltd have a choice of three cheese packing machines, each of which would cost £150,000 and have an estimated useful economic life of five years, with no residual value. Estimate the annual profits for each machine by deducting the annual depreciation charge from the annual cash flows, using the straight-line method. Then calculate the ARR for the three machines and consider this information with the payback periods you calculated in section 20.4.

The first step is to calculate the annual depreciation charge. You will remember that the formula for the straight-line method is:

$$\frac{\text{Cost} - \text{Residual value}}{\text{Useful economic life}}$$

$$\frac{£150,000 - £0}{5 \text{ years}}$$

$$= £30,000$$

The following table shows the deduction of the annual depreciation charge of £30,000 from the annual net cash flows to calculate the annual profit or loss for each machine.

	Machine 1		Machine 2		Machine 3	
	Net cash flow	Profit/(loss)	Net cash flow	Profit/(loss)	Net cash flow	Profit/(loss)
Year	£	£	£	£	£	£
1	60,000	30,000	20,000	(10,000)	10,000	(20,000)
2	50,000	20,000	30,000	0	20,000	(10,000)
3	40,000	10,000	40,000	10,000	30,000	0
4	30,000	0	50,000	20,000	40,000	10,000
5	20,000	(10,000)	60,000	30,000	150,000	120,000
Total		50,000		50,000		20,000
Average (÷ 5)		10,000		10,000		20,000
$\frac{\text{Average PBIT}}{\text{Capital employed}} \times 100$		$\frac{10,000}{150,000} \times 100$		$\frac{10,000}{150,000} \times 100$		$\frac{20,000}{150,000} \times 100$
ARR		7%		7%		13%
Payback period		3 years		4.17 years		4.33 years

In section 20.2 we noted that both machine 1 and machine 2 are expected to give a total net cash flow of £200,000 over the five-year period, which suggests that perhaps either would be a worthwhile investment. However, cash is not the same as profit and you can now see that although both machines will generate an average profit of £10,000 over the life of the project, averages can be misleading. In the case of machine 1, this project will stop making profits after year 3 (breaking even in year 4 and making a loss of £10,000 by year 5). In the case of machine 2, the project will make a loss of £10,000 in year 1, break even in year 2 and not start generating profits until year 3. These differences are not revealed by the ARR, which shows the same low return over the life of the project for both machines.

The ARR for machine 3 suggests that this would be the most favourable investment as it offers almost twice the return of either machine 1 or machine 2. However, when we calculated the payback periods in section 20.3, we ranked machine 3 last because it would take the longest to recover the initial investment (4.33 years compared to 3 years for machine 1 and 4.17 years for machine 2). The directors of The Cheddar Cheese Company Ltd may want to take this into consideration when making a decision, as a short payback period is important if liquidity is a problem, gearing is a concern or borrowing is involved. For example, if debt finance is being used (see Chapter 3), a short payback period means less interest to pay and lower risk to the lender that the business will not be able to repay the loan.

Table 20.2 summarizes the key characteristics of the techniques we have examined in this chapter.

TABLE 20.2 **Comparison of non-discounting methods for capital investment appraisal**

Characteristic	Payback period	Accounting rate of return
Focus	Cash flows	Profits
Nature	Measures time taken to recover investment	Assesses profitability of investment
Assumptions	Value and amount of cash flows	Reliability of annual profits

20.7 conclusions

Capital investment appraisal is a process that provides management with accounting information that helps them choose between different long-term projects that involve the investment of large sums of money. In a business context, owners and managers need to evaluate potential projects carefully and select the investment that is likely to give the highest financial return. One of the main features of capital investment decisions is the difficulty in predicting events that could affect the future returns from an investment project; both financial and non-financial factors need to be considered.

In this chapter we have examined two techniques that provide information for capital investment appraisal. The payback period method focuses on early cash flows and gives information on how soon the capital invested is likely to be recovered by calculating the number of years it is expected for the project to break even. The accounting rate of return method focuses on profitability over the life of the project by expressing average profit as a percentage of the average capital employed. These techniques offer a number of different advantages and disadvantages, but the main drawback is that they do not take account of the time value of money. In the next chapter we will be looking at other methods that address this deficiency.

It is important to remember that the usefulness of the results of capital investment techniques depends on whether the financial estimates are based on realistic predictions. The further into the future the estimate is, the higher the level of uncertainty. We have mentioned a number of times in this book that accounting is not an exact science and you should be aware by now that much financial and management accounting information is based on estimated figures.

practice questions

1. Explain the purpose of capital investment appraisal in general. In addition, explain the purpose of the payback period method and the accounting rate of return.

2. Describe the advantages and disadvantages of the payback period method and the accounting rate of return.

3. The managing director of Jeffery's Boatyard Ltd has £500,000 to invest in a new marine project and has asked you to provide information that will help him choose which is the more favourable of two potential projects. Details of the annual net cash flows are as follows:

Year	Project 1 £	Project 2 £
1	80,000	90,000
2	100,000	110,000
3	180,000	190,000
4	140,000	110,000
5	100,000	80,000

Required
(a) Calculate the payback period for each project.
(b) Recommend which of the two projects is likely to be the better investment, giving reasons to support your advice.
(c) Comment on any limitations of the technique you have used.

4. The owners of Film Animation Ltd wish to expand the business by investing in new technology. They have the necessary capital and have identified two potential projects, only one of which can be financed. The details are as follows:

	Project A £	Project B £
Average sales	318,500	358,000
Average cost of sales including expenses	240,500	264,400
Average capital employed	650,000	780,000

Required

(a) Calculate the accounting rate of return for each project.
(b) Recommend which of the two projects is likely to be the better investment, giving reasons to support your advice.
(c) Comment on any limitations of the technique you have used.

5. Wren Electronics Ltd has capital available for investment in new equipment and the directors are considering two five-year projects, only one of which can be financed. Details of the annual net cash flows are as follows:

Year	Equipment 1 £	Equipment 2 £
1	5,000	20,000
2	17,000	30,000
3	42,000	20,000
4	30,000	20,000
5	10,000	20,000

In both cases, the project will require an average investment of £50,000. Annual profit before interest and tax will be based on net cash flows less annual depreciation on the equipment. This will be based on the straight-line method over five years, with no residual value at the end of the project. You should assume that the annual cash flows shown in the above table arise evenly throughout the year.

Required

(a) Calculate the payback period for each project.
(b) Calculate the accounting rate of return for each project.
(c) Recommend which of the two projects is likely to be the better investment, giving reasons to support your advice.
(d) Comment on any limitations of the techniques you have used.

references

Chittenden, F. and Derregia, M. (2004) *Capital Investment Decision-making: Some Results from Studying Entrepreneurial Businesses*, Briefing paper, London: ICAEW.

Jones, M. J. (2002) *Accounting for Non-Specialists*, Chichester: John Wiley & Sons.

chapter 21

discounted cash flow

When you have studied this chapter, you should be able to:

- Explain the purpose of discounted cash flow techniques

- Calculate and interpret the net present value for an investment project

- Calculate and interpret the internal rate of return for an investment project

- Calculate and interpret the discounted payback period for an investment project

- Describe the advantages and disadvantages of these three techniques.

21.1 introduction

In Chapter 20 we looked at the usefulness of the payback period and the accounting rate of return as tools for providing information when a long-term capital investment decision has to be taken. However, we concluded that both techniques suffer from the serious limitation that they do not take account of the time value of money. Since decisions concerning the investment of large amounts of capital in potential projects are crucial in business, discounted cash flow techniques have been developed to provide managers with more sophisticated techniques that incorporate the concept of the time value of money. (The principle of discounting is now so important that it is also being used in financial accounting.)

In the first part of this chapter we explain the concept of the time value of money. This is a fairly straightforward principle and, once you have mastered it, you will find the calculations in this chapter relatively simple. In the remainder of the chapter we introduce three discounted cash flow techniques that can be used to make a decision when investing in a long-term capital project. These are the net present value, the internal rate of return and the discounted payback period. These techniques are widely used in business and take account of the time value of money. The specific information required for discounted cash flow techniques presents some problems, but if it is available, these methods of capital investment appraisal greatly assist management decision making.

21.2 time value of money

In the last chapter we looked at two of the main methods for aiding capital investment decisions. The simple payback period method focuses on early cash flows and calculates the time it is expected to take to recover the capital invested. The accounting rate of return is a ratio that expresses the average profit over the life of the project as a percentage of the average capital employed in the investment. One of the main criticisms of these techniques is that they do not take account of the time value of money. In this chapter we are going to look at three discounted cash flow techniques that address this deficiency. The main methods for capital investment appraisal are summarized in Figure 21.1.

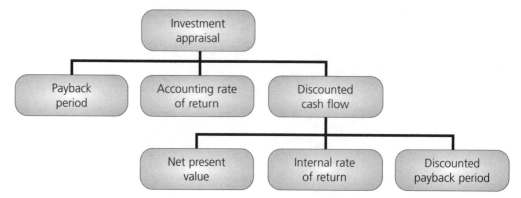

FIGURE 21.1 **Main methods for capital investment appraisal**

The *time value of money* is the concept that cash received at an earlier date is worth more than a similar amount of cash received later. This is because the cash received earlier can be invested to earn interest in the intervening period. The interest forgone in this way is known as the *opportunity cost of capital*. Similarly, because the cash paid out later is not available for investment today, it is worth less than a similar amount received at an earlier date.

KEY DEFINITIONS

The time value of money is the concept that cash received today is worth more than the same amount received at a later date because of the opportunity cost of capital.

The opportunity cost of capital is the interest forgone because the cash was not available for investment today.

The longer we have to wait for the money, the less it is worth. For example, supposing someone wanted to borrow money from you now and promised to pay you £100 in a year's time, how much would you be willing to lend them if the usual interest rate is 10%? One concern you may have is whether you are likely to be paid the £100. If you consider it is doubtful, you may decide not to lend the money or you may decide to charge a high rate of interest because of the risk. If you consider the loan is very safe, you may be willing to lend £90.90. In a year's time this would give interest of £9.10 to make the sum of £100 which you are repaid.

activity

How much would you be willing to lend now, if the interest rate is 15% and the borrower promises to repay £500 in three years' time?

You have probably had to make some complex calculations to arrive at the correct answer of £329. However, there is an easy method that makes use of the present value table in the Appendix, which shows the *present value factors* for future years at a range of different interest rates. For convenience, Table 21.2 shows an extract below.

TABLE 21.1 **Present value table for £1 at compound interest (extract)**

Future years	Interest rate			
	1%	5%	10%	15%
1	0.990	0.952	0.909	0.870
2	0.980	0.907	0.826	0.756
3	0.971	0.864	0.751	0.658
4	0.961	0.823	0.683	0.572
5	0.951	0.784	0.621	0.497
6	0.942	0.746	0.564	0.432
7	0.933	0.711	0.513	0.376
8	0.923	0.677	0.467	0.327
9	0.914	0.645	0.424	0.284
10	0.905	0.614	0.386	0.247

The question we are trying to answer is: What is the present value of £500 received in three years' time, if the interest rate is 15%? Look down the left-hand column until you reach future years 3 and then look along the row to the 15% interest column. The discount factor is 0.658, which is the discount factor for £1. It means that the present value of £1 received in three years' time is only £0.658. If you multiply £500 by the discount factor of 0.658, the result is £329, which is the amount you would be willing to lend now. You can check this by working out 15% compound interest on £329 for three years.

Compound interest (15%)		
Year		£
0	Principal	329.00
1	Interest	49.35
		378.35
2	Interest	56.75
		435.10
3	Interest	65.27
	Total	500.37

The time value of money underpins all discounted cash flow techniques, which makes them more sophisticated tools for appraising capital investment projects. Such techniques convert future net cash flows into present-day values and this is known as *discounting*.

KEY DEFINITION	Discounted cash flow (DCF) is a method that predicts the stream of cash inflows and outflows over the estimated life of a project and discounts them to present values.

The basic assumptions of *discounted cash flow* are as follows:

- Cash is invested at the start of the year (year 0).
- Future annual cash flows are certain (but in reality they are estimates).
- There is no inflation.
- Interest rates for lending and borrowing are the same.
- The interest rate is constant throughout the period.

We are now ready to look at the first technique.

21.3 net present value

The *net present value (NPV)* technique uses discounting to convert the future cash flows of a project into present-day values. The *discount factor* is chosen on the basis of the required interest rate. Therefore, the NPV tells us how much better the return on a capital investment project will be than an alternative low risk investment.

KEY DEFINITION
Net present value (NPV) is the difference between the sum of discounted values of the predicted net cash flows and the capital invested in a proposed investment project.

When comparing capital investment projects, the project with the largest positive net present value is the one preferred.

activity

Keith Hackett is considering whether to buy computer-aided design equipment that will improve his net cash flows by £30,000 per annum for the next five years. At the end of this time, the equipment will have reached the end of its useful economic life as it will be out of date and have no residual value. The equipment will cost £75,000 and will be bought for cash. The interest rate that Keith thinks is suitable is 15%. Calculate the NPV of this investment project using the following pro forma and the present value factors in the Appendix.

Year	Net cash flow £	Discount factor at 15%	Present value £
0	(75,000)	1.000	(75,000)
1			
2			
3			
4			
5			
		NPV	

If you had problems with this activity, you may find the following comments helpful:

- The initial investment takes place in year 0, which refers to the start of year 1. It is shown in brackets because it is a negative cash flow.
- The discount factor is 1.000 in year 0 because this is the present year and not a future year.
- The NPV is the difference between the total of the present value (PV) of the future net cash flows expected from the project (the discounted net cash flows) from the project and the initial capital invested ('net' always means something has been deducted).

The solution is as follows:

Year	Net cash flow £	Discount factor at 15%	Present value £
0	(75,000)	1.000	(75,000)
1	30,000	0.870	26,100
2	30,000	0.756	22,680
3	30,000	0.658	19,740
4	30,000	0.572	17,160
5	30,000	0.497	14,910
		NPV	25,590

The results show that the NPV of the project is a positive £25,590, which means that Keith will be getting a return on his investment of 15% plus this amount. If the NPV had been 0, his return would be 15%. If the project had shown a negative NPV, the return would be less than 15%. If 15% represented the return on an alternative low risk investment, a negative NPV would indicate that the project under consideration would not be worthwhile. Therefore, the decision rule is to accept the project with the highest positive NPV.

21.4 internal rate of return

The *internal rate of return (IRR)* uses the same principles as the NPV method, but the aim is to find the interest rate which gives an NPV of 0 for the project. In other words, instead of measuring the return partly as a percentage and partly as a financial figure, the aim is to show the return on the investment entirely as a percentage.

KEY DEFINITION	The internal rate of return (IRR) is the interest rate at which the sum of the discounted values of the predicted net cash flows is equal to the capital invested in a proposed investment project.

When evaluating a single project, the IRR will be chosen when it is higher than the cost of capital. When comparing projects, the project with the highest IRR is preferred.

activity | In the previous example, we concluded that at an interest rate of 15%, a positive NPV of £25,560 made Keith's investment worthwhile. In other words, Keith would be getting a return on the project in excess of 15%. Using the following pro forma and the present value factors in the Appendix, calculate the NPV for the project using interest rates of 20%, 25% and 30%.

Year	Net cash flow £	Discount factor at 20%	Present value £	Discount factor at 25%	Present value £	Discount factor at 30%	Present value £
0	(75,000)	1.000	(75,000)	1.000	(75,000)	1.000	(75,000)
1	30,000						
2	30,000						
3	30,000						
4	30,000						
5	30,000						
			NPV _____		NPV _____		NPV _____

Check your answer against the following:

Year	Net cash flow £	Discount factor at 20%	Present value £	Discount factor at 25%	Present value £	Discount factor at 30%	Present value £
0	(75,000)	1.000	(75,000)	1.000	(75,000)	1.000	(75,000)
1	30,000	0.833	24,990	0.800	24,000	0.769	23,070
2	30,000	0.694	20,820	0.640	19,200	0.592	17,760
3	30,000	0.579	17,370	0.512	15,360	0.455	13,650
4	30,000	0.482	14,460	0.410	12,300	0.350	10,500
5	30,000	0.402	12,060	0.328	9,840	0.269	8,070
			NPV 14,700		NPV 5,700		NPV (1,950)

The information we now have can be summarized as follows:

- Using an interest rate of 15%, the NPV is a positive £25,590.
- Using an interest rate of 20%, the NPV is a positive £14,700.
- Using an interest rate of 25%, the NPV is a positive £5,700.
- Using an interest rate of 30%, the NPV is a negative £1,950.

Looking at this, you can see that the higher the interest rate used to discount the future cash flows, the smaller the NPV becomes, until it eventually becomes negative somewhere between 25% and 30%. The IRR lies at the point where the NPV changes from positive to negative, which is where the NPV is 0. This can be illustrated by plotting the NPVs on a graph against the appropriate interest rates. The interest rates are marked on the x axis, and net present values on the y axis.

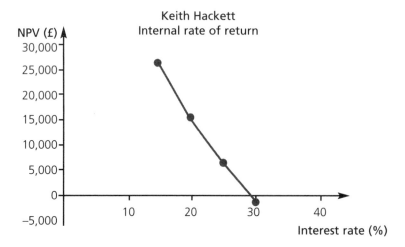

You will see that the line joining the four points is a slight curve, but for all practical purposes, we can assume that it is a straight line, provided the points are not too far apart. We shall use the data at 25% and 30% interest rates. The interest rate at which the line crosses the x axis, where NPV is 0, is somewhere between 25% and 30%; in other words, 25 + a number between 0 and 5 (30 – 25). The calculation of the IRR involves linear interpolation (linear, because it assumes a straight line) and the formula is as follows:

$$\text{Positive rate} + \left(\frac{\text{Positive NPV}}{\text{Positive NPV} + \text{Negative NPV}} \times \text{Range of rates} \right)$$

$$= 25 + \left(\frac{5{,}700}{5{,}700 + 1{,}950} \times (30 - 25) \right)$$

$$= 25 + (0.745098 \times 5)$$

$$= 28.73\%$$

The calculation shows that Keith will get a return of 28.73% on the project. The figures in brackets represent the proportion of 5 that we require to be added to 25. The difference between the two NPVs (£5,700 positive and £1,950 negative) is actually the sum of the two figures, because we are ignoring the fact that the second figure is negative. If you find this difficult to understand, the following explanation may help. If you had £100 in the bank yesterday (a positive figure), and today find that you have an overdraft of £50 (a negative figure), how much money have you drawn out of the bank since yesterday? The answer is:

£100 + £50 = £150

21.5 discounted payback period

In the previous chapter we explained that the payback period method is widely used because it is important for the owners and managers of a business who are considering an investment project to know how long it will take before the capital invested has been recovered and the project begins to pay for itself. However, the drawback of the simple technique we demonstrated is that it ignores the time value of money. This can be overcome by discounting the future net cash flows.

KEY DEFINITION The discounted payback period is the time required for the predicted discounted net cash flows to equal the capital invested in a proposed investment project.

The project taking the shortest possible time is the one preferred.

activity

Return to the example of The Cheddar Cheese Company Ltd in Chapter 20 where we compared the simple payback period for three projects that involved investment in a packing machine. Using a spreadsheet and the following layout, calculate the discounted payback periods for each project. Then compare them with your earlier results and make recommendations to the directors.

	Net cash flow	Discount factor	Present value	Cumulative net cash flow
Year	£	at 10%	£	£
0				
1				
2				
3				
4				
5				

Check your calculations against the following:

	Machine 1			
	Net cash flow	Discount factor	Present value	Cumulative net cash flow
Year	£	at 10%	£	£
0	(150,000)	1.000	(150,000)	(150,000)
1	60,000	0.909	54,540	(95,460)
2	50,000	0.826	41,300	(54,160)
3	40,000	0.751	30,040	(24,120)
4	30,000	0.683	20,490	(3,630)
5	20,000	0.621	12,420	8,790

Discounted payback period: 4.29 years $\left(4 \text{ years} + \dfrac{3,630}{3,630 + 8,790} \right)$

Simple payback period: 3 years

Machine 2

Year	Net cash flow £	Discount factor at 10%	Present value £	Cumulative net cash flow £
0	(150,000)	1.000	(150,000)	(150,000)
1	20,000	0.909	18,180	(131,820)
2	30,000	0.826	24,780	(107,040)
3	40,000	0.751	30,040	(77,000)
4	50,000	0.683	34,150	(42,850)
5	60,000	0.621	37,260	(5,590)

Discounted payback period: investment not recovered
Simple payback period: 4.17 years

Machine 3

Year	Net cash flow £	Discount factor at 10%	Present value £	Cumulative net cash flow £
0	(150,000)	1.000	(150,000)	(150,000)
1	10,000	0.909	9,090	(140,910)
2	20,000	0.826	16,520	(124,390)
3	30,000	0.751	22,530	(101,860)
4	40,000	0.683	27,320	(74,540)
5	150,000	0.621	93,150	18,610

Discounted payback period: 4.8 years $\left(4 \text{ years} + \dfrac{74,540}{74,540 + 18,610}\right)$

Simple payback period: 4.33 years

This exercise illustrates the difference it makes to the choice of project when the time value of money is taken into consideration in the calculation of the payback period. With an interest rate of 10%, you can see that the investment in machine 1 will not be recovered at the end of year 3 after all; instead, the directors will have to wait for 4.29 years, which is the first quarter of year 5. If you look at machine 2, the simple payback period was 4.17 years but now you can see that once the annual net cash flows are discounted, the capital will not be recovered at all. Finally, the results for machine 3 show that instead of being paid back in 4.33 years, the discounted payback period shows it will not be paid pack for 4.8 years and they will have to wait until the last quarter of year 5 to recover the capital.

You should have recommended machine 1 as being the most favourable project in terms of its discounted payback period. Not only does this method consider the time value of money, but it also takes account of more of the future net cash flows, since the discounted payback period is always longer than the payback period using the simple method.

21.6 advantages and disadvantages

The main *advantages* of discounted cash flow techniques are as follows:

- They use the concept of the time value of money.
- The NPV and IRR methods take account of the entire life of the project (the discounted payback period only considers the project up to the payback period).
- They permit comparisons with other opportunities to be made.

The main *disadvantages* are:

- It is difficult to determine the appropriate interest rate to use.
- The calculations are complex.
- Some managers may have difficulty in understanding the results.

So, we can conclude that although the net present value, internal rate of return and discounted payback period are useful techniques, they are also complex and managers with little knowledge of accounting may have difficulty in understanding them. The main purpose of management accounting is to help managers by providing information that will help them carry out their responsibilities of planning, controlling and decision making. Therefore, giving information that is hard to interpret makes it less useful.

activity

> What sort of problems do you think might be associated with investment appraisal techniques based on discounted cash flows?

As well as the management team having problems in understanding the results of the calculations, the accountant may have difficulty in obtaining the figures to do the calculations. Indeed, this is a problem that is common to all investment appraisal techniques. As far as discounted cash flow techniques are concerned, the difficulty lies in predicting the amount of cash inflows and outflows over the life of the project. Some projects last for many years and it will not be possible for the accountant to forecast the amounts with any certainty. For this reason, many firms prefer the payback period, because it is based on the earliest cash flows. One cash flow that can arise at the end of a project is the sale of the machinery and equipment that was originally purchased for the project. With a large investment in machinery, the *residual value* (the second-hand or scrap value) may be very high, even after many years of use. The expected proceeds from the sale of such assets must be shown as a cash inflow in the calculations.

Another problem is the choice of *discount factor*. In this chapter we have used a number of different rates as illustrations, but management (with advice from the accountant) must decide which rate to use. You will appreciate that the choice of discount factor is critical to the results. Most commonly, businesses base their choice on the current rate of return received on capital employed, the current cost of capital, the return on other projects available or the rate that could be received if the business were to invest the capital externally. When answering questions on capital appraisal, it is easy for students to concentrate on the calculations and forget these other aspects. The calculations are relatively easy, but the above issues make capital investment appraisal techniques complex. However, it is vital that the management accountant makes use of them, as they assist management in determining the likely return they will get from a long-term project and deciding whether it is acceptable in view of the risks involved.

Research in innovative small, medium and large firms (Chittenden and Derregia, 2004) shows that payback period, net present value, internal rate of return, sensitivity and scenario analyses are used to assist capital investment decision making. (These last two methods are beyond the scope of this book, but you may come across them if you continue your study of accounting to a higher level.) The findings show that producing numerical estimates of expected investment performance measures is important, but qualitative assessments are used to evaluate opportunities in the absence of reliable figures. As mentioned in the previous chapter, among some of these entrepreneurial firms, market mechanisms such as leasing, renting, outsourcing and subcontracting are used. This reduces the effect of uncertainty on decisions, increases the resources available for a much lower initial outlay and avoids capital investment decisions in connection with fixed assets that can be obtained in this way.

Table 21.2 summarizes the key characteristics of the techniques we have examined in this chapter.

TABLE 21.2 **Comparison of discounting methods for capital investment appraisal**

Characteristic	Net present value	Internal rate of return	Discounted payback period
Focus	Cash flows	Cash flows	Cash flows
Nature	Measures present value of net cash flows	Determines rate of return at which investment breaks even	Measures time taken to recover investment
Assumptions	Value and amount of cash flows and the interest rate	Value and amount of cash flows and the interest rate	Value and amount of cash flows and the interest rate

21.7 conclusions

There are a number of different investment appraisal techniques that can provide useful information to aid capital investment decisions. In the last chapter we introduced the simple payback period method and the accounting rate of return. In this chapter we have described three techniques that are based on discounting projected cash flows: net present value, internal rate of return and discounted payback period. Each technique provides different information and offers different advantages and disadvantages. However, the specific information required for discounted cash flow techniques presents some problems, but if available, these more sophisticated methods of appraisal offer the advantage that they incorporate the time value of money in the calculation of return. Guided by the accountant, management will have to decide which techniques are appropriate to use in the circumstances and in many cases more than one will be used.

practice questions

1. Describe the advantages and disadvantages of using discounted cash flow techniques for capital investment appraisal.

2. Compare the net present value method with the internal rate of return.
3. Kerry Melrose is considering an investment in hi-tech audio visual equipment costing £10,000 for her business, Melrose Events. With the help of her accountant, Kerry has done her calculations on a cash basis and is assuming that the following annual cash flows will take place evenly throughout the year. She anticipates that the project will require the business to spend £5,000 on advertising in the first year, but it should generate £1,000 in revenue. The advertising costs are expected to reduce to £3,000 in the second year and generate £2,000 worth of business. In the third and fourth years, no advertising will be required and the revenue generated is expected to be £3,000 in year 3 and £6,000 in year 4. In year 5 the project will generate £8,000 worth of business, but by the end of the year she expects the equipment will be obsolete, with no residual value.

Required
(a) Calculate the simple payback period and the net present value for the project using an interest rate of 12%.
(b) Interpret your results and recommend whether Kerry should go ahead with the project, giving reasons to support your advice.
(c) Comment on any financial considerations Kerry should bear in mind.

4. The managing director of Jeffery's Boatyard Ltd has £500,000 to invest in a new marine project and has asked you to provide information that will help him choose which is the more favourable of two projects. Details of the annual net cash flows are as follows and these are assumed to arise evenly throughout the year:

Year	Project 1 £	Project 2 £
1	80,000	90,000
2	100,000	110,000
3	180,000	190,000
4	140,000	110,000
5	100,000	80,000

Required
(a) Calculate the discounted payback period for each project and the net present value of each project using an interest rate of 6%.
(b) Recommend which of the two projects should be chosen, giving reasons to support your advice.
(c) Comment on any limitations of the techniques you have used.

5. Your aunt Laura owns Bloomfield Laundry Ltd and has £50,000 to invest in new dryers. She has asked you to advise her on the financial viability of the project and tells you that she requires a 15% rate of return. The following projected annual net cash flows are expected to arise evenly throughout each year:

Year	£
1	10,000
2	25,000
3	25,000
4	20,000
5	10,000

Required

(a) Calculate the discounted payback period, the net present value and the internal rate of return from the purchase of the new dryers.

(b) Interpret your results and advise your aunt.

(c) Comment on any limitations of the techniques you have used.

references

Chittenden, F. and Derregia, M. (2004) *Capital Investment Decision-making: Some Results from Studying Entrepreneurial Businesses*, Briefing paper, London: ICAEW.

present value table for £1 at compound interest

Present value table for £1 at compound interest

Future years							Interest rate								
	1%	2%	3%	4%	5%	6%	7%	8%	9%	10%	11%	12%	13%	14%	15%
1	0.990	0.980	0.971	0.962	0.952	0.943	0.935	0.926	0.917	0.909	0.901	0.893	0.885	0.877	0.870
2	0.980	0.961	0.943	0.925	0.907	0.890	0.873	0.857	0.842	0.826	0.812	0.797	0.783	0.769	0.756
3	0.971	0.942	0.915	0.889	0.864	0.840	0.816	0.794	0.772	0.751	0.731	0.712	0.693	0.675	0.658
4	0.961	0.924	0.888	0.855	0.823	0.792	0.763	0.735	0.708	0.683	0.659	0.636	0.613	0.592	0.572
5	0.951	0.906	0.863	0.822	0.784	0.747	0.713	0.681	0.650	0.621	0.593	0.567	0.543	0.519	0.497
6	0.942	0.888	0.837	0.790	0.746	0.705	0.666	0.630	0.596	0.564	0.535	0.507	0.480	0.456	0.432
7	0.933	0.871	0.813	0.760	0.711	0.665	0.623	0.583	0.547	0.513	0.482	0.452	0.425	0.400	0.376
8	0.923	0.853	0.789	0.731	0.677	0.627	0.582	0.540	0.502	0.467	0.434	0.404	0.376	0.351	0.327
9	0.914	0.837	0.766	0.703	0.645	0.592	0.544	0.500	0.406	0.424	0.391	0.361	0.333	0.308	0.284
10	0.905	0.820	0.744	0.676	0.614	0.558	0.508	0.463	0.422	0.386	0.352	0.322	0.295	0.270	0.247

Future years							Interest rate								
	16%	17%	18%	19%	20%	21%	22%	23%	24%	25%	26%	28%	30%	40%	50%
1	0.862	0.855	0.847	0.840	0.833	0.826	0.820	0.813	0.806	0.800	0.794	0.781	0.769	0.714	0.667
2	0.743	0.731	0.718	0.706	0.694	0.683	0.672	0.661	0.650	0.640	0.630	0.610	0.592	0.510	0.444
3	0.641	0.624	0.609	0.593	0.579	0.565	0.551	0.537	0.524	0.512	0.500	0.477	0.455	0.364	0.296
4	0.552	0.534	0.516	0.499	0.482	0.467	0.451	0.437	0.423	0.410	0.397	0.373	0.350	0.260	0.198
5	0.476	0.456	0.437	0.419	0.402	0.386	0.370	0.355	0.341	0.328	0.315	0.291	0.269	0.186	0.132
6	0.410	0.390	0.370	0.352	0.335	0.319	0.303	0.289	0.275	0.262	0.250	0.227	0.207	0.133	0.088
7	0.354	0.333	0.314	0.296	0.279	0.263	0.249	0.235	0.222	0.210	0.198	0.178	0.159	0.095	0.059
8	0.305	0.285	0.266	0.249	0.233	0.218	0.204	0.191	0.179	0.168	0.157	0.139	0.123	0.068	0.039
9	0.263	0.243	0.225	0.209	0.194	0.180	0.167	0.155	0.144	0.134	0.125	0.108	0.094	0.048	0.026
10	0.227	0.208	0.191	0.176	0.162	0.149	0.137	0.126	0.116	0.107	0.099	0.085	0.073	0.035	0.017

glossary of terms

Absorption costing A method of costing that, in addition to direct costs, assigns a proportion or all the production overheads to the cost units. Costs are first allocated or apportioned to the cost centres, where they are absorbed into the cost unit using one or more overhead absorption rates.

Accounting The process of identifying, measuring, recording and communicating economic transactions.

Accounting equation Assets = Capital + Liabilities

Accounting rate of return (ARR) Measures the predicted average profit before interest and tax as a percentage of the average capital employed in a proposed investment project.

Accounting standard An authoritative statement of how a particular type of transaction or other event should be reflected in the financial statements. Compliance with accounting standards is normally necessary for the financial statements to give a true and fair view.

Accumulated depreciation The total depreciation charged to date.

Accrual An estimate of a liability that is not supported by an invoice or a request for payment at the time when the accounts are prepared.

Accruals concept The principle that revenue and costs are recognized as they are earned and incurred and they are matched with one another and dealt with in the profit and loss account of the period to which they relate, irrespective of when cash (or its equivalent) is received or paid.

Activity-based costing (ABC) A method of costing in which overheads are assigned to activities and cost drivers are used to attach the activity cost pools to the cost units.

Activity cost pool A collection of all the elements of cost associated with an activity.

Appropriation account A record of how the net profit/(or loss) for the period has been has been distributed.

Asset A resource controlled by the enterprise as a result of past events and from which future economic benefits are expected to flow to the enterprise (IASB, 1989, para. 25)

Bad debts An amount owed by debtors that is considered to be irrecoverable. It is written off as a charge against profit or against an existing provision for doubtful debts.

Batch costing A method of costing for specific orders in which costs are attributed to a group of similar items that maintains its identity throughout one or more stages of production.

Breakeven point (BEP) The level of activity at which there is neither a profit nor a loss, as measured by volume of production or sales, percentage of production capacity or level of sales revenue.

Budget A quantitative or financial statement that contains the detailed plans and policies to be pursued during a future accounting period.

Budget centre A designated part of an entity for which budgets are prepared and controlled by a manager.

Budgetary control The process by which financial control is exercised by managers preparing budgets for revenue and expenditure for each function of the organisation in advance of an accounting period. It also involves the continuous comparison of actual performance against the budget to ensure the plan is achieved or to provide a basis for its revision.

Capital The money invested in the entity by the owner(s) to enable it to function.

Capital employed Fixed assets plus net current assets less creditors: amounts due after more than one year.

Capital investment appraisal The evaluation of proposed investment projects, with a view to determining which is likely to give the highest financial return.

Cash deficit The net cash position where cash outflows exceed cash inflows.

Cash inflows Cash transactions that bring money into the business.

Cash outflows Cash outflows are cash transactions that take money out of the business.

Cash surplus The net cash position where cash inflows exceed cash outflows.

Conceptual framework A statement of theoretical principles that provides guidance for financial accounting and reporting.

Consolidation The process of adjusting and combining financial information from the individual financial statements of a parent undertaking and its subsidiary undertakings to prepare consolidated financial statements that present financial information for the group as a single economic entity.

Continuous operation costing Methods of cost accounting used where products or services are produced as a constant operation.

Continuous weighted average (CWA) A method of costing for direct materials based on the weighted-average price at which materials are received, which is recalculated every time a new consignment is received.

Contract costing A method of costing for specific orders in which costs are attributed to individual long-term contracts.

Contribution Contribution is the sales value less the variable costs and is based on the assumption that the sales value and the variable costs will be constant.

Cost Cost is the amount of expenditure incurred on goods and services required to carry out the economic activities of the entity.

Cost accounting The process of collecting, processing and presenting financial and quantitative data within an entity to ascertain the cost of cost centres and cost units.

Cost centre A cost centre is a designated location, function, activity or item of equipment for which costs are collected.

Cost driver Any factor that causes a change in the cost of an activity. An activity may have multiple cost drivers associated with it.

Cost unit A unit of production for which costs are collected.

Creditor A person or entity to whom money is owed as a consequence of the receipt of goods or services.

Cumulative cash brought forward (b/f) The cash surplus or deficit at the start of the month that has been brought forward from the previous month.

Cumulative cash carried forward (c/f) The cash surplus or deficit at the end of the month that is carried forward to the next month.

Current assets Cash or other assets held for conversion into cash in the normal course of trading.

Debtor A person or entity owing money.

Depreciation The systematic allocation of the cost (or revalued amount) of a tangible fixed asset, less any residual value, over its useful economic life.

Direct costs Expenditure that can be directly traced to a cost unit.

Discounted cash flow (DCF) A method that predicts the stream of cash inflows and outflows over the estimated life of a project and discounts them to present values.

Discounted payback period The time required for the predicted discounted net cash flows to equal the capital invested in a proposed investment project.

Double-entry bookkeeping Double-entry bookkeeping is based on the principle that every financial transaction involves the simultaneous receiving and giving of value, and is therefore recorded twice.

Equity The residual interest in the assets of the enterprise after deducting all its liabilities (IASB, 1989, para. 25).

Expenses Decreases in economic benefits during the accounting period in the form of outflows or depletions of assets or occurrences of liabilities that result in decreases in equity, other than those relating to distributions to equity participants (IASB, 1989, para. 70).

Finance 1. The practice of manipulating and managing money.
2. The capital involved in a project, especially the capital needed to start a new business.
3. A loan of money for a particular purpose, especially by a financial institution, such as a bank.

Financial accounting A branch of accounting concerned with classifying, measuring, and recording the economic transactions of an entity in accordance with established principles, legal requirements and accounting standards. It is primarily concerned with communicating a true and fair view of the financial performance and financial position of an entity to external parties.

First in, first out (FIFO) A method of costing for direct materials that uses the price of the earliest consignment received for all issues to production until the quantity received at that price has been issued, then the price of the next consignment is used.

Fixed assets Assets the business owns and plans to keep in the long term

Fixed budget A budget that is not changed merely because the actual activity level differs from the planned level of activity.

Fixed cost An item of revenue expenditure that is unaffected by changes in the level of production or sales activity in the short term.

Flexible budget A budget that changes in accordance with activity levels and reflects the different behaviours of fixed and variable costs.

Generally Accepted Accounting Principles (GAAP) In the UK, these are the accounting standards, the requirements of company legislation and stock exchange rules.

Goodwill The difference between the value of the separable net assets of an entity and the total value.

Gross profit The difference between the sales revenue and the cost of goods sold.

Income Increases in economic benefits during the accounting period in the form of inflows or enhancements of assets or decreases in liabilities that result in increases in equity, other than those relating to contributions from equity participants (IASB, 1989, para. 70).

Indirect costs Revenue expenditure that cannot be traced directly to a cost unit and is therefore an overhead cost.

Intangible fixed assets Fixed assets do not have a physical form.

Internal rate of return (IRR) The interest rate at which the sum of the discounted values of the predicted net cash flows is equal to capital invested in a proposed investment project.

Job costing A method of costing for specific orders in which costs are attributed to individual jobs.

Liability A present obligation of the enterprise resulting from past events, the settlement of which is expected to result in an outflow from the enterprise of resources embodying economic benefits (IASB, 1989, para. 25).

Limiting factor A limiting factor is any constraint that limits the business from achieving higher levels of performance and profitability.

Management accounting A branch of accounting concerned with concerned with collecting, analysing, interpreting quantitative and financial information. It is primarily concerned with communicating information to management for planning, controlling and decision making.

Marginal cost The variable cost per unit of production.

Materials The supplies of raw materials, components or subassemblies used to make a product.

Net book value (NBV) Cost of a fixed asset less the accumulated depreciation.

Net current assets The difference between current assets and creditors: amounts due within one year.

Net present value (NPV) The difference between the sum of the predicted discounted cash inflows and outflows for a proposed investment project.

Net profit The amount of income earned after deducting all expenses.

Net realizable value (NRV) The sales value of the stock minus the additional costs likely to be incurred in getting the stocks into the hands of the customer.

Opportunity cost of capital The interest forgone because the cash was not available for investment today.

Output costing A method of cost accounting used where only one product is manufactured.

Overhead absorption rate A means of attributing production overheads to a product or service.

Payback period The time required for the predicted net cash flows to equal the capital invested in a proposed investment project.

Prepayment Revenue expenditure made in advance of the accounting period in which the goods or services will be received.

Process costing A method of cost accounting used where the production process is carried out as a sequence of operations.

Provision for depreciation An amount charged against profit and deducted from the net book value of the asset.

Provision for doubtful debts An amount charged against profit and deducted from debtors to allow for the estimated non-recovery of a proportion of debts.

Ratio analysis Ratio analysis is a technique for evaluating the financial performance and stability of an entity, with a view to making comparisons with previous periods, other entities and industry averages over a period of time.

Relevant range The activity levels within which assumptions about cost behaviour in breakeven analysis remain valid.

Service costing A method of cost accounting used where specific services or functions are provided.

Specific order costing Methods of cost accounting used where a different product or service is produced for each order.

Standard costing A method of control in which standard costs and revenues are compared with actual performance to identify variances, which can be used to improve performance.

Tangible fixed assets Fixed assets that are non-monetary in nature and have a physical form.

Time value of money The concept that cash received today is worth more than the same amount received at a later date because of the opportunity cost of capital.

Total net assets Fixed assets plus net current assets less creditors: amounts due after more than one year.

Trial balance A list of the balances of all the accounts in a double-entry bookkeeping system, with debit balances in the left-hand column and credit balances in the right-hand column. If the recording processes have been accurate, the totals of each column should be the same.

Variable cost An item of revenue expenditure that varies directly with changes in the level of production or sales activity.

Variance The difference between the predetermined cost and the actual cost, or the difference between the predetermined revenue and the actual revenue.

Working capital Current assets less creditors: amounts due within one year.

* Unless indicated otherwise, these definitions are adapted from the following sources:

CIMA (1996) *Management Accounting Official Terminology*, London: Chartered Institute of Management Accountants.

Hussey, R. (ed.) (1999) *Oxford Dictionary of Accounting*, Oxford: Oxford University Press.

index